35th Annual Pacific Northwest Software Quality Conference 2017

Scaling Quality Software

Portland, Oregon, USA
9 – 11 October 2017

ISBN: 978-1-5108-5220-4

Printed from e-media with permission by:

Curran Associates, Inc.
57 Morehouse Lane
Red Hook, NY 12571

Some format issues inherent in the e-media version may also appear in this print version.

Printed by Curran Associates, Inc. (2018)

For permission requests, please contact PNSQC/Pacific Agenda at the address below.

PNSQC/Pacific Agenda
PO Box 10733
Portland, OR 97296-0733
USA

Phone: 503 223-4630

www.pnsqc.org

Additional copies of this publication are available from:

Curran Associates, Inc.
57 Morehouse Lane
Red Hook, NY 12571 USA
Phone: 845-758-0400
Fax: 845-758-2633
Email: curran@proceedings.com
Web: www.proceedings.com

Monday, October 9, 2017

7:00-8:00 AM	**Registration and Wake Up with Coffee & Tea** Level 2 Mezzanine			
8:00-8:15 AM	**Welcome and Highlights for the Day** Level 3 Auditorium			
8:15-9:45 AM	**Keynote** (Auditorium Level 3) Quality Engineering 2017: Trends, Tricks, and Traps Penny Allen, Recreational Equipment, Inc. (REI)			
9:45-10:15 AM	**Break in Exhibit Hall** Level 2 Mezzanine			
	Level 3 Auditorium	**Level 1 Plaza Room**	**Level 2 Mezzanine Room**	**Level 3 Skybridge Room**
	Invited Speaker	***Testing & SQA***	***Management***	***Development***
10:15-11:00 AM	**INVITED SPEAKER** The Power of Doubt - Becoming a Software Skeptic Zeger Van Hese, Z-sharp N/A	Is Your Automation Any Good? Finally an Answer Wayne Roseberry, Microsoft 1	Four Years of Scrum: The Good, The Bad, and The Ho-Hum Heather Wilcox, NWEA 17	Architect as an Agent of Quality Brian Walker, Tektronix 27
11:10-11:55 AM		Utilizing Data Science To Assess Software Quality Renato Martins, Groupon Inc. 40	Influencing Change Levi Siebens, Vertafore 50	Senses Working Overtime: Improve Software Quality Through Accessibility and Inclusive Design Michael Larsen, Socialtext 57
12:00-1:25 PM	**Lunch Program - Grab & Go lunches with scaling quality demonstrations or thought-provoking games.**			
12:00-1:25 PM	**Game on! Mind Challenges** - Skybridge Terrace Level 3		Scaling Back on Square Footage, Joan Grimm, PAD, Mezzanine 2-4, Level 2 N/A	Mountaineering: The only sport where we celebrate at half time, Sarah Bradham, Mazamas SkyBridge A-B, Level 3 N/A
	Level 3 Auditorium	**Level 1 Plaza Room**	**Level 2 Mezzanine Room**	**Level 3 Skybridge Room**
	Invited Speaker	***Development***	***Management***	***Testing***
1:30-2:15 PM	**INVITED SPEAKER**	AI and Machine Learning for Testers Jason Arbon, Appdiff 65	Pre-mortems: keeping your project off the autopsy slab Christopher Cowell, HealthSparq 84	Help Your Developers Help Themselves Scott Stancil, Automattic, Inc 97

2:25-3:10 PM	Trimming Down your QA Effort While Maintaining Quality N/A Clyneice Chaney, Mitre	How Golf Taught Me to Be a Better Software Professional 105 Alan Ark, Duo Security	Building a Customer Quality Dashboard – A Case Study 116 John Ruberto, First Data	Data Quality? Yes Please! 129 Bovard Doerschuk-Tiberi, Workiva
3:15-3:45 PM	**Break in Exhibit Hall** Level 2 Mezzanine			
	Level 3 Auditorium	**Level 1 Plaza Room**	**Level 2 Mezzanine Room**	**Level 3 Skybridge Room**
	Invited Speaker	***Development***	***Management***	***Testing***
3:45-4:30 PM	**INVITED SPEAKER** Quality in the Data Center: Data Collection and Analysis Kingsum Chow, Alibaba Infrastructure Services 146	End to End Quality with the Sonar Ecosystem and the Water Leak Metaphor 165 G. Ann Campbell, SonarSource SA	How Does Pervasive Leadership Improve Agility? 185 Jean Richardson, Azure Gate Consulting	Supporting Continuous Integration in Embedded Systems 195 Andrew Graham Techtronix
4:40-5:20 PM		Testing Lessons from Lean Startups 204 Lee Copeland, TechWell Corp.	Hard Conversations: Project Quality & Project Sponsorship 210 Payson Hall, Catalysis Group, Inc	Roadmap to Enterprise Quality 217 George Nelson FarmCredit Services
5:30-6:30 PM	**Networking, Groups Discussion, Mezzanine Level 2**			
6:30 PM	**Portland Dine Around Dinner**			

Tuesday, October 10, 2017

Time	Level 3 Auditorium	Level 1 Plaza Room	Level 2 Mezzanine Room	Level 3 Skybridge Room
7:00-8:00 AM	**Registration and Wake up with Coffee & Tea** Level 2 Mezzanine			
8:00-8:15 AM	**Highlights for the Day** Auditorium Level 3			
8:15-9:45 AM	**Keynote - Auditorium Level 3** Who Owns Quality in Agile? Katy Sherman, Premier, Inc.			
9:45-10:15 AM	**Break with Poster Papers** Level 2 Mezzanine			
	Level 3 Auditorium	**Level 1 Plaza Room**	**Level 2 Mezzanine Room**	**Level 3 Skybridge Room**
	Invited Speaker	***Testing & SQA***	***Security***	***Process***
10:15-11:00 AM	**INVITED SPEAKER** Product Ecology for the Elicitation of Requirements Ruud Cox, Improve Quality Services N/A	An Empirical Analysis of Java Performance Quality 229 Simon Chow, Lincoln High School	Unit Level secure by design strategy 240 Vasantharaju M S, McAfee & Joshua Rebelo, McAfee	What's next for traditional Functional QA Managers? 255 Jim Trentadue, Independent QA Management Consultant
11:10-11:55 AM		Feeling Like a Fake - The Impostor Syndrome Berglind Bergsdóttir, Kolibri 265	Requirements Based Web Application Security Testing – A Preemptive Approach! Bhushan Gupta, Gupta Consulting, LLC. N/A	How a Technology Client became 1st in North America to be TMMi Suresh Chandra Bose Ganesh Bose, Cognizant Technology Solutions 278
12:00-1:25 PM	**Lunch Program - Meet the Speakers - A plated lunch to eat and meet. Skybridge Terrace Level 3**			
	Level 3 Auditorium	**Level 1 Plaza Room**	**Level 2 Mezzanine Room**	**Level 3 Skybridge Room**
	Invited Speaker	***Testing & SQA***	***Security***	***Process***
1:30-2:15 PM	**INVITED SPEAKER** The Future of the Testing Role James Bach N/A	How to get your enterprise to be agile Henry He 287 MatrixCare Inc.	How do you measure success rate of large scale agile process? 292 Bhageerathi Bai, Intel Tech India Pvt Ltd	Building Quality In - Ten Years Later 308 Kathy Iberle, Iberle Consulting Group, Inc.
2:25-3:10 PM		Scalable, Humane Code Review N/A Ian Dees	Embedding Security in Product Lifecycle 323 Arvind Srinivasa Babu, McAfee LLC & Deepti Chauhan, McAfee LLC	QA? Who needs that? Konnor Willison, Salesforce 340
3:15-3:45 PM	**Break with Poster Papers** Level 2 Mezzanine			

3:45-4:45 PM	**CLOSING KEYNOTE** (Auditorium Level 3) Build A Workplace People Love - Just Add Joy Rich Sheridan, Menlo Innovations N/A
5:00-6:00 PM	**Social & Networking - Skybridge Terrace Level 3**

Wednesday, October 11, 2017

7:30 - 8:30 AM	**Workshop Registration Opens**					
Breaks 10:00AM and 2:45 PM, Level 2 Mezzanine Lobby						
Lunch 12:30-1:30 PM Level 3 Skybridge Terrace						
Plated service on the covered terrace, please dress for the weather.						
8:30 AM – 5:30 PM	**W1** Pursuing World Class Quality: Transforming Your Organization Clyneice Chaney, N/A Mitre	**W3** Improving Alignment In Your Project Team Rich Sheridan, Menlo Innovations N/A	**W5** Risk-based Testing and Agile Rex Black, RBCS N/A	**W7** Scaling Software Performance Kingsum Chow, Alibaba Infrastructure Services N/A	**W9** Pragmatic Web Application Security Testing Bhushan Gupta, Gupta Consulting N/A LLC.	**W11** Let's Get Visual – Discover the Power of Visualization Zeger Van Hese, Z-sharp Ruud Cox, Improve Quality N/A Services
	W2 Agile Testing: How Lean Can You Be? Clyneice Chaney, Mitre N/A	**W4** Using Pairing to Solve Your Business Problems Rich Sheridan, Menlo Innovations N/A	**W6** Meaningful Metrics for Test Results! Rex Black, RBCS N/A	**W8** Software Performance in the Cloud Kingsum Chow, Alibaba Infrastructure Services N/A	**W10** Essential Web Application Security Test Tools – Get Most Bang for Your Buck! Bhushan Gupta, Gupta Consulting N/ALLC.	**W12** Let's Get Visual – Using Models in Testing Ruud Cox , Improve Quality Services Zeger van Hese, Z-Sharp N/A

PNSQC™ 2017 President's Message

It's my pleasure to welcome you to the 35th Pacific Northwest Software Quality Conference. The theme of Scaling Quality is an appropriate one for our anniversary. Since 1983, we have seen the conference grow from a handful of industry experts and academics to the diverse group of practitioners you see here today. We've also seen the software industry grow from semiconductors and embedded systems, to personal computers, to web and mobile applications. It has been an amazing time.

For the past 35 years, PNSQC has marked the changing scale and importance of software with an outstanding roster of speakers, including Bill Hetzel, John Musa, Richard Fairley, Victor Basili, Boris Beizer, Timothy Lister, Nancy Leveson, Ward Cunningham, Watts Humphrey, Cem Kaner, Tom DeMarco, Tom Gilb, and Steve McConnell. In 2017, PNSQC continues to attract industry experts to build on this body of knowledge and share their experiences with their peers. As the longest running software quality conference in the country, PNSQC has been a reliable partner providing professional training, generating new ideas, and helping software organizations with the tools, methods, and measures to scale appropriately.

PNSQC has been successful for as long as it has because of the strong community of practice in the area and the dedication of our volunteers. It is awe inspiring to see the scale of commitment many of our volunteers have made over decades of involvement with PNSQC. Many are here with us today. I hope that it will inspire you too to think about sharing your time and expertise with PNSQC to ensure its ongoing success.

We are delighted to have Zeger Van Hese return this year. He has been a popular speaker in the past and we look forward to hearing what he has to say this year. We are also excited to have Penny Allen with us this year to hear about the trends in tools and techniques that are driving the Quality Engineering efforts at REI. I am personally excited to attend Kingsum Chow's talk on data collection and analysis. We both presented at PNSQC in 1996. Our lunch program this year features Sarah Bradham, who is scaling mountains as the Marketing & Communications Director for the Mazamas, and Joan Grimm, who is leading efforts to scale housing as part of the Tiny House movement.

We hope you find the conference engaging and relevant. We look forward to your feedback and opportunities to improve the conference and sustain it for at least another 35 years. We would love to have your help making the conference a success in 2018.

Sincerely,

Tim Farley
President, PNSQC 2017

Is Your Automation Any Good? Finally, An Answer.

Wayne Roseberry

wayner@microsoft.com

Abstract

It is time for a monstrous change in how we treat test automation.
Test automation has always been difficult to justify. The effort, the cost, the analysis - is it worth it? Sure, you find bugs, but are they the important bugs? Many people see the time and expense and wonder if it should be spent elsewhere. Those days can end. Using data analysis and customer telemetry, it is completely feasible to assign direct value to how the test automation relates to the real business value of faster delivery of what the customer really needs with higher quality. The key is to turn the test automation activity into part of the product itself, and the tests into just one more user of your system - a user that YOU control. You can know, for certain, which test activities are important, which ones are helping you go faster and which ones are finding the issues the users will care about because you will think about the test results the same way you think about end users.
This presentation will describe how the Microsoft Office team bridged the gap and collapsed the silos between product and test automation. It will show how the telemetry signal and analysis features and services that are a regular part of the Office product were the critical component to finally solving the age old problem of tests completely disconnected from customer needs and business value. It will show how individual product teams within Office use insights gained from bridging that gap to identify real problems earlier and ship with confidence faster and more often.

Biography

Wayne Roseberry *is a Principal Software Engineer at Microsoft Corporation, where he has been working since June of 1990. His software testing experience ranges from the first release of The Microsoft Network (MSN), Microsoft Commercial Internet Services, Site Server, and all versions of SharePoint. Previous to testing, Wayne also worked in Microsoft Product Support Services, assisting customers of Microsoft Office.*

Previous to working for Microsoft, Wayne did contract work as a software illustrator for Shopware Educational Systems.

In his spare time, Wayne writes, illustrates and self-publishes children's literature.

1 Introduction

Shipping faster and more often necessitates rich, in-depth telemetry. The necessity of the feedback loop, the need to understand the customer quickly and thoroughly drive the creation of telemetry collection and analysis capabilities in any modern software team. Inevitably we will turn these same capabilities toward product testing.

We have less time to test, which motivates toward as much testing and issue discovery as possible via automated tests. This need for more automation increases the need for higher quality automation that is better at discovering issues sooner and is more relevant to business and customer needs. The same product telemetry capabilities that allow us to understand and analyze customers can do the same for our automated tests. We can better align the testing activity to customer activity and improve our ability to detect issues and bugs much sooner and faster.

2 Aligning the Tests with The Customers

2.1 When is a test any good?

For sake of this paper, a test is any good when:

1. It helps us discover and understand issues important to our customers and the business
2. We understand how it relates to behaviors and needs important to the customer and business
3. We understand what it does, how and when to execute it

There may be other criteria for a test being good or not, but this paper focuses on these points above.

2.2 Tests vs. Customer Separation

Automated tests and customers have always been separate.

We find it difficult to know whether test behaviors and results are relevant to the customer experience. It is difficult to create tests which cover the same experience one expects of users. A test engineer often guesses the value of a sequence or set of test steps. Would a customer actually do this, or would the issues found matter to the customer? Would the customers frequently do something missing from the tests?

We also find it difficult to understand test behavior after execution when we examine results. Short of reading test source code or logs, test behavior largely remains opaque. What actually happens inside the product when a test runs may be complex, rich and variant. This makes it even more difficult to determine how a given test outcome relates to the customer experience.

We used to address this separation by consuming test engineer resources and time. Allocate someone to spelunking the test results, wading through the details, and doing the best they can to report the right bugs and ignore the others all while trying to keep the customer in mind. This extra effort fit in long schedules with ample amounts of time. That time doesn't exist when shipping quickly, so the gap must close.

2.3 Telemetry Signal Makes Tests & Customers Speak Same Language

Telemetry gives us a medium to compare humans and tests.

Human use the product to satisfy their own needs or interests. Product telemetry generates data we analyze to understand customer behavior patterns, issues, problems and trends. We can anticipate adoption rates, spot rising anomalies that identify failure, assess if new feature changes are popular, or simply understand which behaviors are most common or important. This analysis is a specialized skill, but once we have learned it we can apply it to anything where the telemetry is collected.

If the product already has a rich telemetry signal in place that signal ought to be collected in both regular customer usage and automated test usage. This creates an important transformation in the way we can think about tests.

2.4 Tests Become Users You Control

When tests and customers both speak the language of telemetry we can classify them under the same category. We can think of telemetry as "a data signal produced by users" and have two types of users – humans and automated tests. Biological and synthetic. Users we do not control, and users we do control.

We can compare the two types of users to consider how to think about them:

Comparing Types of Users		
	Automated Tests	**Humans**
Behavior	You can control behavior	You cannot control behavior
Priority	Priority/Reality of behavior unknown	Priority of behavior known All behavior real

Figure 1 Comparing Human and Test Users

We control automated tests, but we are uncertain of the realism or priority of the test behavior. We cannot control humans, but we are certain every behavior we observe is real and can establish priority of the behavior using relatively simple analytical models.

We should use these differences to our advantage. There are human behaviors we can force to happen via automated tests as a means of discovering bugs and issues prior to release. There are automated test behaviors we can prioritize by comparing to the human behavior patterns. All of this becomes possible when we think of both tests and humans as the same class of entity because they speak the same language (telemetry).

3 Aligning Via Telemetry

There are technical requirements and best practices to consider when collecting product telemetry along with automated tests.

3.1 Use the Same Code, Channel and Tools

You want to take full advantage of every investment made in the existing product. You want the telemetry data to look identical whether it is a test or a customer (qualifications later on this point). You want people to use the same tools to analyze the data from the same locations. You want to have every investment in fixing and maintaining the telemetry code, pipeline and tools to accrue to the automation test effort. You do not want to compete with time or resources between test telemetry and product telemetry. With that in mind, follow these guidelines:

1. Product code, not some separate test only code, should emit the telemetry
2. Upload through the same pipeline/mechanism as would normally happen with customers. At least make sure whatever code executes the pipeline is identical and not a separate pipe or service
3. Persist to the same data store as customer telemetry

4. Query, reporting and analysis tools should be identical as per product telemetry

Hopefully your automation and product telemetry are already in a state where the above naturally happens. If not, it is worth the time and effort to change and get automation and customer telemetry in sync. Any deviation will create unnecessary friction.

3.2 Emit Test Specific Telemetry and Make Product Testing Aware

The real power of capturing product telemetry during test automation is the ability to correlate the telemetry data back to the test specific data. This means that there will be telemetry data specific to running a test. The product needs to change to recognize when it is running a test. For example, Office added a specific event to its set of telemetry events that carries data about the test. The following data is uploaded by the Office client applications at startup if an automated test is running:

- An identifier for the specific instance of the test running, and an identifier for the job it was running in
- An identifier for the specific test running
- A tag to indicate if the test was running in lab or on an engineer's own machine
- A tag identifying the type of test job that was running (Office has different test types for different purposes)

The above fields are meaningful to Office and would likely change based on how a given team manages and executes their automated tests. Most of the identifiers specified above can be joined to other systems that provide more context, such as who ran the job, what branch version it was run under, and other data that relates to Office's engineering and release processes.

Probably the most useful of the test specific data is the test identifier. This allows later analysis that can correlate product behavior captured in the telemetry to a given test or set of tests. This correlation is the basis for comparing user activity to test behavior, analyzing coverage, predicting failure rates, redundancy and ROI on execution and a variety of other useful topics.

4 Applying the Telemetry

Once the automation and the telemetry are aligned, there are many useful questions you can answer.

4.1 Do we have sufficient coverage to ship?

Office releases product to a progressively growing set of users, referred to as "rings." The rings start with the product team (called the "dogfood ring", as in "eat your own dogfood"), then all of Microsoft, followed by select external customers that agree to get non-final builds, and finally all users in market. Slow usage patterns in the earlier user rings present a key challenge. Waiting for users to generate sufficient command usage to pass release criteria can add several days to ring promotion.

Some engineers check the coverage with automation. If humans do not use some commands enough then release engineers check the automation telemetry see if the same commands are getting test coverage. This helps the team decide if the volume of failures collected from the telemetry provides sufficient information to inform the promotion decision. The screenshot below depicts an actual dashboard that reports different commands inside one of the client applications as observed during test automation. According to the engineering manager on the team using this dashboard:

It gives us confidence around audience promotion. If we don't have human coverage per feature (by threshold) then we fall back to automation because we can feel good about the automation as a signal of usage as well... Both human and automation coverage is critical."

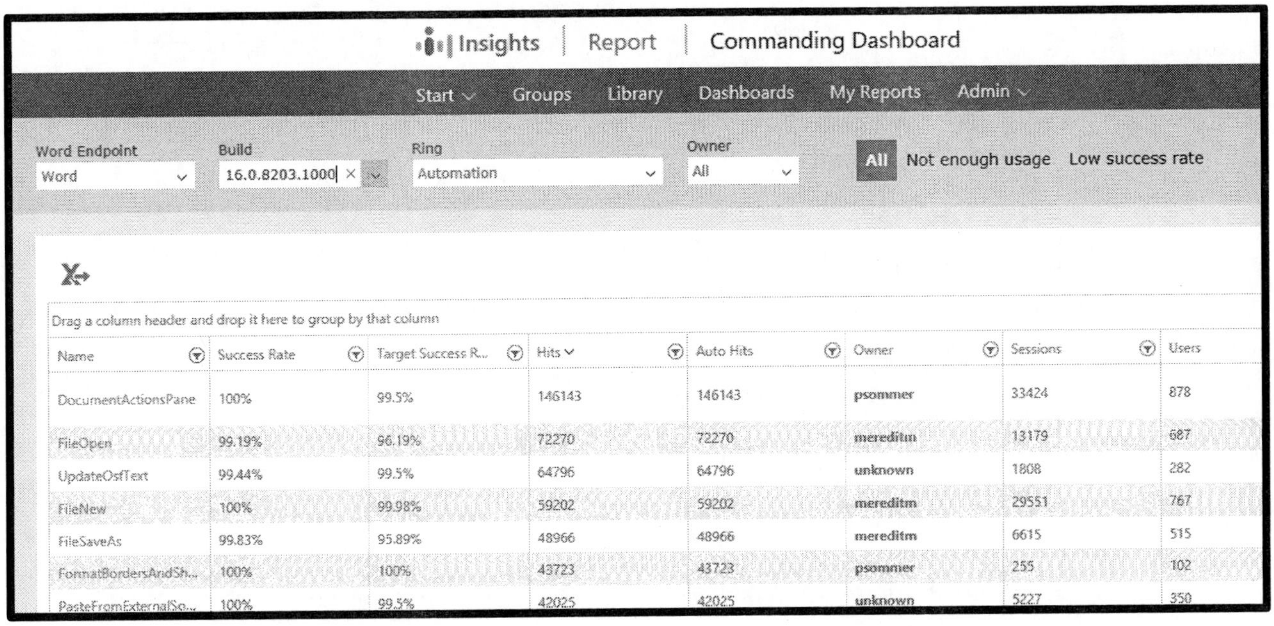

Figure 2 Command Usage Dashboard Depicting Automation Coverage

4.2 What did this test do?

Sometimes an engineer or a product team triaging test failure wants to know what a test did. Test logs only indicate test behavior from the test's point of view, they don't expose the inner behaviors of the product under test.

4.2.1 Test activity is no longer a mystery, the telemetry can describe the test

This is where product telemetry can help people understand what happened when a given test executed. The mystery is gone, as the events recorded in the telemetry will show how far the application got, what exact errors occurred when. Below is an example of a test result investigation page from the Office automation system's web UI showing events captured during a copy/paste test from one of the client applications:

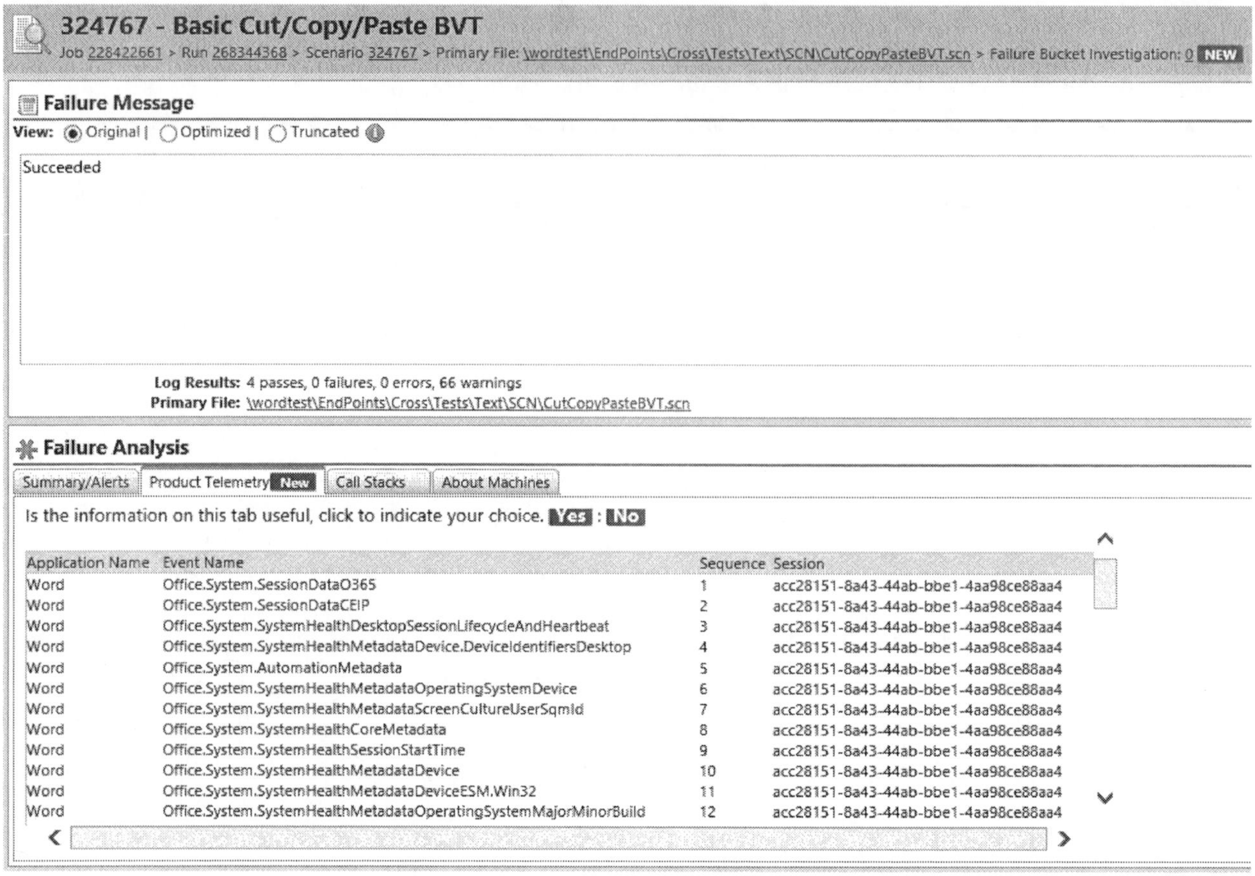

Figure 3 Automation Results UI Showing Telemetry Collected During Test

4.2.2 Makes variance more visible – not just pass/fail bug variance, but actual behavioral variance

Something that becomes apparent very quickly when comparing product telemetry across executions of the same test is that even when the test itself has no variance at all in its own behavior, the application underneath will vary a great deal in terms of exactly what events fire and in what order.

A six hour sample of all of the Office automation shows some interesting trends:

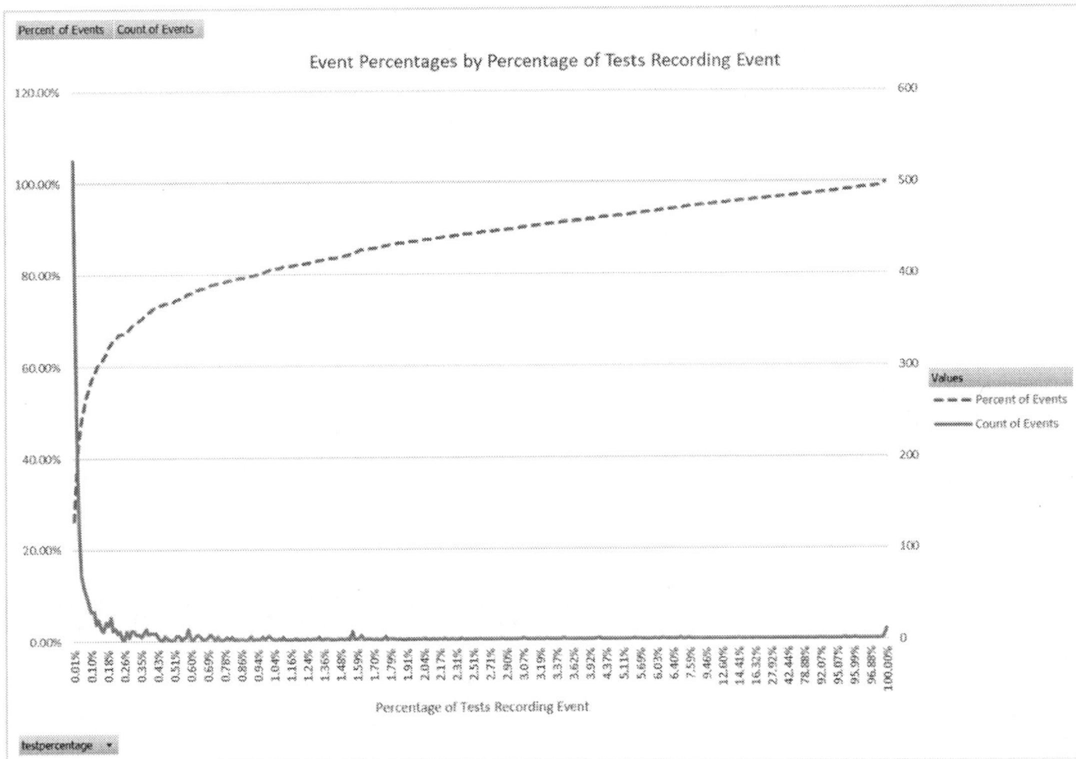

Figure 4 Event Distribution by Percent of Tests

The chart above shows the distribution of events by how many tests recorded them. Over half of the events affected only .06% of the tests, while approximately 3% of the events were recorded by 80% of the tests. This suggests a high degree of event differentiation between tests, but also that for any given test, at least 3% of the events recorded are not distinctive to that test.

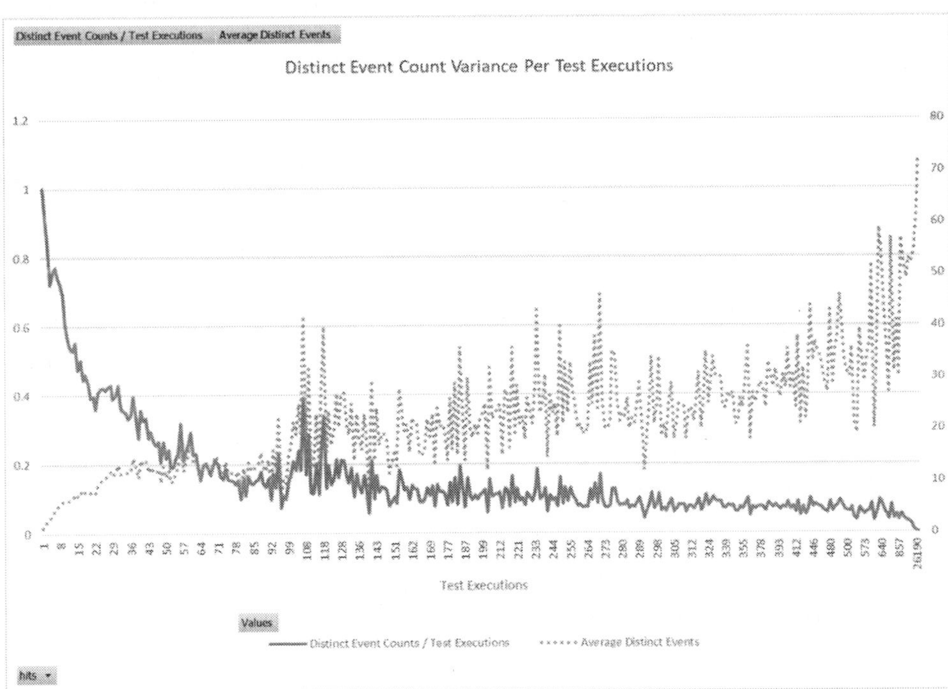

Figure 5 Event Count Variance Per Test

The chart above demonstrates the intrinsic variance in product behavior during test execution. For example, a test may record 30 distinct events during one execution, 31 in the next, 29 in the next and so on. As the number of test executions increase, the number of distinct events recorded per test trends toward 10% of the total number of executions. The trend continues upward, so long as the number of executions of the test increases. The interesting observation is that product behavioral variance in terms of combinations of events captured during a session continues as many times as a test is re-executed. Not shown, but event sequence variation trends to ~.99 of executions, so every time the test is executed, the sequence of events will be new.

4.3 Test Characteristics and Stopping Failures from Escaping to Customers

Once you can tie failures seen by tests to failures seen by customers and which tests suites the tests come from you can begin to understand the value of the different tests suites for serving different purposes.

In the table below "How Found" indicates different tests run by the Office team. "Escaped" means a human user later hit the a crash found by the test suite and "Stopped" means the crash was not seen later by human users.

How Found	Escaped	Stopped	Stop Rate	Notes
Developer Manual Tests	229	298	57%	No required stability or fix bar, no bugs ever filed
Product Team Full Suite	64	46	42%	No required stability or fix bar, bugs manually created
Product Team Check in Suite	11	25	69%	Checks quality of team branch, some teams auto-bug, usually gates main branch integration
Build Verification Suite Reliability Run	6	11	65%	Measures reliability of build verification tests, tests must be 98% reliable or disabled, bugs automatically filed
Dogfood Gating Verification Suite Reliability Run	2	1	67%	Measures reliability of dogfood gating suite, tests must be 99%, bugs filed on failures
Build Verification Suite	2	9	82%	Blocks release of build to product team, bugs automatically filed, failure locks team from checking integrating main branch
Dogfood Gating Suite	0	0	NA	Blocks promotion of build to dogfood users, tests must be 99% reliable or disabled, tests run twice to reduce intermittent failures blocking deployment

Table 1 Crash Discovery and Escape Rate by Test Suite Type

The tests in the suite increase in reliability as they are used for more and more stringent gating processes. As reliability and response to a failure increase, the likelihood a crashing bug will be found decreases. With this comes the likelihood that bugs found will be stopped before escaping to human users.

This is an important principle to recognize, and the data reinforces principles discussed in previous papers regarding managing test suite reliability (Roseberry, 2016). Test suites that are stabilized provide reliable, fast, high precision information that can be used for managing process gates, but they lose the capacity to discover failures. As tests gain ability to find more failures, they also increase in noise rate and processes that normally ensure low escape rate (automatic bug filing, locking zones for changes, blocking build promotion, etc.) overwhelm team ability to respond. It is clear that a complementary set of test automation is necessary, rather than focusing exclusively on tests that are 100% reliable.

I am predicting that we will begin to see increased innovation over the next several years over precisely this dilemma. The pressure to ship faster, with a more certain signal will motivate us to apply better and better analysis to the noisy pile of less reliable tests to more quickly determine which failures merit our attention.

4.4 What tests hit this event?

Imagine you know which telemetry events to expect for a given user scenario. Or imagine you have changed a block of code, and you know which telemetry events ought to fire when that code is executed, or you know of several different ways the code is used and those ways are indicated by different patterns and markers in the product telemetry.

Do you have tests which cover each of those cases?

Product telemetry from test automation serves as a code coverage proxy. It won't get down to the block level accountability we are used to with most code coverage tools, but it will account for whatever level of telemetry instrumentation exists in the code in question. The screen image below depicts a query in Microsoft Insights and Analytics showing tests in the last day that invoked Microsoft Word's "ApplyHeading1" command.

```
let after=ago(1d);
Office_Word_Commanding_ApplyHeading1 |  where Event_ReceivedTime > after and Release_AudienceGroup == "Automation"
| project Session_Id, Event_Name | take 100
| join kind= inner (database("Office System").Office_System_AutomationMetadata | where Event_ReceivedTime > after
   | project Data_TestId , Data_JobId, Data_JobProperties , Session_Id ) on Session_Id
| summarize any(Data_JobProperties) by Event_Name, Data_TestId
```

Event_Name	Data_TestId	any_Data_JobProperties
Office.Word.Commanding.ApplyHeading1	206995	{"JobID": "235351779", "ClassificationID": "1826", "ScenarioId": "206995", "ScenarioName": "NavPaneTabInsertAboveBelow", "ScenarioPath": "OfficeVSO\OC\Word\Layout and Display\View\Navigation Pane",
Office.Word.Commanding.ApplyHeading1	223429	{"JobID": "235425620", "ClassificationID": "-37", "ScenarioId": "223429", "ScenarioName": "NavPaneTabPromoteDemote", "ScenarioPath": "OfficeVSO\OC\Word\Layout and Display\View\Navigation Pane",
Office.Word.Commanding.ApplyHeading1	274816	{"JobID": "235452512", "ClassificationID": "1826", "ScenarioId": "274816", "ScenarioName": "NavPaneDragDropTabs", "ScenarioPath": "OfficeVSO\OC\Word\Layout and Display\View\Navigation Pane",
Office.Word.Commanding.ApplyHeading1	206996	{"JobID": "235351779", "ClassificationID": "1826", "ScenarioId": "206996", "ScenarioName": "NavPaneTabitemDelete", "ScenarioPath": "OfficeVSO\OC\Word\Layout and Display\View\Navigation Pane",

Figure 6 Query Showing Which Tests Hit a Given Event

4.5 How do test users compare to human users?

One of the questions a product team wants to know is whether or not their tests actually cover what their users do. How much of a gap is there between the user experience and the test coverage?

4.5.1 Ring hit comparisons – developers vs automated tests vs humans in different rings

Comparing user behavior to automation coverage can be pretty straightforward once the telemetry is collected in the same place and is analyzed with the same tools. One need only count the distinct events collected on a per ring basis.

The following charts are examples of event comparisons between tests developers ran on their own desktop, tests run via automation in test labs and events collected via regular usage from human users of the product.

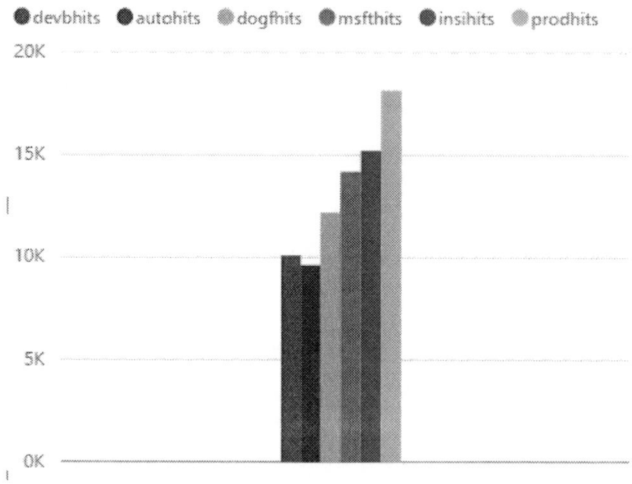

Figure 7 Distinct Event Count By Ring

The above chart demonstrates that production users (prodhits) generated nearly twice as many distinct telemetry events as seen by test automation (autohits). Meanwhile, developers performing their own tests generated slightly more events that test automation run in the lab (devbhits).

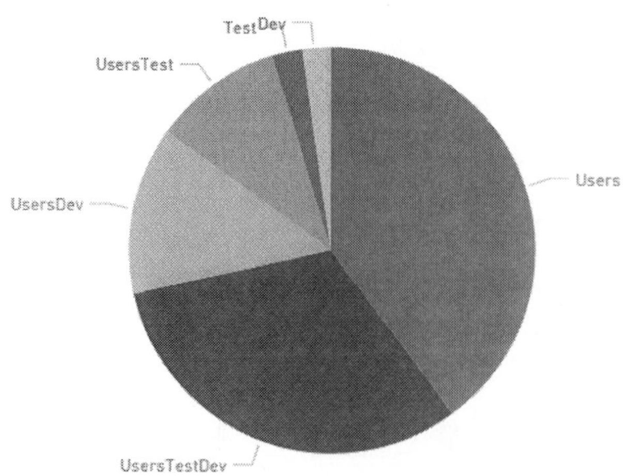

Figure 8 Event Overlap Based on Developers, Automation and Human Users

This chart compares event overlap. All the rings that comprise humans using the product (dogfood, Microsoft, insiders, Production) are collapsed into a single category called "Users." Each wedge indicates the number of distinct events seen by each category. From here, there is nearly 40% of distinct events that only ever seen by human users. Meanwhile, about a third of events are seen by users, automated tests and developers. The remaining quarter is split between events tests hit that developers did not and vice versa.

One can use charts like the above to establish how large a gap exists between the test automation and different groups of users. One can also see how automated test activity and individual developer activity are distinguished by coverage.

4.5.2 Failure Hit Comparisons –crashes seen by humans versus by developers and tests

One can also compare coverage of specific failure types. For example, if the product telemetry system collects crash data, then one could compare which crashes were seen by automation or human users.

Office collects crash information from Windows. Each crash is assigned a unique hash tag based on the location of the crash inside the product source code. This has tag is persistent across builds of the product, so it is possible to track the historical record of a crash, but also to compare crashes seen in only internal builds versus crashes seen in released builds.

The following chart shows a crash that was detected during a product team private run of their entire automation suite (this is what "Comprehensive" refers to, versus "Comprehensive Official", which is a run off the main trunk build across all Office check integrated changes). The crash was detected in automation one day prior to being seen by any human users, and two days prior to being seen in the centralized runs. In terms of process, this is interesting to the Office team, because the "Comprehensive Official" run has no gates assigned to failure, and the size of the suite is such that the official run occurs only once a week. So we have a case here were central runs straddled release of the code to dogfood, but the product team private run was able to see the crash first.

789f2482-cd6e-9117-0f6a-c7c616f6c480	30-Apr	16.0.8128.1000	Automation	Comprehensive	2
	1-May	16.0.8128.1000	Dogfood	Usage	4
	2-May	16.0.8128.1000	Automation	Comprehensive Official	2

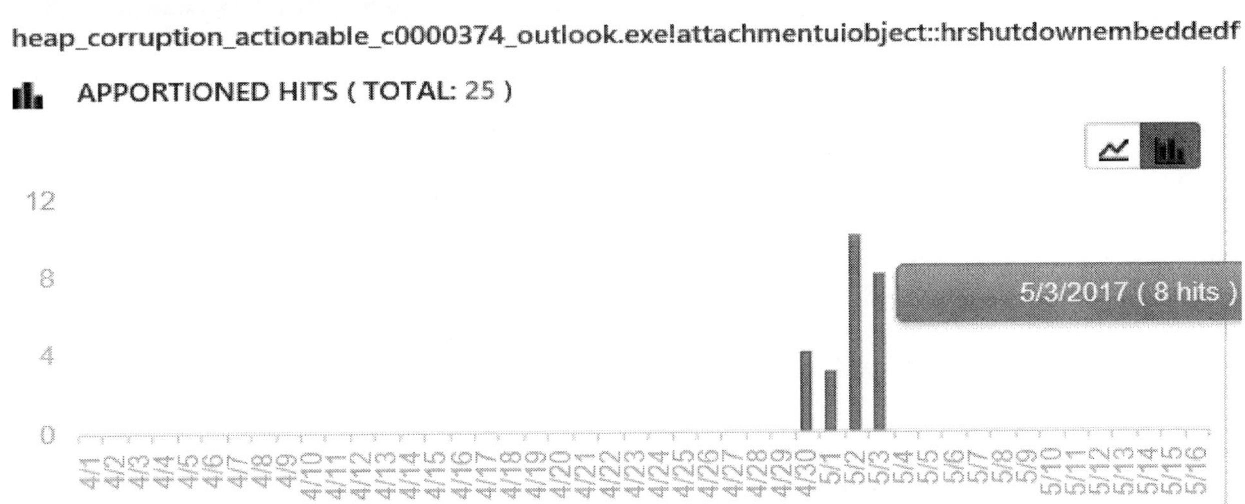

Figure 9 Crash seen in automation and dogfood

4.5.3 Anomaly Detection, Tests vs. Humans

A key benefit of using the same telemetry as the product is taking advantage of the analytical tools already developed for end users. The image below depicts an anomaly detection tool shows how activities within the Office client applications vary in behavior across different dates, builds, or groups of users (among other parameters). If certain attributes, such as activity failure rate or performance measurements fall outside expected ranges then they are highlighted as anomalous. Product team engineers create alerts on specific events of interest to them and if they feel a detected anomaly is a problem the tool will file the bug for them with all the relevant information. By framing "Automation" as a type of user, we can easily compare test automation against any other class of users and see if there are any issues we can spot in the differences.

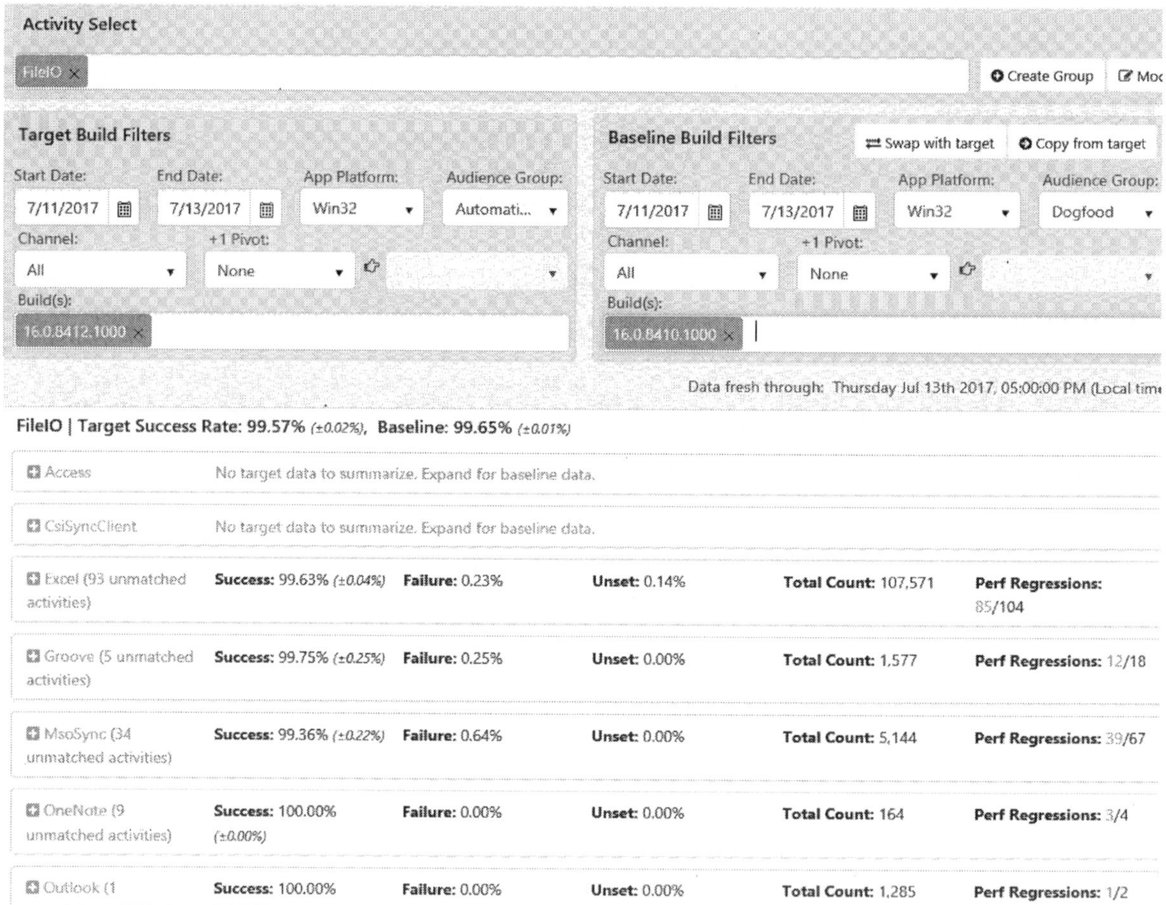

Figure 10 Anomaly Detection Automation vs. Customer Usage

4.6 Test Creation

4.6.1 See the Gap, Write the Test

One of the things people do when they compare event and telemetry coverage between real world usage and automated tests and see the gaps in the test automation coverage is plan authoring tests to address that gap. This is further assisted by measuring the occurrence rate of certain events, and addressing the most common events first. With deeper analysis of the customer experience, one ought to be able to correlate certain events or event sequences with failure modes or decreasing customer satisfaction, which should also motivate more automation coverage against those behaviors.

This is a great low hanging fruit opportunity, and is usually easy to address right away. The task ought to reap early rewards, but it is also likely that there is a long "final mile" that becomes difficult to keep up with. Writing automation code manually is expensive, and chances are the uncovered events were uncovered for a reason. Teams tend to automate the easiest tasks first.

Also, bugs frequently exist not in the single action of one event at a time. The often exist in the combinations of different behaviors mixed together. Single, one at a time, automated tests do not handle this kind of approach well.

4.6.2 Markov Chain Models driving Automation

Another way to approach the test automation is to use the product telemetry to build a model that drives the testing behavior. A typical way of doing this approach is to sample telemetry sessions and build Markov Chain models of the frequency of transitions between different events. That model is then given to a test automation driver which executes single test actions as depicted by the model.

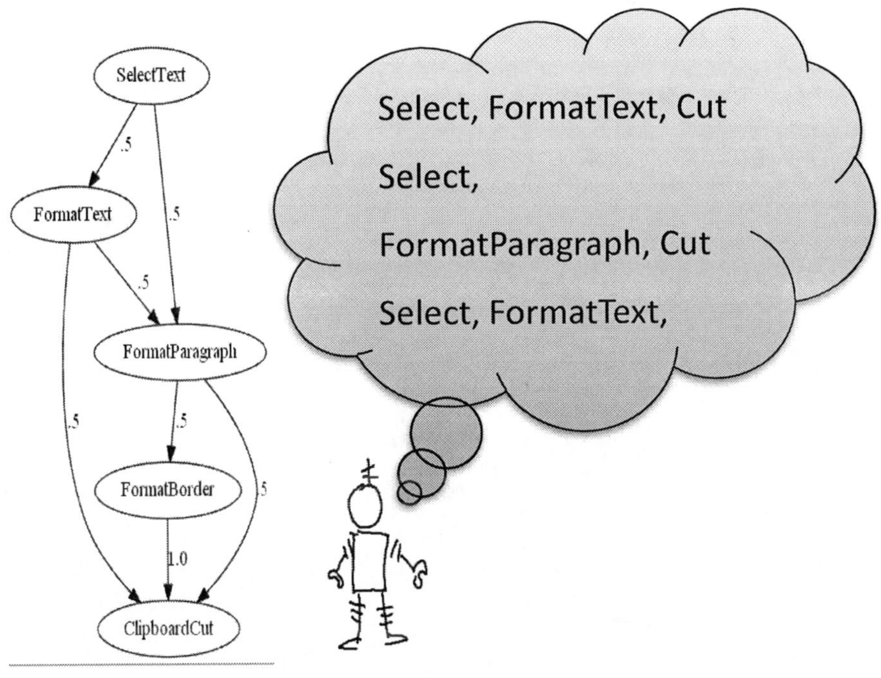

Figure 11 Comically amusing depiction of a Markov chain driven test

The approach is not like typical tests where each test is checking outcomes for a specific sequence. Instead, the test code is designed purely to drive the product behaviors. The "validation" happens by monitoring artifacts of product behavior, which can involve system event logs, memory monitoring, network monitoring, product logs and – of course – product telemetry. The exact sequence is more stochastic in nature. Not predictable or the same every time, but more seemingly random – but biased according to a model describing the frequency of user behaviors.

This is a common approach used often in server load, stress and capacity testing. In prior PNSQC sessions, I shared a methodology the Microsoft SharePoint team designed for building similar models based on web server logs (Roseberry, 2010).

In the past, such testing usually came at a high cost to set up a test bench, run and monitor the tests, and then spend several days mining all the likely sources of failure evidence to discover bugs. With the push for faster releases, it is a good bet to predict a significant investment in innovation around automatically discovering failures from the telemetry and other artifacts. There is already investment in machine learning via anomaly detection and error prediction from real-world customer behaviors, so it is easy to imagine turning the same tools and techniques against synthetic load as well.

4.6.3 Teach the computer to test

Let's have fun and add an idea that is a little crazy, but not too far outside the realm of probable. At StarWest 2017, there is a session with the intriguing title "Machine Learning, Will it Take Over Testing?" (Merril). Indeed, will it?

On YouTube, there is an amusing video that demonstrates using genetic algorithms to teach a computer to play SuperMario. The key principle relevant to this topic is that prior to training, the machine had no understanding of the game SuperMario at all. All it did was emit numbers that were translated into movement commands, and based on that it was fed data that described the screen and score, although the machine did not understand it as such. The algorithm was trained over and over, optimizing on higher score values and keeping the game running (i.e. Mario not dying). Eventually, the machine learned how to win SuperMario.

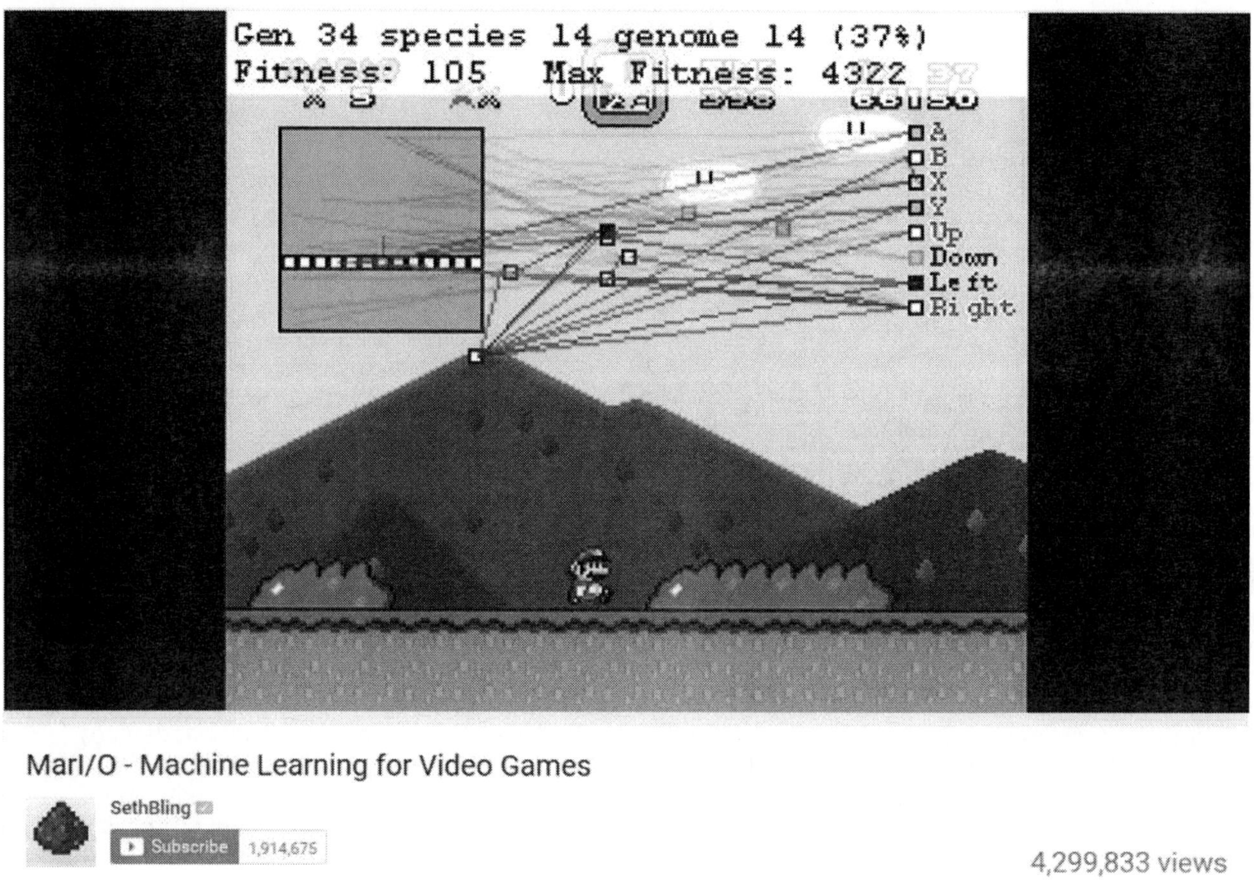

Figure 12 Screen shot of MarIO video

Let's extend this to testing. There are two things we can imagine: 1) training a machine to manipulate a product under test (click commands, type, etc.), 2) optimizing toward some test goal.

Clearly a typical software product is more complex than SuperMario, but in the same vein, the typical software team has more resources at their disposal than a home hobbyist playing with machine learning toolkits. It does not seem outside the realm of possibility that using a similar approach, a machine learning algorithm could teach itself to operate a given software product.

So now comes the question of what goal to seek. This is where the product telemetry is a useful input. Given an understanding of how telemetry manifests under test and real users, one could optimize for many different outcomes:

- Match user frequency patterns
- Maximize distinct event coverage
- Maximize distinct event sequences
- Optimize for higher failure rate per steps
- Maximize for distinct failures

The possibilities are broad, and it doesn't defy credibility too much to imagine the ability of such a system to vastly accelerate our ability to achieve much larger coverage, and hence failure discovery, in less time and with less human effort required.

5 Conclusion

Testing software is going to become more difficult as the demand for faster release velocity increases. It is time we apply the same discipline we have toward the software to the tests; better telemetry and deeper analytics applied to the actual product engineering and behavior. Once we align the automation with the product via telemetry the tests unify the gap between product and customer via the tests. This unification creates an opportunity for much better test quality and coverage than we have had before.

References

Paul Merrill, Starwest 2017, "Machine Learning, Will it Take Over Testing?" https://starwest.techwell.com/program/concurrent-sessions/machine-learning-will-it-take-over-testing-starwest-2017

SethBling, June 13, 2015, "MarI/O – Machine Learning for Video Games", https://www.youtube.com/watch?v=qv6UVOQ0F44

Wayne Roseberry, PNSQC 2010, "Simulating Real-world Load Patterns When Playback Just Won't Cut It", https://www.pnsqc.org/simulating-real-world-load-patterns-playback-just-wont-cut/

Wayne Roseberry, PNSQC 2016, "Winning with Flaky Test Automation", https://www.pnsqc.org/winning-flaky-test-automation/

Four Years of Scrum: The Good, The Bad, and The Ho-Hum

Heather M. Wilcox

heatherwilc@yahoo.com

Abstract

Three years ago, a paper was presented at the 2014 PNSQC titled, “How to Fail at Agile Without Really Trying”. It was based on the concept of achieving a successful implementation of Agile Scrum by leveraging the “lessons learned” from failure.

The company in question is now over four years into using the Scrum Methodology. Some things have changed significantly since the original launch and implementation. Some things have remained remarkably the same.

This paper examines what Scrum looks like when the newness has worn off and the process matures. It also addresses what we’ve learned about when Scrum really works and when it really doesn’t.

Biography

Heather has spent over 20 years working and learning in the software industry, choosing to focus primarily on start-up and small companies. As a result, she has had a broad range of job descriptions which include, but are not limited to: Tech Support Engineer, IS Manager, Technical Writer, QA Engineer, QA Manager, and Configuration Management Engineer. This has given Heather a wide range of experiences to draw from in her current roles as a Senior Quality Assurance engineer and Scrum Master.

1 Introduction

Three years ago, I presented a paper at the 2014 PNSQC titled, "How to Fail at Agile Without Really Trying". It was based on achieving a successful implementation of Agile Scrum by leveraging "lessons learned" from failure. At the time the paper was presented, I promised to return at some point and report on how everything evolved. Since then, enough time and change has happened that it feels like there are lessons worthy of sharing.

The company in question is now over four years into using the Scrum Methodology. Some things have changed significantly since the original launch and implementation. Many of these changes have been the result of a rededication to Scrum process and knowledge achieved through trial and error. Some things have remained remarkably the same – again as the result of lessons learned through trial and error. However, some less positive issues have remained and have not improved over time.

This paper examines what Scrum looks like when the newness has worn off and the process matures. It also addresses what we've learned about when Scrum really works and when it really doesn't.

2 Where We Were

Three years ago, at the point "How to Fail at Agile Without Really Trying" was published and presented, the company in question was still figuring out how to make its Scrum implementation work. A few critical errors were made during the initial rollout: Not training everyone on the Product Development team, not training the rest of the Company on Agile Scrum (or even giving more than a cursory explanation of what it might be about.), changing up and/or reorganizing teams every 6 months or so, and temporarily robbing people from one team and assigning them to others to increase productivity on current projects which, in turn, stunted progress on future works. Not every team had its own Business Analyst (BA) and, on some teams, the Product Owner (PO) exclusively drove feature work. There was also a generalized undercurrent of chaos which, in hindsight, was likely due to trying to figure out how to make scrum work in our organization given the rules we were initially given.

We also had a very "top down" approach to scheduling, which meant that points were nearly worthless. The expectation that certain features had to be available at certain times was the driving force behind all projects. Whether there was sufficient time to get the work done wasn't an integral part of the discussion, so putting points on stories was seen as a waste of effort and, therefore, wasn't done.

3 Where We Are Now

Since that first year, we've evolved significantly. During the second year, after the paper was published (although not necessarily as a direct result of the paper), Product Engineering rededicated itself to Scrum. We also reorganized our processes and made changes with respect to the personnel associated with each team.

3.1 Things that Changed

Each Scrum team now has a Business Analyst that works directly with the Team's assigned Product Owner. Interestingly, BAs do not serve as Product Owners. The PO position is occupied, in most cases, by a project manager or, in some cases, a people manager. We also have at least one POs who is a Senior Quality Engineer. In all cases, BAs or Marketing do not drive the pace of development although they do have influence on it. A PO works with the team to come up with a loose estimate on the number of sprints required for a particular Epic or Feature. From there, the PO confers with the BAs to create and rank stories that encapsulate the work to be done. Each team then refines the stories to suit their unique needs. During the final step, the PO works with the team to determine which stories are brought in to each sprint. So, in that respect we now schedule our projects from the bottom up, which is much more Scrum-like that our previous "top down" approach.

This has meant that our once irrelevant story points are now wholly relevant. Regular grooming sessions are used by most teams to make sure their stories are pointed out in advance. Additionally, estimated points are used to prioritize and schedule project work, so getting a good estimate for story points is now a vital part of our process.

Instead of holding several different meetings to keep work activity across all teams synched up, we've split our scrum teams up under business units. To spare us from spending time worrying about how to keep everyone's work lined up, we now have a top-down driven "Seating Plan", which prioritizes activities for each business unit for the coming year. Teams within a business unit are coordinated by their Project Managers and POs. Any coordination that needs to happen across business units is normally handled by the Product Owners.

We now use a tool called Target Process to manage our Epics, Features, User Stories, Test Cases and Test Plans. This has helped us to unify some of our processes across teams and has enabled more precise measurement of and metrics for test cases, test plans, test runs, and other valuable data. Although the tool isn't ideal, it does serve its purpose reasonably well and has provided a framework upon which we could build our Scrum process.

Finally, team membership is now much more constant. People occasionally trade groups as they tire of working on the same project but, for the most part, teams stick together and have sufficient time to not only jell but to get a solid understanding of how each person works best and how to most effectively leverage their skillset.

3.2 Things That Stayed the Same

"The more things change, the more they stay the same…." This is certainly true in our case. Some of the best parts of the Scrum process have stayed with us throughout our journey. Each team is still expected to demo any new work at the end of each sprint. We are also expected to write and keep track of our stories, have planning meetings and hold retrospectives. The basic tenets of scrum are still in place for every group, even if each one handles those requirements differently. As explained above, every team has a Scrum master, a product owner, and a Business Analyst who all work together to guide development work.

Unfortunately, some of the less positive things stayed around too. We don't have a consistent Scrum onboarding process for our new hires. Once an employee is brought in, they are invited to all the relevant meetings and then dumped into the mix to learn as they go. Some teams have a more formal indoctrination procedure than others but the one constant is that our Scrum training is inconsistent at best.

3.3 What Our Teams Look Like Now

As it turns out, our scrum teams have become very siloed both between and, in some cases, within business units. Each team has evolved its own version of Scrum process based on what was originally defined for us four years ago.

I sent out a short survey to all of the Scrum Masters. As it turns out, a few teams are using Kanban. Some adhere to a reasonably formal definition of Scrum process. Others "wing it" and follow the rules as they can but either can't or don't choose to follow Scrum process very closely. Most teams use two week sprints but a few utilize a one week sprint. All teams follow some sort of Scrum or Scrum-like process and no teams have reverted to a full waterfall format. However, the level at which the teams adhere to "true Scrum" clearly varies widely.

3.4 What My Team Looks Like

Since receiving the initial training in 2012, I've gotten five solid years of Scrum Mastering under my belt. As a result, I've formed some opinions about what I think works and what doesn't. The process below is the result of the opinions of myself and my teams translated into our work paradigm.

3.4.1 Standups

My team does some sort of standup every day. Since we have a few folks that work from home, we usually do a quick "Standup Status" email on Tuesdays and Fridays (the most common WFH days.) Mondays, we "walk the board", meaning that we look at our task board and get an actual status on each story. On Thursdays, we do a quick status based standup that usually takes less than five minutes. If we can't solution an issue quickly, it gets moved to a separate offline conversation. Wednesdays are a little different and will be explained separately. Ultimately, however, the goal of each of these interactions is to ensure that nobody is "in the weeds" and that there are no blockages. In other words, we stick to a pretty traditional version of the Standup meeting most of the time.

3.4.2 Planning Meetings

Although my team runs two-week sprints that end on a Tuesday, we have a one-hour planning meeting EVERY Wednesday. The first Wednesday of our sprint is a true planning meeting, where we step through our stories to verify which ones are finished and determine which ones need to be carried over from the previous sprint. Then we add enough stories to (we hope) get us through the whole two weeks. If there is any planning time left over, we work with our PO and BA to groom upcoming stories.

The second Wednesday of every sprint is more of a check-in and grooming meeting. We start by walking the board, which lets us know whether we're behind, on, or ahead of schedule. If we are ahead of schedule, we use the opportunity to add enough stories to keep everyone busy for the rest of the sprint. We tend to end up with more leftover time in the Second Wednesday meeting, so it often becomes primarily a story grooming session.

Theoretically, we understand that we should only need one planning meeting per sprint, but what we've discovered is that theory and reality don't always jive. To the good, we are often ahead of schedule and people feel like they might run out of work, so we have our PO handy to help us decide what should be pulled in next. During those times when we are behind schedule, the planning then serves two purposes – our PO gets an early warning that we may be falling behind but she also then helps us re-prioritize the remaining work so that the most important things really do get done.

An interesting side effect of this meeting schedule is that we have eliminated additional story grooming meetings. We occasionally meet with our PO to do broad estimates on upcoming Epics, but the days of marathon backlog grooming meetings are gone!

3.4.3 Demos

When we first started, many of my teams insisted (myself included) that we should demo something EVERY Sprint. What we ended up with was more than a few ten-minute demos that didn't really provide anything interesting and that took far more time to prepare than we spent showing our work. This made demos an expensive proposition.

What we settled on was waiting until we had real and valuable features to demo. Sometimes we go two or three sprints without showing anything. Sometimes we demo several sprints in a row. We don't save things up, but we also don't have a demo just for the sake of having it. What we've discovered is that, since we have fewer demos, people are more interested when we do hold an event, so our participation levels are much higher and those who attend are strongly engaged in the presentation.

3.4.4 Retrospectives

My team holds a retrospective every sprint. The rule I have for retrospectives is to use the same technique for as long as it works. Once the valuable input slows or stops working, I switch it up. I believe I've been fortunate in that my team takes the retro process very seriously and they work hard to come up with valuable output. Having a similar format every sprint saves time in that I don't have to explain a lot and my team is prepared for what is coming. However, eventually the format stops working. I then come up with a new technique, or revisit something that we haven't done in a long while.

Currently, I'm using a very simple retro format which is producing good results:

- Draw an emoticon that expresses how you think this sprint went.
  - This gives me a heads-up on how everyone is feeling about our current work and conditions
  - It gets everyone laughing and engaged immediately.
- Write down one thing that has had a significant effect on you this sprint.
  - It can be anything – an event, a conversation, a rule sent down from Upper Management, etc.
  - This forces people to really think about the sprint and all the events in it.

This retro usually takes 30-45 minutes (sometimes less than 30) and, so far, has been extremely productive in exposing issues that need attention. If this format does as well as my previous method, I should be able to get at least six to twelve months use out of it before I need to invent or locate a new retro technique.

3.4.5 Chartering

Whenever I am moved to a new team or if the team I'm on has a significant membership turnover, I take the group through a chartering exercise. Initially, the teams tend to feel like this is a waste of their time. However, I've discovered that, if a team has created certain artifacts, they can and will reference them when they feel like they've lost touch with what they're supposed to be doing or how they're supposed to be doing it. When I explain this value, most teams then become more willing to step through the process. Through some trial and error, I've learned that certain portions of the Chartering process are more valuable to my teams. I focus specifically on Vision, Mission, Mission Tests, Shared Values/Simple Rules, and working statements. For whatever reason, these seem to be the touchstones a team needs when they lose their way.

3.4.6 The Goal

As our team's process has evolved over time, our goal has consistently been to respect and preserve the ceremonies of Scrum while also being as mindful of time as possible. We know that each step in the process serves a specific and important purpose for our team. However, we also balance the time required for each ceremony against our workload and available bandwidth. So far, this has worked well for us as we have been able to successfully hold all the required scrum events but we have also managed to prune them down to the point where we have all the time we need but that time is nearly always an hour or less.

4 What We Learned

4.1 When Scrum Really Works

One of the things that has become clear to us is that, when the availability of a feature or epic needs to be predictable, but doesn't have a hard and fast delivery date AND the feature or epic is of "reasonable" size (typically less than 6 sprints), scrum works very well. This is especially true when we are doing incremental additions or fixes to an existing product. The team can follow all the rules of Scrum and complete the project "on time" and with an elevated level of quality. These are, by far, our most enjoyable sprints.

4.2 When Scrumfall Works Better

Over the last four years we have had a few occasions where the team has had to temporarily abandon true Scrum in favor of a technique we call "Scrumfall". We found that this tends to happen when we have an excessively large project. (e.g. Code refactor of an entire application.) A large project combined with a hard completion deadline usually assures the transition to "Scrumfall".

In the "Scrumfall" process, we tend to abandon true planning sessions and, instead, we bring every story we need to complete into the sprint in prioritized order. From there, we simply work through all the stories until they are done. At the "end" of the sprint, all incomplete or un-started stories are pushed to the next sprint. This eliminates the need for full planning meetings and backlog grooming. We still hold standups and the regular planning meetings, but they become more of a check in/status/strategy meeting than actual planning and backlog grooming. Along with the modified meeting structure, we also tend to jettison sprint retrospectives in favor of an end-of-project retro. This saves the team precious hours in meetings but allows us to deliver a high-quality product within the desired time frame.

In some respects, "Scrumfall" could be thought of as the team coasting on previous good habits. Our backlog is almost always in shape enough that we can go without grooming and regular ceremonies for several sprints in a row and then, at the end of the project, resume our normal Scrum processes without really skipping a beat. To take this whole concept a step further, it could also be considered a very Scrum-like adaptive strategy put in place to deal with a unique set of circumstances. I've often found myself reminding my teams that, even though we're trying something new, we're only committing to it for two weeks. So, if it doesn't work, we're not stuck forever and nobody dies. (This was especially true during the earliest part of our Scrum adoption.) The ability to switch seamlessly from Scrum to Scrumfall and back again, is a clear demonstration that, at least my current team has truly internalized that concept.

Finally, I should emphasize that "Scrumfall" events are rare. We work hard to not take on projects of a magnitude that forces so much change in our process. This is partially because that sort of project is inconsistent with what we know Scrum to be. Also, that type and mode of work is draining. To do a project like that very often would quickly burn out a development team.

4.3 Points Matter

As discussed previously, when we first implemented Scrum, we went through a stage where we didn't attempt to put points on stories. We were given deadlines for the completion of work, so it didn't make sense to spend time pointing stories because we already knew when we needed to be done. However, over time we have, happily, evolved into a more "bottom up" planning process. We now do an initial low-confidence estimation on epics that is used for long term project planning. Once the work has been "seated" (or put on the schedule), we work with our Business Analyst and PO to divide each epic up into small, feature-based stories.

Now that we're more Epic/Feature driven, we can confidently plan and agree to a set of features that we are able to deliver on a specific monthly release train. In most cases, we have been very successful in meeting our commitments. A large part of this success is due to diligent and consistent pointing for every story along with a good understanding of the point completion capabilities of the team under both normal and dire circumstances. Additionally, we have become extremely diligent about kicking back stories that we feel do not have all the information we need and splitting stories that are too large. We have found that any story larger than five points is, in most cases, too big and needs to be split. Occasionally, we get an odd large story (five to eight points) that must be tackled whole, but this is rare.

Lastly, given our "obsession" with small stories, we've let go of the Fibonacci numbers for pointing. For some reason, we have stories that we feel must be four points. They are clearly bigger than three, but not as large as five. So, we now have four-point stories periodically. We also don't usually use .5 (half) point stories. We tend to round up to one just to ensure that there's sufficient time to do a thorough job of testing. As a result, we have a lot of one, two, three, and five-point stories, but we also have more than a few four-point stories.

The result of all of this is that, in the last ten or so sprints (and often before that), we've only missed our "finish within five points of the estimated sprint work" goal once and, most of the time, we're within one or two points of our original estimate. Sometimes we even complete more work than we originally estimated.

5 Things We have Questions about or are Still Questioning

Since we've adopted this process, we've had a few questions come up that we either haven't answered completely or the answer isn't completely satisfactory.

5.1 Is Continuous Improvement Continuously Necessary?

We are currently mandated to provide at least one "item for improvement" out of our retrospective for every sprint. The idea is that, by requiring an action item, the teams will be driven to constantly improve themselves. I and my team have been torn on this subject. We find that our retrospectives now tend to gravitate towards brainstorming mostly on our needed "item for improvement." The fear is that this is happening at the expense of other discussions that, although they might be equally or more important, won't provide the required resolution.

To the good, the team has been able to consistently come up with a thing each sprint that we could improve or fix so there is definite value in the exercise, but again, at what cost?

5.2 Is it Okay for Every Team to be Different?

Within the Company, there are currently fourteen scrum teams. Five of those are "Reporting" teams, which my group is a part of. Even within those five teams, the Scrum process varies widely from "pretty formal" to completely informal. Across the entire fourteen teams, the variation is even wider, with some groups using Kanban methodologies, one-week sprints, permanent Scrumfall.... Essentially, each team has adapted the original scrum process to suit its own needs. However, is that wide variation acceptable? Other than the learning curve associated with transferring between groups, is there any other harm that's being done? Are there any parts of the process that we should force teams to adhere to? These topics come up for discussion periodically. So far, we've not come to any specific resolutions. Perhaps that lack of decisiveness is its own answer. Maybe we haven't answered those questions because there isn't a problem that's forcing us to come to a resolution?

5.3 How To Temporarily Join Two Teams?

Within our group of five related Scrum teams, we've had a couple of projects where teams were temporarily combined. For one reason or another, this process has never been as smooth as it probably should have been. Scrum masters accidentally step on each other's toes. QA and Dev leaders suffer the same issue. On the QA side, we did figure out a solution to the squashed toes problem. Even though there are five teams in our business unit, we ship all our software together. To prevent one person from getting stuck with all the work for every release, we now have a rotation within the QA team. A "Shepherd" is designated for every deployment. This person is responsible for attending all meetings and completing any artifacts that are required. We've found this process eases at least some of the pains associated with combined releases. The Dev team has a similar arrangement. However, even though these agreements are in place, we still have sticky issues associated with combining teams and, sometimes, things still fall through the cracks because each group does things just a little differently.

5.4 How bad is it really for a Manager to come to a Retrospective?

I have a running debate with a manager who claims that, if they are doing their job properly, it should be fine for managers to attend retrospectives. He also claims that the retrospective isn't an appropriate venue to address management issues. My response is that sometimes, the Manager isn't doing their job properly and the retro may be the only opportunity for people to voice their concerns, regardless of whether it is wholly appropriate. I also have stated my belief that, even if someone has a good relationship with their manager, the presence of a high-ranking person may inhibit or prevent some conversations. So far, he hasn't budged and neither have I. I always extend a courtesy invite to managers for our retrospectives but I also encourage them not to attend.

6 Conclusions

6.1 The Good

Scrum is working. Despite variations in usage, all the teams are getting work done in a timely matter and producing the required documentation. Whatever process each group is using, they are consistent and predictable. Teams are putting points on their work and they are providing items for continuous improvement. We don't go dark for months –features and fixes are released regularly. This has had a positive effect on our Sales and Marketing staff as they know that many features and most bug fixes are never more than a few weeks away.

6.2 The Bad

Not everything is perfect – not even close. As previously discussed, there is a lot of variability in how each of the groups runs itself. Sometimes this is a non-issue, but switching from one scrum team to another can be confusing. Additionally, internal processes vary widely. Some teams document every test case, some groups don't document test cases at all. Test automation is very inconsistent, both in technology and in the amount of code coverage. Some teams rely heavily on their Business Analysts, some rely heavily on their scrum masters, some are more harmonious and rely on both roles equally and appropriately. Lastly, as I mentioned earlier, we don't have a good program for indoctrinating new hires into our Scrum process.

6.3 The Ho Hum

The boring (and best) part of all of this is that work is getting done and, by in large, it's getting done Scrum-style. More importantly, when a team constructs a good process and sticks to it, the entire thing becomes part of the background. When we first started down this path, Scrum was the beginning and end of a lot of conversations. Development happened but we were very clearly USING SCRUM TO MAKE SOFTWARE. Four years in, we have a solid foundation in Scrum, so now WE DEVELOP SOFTWARE and Scrum is simply the device we use to do it. Scrum has been relegated to the background, where it belongs.

Few of the processes we use are innovative. The development tools we leverage are as "technology forward" as we can make them, but our Scrum methods (even though they vary widely) are still very much "by the book". We've tuned our processes to the best of our abilities and now we abide by them religiously. There is comfort in the consistency and challenge in improvement.

Interestingly, we're bringing in a Scrum coach to audit our processes. It will be exciting to hear their verdict on our adaptation of Scrum. My hope is that the coach will answer some of the questions posed earlier in this paper.

6.4 Winning Is Possible

The end goal of a software company is to successfully build and ship software and to make money in the process. This industry wants to be (and often must be) all about innovation. So, as soon as we master a technology or a process, instinct tells us that it's time to move on and invent or find the "Next Great Thing" – always skating the bleeding edge. However, sometimes the tried and true process is the best thing to use. The Waterfall development methodology is still appropriate in certain situations. Like Waterfall, Scrum may not be a bleeding edge technique any more, but it is reasonably easy to learn, extremely adaptable to many situations, and certainly enables the fast construction of quality software. That, by any measure, is a win.

7 Thanks

As always, I am thankful for the patience of my employer, who allows me to continue to write and publish papers as part of my normal job duties. I am especially gratefully to my manager who, not only allows me to get away with writing during company time, she includes it in my annual goals so that I must do it! Finally, I wish to thank my husband, Justin, who still doesn't really get all this technology doo-dah, but puts up with me talking about it all the time anyway.

References

Wilcox, Heather M. 2014. "How to fail at Agile Without Really Trying", Proceedings of the 2014 Pacific Northwest Software Quality Conference, http://www.uploads.pnsqc.org/2014/Papers/t-014_Wilcox_paper.pdf

Software Architect as an Agent for Product Success

Brian Walker

walkerb@mac.com

Abstract

As software development projects become larger and more complex the need for a development roadmap becomes imperative. A software architecture provides the necessary roadmap to guide development and provides a high-level view of the system design and construction. The role of software architect provides a vital influence for the quality of a system. As guardian of the architecture, the architect can be a champion for software quality within a development team.

Biography

Brian Walker is Software Architect for the Video Product Line at Tektronix developing professional video monitors for television stations, cable operators and video content producers around the world. For the past 19 years, he has been the lead architect for a software architecture that started its life running on a real-time, embedded PowerPC processor within the first WVR video monitor product and has evolved through time to run on full desktop Linux system with a brief foray into embedded ARM processors. During that time, the architecture survived memory-constrained systems, handheld products and the transition from a big-endian to little-endian hardware architecture and evolved to meet the needs of current shipping products.

1 Introduction

Good design leads to quality. Although there are many paths that one can follow to realize a quality product, the one constant is that quality product follows from a good design. Whether that design derives from a top-down development pattern where a carefully constructed design is faithfully implemented or from a. Test Driven Development pattern where a design is discovered through frequent refactoring, quality follows design.

As projects become larger and more complex, the effort to design a product grows in complexity as well. Whereas a small system could simply evolve over time and their function could be easily understood by a single developer, complex systems defy the ability for a single person to intimately know the details of the entire system. No longer can the design of the system simply emerge after serious coding sessions or be briefly sketched on a napkin. As more developers are needed to construct a system, more people must become involved in the design of the system and their efforts must be coordinated and consistent. Large systems, therefore, need an architecture to define the overall design of the system, its parts and how those parts interact with each other to produce a unified whole.

The architecture requires the attention of a dedicated individual or team to create, manage, guide and protect the architecture to provide the necessary foundation, conceptual framework and roadmap for the development of a software system. An architecture may integrate existing products into a unified whole or it may establish the foundation for an entirely new system. The role of the architect is to assemble or create the architecture and communicate it to the team. Once development starts, the architect should guide the product development and champion the integrity of the architecture. The architect manages the evolution of the architecture to ensure that the architecture remains relevant and continues to serve the needs of the development team and happy customers.

2 Role of the Architect in an Organization

The architect is uniquely positioned to be a champion for the quality of a system. In a Scrum team, the participants typically have an area of interest that determines their focus.

The Product Owner is often focused on delivering value to the customer. The Product Owner might have technical expertise but often they bring the domain expertise of the customer to the team and must be able to understand and express the needs of the customer. Those needs are often expressed as features that the product will deliver to the customer and can be expressed by User Stories.

The Scrum Master works with the Product Owner to groom the backlog. The Scrum Master oversees and manages the Scrum process by which the product team delivers stories to the customers. Those stories tend to have an external focus since they are told from the perspective of the customer.

The Scrum team is charged with implementing the stories in each sprint. The team must add technical stories to define the infrastructure that is necessary to realize the user stories because they are the domain experts in the matters of product development. In the early stages of product development, the technical stories often outnumber the user stories. The team is often measured by their sprint velocity and by the amount of technical debt that they accumulate or remove during a sprint.

The interest for the architect is the architecture of the system and the architect's focus is delivery of the architectural vision. The architect works with the Product Owner and the Scrum team to develop the architecture. The architecture provides the overall scope of the project and the basis for early story estimation in the form of T-shirt sizing. The architect may work with the Scrum Master and the Scrum team to define Epics which can be placed in the backlog.

While the effort to implement features can easily be measured in story points, matters of quality are hard to measure in terms of story points. Granted, defects can be used as a measure of technical debt or lack of quality, but, defects are a lagging indicator. Acceptance criteria allows teams to determine when the story has been completed so that it may be accepted by the Product Owner. Quality can be unknown until defects are discovered. A proactive approach to remove risk of defects in a system through a consistent architectural definition improves system quality by preventing defects.

Conformance to an architecture can be an indicator of system quality. Each unit of work should follow a design which is derived from the architecture. The architecture should define the interactions, the processes and interfaces between units such that units that adhere to that interface will interact correctly and reliably with others. An architect should review system design and measure how faithfully it follows the framework defined by the architecture.

As the guardian of the architecture, the architect can be a champion of quality. With a focus of architectural integrity, the architect promotes consistency with the software. Consistency reduces variations that produce opportunities for defects and increase the cost of testing. The architecture defines common infrastructure which is reused within the product. Through consistency and reuse, the architecture contributes complete and tested components that increase system stability.

The architect's job is not complete when the architecture is finished. The architect's roles transitions from defining the architecture to guiding the implementation of the architecture through product development. The value of an architecture is determined by its reuse, its adoption and its development beyond the needs of its first product.

3 Design of a Large System

3.1 Nature of Human Design

For a small, discrete system, one can discover the design through trial and error and repeated refactoring. The process quickly becomes unwieldy in larger systems. Where multiple systems interconnect, the job of coordinating the system requires a conceptual vision to explain the construction and function of the system as a whole. People specialize because it is the most efficient way to work in groups so there is a need within a large group to break problems into manageable pieces. An architecture describes the overall design of a system, specifies its parts and provides a reference for what is available and what still needs to be created so that developers can focus their efforts on providing value instead of reinventing infrastructure.

As humans, we all have different biases and experiences that produce a diversity of solutions. That diversity of ideas is a strength that teams use to construct novel approaches for solving problems. Unbounded, that diversity of opinions produces chaos through conflicting designs and undiscovered dependencies. An architecture provides a common vision of the system that focuses the solutions into a unified strategy. It promotes reuse and consistency by restricting the design and implementation of the system component to a known set of patterns. Those patterns allow developers to move between components and aids in the knowledge and understanding of the system. An architecture documents those patterns to remove mystery and surprise from the effort.

By definition, there is no perfect architecture. Otherwise, we would all be using it and there would be no need to discuss best practices or optimal solutions. The architecture should be the best fit for the particular problem space within the constraints of the business and available resources. Each team member may well develop the most perfect design for an individual component within the system and that design could be in complete conflict with the equally elegant and refined solution developed by her teammate. The architect must choose, from among the available solutions, to define a framework that defines the interfaces and common elements of the system. The architecture will not be perfect, but it will provide a common design philosophy that can be carried through the entire system and unite the disparate pieces into a unified whole.

3.2 Elements of Architecture

First and foremost, an architecture provides a high-level perspective of the system design. It defines the basic system strategy for interactions such as message passing, central database or client-server transactions. It describes data flow within the system, protocols for sending and receiving data, interfaces for system-to-system and user-to-system interactions and how elements will be reused or created for the system.

From there an architecture defines a framework for design and development. It defines the components of the system and their hierarchy. It lists the types of components, describes their character and relationships and specifies how they interact with others. It describes common infrastructure including common interfaces, connective components, base classes and resources.

An important consideration for the architecture is the hierarchy of authority within the system. Each resource within the system should have a single owner with authority over it. When authority is not clearly defined, multiple agents can attempt to exert authority over the same resources. When not well managed, these conflicts can produce race conditions that cause unexpected and unstable system behavior. In the classic race condition, the result is determined by which agent finishes last. Execution order may vary because of slight differences in timing. The confused software engineer may then be confronted with a system that works correctly in the debugger only to fail intermittently under normal conditions. Race conditions are notoriously difficult to diagnose and debug so the best solution is prevention. An important role of the architecture is to clearly define the resources of the system and which agent controls that resource and where that control originates.

The architecture serves as a framework for detailed design. At inception of a project, the architecture should minimally define and describe the core features of the system infrastructure with enough detail to allow in-depth design of system components. The architecture should evolve over time as new problems are discovered or expected problems become evident as product requirements are more fully defined and understood. When limitations are discovered in the architecture, the architecture should evolve and its evolution should be documented so that it continues to be relevant and provide guidance.

The architecture serves as a development roadmap allowing the development team to quickly discover what needs to be accomplished to bring a large system to life. It should be a focus of discussion to determine what the system is and how it will be constructed. It must guide the in-depth design of the system. Designs that are contrary to the architecture need to be reevaluated and revised or the architecture must evolve. One could develop without a roadmap, and some may aspire to do so, but it would be easy to get lost without one.

3.3 Modular by Nature

By its nature, an architecture is modular in since it provides a high-level description of a system by identifying its parts. A monolithic design might be reasonable for a small system but as the size of a system grows, the interactions and, therefore, connections between units grows at a rate of $n \cdot \log(n)$ which is faster than the growth in the number of its parts. The complexity of that system would quickly overwhelm the ability of people to accurately understand it. Rarely will you find a complex program that follows a single sequence of operations. There are always exceptions and deviations in a process. Minimally, a system that interacts with users must account for errors and basic human interaction. Without modularity, software quickly turns into what is affectionately and derisively known as spaghetti code.

Modularity minimizes the number of connection points and, if done well, defines their interfaces to produce well-defined APIs. Modular units may be tested in isolation with unit tests providing predictable and consistent units of functionality. A well-defined set of units with consistent behavior and spheres of influence simplifies the organization of a system making it accessible and understandable. Modularity allows people to focus their attention on discrete units within the system. A well-defined module has a discrete purpose, defined behavior and known interface.

3.4 K.I.S.S

Modularity promotes simplicity and simplicity should be a goal of every architecture. An architecture that requires complex interactions will induce, rather than reduce, errors in a system. The architecture should hide the complexity of a system in well-tested interfaces so that the complex operations can be used within the system without the need for individual developers to know the details of that complexity. Much like the libraries of a modern programming language, the infrastructure of an architecture should make it simple for developers to use the architecture so that they can focus on producing value for the customer.

In practice, I have seen many examples of complexity for the sake of complexity. It is tempting to build complex structures with several layers of nested objects and complex interactions of parts. Complexity in design is often a symptom of not truly understanding the problem or sufficiently developing a solution.

In the process of developing a solution, it is often helpful to throw down a prototype design as a brain storming exercise to start the design process. From there, the designer works with the design to discover its patterns and iteratively refines and reforms the design. Too often, inexperienced designers start coding immediately and become too vested in the implementation to adequately refine the design. They attempt to force the prototype design into a finished design by adding layers of complexity. Simplicity takes time, thought and contemplation to discover the interactions between components and reduce the design to its core. The process of design prototyping, refactoring and refinement is best accomplished on paper where the process can unfold without the being vested too early in the implementation of the design.

As a developer, when faced with a complex design, my first impulse is not to delve in and try to make sense of the design for the good of the team. My first impulse is to run away as quickly as possible to avoid the inevitable frustration of confusion and prolific cursing. In the face of complexity, the natural impulse of the sane developer is to seek a better solution that can be understood and maintained.

Simplicity should be the goal of every architect because simple is easier to understand, easier to explain, easier to use and easier to avoid mistakes. There may be complexity behind the curtain but the interfaces that the architecture provides should be simple and approachable. Simplicity is also the hallmark of elegance and for an architect, that can be quite satisfying. So, the architect should follow the edict of Keep it Simple, S....

3.5 Environment Influences Software Architecture

An architecture does not stand on its own. It is driven by needs of the customer, the needs of the developers and the needs of the business. The architecture may be the first step in the delivery of a roadmap of products that can sustain a business into the future or it may be the continuation of a product platform for continued development. It may be structured around a process of continuous delivery or by the periodic release of functional boxes. Products that are purely software will be constrained by the hardware that they run on and whether the hardware is handheld, desktop or virtual. Products that include both hardware and software will be both constrained by the hardware and the need to support the hardware through its expected life cycle and freed by the ability to define the hardware to fit the needs of the product.

There may also be regulatory requirements such as FDA certifications and compliance to industrial standards for safety critical systems that regulate not only the behavior of the product but the process of developing and testing the product. Where safety is a critical concern, the architecture must be structured to facilitate rigorous processes and development standards.

3.6 Platform Development

Often, the worst thing a business can do is build a platform. I have seen several platform efforts fail through lack of focus and vague requirements. The nature of a platform is to deliver a complete architecture but that effort makes the grand assumption that the extent and capabilities of a platform are known before any products are developed and usually before customers are consulted. The chief failure of a platform development effort is the lack of a concrete definition of doneness. A platform development effort is often the pretext for allowing the architect to go wild and throw in everything that might be needed for a platform, including the proverbial kitchen sink.

Another risky proposition for a business is to develop a platform in a central group. It makes sense to share and reuse software but a centralized platform effort may be delivered as an edict from management to reuse software developed by an isolated group attempting to serve too many stakeholders. Such efforts run the risk of producing edifices to system complexity as they attempt to address conflicting and misunderstood product requirements.

The result of a platform development effort is often a platform that does not fit the target product category. It often fails by delivering too much but not enough of what the product really needs. In the past, I have observed a platform development effort that resulted in the acquisition of expensive shelfware after the development team bought into a promise of blissful development through technologically advanced tools. In another, the platform was simply too big and too expensive to build into a product.

When given the opportunity to define and develop a new product, I and the other members of my team rejected the existing platform and decided instead to develop our own. In our calculation, the platform simply did not fit our needs and the effort to fit the platform to our needs would be wasted. The existing platform was simply too expensive and too complex. We chose a simpler path are much happier for the effort.

The architect must remind the team and the business leaders that platforms and architectures are not static creations. They grow and evolve over time. The best architectures are tailored to serve the products. The best platforms accelerate product development rather than constrain products into a particular mold. At the end of the day, the business must deliver a product to the customer. A properly designed and fitted architecture makes that effort possible.

3.7 Just in Time Platform Development

When developing what eventually became our new product platform, our mantra was "product first, but leave the door open." That mantra expressed the view that the product development team should focus on the development and delivery of a product that the business could sell. At the time, it was a very agile philosophy before agile became popular. That focus on product allowed the development team to focus architectural development on features that were most needed by the product that used it. But, in developing that architecture, the team chose options that did not overly constrain the architecture and allowed for current and future flexibility. That flexibility allowed the architecture to evolve over time. As new features were added to the platform, the architecture evolved.

Flexibility in the platform manifested itself in several elements of the architecture. We chose a message passing architecture based on experiences with imitation in the previous architecture. We specified that message transactions were atomic to limit the interactions between modules and defined "datatags" to identify the data that was modified by those messages. We defined those datatags in "schema" files that were specifically not written in C so that the user interface could be decoupled from the core application. That decoupling allowed user interface development to proceed in parallel or in advance of development of lower-level code as long as the datatag was added to the schema file. Schema files defined the data that formed the primary interface for every module of the system to provide a consistent and universal interface.

Message types described the actions that could be performed the data identified by the datatags. Like the SNMP protocol, the initial message request types were Get and Set with response types of Response, Error, ACK and NAK. As the system evolved we added Alarm and Status messages to account for asynchronous events and by-products of other operations. The current system adds Data and Post message to limit the exposure of messages sent internally within the system and to manage message traffic.

Type	Class	Description
Get	synchronous request	A message sent to request the value of a system variable, parameter or hardware status.
Response	unicast response	A message sent in response to a successful Get request. The message payload contains the value requested by the application.
Error	unicast response	An error message in response to an unsuccessful Get request. The payload contains an errno value.
Set	synchronous request	A message sent to set a parameter or value or to initiate an action within a supplier.
ACK	broadcast response	An acknowledgement message sent in response to a successful Set message. The payload contains the actual value used by the supplier. ACK messages are broadcast to all interested clients.
NAK	unicast response	An error message sent in response to an unsuccessful SET request. The payload contains an errno value.
Post	asynchronous request	A message sent to set a parameter or value or to initiate an action without generating a response for the action.
Status	asynchronous broadcast	An asynchronous message sent to announce a new value for a system variable, parameter or hardware status. A status message reflects a change in instrument state as a side effect of a related Set operation or in response to an external event. Status messages are broadcast to all interested clients.
Data	asynchronous unicast	An asynchronous message sent to provide data within the system. One typical use for this type of message is to transfer data from hardware to an application service for further processing.
Alarm	asynchronous broadcast	An asynchronous message sent to announce an exception or fault (one-shot). The payload contains alarm parameters describing the specific circumstances of the alarm.
Alarm Start	asynchronous broadcast	An asynchronous message sent to announce the start or change in a continuous alarm condition. The payload contains alarm parameters describing the specific circumstances of the alarm.
Alarm End	asynchronous broadcast	An asynchronous message sent to announce the end of a continuous alarm condition. The payload contains alarm parameters describing the current circumstances of the alarm.

Originally, messages were defined as a C structure with a basic header and a flexible payload. The payload was a union which required the software to know how the size and number of the values in the payload. The architecture quickly added a database so that software could use accessor functions to extract values from the message payload. The current message implementation is a C++ object that encapsulates the payload within the message and removes direct access to the payload. It stores the payload type within the message instead of relying on a database so that the message object can translate itself to and from JSON and manage its own payload. The message provides a reference payload type so that arbitrarily large objects can be allocated, attached to a message, distributed throughout an application and then automatically deleted.

Nineteen years ago, that architecture defined a single application written in C and C++. Along the way, the architecture moved from a big-endian PowerPC microcontroller to a little-endian ARM embedded processor and finally to an Intel desktop processor. Today, that architecture describes a constellation of applications that are written in C++, Python and JavaScript. The decoupling that was inherent in the system enabled messages to leap between application. Formerly primitive message structures evolved to become message objects that could translate themselves to and from JSON.

The combination of focus on product development with flexibility for the future allowed that architecture to evolve and continue to meet the needs of the development team, the business and customers. The most recent product development effort had a very aggressive timeline but the business was confident that they could achieve the targets because it could rely on an established, mature body of software. Product development is hard but it would be even harder without a stable foundation on which to build.

4 The Influence of an Architect on Software Quality

Incidental to the development of the architecture, the architect affects software quality in other ways.

4.1 Requirements

The architect is often the first member of the development team to be engaged in the product definition and design of the product. While the Product Owner brings customer domain expertise, the architect brings technical expertise. At inception of a product development effort, the architect begins by interacting with the Product Owner to gather and define system requirements.

Whether they are written as stories or as formal requirements, understanding non-functional requirements is crucial to development of the system architecture and determining the tradeoffs that are inherent in the definition of an architecture. The architecture provides the first effort to define the system in a holistic manner and requires broad analysis of the system requirements. The effort to use the requirements to define the system creates a necessary push back to refine and develop the requirements. It challenges the Product Owner to more fully define the requirements and engage in discussions the further define the product and its value to users. The collaborative effort between Product Owner and architect provides an important tool to allow the process of generating requirements to stay ahead of the development effort.

It is advantageous for the architect to actually write product requirements because the architect can bring a technical rigor to the process. As a consumer of the requirements, the architect is familiar with the kind of details that developers need to implement the requirement in software. It is also a convenient way to clarify the understanding of the requirements for the architect to express his understanding of the user stories to the Product Owner through the writing of requirements.

4.2 Architectural Evaluation

As a matter of due diligence, it is incumbent on the architect to validate the architecture. For validation of efficiency and performance, that evaluation may require building a prototype to verify the performance expectations of the completed system. When done correctly, prototyping removes risk from the architecture and allows the development team to make informed decisions. However, the findings of a badly executed evaluation can have serious repercussions on the success of the architecture and product.

Our architecture once had a flirtation with Java. The performance of Java on our embedded ARM processor was a concern for the development team but the designated architect at the time had a fondness for Java. The cursory evaluation of Java performance appeared to be adequate and thus the decision to proceed was granted. However, after the system was implemented, it became quite apparent that processor was not up to the task. The performance evaluation failed to account for the prolific use of floating point operations in the Java libraries. On an embedded microprocessor that did have floating-point support in hardware, those operations had to be emulated in software. It also failed to test performance in a multithreaded environment that resulted in sluggish user interface performance and very frustrated users.

After the several attempts to salvage the situation, the product was shipped late to market. However, plans to remove Java from the platform began well before the product shipped. The flirtation with Java resulted in years of wasted man-months of effort and many lost weekends in a valiant effort to ship the product as promised despite the high hurdles imposed by an architectural decision.

4.3 Selections of Tools and Environments

Two key elements of the architecture are the tools and environment in which that architecture lives. Often that choice is dictated by the platform. Where there is a choice, the decisions of the architect can have a profound influence on the quality of the code.

For example, in embedded system, the common myth is that C++ is too big and inefficient to run within the constraints of an embedded system with its limitations of memory and CPU. That may be relevant for tiny 8-bit processors and it may have been relevant before GNU compilers became the compiler of choice for many embedded processors. However, the more rigorous type checking available in a C++ compiler allows the compiler to protect against a wide variety of errors especially in systems that often use integers of specific sizes, like embedded systems.

I once worked on a product that reused user interface code from a previous product which was written in C. However, the new product design provided a tiled display so that instead of one instance of the UI, there were essentially four instances on the screen at the same time. The developer decided to expand the original UI by replicating the parameters of each instance in an array rather than encapsulate the instances of each interface in separate objects. Instead of a neat modular construction of discrete objects the resulting monolithic spaghetti code was plagued by inconsistencies due to crosstalk between the tiles. Programs written in C tend to follow very functional constructs. While object-oriented programming is possible in C, the language does not lend much support for the effort.

As a first step in the evolution of the UI, we changed all the file name extensions from .c to .cpp so that we could compile them with the C++ compiler. After fixing compiler warnings, we then proceeded with the real task which was to re-implement the spaghetti as objects. The choice to allow C for development was pragmatic but it led to the development of a monolithic and enormously complex code. The effort to refactor the UI was a three-month hit on the schedule that was welcomed by management as a necessary exercise to stabilize the product and enable further development.

In the current iteration of the architecture, the core application has been standardized on C++11. I once described C++ as "C with object-oriented extensions." As architect, I chose C++11 because it is the first fully object-oriented implementation of C++ because it includes the standard library as an integral part of the language. Using C++11 allowed me to implement new capabilities in the architecture to make it simpler to use.

Another important consideration for the architecture is whether to build or buy. In that sense, "buying" includes the use of open source software. However, in choosing to "buy", the team needs to know the quality of the code. Buying code for mission critical components of the architecture has inherent risk especially if there are few alternatives. Open source software is not free but it is provided "as is" which means that the product team assumes responsibility for maintenance. Some open source also have licensing provisions that could place the entire source code at risk if used in a way that allows copy-left provisions to attach to proprietary code. Good acquisitions can significantly reduce time to market and provide proven, tested code. Bad acquisitions can increase risk and eat time and effort in debugging that could have been better spent on creating value for customers.

4.4 Documentation

The architect must document the architecture because if it isn't documented it does not exist. The architecture is the basis for all design so it must be well understood by the development team. The architect should strive to remove ambiguity and that happens best when the architecture is described in terms that can be understood, reviewed and critiqued. The architecture document should also document the tradeoffs that shaped the architecture to ensure that they don't come back to haunt the development team. A successful architecture will also be adopted for succeeding products and by other products.

My tools of choice for an architecture document are a good document editor and a graphing program. I use Word and Visio because they are available. I generally start with the Visio document because I think better in pictures. The Visio document generally provides a summary of the architecture and provides pages that are well suited for plastering cubical walls and conference rooms. The word document incorporates the images from the Visio document and provides additional details about the architecture.

Both documents are stored in the revision control system because if it isn't controlled, it will be lost. The revision control system provides a history of the evolution of the architecture and an authoritative source for the current revision of the document so that people know where to find it and won't be confused by old copies stuffed away in a filing cabinet. The document is periodically updated to reflect the current state of the architecture.

An architectural document is also a valuable tool in the process of on-boarding new team members. By offering training, the architect can set the stage for the architecture and share the architectural vision with the team.

4.5 Guardian of the Architecture

The architect defines or chooses the architecture and acts as its guardian but does not own the architecture. Some may choose to impose an architecture or perhaps the team chooses an existing architecture that they do not control. It is usually better to work collaboratively to create and refine an architecture. The architect must achieve buy-in from the development team because they are the ones who must live within its constraints.

As guardian of the architecture, the architect has a responsibility to ensure that the architecture is faithfully implemented. He or she continues to encourage team members to follow its guidance and collaborates with developers to ensure that it is implemented with integrity. The architect must address flaws in the architecture and be flexible to adapt the architecture as needed so that the architecture remains relevant and useful. After all, there is no perfect architecture and the architecture should evolve.

However, sometimes it is the role of the architect to say "no". If the architect is too flexible, the architecture may become unfocused and divergent. But, in saying "no", the architect must explain why that response is best for the architecture and not just a personal bias. Sometimes, that reason is in the service of consistency. Where necessary, the architect may provide guidance in the use of the architecture in the form of examples, coaching or training.

4.6 Quality Assurance

As part of the process of defining the architecture, the architect may also establish coding standards and design principles. Coding standards are not necessarily the same as code style. Coding standards include such standards as the MISRA standards for C and C++ which began life subset of the C language for preventing defects in automotive control software and has since been adopted by other mission critical applications.

An architect may also establish a build environment which includes a framework for automated unit tests or implement automated source code analysis that tests against known, insecure coding particles from the Common Vulnerabilities and Exposures database.

An architect should participate in design, code and test plan reviews. Design reviews allow the architect and team members to participate in the refinement of the architecture. Detailed code reviews provide a valuable tool for an architect to monitor the implementation of the architecture and to provide insight and advice on its implementation. Test Plan reviews allow the architect to ensure that system requirements have been adequately specified and provide insight for test coverage

As a senior member of the development team, the architect also can provide the benefit of a wealth of experience for other members of the team. As an active member of the team, the architect can share that experience with fellow team members.

4.7 Implementation

An architect benefits from participation in the implementation of the architecture. Through personal experience, the architect can "feel the pain" and quickly determine whether the architecture is sufficient or deficient. Personal experience can often lead the architect to proactively enhance the architecture to better fit the needs of the developers.

As a senior developer, the architect may also be the most capable person to implement key infrastructure components of the architecture. Part of that is aided by first-hand knowledge of the architectural intentions and an appreciation for how that work fits into the whole.

4.8 Qualities of an Architect

An architect is a seasoned technical leader with years of experience that provides technical insight to conceive and construct the overall design of a system. An architect must work at a detailed level without becoming lost in those details or lose sight of the larger picture. An architect must be creative to imagine novel solutions but disciplined to focus on the crucial elements of the design. An architect must organize the design in a meaningful and approachable form and communicate that vision to others. An architect must listen for concerns and requirements so that they may be addressed by the design. An architect must collaborate to incorporate the best ideas and negotiate to find the most acceptable trade-offs. An architect must be confident in advocating for the architecture but diplomatic in managing and protecting its integrity. An architect must be critical to adequately assess the strengths and weaknesses of the architecture and humble enough to continuously work to improve it.

5 Challenges for an Architect

Life, however, is not without its challenges and the business pressures may interfere with the ability of the architect to fully fulfill his obligations.

5.1 Time-to-Market Pressures

Agile processes are efficient in focusing the team to quickly adapt to market needs and drive development teams to produce more quickly and efficiently. However, that same drive to deliver quickly may also drive the development team to take shortcuts. In some cases, code intended to prototype a behavior may be deemed good enough to ship regardless of the technical debt that would be incurred by that decision.

While it is an advantage for an architect to participate in the product development, they may also be consumed by it. When an architect is enmeshed in the day-to-day process of delivering story points and contributing to the sprint velocity of the team, the needs of the sprint may override his obligations as guardian. In the Scrum process, burn up and burn down charts measure the progress of the sprint. Management may look upon those values exclusively simply because they are available and easy to measure. The role of the architect is less easy to measure because the process lacks a metric for architectural integrity.

The challenge for the architect is to strike the happy medium of being engaged in the development effort but not to be so consumed by it that he cannot fulfill his role as guardian of the architecture. The architect must also balance the need to define the architecture for the next project while the development team is feeling the pressure to finish and deliver the current project as quickly as possible.

5.2 Distributed Project Teams

Distributed project teams also present a challenge because of the lack of one-on-one interactions with team members in remote locations. The architect must be able to share his vision with those team members despite the distance or even differences in time zones. For interactions with team members in a remote location, the architect must rely more on written communications including the architecture document.

Depending on the nature of the product, the architect may also have to interact people outside the company such as contractors or even customers who must interact with the architecture through more formal definitions and interfaces.

6 Conclusion

In any large endeavor, one can choose to simply dive in and start implementation without the benefit of a road map. Certain aspect of the design will certainly reveal themselves but it is also easy to lose one's way.

An architecture provides a roadmap for development and a framework for design and implementation. It provides the high-level perspective that can guide and focus an effort. The infrastructure that an architecture provides can simplify implementation and allow developers to focus on adding value to the software. Using an evolutionary approach, an architecture can evolve with the products that it supports. The architecture may also live beyond the span of a single product not only providing the consistency within a project but across an entire platform of products.

As guardian of the architecture, the architect plays a key role in fulfilling the promise of the architecture in the product development effort. The level of integrity with which the software implements the architecture improves software quality through consistency of design and familiarity of implementation that produces software that is easier to review and easier to test. Adherence to an architecture can be a measure of quality within the system. The architect encourages a shared vision that forms the basis for development. The production of an architecture document provides a vital resource for the team that enables new team member systems to quickly gain an understanding of the system.

As a senior member of the development team, the architect can be a positive influence for quality by encouraging good design and sharing the wealth of his experiences.

References

Webb, Brian. "Programmer vs Engineer vs Architect." http://brianwebb.org/programmer-vs-engineer-vs-architect/ (accessed 6 July 2017)

Brown, Simon, 2010, "Are You a Software Architect." InfoQ. https://www.infoq.com/articles/brown-are-you-a-software-architect (accessed 6 July 2017)

Kostenko, Constantin. "Responsibilities of a Software Architect." SoftwareArchitectures.com. http://www.softwarearchitectures.com/responsibilities.html (accessed 6 July 2017)

Perrin, Chad, 2010. "The danger of complexity: More code, more bugs." Tech Republic. https://www.techrepublic.com/blog/it-security/the-danger-of-complexity-more-code-more-bugs/ (accessed 6 July 2017)

MISRA C 2012: Guidelines for the Use of the C Language in Critical Systems. Nuneaton: MISRA Limited, 2013.

MISRA C++ 2008: Guidelines for the Use of the C++ Language in Critical Systems. Nuneaton: MISRA Limited, 2018.

Jones, Nigel, 2002 "Introduction to MISRA C", embedded.com. http://www.embedded.com/electronics-blogs/beginner-s-corner/4023981/Introduction-to-MISRA-C (accessed 14 August 2017)

Utilizing Data Science To Assess Software Quality

Renato Martins

renatopmartins@gmail.com

Abstract

Data Science is a "hip" term these days. Most people automatically associate Data Science with financial and customer behavior applications. It turns out that Data Science provides a set of very powerful tools that can be used to assess software quality, especially in the cloud/online world.

Most cloud companies that supply online applications use the “canary” release technique to assess release quality on a limited set of hosts before fully deploying a new release candidate. These online applications also provide a great wealth of metric data that can and should be used to assess the quality of the release candidate before it is fully deployed. A green set of passing test case results is not enough to make the deployment call. Many release engineering teams find themselves staring at graphs trying to assess if the new release candidate build is at least as good as the current production build. Sometimes what they think they see is not what it really is.

This paper will go over breaking down metric data and statistical methods that will aid in making quality decisions and boost confidence on go/no-go deployment decisions. It will cover recommended methods, the process used to select the methods, and key learning points.

Biography

Renato Martins has over 15 years of experience in the software industry where he has worked on many types of devices and applications, from embedded systems to highly available and scalable cloud systems. He spent 11 years at Microsoft in many different software quality roles. He was also the CTO and Co-Founder of Stringr Inc, a crowd-sourced video marketplace for media outlets, and he also ventured outside of the software industry by co-founding and operating a Craft Brewery in Seattle, WA. Renato currently works for Groupon, Inc. as a Senior Engineering Manager on the set of services that form Groupon’s Relevance platform.

Renato holds a bachelor’s degree in Electrical Engineering from Inatel, a master’s degree in Computer Science from DePaul University, and a master’s degree in Business Administration from the Wharton School at the University of Pennsylvania.

1 Introduction

Most Cloud Companies utilize a "canary" release technique to assess the quality of a new release before it is rolled out to all of the production hosts. This technique, allegedly, comes from underground mining. Before high tech sensors and other sorts of elaborate protection mechanisms, miners brought a canary (a kind of bird) down to the mining grounds. Every now and then one would "poll", or observe, the canary. If the bird was lively, they'd carry on. If the bird was lethargic or even dead, they'd get out of there as soon as possible, hopefully remembering to bring the bird along if it was still alive.

In cloud computing we use a similar technique in which we deploy a new release candidate to a small set of hosts, the least amount possible, and then we compare the metrics between a host running a new release candidate and one running the current production release. In doing that we find ourselves staring at graphs and trying to determine if what we are looking at is okay or not. That's easy when we're looking at very stable metrics, like disk utilization. But when it comes to more volatile metrics, the decision making process is not always simple and we find ourselves drawing lines and other types of artifacts to help us make a decision.

In order to improve this decision-making process and help make decisions one would not regret later, we can adopt Data Science concepts and tools. With the adoption of such concepts and tools, the release process reliability has been shown to improve dramatically as well as the level of confidence in making go/no-go decisions.

2 Picking The Tools

When looking at the realm of Data Science tools we can find ourselves overwhelmed by the sheer amount of tools available out there. Naïve Bayesian models, K Clustering, Linear and Logistic Regression, etc. It's easy to get lost and be overwhelmed. Where do we start? How do we decide which are the right and best methods? We have to get down to the basics and use the KISS (Keep It Simple S...) concept. The rest will follow.

Take a look at the graphs below showing error rates of two different hosts running two different builds; one is a canary and one is a reference host. They compare the 3XX, 4XX and 5XX error rates between the two hosts. If you had to pick the best one, which one would you pick? Why?

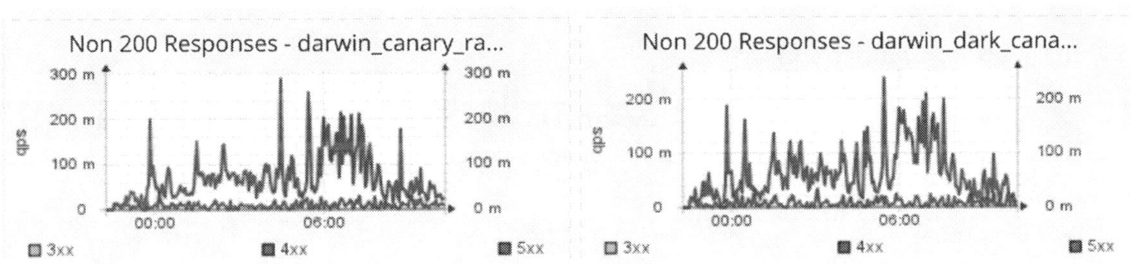

Figure 1 - Error Rates From Canary And Reference Hosts

Sometimes things are not really what they appear to be. Or are they? The goal of this paper is to remove any guessing from the picture by teaching the reader to utilize tools to bring better visibility into the data and make better informed decisions that can stand challenges.

2.1 Percentiles, Mean, Median, and Standard Deviation

We are able to easily calculate these metrics for each data set, so why wouldn't we? This is like putting an X-Ray through the data to help us see where it's more volatile and where it differs the most between the reference and the canary.

The percentiles to be used need to include some basic reference ones, like 25th, 75th, and 95th percentiles. The other percentiles depend on what metric you're using and what is the expectation your clients have about that metric. For example, if your service needs to have 99% availability, then you need to calculate the 99th percentile as well to make sure that the data up until that point meets the *fill in the metric* expectations.

Let's take the previous two graphs showing the same metrics for the same period of time. How do you figure out which one is better? Is one even better than the other or about the same? Take a look. Can you tell?

2.1.1 5XX Metrics Comparison

Metric	Canary Host	Reference Host
00th percentile	0.00000	0.00000
25th percentile	0.00002	0.00004
75th percentile	0.00355	0.00471
90th percentile	0.00643	0.00890
95th percentile	0.00923	0.01172
Mean	0.00236	0.00300
Median	0.00110	0.00159
Standard Deviation	0.00317	0.00377

2.1.2 4XX Metrics Comparison

Metric	Canary Host	Reference Host
00th percentile	0.00000	0.00000
25th percentile	0.01020	0.01029
75th percentile	0.02911	0.02823
90th percentile	0.04800	0.04993
95th percentile	0.06251	0.05956
Mean	0.02202	0.02193
Median	0.01739	0.01697
Standard Deviation	0.01734	0.01772

2.1.3 Source Of Metrics

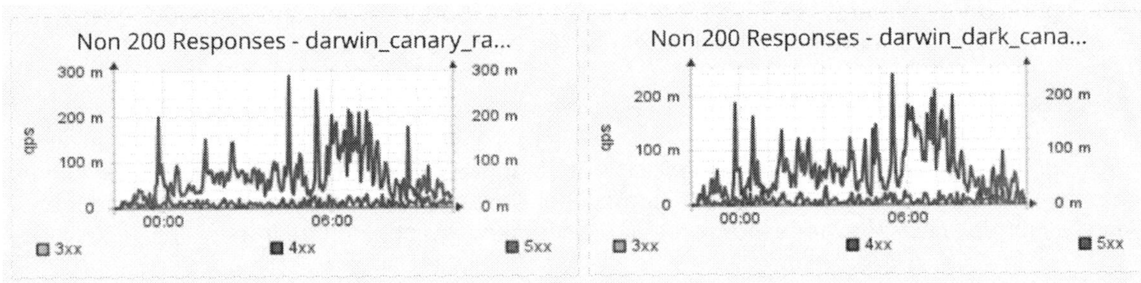

Figure 1 - Error Rates From Canary And Reference Hosts

2.1.4 Conclusions from the breaking down of percentiles, mean, median, and standard deviation

2.1.4.1 5xx

In terms of 500s, the canary host appears to be better. How can we tell? All metrics are better, varying from up to 40% better in the case of the 25th percentile, down to about 16% better in case of standard deviation. Because of that, it is already safe to assume that the build under test there improves this metric by non-trivial amounts, and therefore it should be considered for deployment.

2.1.4.2 4xx

In terms of 400s, the canary host is almost identical, without any significant difference in the metrics between the two hosts. Because of that, it is safe to assume that the new build under test there does not significantly impact this metric; therefore it should be considered for deployment.

2.2 Percentiles, Mean, Median, and Standard Deviation Ratios

Now that we have started breaking down the percentiles, mean, median, and standard deviation of the data, it only makes sense to calculate ratios (new/reference), so it's even easier to spot and quantify differences.

The previous section surfaced that the 5XX metric is better, so let's take a look at the ratios.

2.2.1 5XX Metrics Comparison With Ratios

Metric	Canary Host	Reference Host	Canary/Reference
00th percentile	0.00000	0.00000	0.00000
25th percentile	0.00002	0.00004	0.42086
75th percentile	0.00355	0.00471	0.75467
90th percentile	0.00643	0.00890	0.72199
95th percentile	0.00923	0.01172	0.78787
Mean	0.00236	0.00300	0.78600
Median	0.00110	0.00159	0.69066

Standard Deviation	0.00317	0.00377	0.84007

By adding the ratios, we now have a quantifiable way to express how much better each metric is and thus make a much more informed decision on the merits of shipping this build or not.

2.3 Boxplot

Sometimes looking at a table full of numbers is not so appealing and it can also make it difficult to determine when differences are too much or too little. Boxplots remove that guesswork and the saying "*a picture is worth a thousand words*" (source unknown) couldn't be truer.

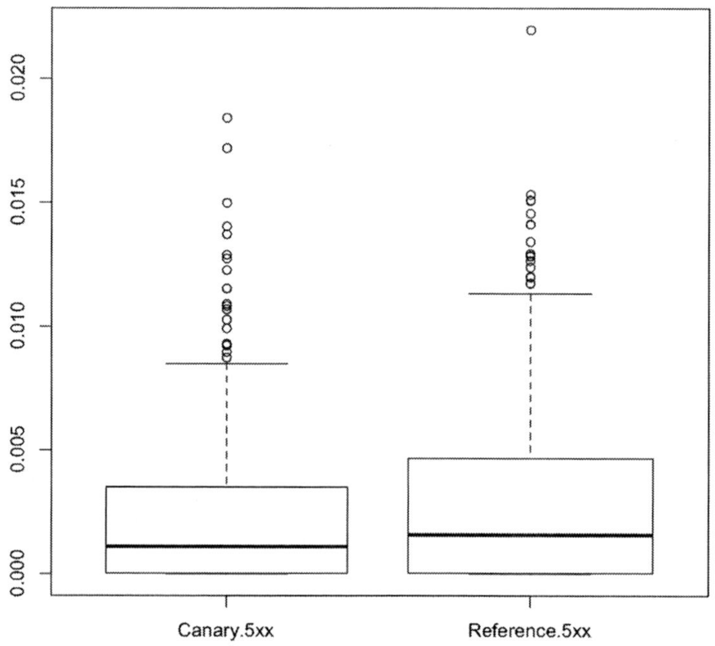

Figure 2 - Boxplot Showing Data Distribution Of Canary And Reference Hosts

The boxplot above gives us a few extra insights here:

- The canary mean is below the reference build.
- The canary's 75th percentile is below the reference build.
- The canary's max percentile is below the reference build.
- The canary's outliers also seem to be consistently below the reference build.

The conclusion from this boxplot comparison is that the canary build is slightly better than the reference build and thus should be considered for deployment.

2.4 Histograms

Following on the thought and subsequent conclusion that a picture is worth a thousand words, we can plot out histograms of the data so we can observe any yet unnoticed insights about the data.

Histograms can be a very powerful tool because, if done right, they'll always be unique for each data set and that, invariably, gives us new insights. Some of those insights include the following:

- The data should not be normally distributed.
- Are there any meaningful gaps in the data set?
- Where is the highest concentration of samples?
- Where is the lowest concentration of samples?

Let's take a look at the current data set and see what their histograms show us.

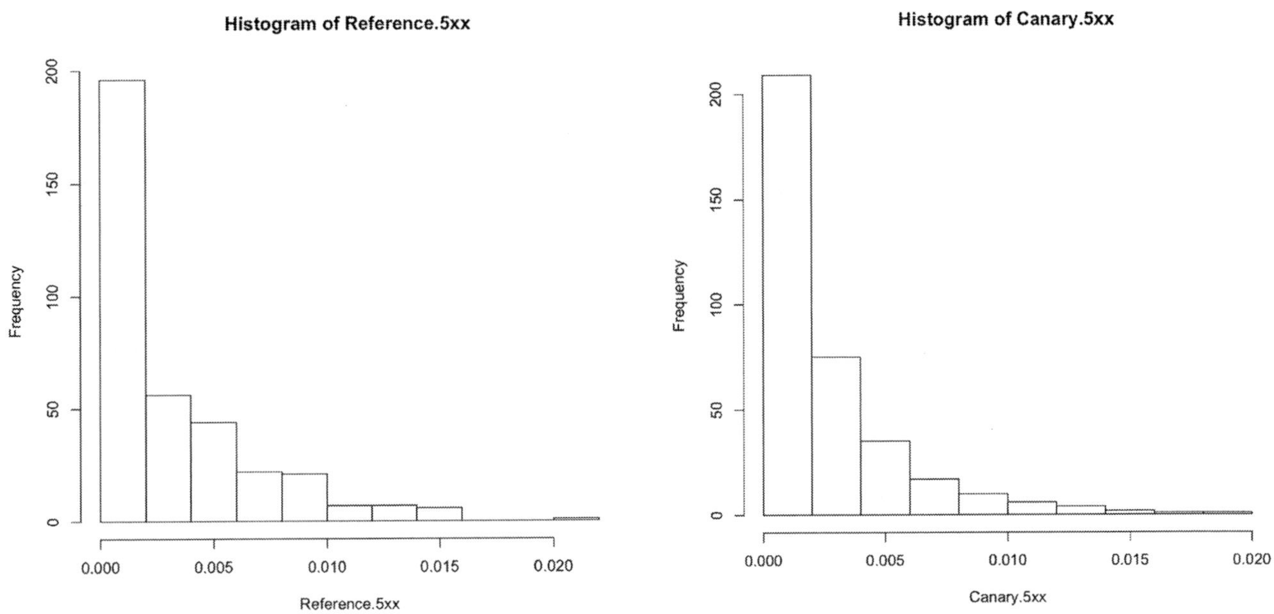

Figure 3 – Histograms Showing Distribution Of Data For All Hosts

Analyzing the data that we have here helps us notice the following:

- Canary has a higher concentration of samples at the lowest percentile of the data set.
- The reference host seems to have a set of outliers at the highest percentile.
- The canary seems to have a better distribution of the data as it progressively drops as values go up, whereas the reference host's data seems grouped across two or more bins.

2.5 ANOVA – Analysis of Variation

Now that we have looked at the meaningful percentiles and other metrics, we can start working with means and ANOVA is a great statistical test tool to start with.

According to Wikipedia[1], ANOVA "is a collection of statistical models used to analyze the differences among group means and their associated procedures (such as "variation" among and between groups), developed by statistician and evolutionary biologist Ronald Fisher"

If we run ANOVA on the data that has been plotted in the two graphs, we get the following result:

[1] https://en.wikipedia.org/wiki/Analysis_of_variance

```
              Df   Sum Sq   Mean Sq F value Pr(>F)
ind            1 0.000073 7.304e-05   6.032 0.0143 *
Residuals    718 0.008695 1.211e-05
---
Signif. codes:  0 '***' 0.001 '**' 0.01 '*' 0.05 '.' 0.1 ' ' 1
> TukeyHSD(anova_results)
  Tukey multiple comparisons of means
    95% family-wise confidence level

Fit: aov(formula = values ~ ind, data = stacked_errors)

$ind
                                 diff          lwr         upr     p adj
Reference.5xx-Canary.5xx 0.0006370231 0.0001277988 0.001146247 0.0142855
```

Figure 4 - ANOVA Test Output

While the sheer amount of data from this output might seem overwhelming at first, there are some key pieces which we must focus on and determine which other numbers we should look at, if any. The obvious first metric to look at is the p-value, which indicates the probability of a value of F greater than or equal to the observed value. The null hypothesis is rejected if this probability is less than or equal to the significance level. In this case our p-value is well within the confidence interval (95%), so we now turn our attention to the F-stat, which has a value of a bit over six. Ideally this metric should be as close as possible to one, but while it isn't, it still isn't far enough for us to reject the null hypothesis of no significant difference in variance between the two data sets.

2.6 Welch's T-Test

Continuing with our analysis of means, we'll use this test for its ability to remove any guessing that we could still have on the comparison of the data sets.

According to Wikipedia[2], "in statistics, Welch's t-test, or unequal variances t-test, is a two-sample location test which is used to test the hypothesis that two populations have equal means."

The null hypothesis here is that there is no significant difference in the means of the two data sets. As we have already calculated in section 2.2.1, we have noticed a lower mean in the canary data set when compared to the reference host. So let's see what a statistical test that checks difference in means says about that.

```
        Welch Two Sample t-test

data:  values by ind
t = -2.456, df = 697.29, p-value = 0.01429
alternative hypothesis: true difference in means is not equal to 0
95 percent confidence interval:
 -0.0011462730 -0.0001277733
sample estimates:
   mean in group Canary.5xx mean in group Reference.5xx
                0.002359227                 0.002996250
```

Figure 5 - T-Test Output

Just like in the ANOVA test looked over in the previous section, there is a great deal of data that the test outputs and that can be overwhelming to look at first. But like in that case, there are key pieces of data we look at first to determine if the rest of the data set matters or not. The first piece of data we look at is the p-value, which here is well within our 95% confidence interval. That

[2] https://en.wikipedia.org/wiki/Welch%27s_t-test

indicates the t-stat is significant. The t-stat is -2.456, which is a good result since we want that number to be around two. Like in the ANOVA test, we don't want a number that is too large here, so the null hypothesis is not rejected which means, according to this test, the true difference in means is equal to zero.

3 What We Have Learned

3.1 What Percentiles to Calculate

Picking the percentiles was pretty straightforward and didn't really yield a lot of learning opportunities. The biggest takeaway here is that we should err on the side of caution and should calculate as many percentiles as possible. It's also important to strike a balance and not generate too much data that overwhelms us. The most meaningful percentiles when it comes to decision-making are the higher percentiles because they usually are the most volatile ones. It's best to always calculate the 90th, 95th, 99th and max (or 100th) percentiles so we can more clearly and easily assess the volatility of the data in question.

More importantly, for cloud systems that need to have over 99% reliability, we need to make sure that we're always looking at the higher percentiles to make sure we're not regressing this very important metric. Mean, median and lower percentiles may all be the same, or even better, but that doesn't necessarily imply that the 99th and above percentiles are also better. **Takeaway: never make assumptions without generating the actual numbers.**

3.2 How Much Data Is Needed

This is the question one struggles with the most. In a recent project we started collecting and comparing 12 hours of data, but that proved to be too much. Figuring out the ideal data set size was a long and laborious process. We started at 12 hours of data and went down in one-hour increments, calculating the metrics and running the tests for each of them. In the end it became clear that a data set of at least three hours had enough data for us to run the tests. We also noticed that we wanted to have less than six hours of total data, so there is such a thing about having too much data. Because the number of samples over time will vary on logging solutions and policies, in terms of numbers of samples, we want to have around 160 samples.

Samples	t-stat	p-value
360 (12hr)	3.8951	0.0001078
260 (9hr)	3.5781	0.0003806
160 (6hr)	2.9022	0.003972
100 (3.1hr)	2.9415	0.003676
90 (3hr)	3.2008	0.001642
60 (2hr)	2.1255	0.03568
50 (1.6hr)	1.4877	0.1401

Table 1 - Samples, Time, And Test Results

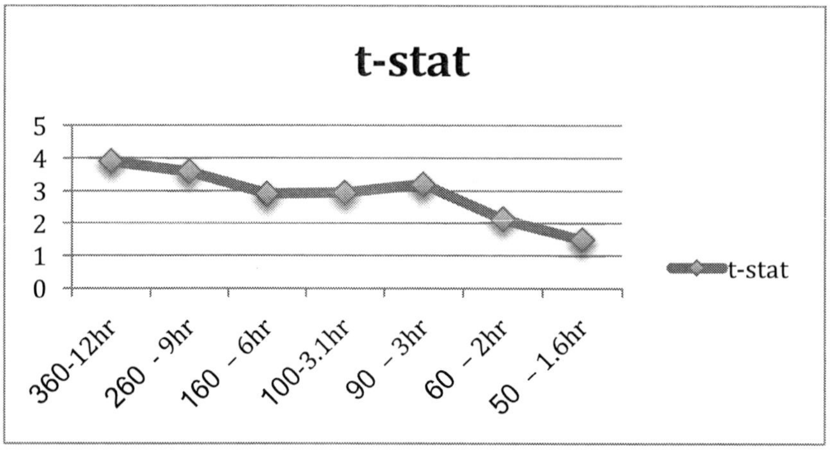

Figure 6 - Plot Of T-Stats x Samples - Time

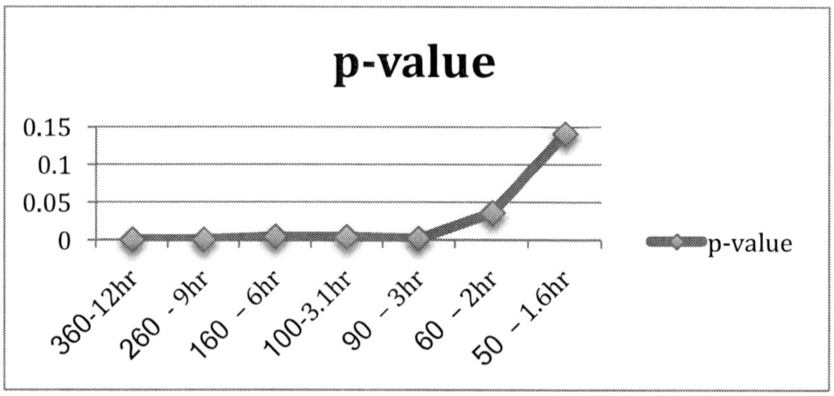

Figure 7 - Plot Of P-Values x Samples - Time

In the table and graphs above we can see t-stat values increasing with the number of samples and p-values dropping instead. It's easy to see that once we have too many samples, we end up with high confidence intervals, and as a result we have difficulty rejecting data unless it's extremely different. That is not ideal for high availability systems where the slightest shifts can make a big impact.

3.3 What Time Frame Is Best To Collect Your Data

In the previous exercise we discovered that more is less, but we didn't determine what time intervals are best. Is data taken from 2:00 AM to 5:00 AM ideal? Or is data from 9:00 AM to 12:00 PM better? The real answer is: *it depends*. The data should come from the time interval that has the most traffic. Why? Because you want to analyze the data under the most demanding conditions as those are more likely to yield the most valuable data. We should already know that testing under ideal conditions usually yields ideal results, often failing to expose issues uncovered by less than ideal conditions. If we take data when things are quiet and not really stressing out the service much, then it's less likely to expose problems simply because there isn't enough traffic to expose them in the first place.

The sampling of the data is up to you. Anything that is less than a metric sample for every 5 minutes is not recommended. Also, too many samples may be too much. Anything in the one sample every one to two minutes is appropriate for the purposes covered in this paper.

4 Automating This Stuff

There are many tools available that will do this work, spanning a different variety of budgets. This list covers some tools that have been successfully used.

4.1 Excel

The basic metrics come built-in and the rest can be done via many available statistics add-on packages, including some free versions. Unfortunately this support is not uniform across all operating systems. The Mac version of Excel has less statistics packages available and less free versions as well.

4.2 R

This is a popular open source statistics tools package. It's very powerful and covers all of the metrics and tests covered in this paper. This tool is supported across multiple operating systems with very similar functionality and best of all, it's completely free!

This was the tool used to generate all the statistical data present in this paper.

4.3 Python

Python has some very powerful libraries capable of calculating all of the metrics listed here and many more. Because it is a programming language with plenty of other libraries and capabilities, it then becomes the best option for automation.

Here are some libraries that we have successfully used for calculation of data and execution of tests listed in this paper:

- Pandas
- Numpy
- SciPy

5 Conclusion

In my most recent project, these tools and methods covered in this paper have been used for daily decision making for over six months and there is absolutely no turning back. Ever since adoption of the methods described in this paper, no release has gone out that significantly regressed a tested metric and no releases have had to be rolled back either.

Ongoing work involves increasing the number of metrics being analyzed and automation of the procedure so this can become an integral part of a continuous testing, integration and delivery platform instead of a side tool that simply helps make a decision to pull the plug on a new build or not. More importantly, this has provided the data used to push back when a release needs to go out, however, causing more harm than good. The tools described here very decisively remove any guess-work and speculation from any discussion about the impact of a metric regressing, even ever so slightly.

These powerful tools have helped maintain and increase quality with minimal overhead, while giving its users maximum confidence in their decisions. The experience shows that through the use of easily and readily available tools, great impact can be brought to the quality of the releases! This in turn results in greater customer satisfaction and increased revenue lift!

Influencing Change

LEVI SIEBENS, VERTAFORE

Introduction

- Test / Dev Lead and Senior SDET at Vertafore
- Background in: mobile, web, Windows OS, game testing
- Passion around making things better for people and teams

Why Influence Change?

- "Isn't that something managers do?"
- For Your Career
- For Your Company
- For the Test Discipline
- For You

How To Influence Change

- Know Your Audience
- Have a "Vision"
- Communicate Well
- Trust

Know Your Audience

- How to fail (Mantis experience)
- Who is the idea for?
- How should the idea be "contextualized"?
  - Identify customer characteristics
  - Identify stakeholders / power brokers
  - Document!

Having "Vision"

- "Our company's vision is to create synergistic opportunities by maximizing the vertical and horizontal integrations across the [InsertIndustryHere] industry"

Having "Vision"

- Understand what change looks like
- Understand the direction of the change
- Understand why it is critical
- Provides a focus and something to check the project against

Communicate Well

- Start with answering "Why?"
- Handling Questions Well
- Keep Vision at Center

Trust

- Cannot influence without this
- Build it every day

Identify Contributors

- Who has the most to gain through this change?
- Who asked productive questions when the vision was presented?
- Who would you like to drive this vision forward?

Success!

- Drive, Drive Drive!
- Change happens slower than it seems it should
- It will not follow the "plan"
  - "They say no plan survives first contact with implementation." - Andy Weir, The Martian

Failure!

- Ask, did this fail because the idea / vision needs to change?
- Who / what is blocking you from moving forward?
  - Are there ways to solve these problems? If so, try again!
  - If they cannot be solved today, when can they be solved?
- Is the idea to large to accomplish all at once? Can this idea be iterated in part instead of as a whole?

"Design [, testing] and programming are human activities; forget that and all is lost." --*Bjarne Stroustrup*

[http://www.softwarequotes.com/ShowQuotes.aspx?ID=539&Name=Stroustrup,_Bjarne&Type=Q]

Questions?

Senses Working Overtime: Improving Software Quality Through Accessibility and Inclusive Design

Michael Larsen

mkltesthead@gmail.com

Abstract

Accessibility makes it possible for those with various disabilities to access information and services. Inclusive Design focuses on making choices so that software and services are usable by as many people as possible. They are distinct but complementary facets of software development and delivery, and they are difficult to add to software after the fact. Making software Accessible using Inclusive Design principles at the start, or as early as possible, makes it easier to develop software that can be used by more people, and allows the development team to deliver better quality, better user experience, and happier users all the way around. In this talk, I will demonstrate principles and processes that you can use to help make Accessibility and Inclusive Design a natural part of your development and testing activities.

Biography

Michael has worked on a broad array of technologies and industries including virtual machine software, capacitance touch devices, video game development and distributed database and web applications. He currently works with Socialtext in Palo Alto, CA. He writes a software testing blog called TESTHEAD (http://mkltesthead.com/).

Michael is also a founding member of the "Americas" Chapter of "Weekend Testing". You can follow their progress and tweets at @WTAmericas or email at WTAmericas@gmail.com. Michael served as a member of the Board of Directors for the Association for Software Testing from 2011-2015. He was their Treasurer and then their President. Currently, he helps teach their Black Box Software Testing classes. Michael is also the current producer and a regular commentator for The Testing Show, a podcast produced for QualiTest (available in Apple Podcasts).

1 Introduction

Accessibility and Inclusive Design are related in that they both strive to increase access to systems, but they are achieved in different ways. We want products to be designed so that they allow as many people as possible to access information. We want to do all we can to make sure that people with disabilities are able to have as similar an experience as their normative counterparts. Both Accessibility and Inclusive Design aim to meet these goals but the ways in which those goals are accomplished differ.

Accessibility can be defined as "The design of products, devices, services, or environments for people with disabilityies. Accessibility allows for design compatibility with a person's assistive technology".[i] Inclusive Design can be defined as "The design of mainstream products and/or services that are accessible to, and usable by, as many people as reasonably possible… without the need for special adaptation or specialized design"[ii]

This paper considers ways to include Accessibility and Inclusive Design as part of the standard design, development and quality process.

2 Why Do We Need to Think about Accessibility and Inclusive Design?

Nearly everyone experiences a primary or secondary disability of some sort during their lifetime: sight, auditory, motor, or cognitive, for example.[iii]

According to the U.S. Census, nearly 1 in 5 people have some form of disability[iv]. The World Report on Disability states that more than a billion people in the world today experience disability.[v] Many people not considered disabled have some sort of disability – even if it is simply wearing glasses. Design taken for granted one day may be insufficient the next, so it makes social and economic sense to plan for a better user experience by incorporating these design philosophies.

3 Situational Disabilities

When a user has a persistent issue (low vision, low hearing, limited mobility, cognitive disability) we consider that a primary disability. There are additional challenges that people without disabilities can face, and these are referred to as "situational" disabilities. Examples of situational disabilities include:

- Background noise (hearing)
- Distracted tasking (cognitive)
- Small text/non-scaled web page (vision)
- Foreign language (literacy)

Picture yourself in a country where you can't read the language or even the writing. This is a way to imagine the frustration people with disabilities might feel using a system not designed for Accessibility. Recognition is the first step towards solving the problem.

IKEA's assembly instructions is a good example of Inclusive Design[vi]. By presenting the instructions as pictographs and images they overcome literacy issues. Additionally, in most cases, only one set of instructions is needed, rather than repeating the same series of instructions multiple times in several languages.

4 Ten Principles of Web/Mobile Accessibility

Jeremy Sydik's book "Design Accessible Web Sites"[vii] focuses on "Ten Principles of Web Accessibility". At the time, mobile was a very small market compared to what it is today, but many of the principles that Sydik presented are just as applicable in the mobile space. Those ten principles are:

1. Avoid making assumptions about the physical, mental, and sensory abilities of your users whenever possible.
2. Your users' technologies are capable of sending and receiving text. That's about all you'll ever be able to assume.
3. Users' time and technology belong to them, not to us. You should never take control of either without a really good reason.
4. Provide good text alternatives for any non-text content.
5. Use widely available technologies to reach your audience.
6. Use clear language to communicate your message.
7. Make your sites usable, searchable, and navigable.
8. Design your content for semantic meaning and maintain separation between content and presentation.
9. Progressively enhance your basic content by adding extra features. Allow it to degrade gracefully for users who can't or don't wish to use them.
10. As you encounter new web technologies, apply these same principles when making them accessible.

These principles are helpful when it comes to designing applications and they are also helpful when it comes to framing how they should be tested. When Socialtext started considering Accessibility issues and focusing on better compliance, these principled were implemented as part of testing first and then became part of the general design and development process.

An example can be seen in an enhancement that was made to the Content menu option in Socialtext. Since there are a lot of possible places to have content, it was determined that a submenu would be an easy way to group content and allow users to quickly discover what they wanted to work with, as well as create new pages. With a mouse, this is easy. Click the Content item on the Navigation bar and then select something from the Workspaces, Watchlist, or Recently Viewed submenu listings. Additionally, click on the "plus" button and you can create a new page. With a keyboard, the user could get lost within the submenus and have no indication as to where they were or how to get out of that submenu. By using the Accessibility principles, Socialtext was able to better articulate how to access the submenus options, how to move to the other submenus, and how to escape the submenu.

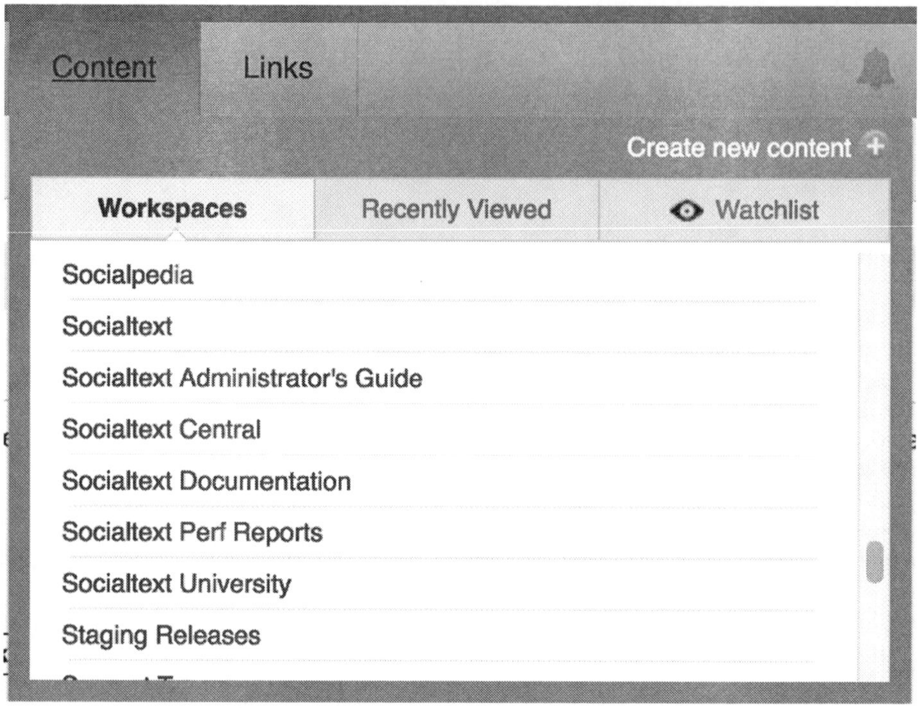

Figure 1: Socialtext application. The submenus within the Content menu listing.

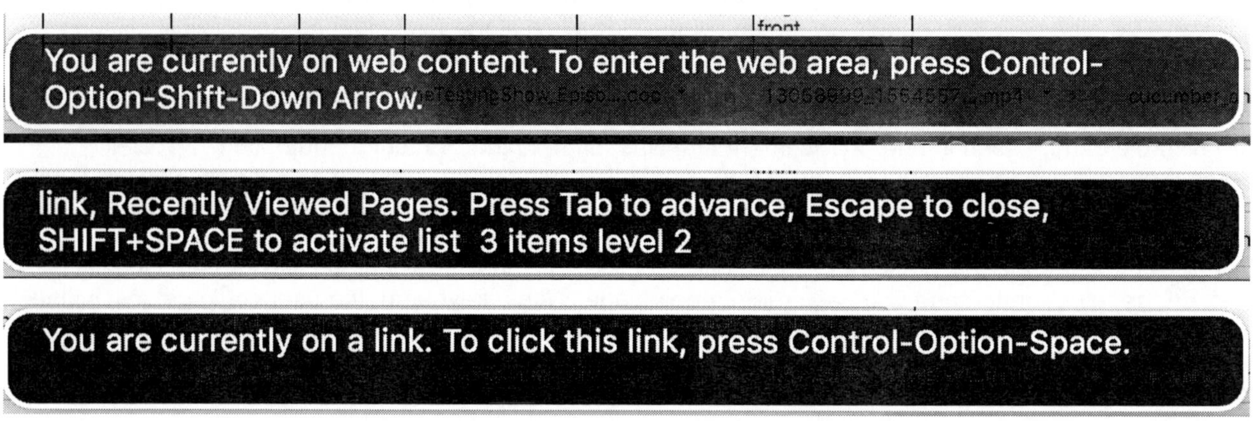

Figure 2: Literal text provided by VoiceOver screen reader to describe the navigation process inside the Content submenu.

5 Practice Empathy: Be "HUMBLE"

It's one thing to advocate about Accessibility or Inclusive Design. It's another to put yourself squarely into the situations you are trying to design for. In "Black Box Accessibility Testing: A Heuristic Approach", Albert Gareev and Michael Larsen describe heuristics to help us think like our users[viii]. One of those heuristics is summed up as "be HUMBLE".

Humanize: Be empathetic, understand the emotional components.

Unlearn: Step away from your default [device-specific] habits. Switch into different habit modes.

Model: use personas that help you see, hear and feel the issues. Consider behaviors, pace, mental state and system state.

Build: knowledge, testing heuristics, core testing skills, testing infrastructure, credibility.

Learn: what are the barriers? How do users Perceive, Understand and Operate?

Experiment: Put yourself into literal situations. Collaborate with designers and programmers, provide feedback.

Looking back at the feature enhancement I described for the Socialtext Content menu, it was important to consider how a user without a mouse or ability to see the screen would interpret the workflow. By stepping away from using the mouse and turning on a screen reader, the person testing could feel the frustration with trying to access a document within those menus, as well as the difficulty of knowing where they were in that menu. What are the prompts a user receives if they enter the submenu? How do they advance through the listings? How do they escape to the upper level of the menu? How can they move to another submenu? Does the application give them prompts to help them remember where they are and what to do?

6 Accessibility and Inclusive Design in Action

There are many ways that software developers and designers can use the principles for Accessibility and Inclusive Design effectively and help make better design and quality decisions. Additionally there are numerous tools that are available to help gather information and experiment with solutions

A high-level audit can be made with the "Web Accessibility eValuation Tool" or WAVE[ix]. This is a website where you can enter a URL. WAVE will then go through and highlight the elements that pass, as well as call out warnings and errors on the page as defined by the Web Content Accessibility Guidelines (WCAG)[x].

There are a variety of Developer Tools available as plug-ins for various browsers. These allow developers and testers to see if a change will be compliant with WCAG guidelines and experiment with the parameters of values such as color contrast. There are specific tool for looking at color contrast, semantic meaning, and overall WCAG compliance.

For those who wish to test pages for non-sighted users, Apple has VoiceOver built into the Operating System, and "NonVisual Desktop Access" (NVDA) is a freely available screen reader for Windows platforms. By turning on a screen reader, you can listen back to the page output as the screen reader is interpreting it.

Examine how your pages will appear to a color-blind user. Realize that there are variations of color-blindness. Color contrast is important. Having an effective and appropriate contrast between colors can help make sure that text and images are not lost in the background.

The "Hemingway" app analyzes the readability of text. This can be helpful for developing content to help people with dyslexia, as well as encouraging greater readability of text in general.

Look at a good example. The World Wide Web Consortium (W3C) has a "Before and After"[xi] demonstration that shows pages prior to being complaint with WCAG and makes a side by side comparison with pages that are compliant. The source code can be viewed and compared, and a variety of Accessibility and Inclusive Design issues and fixes can be reviewed.

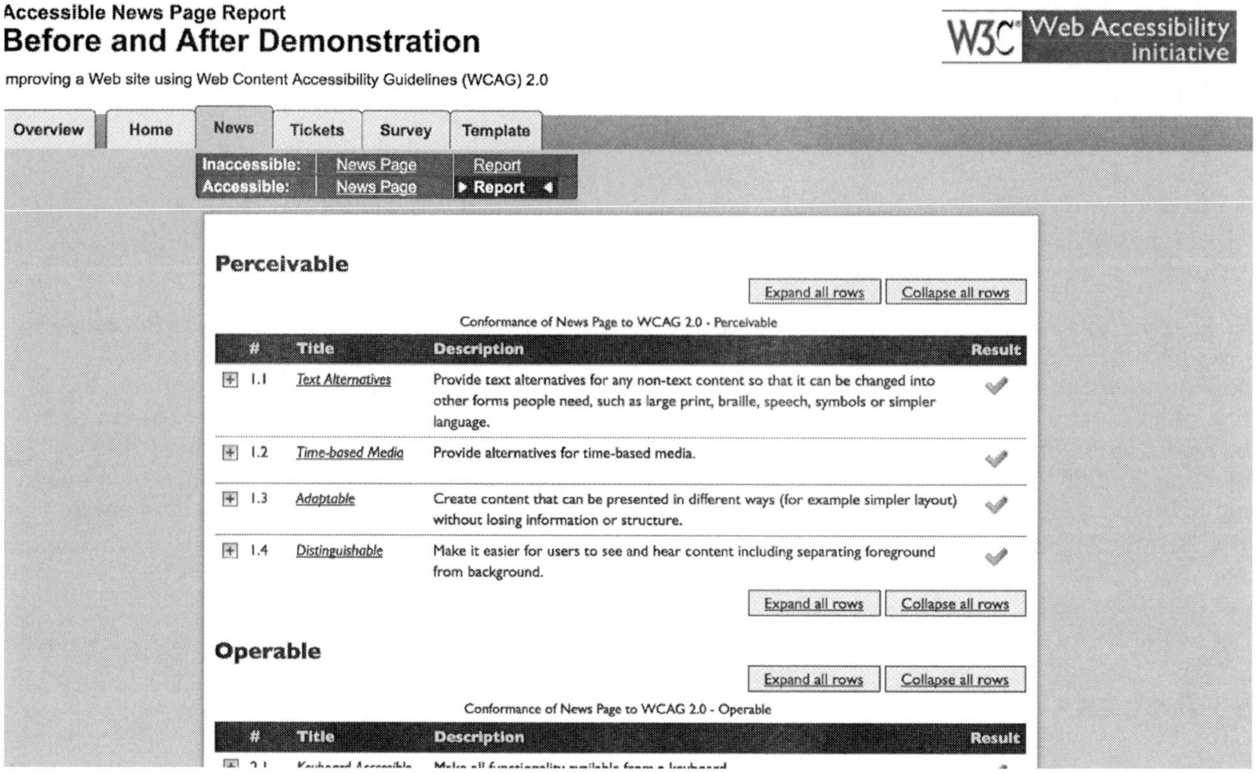

Figure 3: W3C Before/After Simulator with Report

Some additional areas that can help any page are:

- Ensure that images are described with alt tags and that the picture is described meaningfully. Additionally, use alt tags so that repetitive images are not all called out by using the WAI alt decision tree.
- Provide a skip link at the top of the document that will allow users to get to the main content of a page and bypass the navigation menu if desired.
- Use the “lang” attribute in tags to help programs translate or render other languages.
- Make buttons that are scalable and not tied to literal images.
- Use images that have a universal meaning (a smiley face can be rendered once, no translation required).
- Use the div tag sparingly, especially in areas where keyboard focus is important.
- Make content available in a variety of formats. If you have uploaded a video, have an option for closed captioning available. Additionally, include a full transcript of the video’s content.
- If using date fields, allow for multiple ways to enter the date (text field and date picker).
- Allow Pinch-to-Zoom to let the user determine the amount of zoom and focus needed to view the page.
- Make touch areas large enough to interact with without requiring rescaling.
- Encourage the use of proportional fonts.
- Write simply and use space to aid reading.
- Review the contrast recommendations in the WCAG guidelines and encourage high contrast designs.
- Web pages may end up in other media, such as PDF files to be printed. Make sure elements that appear on the screen appear on a printed page, too.
- Remember that simple interfaces are usable interfaces. Do not make navigation or discovery more difficult than necessary.[xii]

One additional consideration is that tools can help us identify issues, but they do not make judgment calls. Automated tools can look for markup tags and provide assert statements with comparisons to ensure that we are using those tags. However, automated tools cannot judge whether the text provided is useful or appropriate. This is an opportunity for testing to evaluate in a mindful way.

7 Conclusion

The design decisions made early in the life cycle of products have the potential to make them excellent solutions to issues they face, or genuine nightmares to use. The farther along a product gets in its development, the more difficult it is to make modifications to its design. Inclusive Design early in the product development can overcome many of those hurdles, and make a more usable product by everyone. Additionally, using Inclusive Design as a guide early on will make those last mile modifications for technologies that assist those with the most profound disabilities much easier to implement.

Think of the applications that you would want to use, and think of yourself in the future, with the possibility that a significant disability (or disabilities) may be part of your everyday experience. The keys to success for Accessibility and Inclusive Design are: remember that not everyone is the same as you; practice empathy; plan to include these design factors into the process from the beginning; and think about the future – you may end up benefiting from your own design.

References

[i] Wikipedia. “Accessibility”. https://en.wikipedia.org/wiki/Accessibility (accessed July 8, 2017)

[ii] British Standards Institute. 2005. “What is Inclusive Design?”. http://www.inclusivedesigntoolkit.com/betterdesign2/whatis/whatis.html#p30 (accessed July 8, 2017)

[iii] Disabled World. “Defining Disability Diversity in Society”. https://www.disabled-world.com/disability/diversity.php (accessed July 8, 2017).

[iv] Census Bureau Reports. Nearly 1 in 5 People Have a Disability in the U.S. https://www.census.gov/newsroom/releases/archives/miscellaneous/cb12-134.html (accessed July 8, 2017)

[v] World Health Organization. World Report on Disability. http://www.who.int/disabilities/world_report/2011/en/ (accessed July 8, 2017)

[vi] North Carolina State University. The Principles of Universal Design. https://www.ncsu.edu/ncsu/design/cud/about_ud/udprinciplestext.htm (accessed July 8, 2017)

[vii] . Sydik, Jeremy J. 2007. "Design Accessible Web Sites: Thirty-Six Keys to Creating Content for All Audiences”. Pragmatic Publishing

[viii] Gareev, Albert and Larsen, Michael. 2015. “Black Box Accessibility Testing: A Heuristic Approach”, http://www.associationforsoftwaretesting.org/wp-content/uploads/Black-Box-Accessibility-Testing-A-Heuristic-Approach-.pdf (accessed July 8, 2017)

[ix] WAVE. Web Accessibility Evaluation Tool. http://wave.webaim.org/ (accessed July 8, 2017)

[x] W3C. Web Accessibility Initiative. Web Content Accessibility Guidelines (WCAG) Overview. https://www.w3.org/WAI/intro/wcag (accessed July 8, 2017)

[xi] W3C. Web Accessibility Initiative. Before and After Demonstration. https://www.w3.org/WAI/demos/bad/ (accessed July 8, 2017)

[xii] Pickering, Heydon. 2016. Inclusive Design Patterns: Coding Accessibility into Web Design”. Smashing Magazine GmbH

AI for Software Testing

Jason Arbon

jarbon@gmail.com

Abstract

Software testing is fundamentally an exercise in applying sample inputs to a system, and measuring the outputs to determine the correctness of the application's behavior. This testing input and output function is very similar to the basic operations of training and executing modern Artificial Intelligence (AI) and Machine Learning (ML) systems. The similarity implies that the field of Software Testing is ripe to benefit from recent advances in AI and ML.

Software Testing and approaches to measure Software Quality have been relatively stagnant over the past decade or so, with only slight technical improvements in test frameworks and methodologies; meanwhile product development, DevOps, and deployment have benefited greatly from increasing availability of compute, network, and storage. Software testing has remained an often linear activity with respect to test coverage--adding tests one at a time or in small batches while products add complexity at a much higher rate, meaning almost no product is tested efficiently. The complexity of products has been growing exponentially, where testing has remained more or less a linear activity with respect to test coverage.

Applying the advancements in AI and ML will help testing 'catch up' with development advances, increase the efficiency, speed and efficacy of software testing, and free testers from many mundane testing tasks. AI and ML, when used to abstract the test input, test execution, and test evaluation problems enable testing at scale, standardization of quality metrics, benchmarking, and a global set of reusable test cases.

Biography

Jason Arbon is the CEO of Appdiff, which is redefining how enterprises develop, test, and ship mobile apps with zero code and zero setup required. He was formerly the director of engineering and product at Applause.com/uTest.com, where he led product strategy to deliver crowdsourced testing via more than 250,000 community members and created the app store data analytics service. Jason previously held engineering leadership roles at Google and Microsoft, and coauthored "How Google Tests Software and App Quality: Secrets for Agile App Teams."

1 Introduction

The software engineering world today is busy applying Artificial Intelligence (AI) and Machine Learning (ML) to solve complex product problems for everything from self-driving cars, smart chatbots, and security. Software quality and testing efforts are also starting to benefit from the early application of AI for classic testing problems, and also waking up to a new world of software testing problems related to testing these new AI-based products.

Software Testing, especially testing applications directly from the user interface, has proven difficult and expensive. So difficult and expensive that many software test automation attempts fail to deliver much value, or fail altogether. In a world of self-driving cars and machines beating the top GO players at their own game, the best software companies and engineers still heavily rely on manual testing, and iterative deploy-identify-fix-deploy loops. Humans are still in this testing loop today because software requires the power of human brain to design, execute and validate complex software systems--but that is about to change thanks to ML.

This paper describes the need for a new approach to software testing, and the problems modern software testers face. It then gives a brief introduction to AI and ML--just enough for the purposes of this paper. Next, several examples of applying ML to generate test input and validation that are more efficient and useful than current methods will be shared. Following that, is an overview of the new software quality and testing problems created by new AI-based products, along with examples of solutions. Lastly, some thoughts on the scope and timing of the impact of these testing approaches and how the testing community can speed up the development and application of AI and ML for testing.

This paper strives to give both an overview of how AI and ML will impact software quality and testing efforts in the coming years, with practical real-world examples from the author's experience.

2 AI and ML Overview for Testers

Artificial Intelligence is the idea of building machines that interact with external data and behave in a cognitive way--actions that appear like human thinking. There are really two branches of AI; Artificial General Intelligence (AGI), which has the goal of building truly generalized thinking, emotive, conscious machines. And then there is the subset of application-focused AI, called Machine Learning, which is what this paper focuses on.

Generally Machine Learning (ML) is used to train a machine to perform a function. In non-AI programming, you design a function thinking of all the if-then and for loops that you need to convert the input data to the correct output data and you write that function. In ML, the idea is inverted -engineers work on gathering many examples of input and output data and show that to a machine which trains itself to build a function that satisfies the Input and Output requirements. This process is called supervised learning, as a human is showing it the correct behavior. Supervised learning is analogous to Test Driven Development (TDD) where the inputs and output tests are defined first, then humans code the functions. In this case the machines 'code' the functions.

Note that this data and training method looks very much like a manual tester, or test automation engineer's job--apply some test input data to the system, and verify:

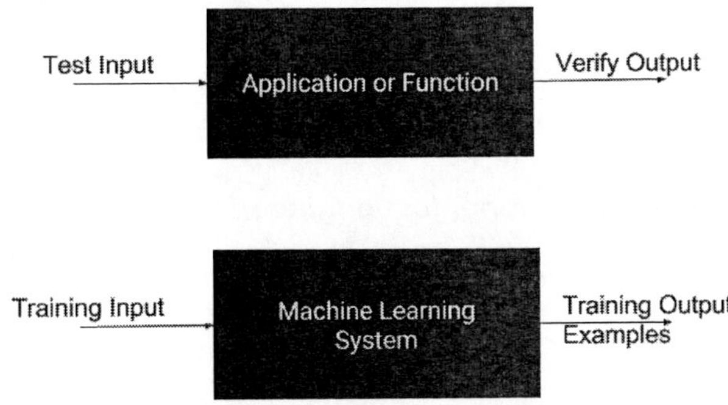

Another variant of ML is called reinforcement-learning, where humans define a reward system to tell the machine when it has done a good or bad thing. The machine builds all sorts of different variations of itself based on this reinforcement. This is analogous to operant conditioning--similar to how people learn task proficiency

For the curious tester, they may want to know how these ML black boxes work. The ML black boxes can be any of ANNs (Artificial Neural Networks), CNNs (Convolutional Neural Networks, SVMs (State Vector Machines), Decision Trees, etc. For purposes of this paper we don't need to know the details of this ML black box, just know that we give it training data and it attempts to build a function that satisfies all the input and output tests it is trained on.

3 Need for AI in Testing

While software engineering and infrastructure has become far easier and scalable thanks to improvements in development languages, tools, processes and cloud computing - software test engineering hasn't seen similar gains in productivity, efficiency or efficacy. Software Test engineering needs similar attention and breakthroughs in technology.

UI testing frameworks Selenium, Appium, and Webdriver were created back in 2004. Most proprietary testing systems such as TestPlant and HP UFT have been around just as long, or sometimes even longer. Even recent variants such as Google's Espresso or Square's KIF test frameworks look, and are used very similar to, test frameworks from 13 years ago. Over the last 10 plus years, the familiar test automation paradigms of leveraging image identification, record and playback, or hand-coding product selectors based on DOM (Document Object Model) trees or accessibility identifiers have only incrementally improved and have been ported to more modern platforms.

The problem is that while not much has changed in testing, the world of software engineering has sped up thanks to tools and processes such as Agile, and the implementation of Continuous Engineering. which produce more code, with far higher frequency of new builds, all requiring testing.

Worse, there is a fundamental disconnect between software engineering and software testing. Writing a simple function or product feature requires a fair amount of testing to verify its behavior. In high-quality applications more engineering time is spent on the testing effort versus the implementation. But, there is an additional test and validation effort as the new feature can affect the behavior of other features. Each new feature can impact some subset of other features.

$$T_{total}(f_n) = T(f_n) + \sum_{i=0}^{n-1} k_i T(f_i)$$

where T is then additional functional test engineering effort for a given feature f.

and ki is the relative risk/impact feature n has on feature i.

Thus, the testing effort for each new feature (f_n) includes the testing required to eliminate the risk to all impacted features. This results in the net testing effort to grow exponentially. Most current testing methods of adding more manual tests, or hand-crafting code for more regression scripts, only adds coverage at a rate linearly proportional to testing effort/cost. Yes, even data-driven tests, delivery linear amounts of test coverage.

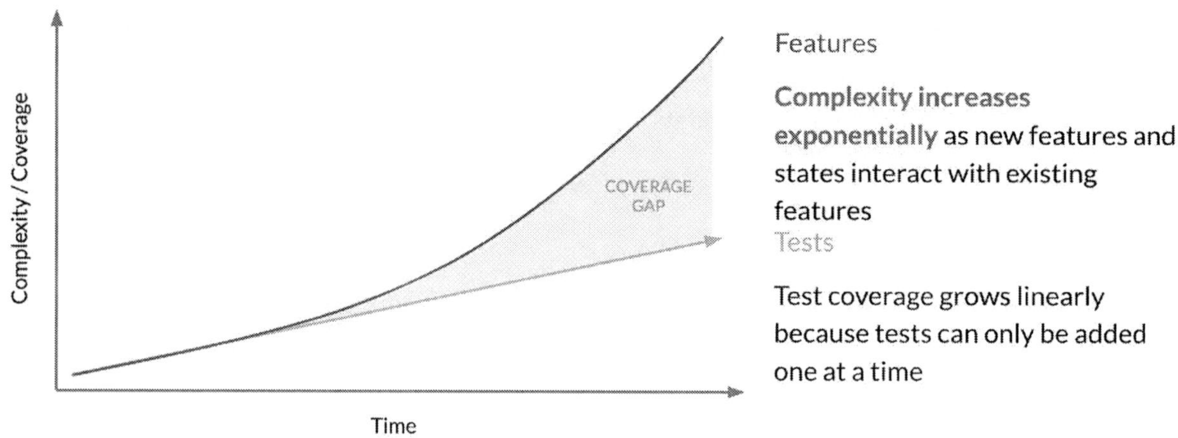

This means every software product suffers from an increasing gap between the amount of complexity that needs to be tested, and the ability to add test coverage. Something has to change to enable a far greater ability to generate test coverage, and I will show that Machine Learning is the only test approach that has the possibility of such exponential test coverage.

How does a Machine Learning approach to testing result in exponential levels of test coverage?

1. ML can be trained to generate test input and test validations for arbitrary applications.
2. ML delivers the ability to execute the same test case against multiple applications.
3. ML test generation and execution can run automatically on exponentially improving storage, network, and compute in the cloud.

Additionally, as we'll see later, a common ML generated test execution environment means quality can be measured and benchmarked against other applications, improving our ability to quantify quality itself.

ML-driven test creation and execution has the possibility of closing the test coverage gap.

4 AI for Test Input and Validation

How do you teach a machine to generate test input? Today, to generate test cases, testers consider the application, and generate test inputs they expect from users to deliver positive test coverage. They then draw upon their past experience of what types of inputs might be interesting or break the application under test. We need to teach a machine to think similarly.

The machine needs to be taught two different things to replicate the human tester's behavior: Recognize the state of the application, and know what inputs are valid or interesting for this application state.

4.1 Training ML: Recognize Application State

Recognizing the application state can be accomplished by giving the machine many screens and labeling the screens as a type of application 'state'. For example, 'login screen', 'search results', 'permissions dialog', etc. If we can teach the machine to recognize what type of state the application is in, much like a tester recognizes the state of the application they are testing, they can intelligently pick what types of inputs to apply to the application.

First, we gather many thousands of screenshots of real world applications. We then consider all the major classes of UI state that applications have. Luckily for machine learning, most apps have similar states, which means we can have many examples to for the ML training.

Labeling is the next step. We need to have humans apply the labels to each screen. A simple application is built which shows one of these screens alongside a list of possible labels. The labeler, a human performing this labeling task, clicks the appropriate labels for each screen in sequence.

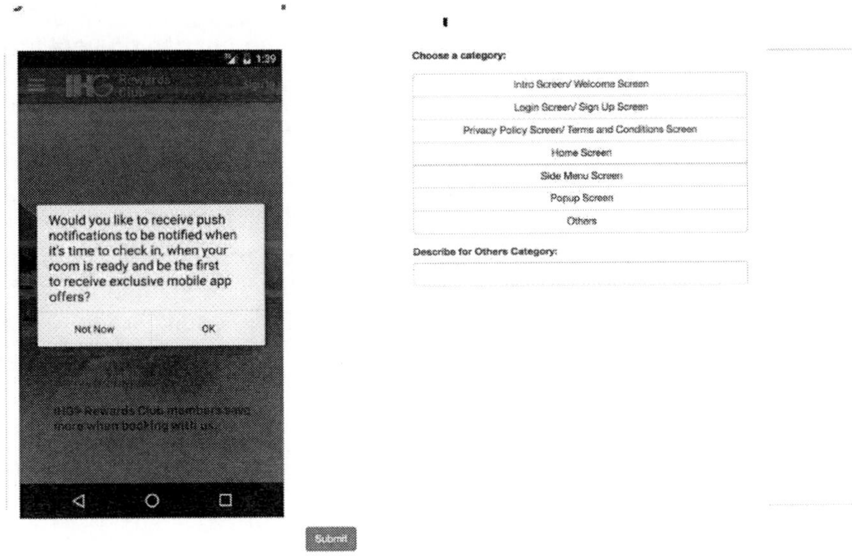

Once all the labels have been saved, there is now a corpus of labeled data with which to train the ML. Again, the detailed mechanics of this work are beyond the scope of this paper, but suffices to say that thousands of pages are shown to the ML program, where the input is a combination of the pixels in the screenshot itself, along with the DOM elements. The training/test data is the labels we got for each screen from the humans.

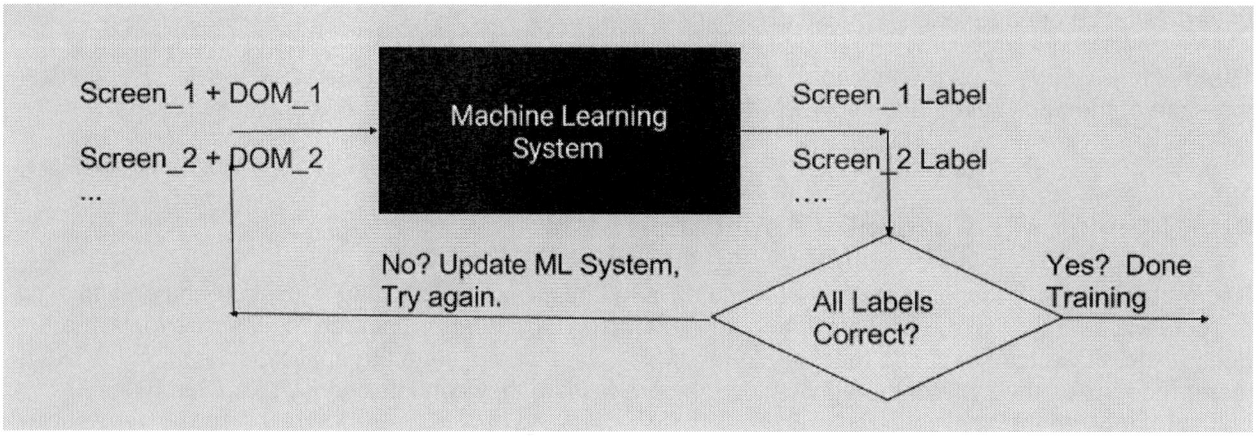

ML Training Input: Image, DOM element information (e.g. <button>, <span>, etc.)

ML Training Expected Output: the correct label(s) per page from humans.

The training process can require hours of computation. With the training system showing the ML machine screenshot after screenshot, determining whether or not the ML machine successfully labeled each screen. Every time the ML gets the label for a screen wrong, it changes its internal structure, and the process is repeated until the ML does the best labeling job it can do.

It is worth noting that training data that is sparse, incorrect, or incoherent can prevent the ML from learning.

Once this process is complete, we now have an ML system that can accept a screenshot and a snapshot of the DOM of the application and not just give the correct label for the screens we have trained it on, but also on screens it has never seen before--just like the human.

When the ML is done training, the quality of the machine labeling is often visualized via a chart that is called a 'Confusion Matrix'. The confusion matrix simply plots each screen label on each axis and shows how often one screen is confused for another--a mistaken label. The results here are from early work after training with about 6,000 screenshots. This approach works fairly well, as lighter blues and smaller numbers mean great labeling.

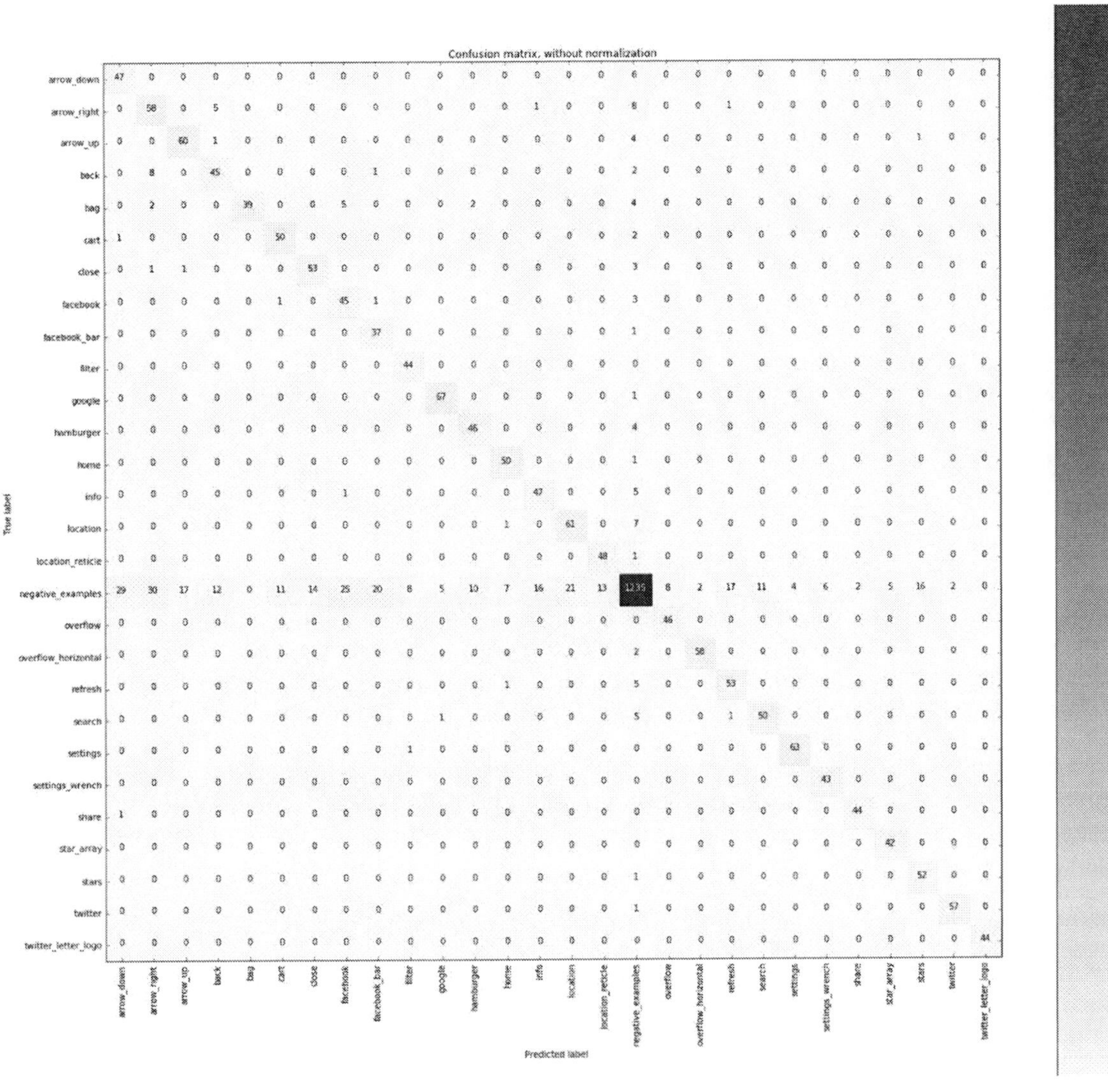

4.2 Training ML: Apply Test Inputs

The next step is to teach the ML how to decide on correct input actions to take based on what screen state the application is in. An individual action is a pair 'element' and 'input'. For example, the element can be an OK button, and the input could be a 'tap', or an element could be a search text box, and the action could be entering the text 'beanie babies'.

Again, we need a large amount of training data, where the input here is the set of all elements on a screen, the label of the screen, and the output is the set of

Input Training Data: ['screen_label':'search', 'elements':'button, textbox, image']

Output Training Data: ['textbox':'enter_text', 'button':'tap', ...]

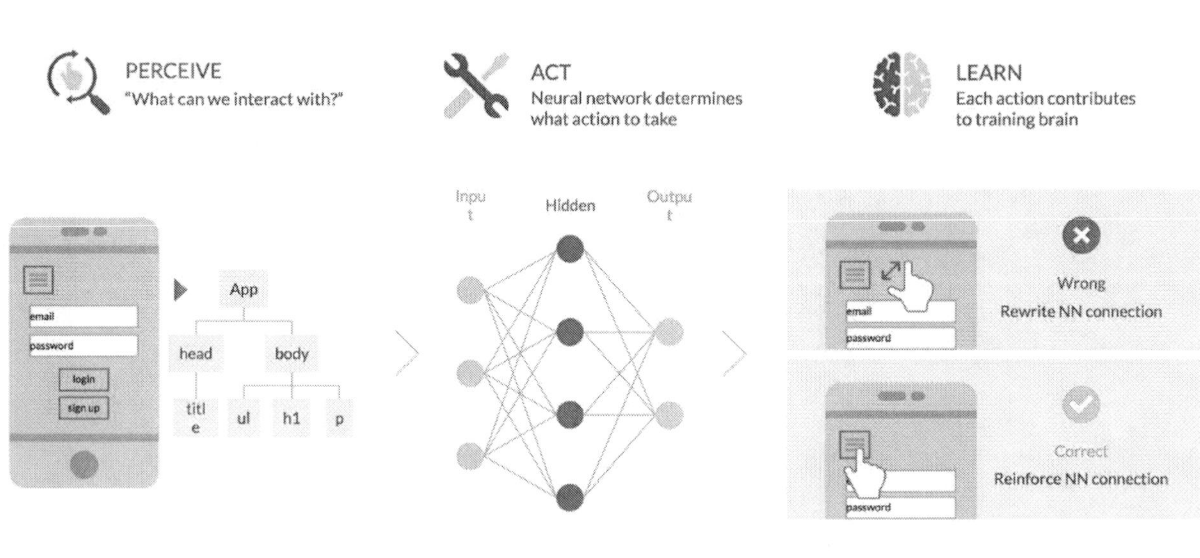

The learning to generate human-like actions on elements is similar to the training label classification. Screen context and a specific element are shown to the network, which guesses at a good action. If the network suggests a strange action, it reconfigures itself and tries again until it starts to behave like a human interacting with the application.

Note that this is a simple version for purposes of this paper, more complex variants deliver more 'intelligent' behaviors if inputs such as previous screens and action taken, or even what 'goal' is being attempted. A goal being a high level intent, such as: 'buy something', or 'search for something', or 'change profile image', etc.

The ML now has the ability to make human like decisions about what action to take on a screen.

It is also worth noting that a general 'fuzz' tester does very poorly when it comes to replicating human like interactions. On average each page has about 150 pairs of plausible element/action pairs. With each new page in a 'flow' of exploring the application there is a branching factor of 150 possible paths. So the total number of possible paths to explore semi-randomly is

num_paths ~= 150^X

where x=number of steps.

To cover all paths in app, say only 35 steps deep, it would require 150^35 = 2^78 test iterations to walk all possible paths.. As there are only ~2^78 atoms in the universe, one can get a feel for the amount of compute it would take a random-walk crawler to explore what an ML trained bot can do in just thousands of iterations. As the ML makes human-like decisions at every step, it prunes the total state space down to something efficient enough for practical applications.

4.3 Executing ML: Real World Apps

Now that the ML can intelligently decide what action to take given an app's state, the question of how the ML 'sees' the app and can take action in the app is worth addressing.

The ML sees, by simply having a bootstrap program that launching the app in a simulator or on a device, takes a screenshot of the application and downloads the current DOM over a debug connection to the app. This can be accomplished with off-the-shelf test automation components and utilities like android 'ADB' utility and executing a command such as 'adb shell uiautomator dump' to get the DOM in xml format, and the command 'adb shell screencap -p /sdcard/screen.png' to get a screenshot. For iOS, the XCUITest framework API allows similar functionality, more generally Appium and Selenium for the Web have this functionality as well. The application driver makes calls to the specific platform driver to request the data and simply passes the information to ML ('brain') to decide what to do next.

Now that the ML has decided what to do next, the output of the ML is a pair of element and action names. The Application driver simply finds the element's location or handle on the screen and based on the recommended action, sends the appropriate tap or text input.

It is worth noting that with only these two pieces of trained ML, we have a system capable to intelligently exploring *any* app. No new training is necessary to exercise human-like paths, and automatically discover crashes or performance issues that would previously only have been done via human manual testing, or humans writing thousands of automated UI test scripts. Best of all, this ML approach is applicable to all apps immediately--no need for humans to manually use the apps, or write test scripts for months.

4.4 Training ML: Verifying Behavior

The ML bots can now intelligently drive the application like a human would, but what of the question of verification? How do the these ML bots know the application is behaving correctly. There are three approaches to enable the ML bots to know if the behavior is correct.

1. Automatically check for common, detectable issues.
2. Train ML on examples of bugs.
3. Human review previous flows, then bots notify of any differences in subsequent test runs.

Automatically checking for common functionality detectable issues is the first line of app verification. At each step, the App Driver checks for any application crashes, error dialogs, etc.

Training a new ML on examples of previously found bugs, to auto classify the next screen in a sequence as a bug. This works for common failures where there are many examples to train on (for example error dialogs) like this one from the UBER app.

With a fair number of similar examples of failures, the ML quickly learns that condition such as screens with few DOM elements, a single dialog that contains the strings ‘sorry’, ‘oops’, or ‘try again’ are very often bugs in the app.

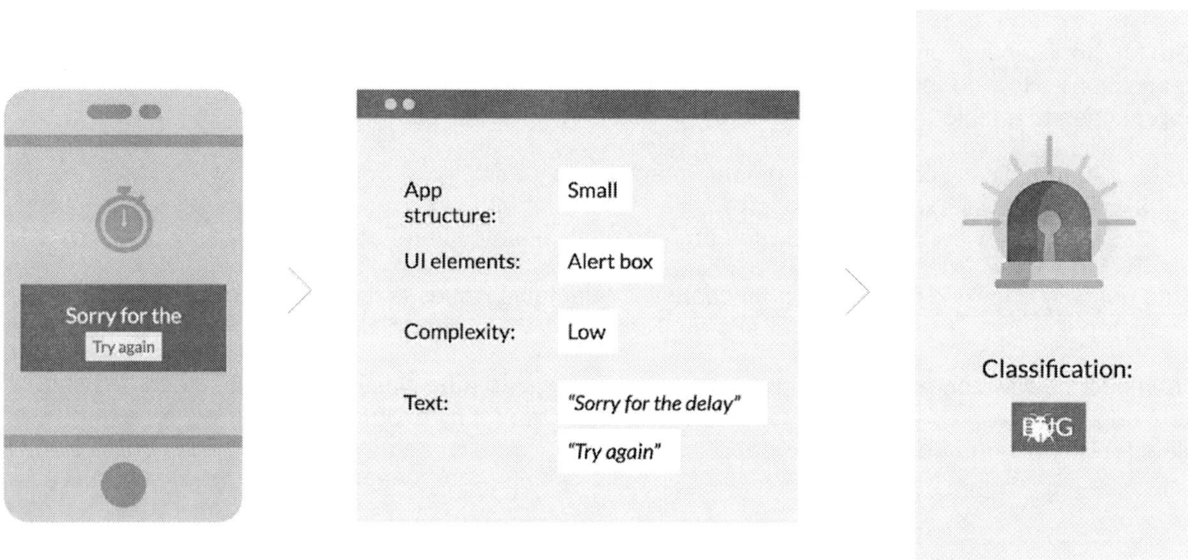

The most powerful method of detecting issues lies in the ability to record every screenshot, DOM and action sequence taken in every test run through the app. Humans then quickly verify these sequences represent good or bad behavior (pass or fail). Then, on subsequent runs, comparing the data between the older run and the newer reveals:

A. The run was identical, the application is still behaving correctly.
B. The run was not identical and revealed a new fault or bug in the applications behavior
C. The run was not identical but discovered a new valid element or path in the application. Humans review for functional correctness, and/or issues.

A subtle but powerful note about the validation that occurs in #3--the ML bots are able to exercise new functionality as soon as it appears the in the app, humans only need review the new behavior, whereas non-ML approaches require the human testers to take note of new functionality or UI in the application, write a manual or automated test cases and execute the test case--much of which in practice just doesn't happen due to the complexity gap, test resourcing and agile practices described above. The generalized ML models on the other hand are robust to changes in the application structure and design, and even recognize new functionality as it is very likely to look similar to that of other apps.in the training set.

ML-based testing system has obviated the need for classical manual or automated regression testing. Human tapping and test code scripts are simply replaced by trained machines that interact with the app via testability APIs.

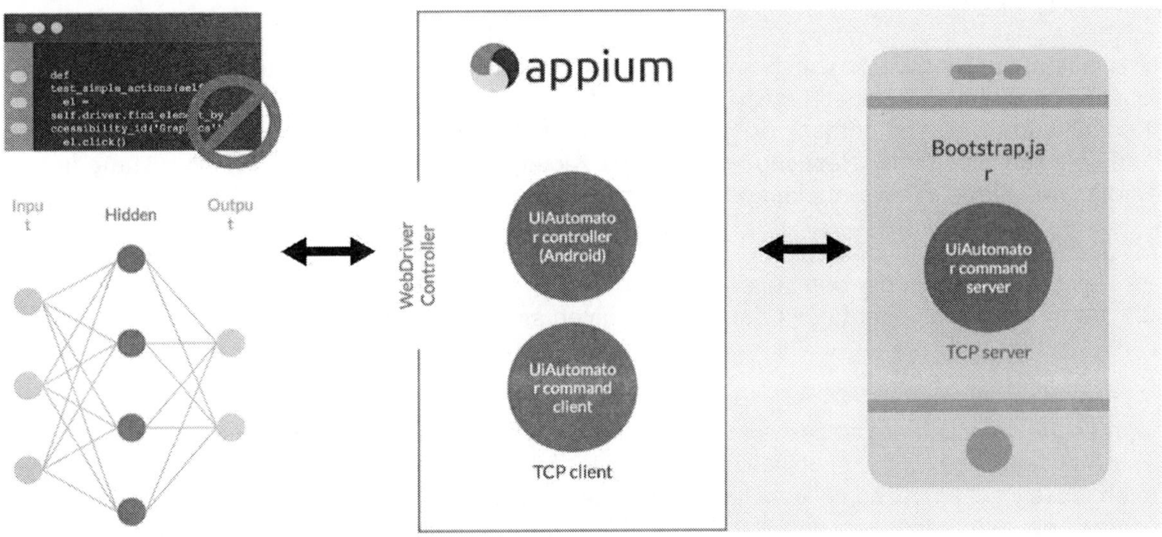

Figure: Replacing traditional, hand-crafted test code logic, with neural networks.

4.5 Benchmarking and Quantifying Quality

Traditionally quality metrics are often simply measured as the percent of available tests that pass or fail, or the load time of a few select pages. Those quality metrics lack context and often aren't motivating enough for app teams to take action and improve them. As ML test bots can test arbitrary apps with little customization, there is now the opportunity to test every app, The reference bot systems I've worked on have executed on over 30k apps, and with all that data we can now benchmark an apps quality against the rest of the marketplace of apps.

From each app test run, data such as performance, stability, and errors can be collected, and associated with labels and application categories. Benchmarks such as 'average login screen load time' or reliability of all apps in the Shopping category enable app teams to understand their app metrics relative to other apps.

Without benchmarking, app teams discover their performance or stability numbers, but are rarely sure how good is good enough. With benchmarking, app teams can be motivated by knowing their app is in the slowest 20% of all apps in their category.

ML also enables the ability to do competitive analysis of app quality. Most app team's can't keep up with the testing requirements for their own app, let alone their competitors apps. With ML, it is possible to run vast regression suites against direct competitors apps, and compare quality metrics in a way that directly relates to the business and is highly motivating to non-engineers to resolve quality issues when presented in a competitive light.

4.6 Abstract Intent Test Cases

The last mile of applying ML to software testing is the ability to have the ML testing bots execute very app-specific test cases, or import legacy test cases for ML execution. The ML bots know how to get to and from differently labeled portions of the application. We now need a way to orchestrate the ML bots to execute very specific, named, test sequences with exacting input and output verification. There are three capabilities needed to execute these specific regression test cases:

1. Named sequences of steps.
2. Specific test input per app state
3. Verify specific app features or strings in a given state.

To address the definition of test cases at this level of abstraction (labeled states and elements), I propose a new formal test case format specifically designed for ML test execution. Traditional manual test cases are often loosely schematized collections of test case names, test steps, validations, and categorization metadata. Test automation test cases are often either encoded directly in a procedural coding language with very little structure, and/or represented in schemas similar to manual test cases in a formatted file, or formal Test Case Management System. As ML tests are able to execute on arbitrary applications, we want to ensure there is a declarative format that doesn't bind the test case logic to the specific application.

It borrows heavily from Gherkin, but has additional specificity in that it allows for the actions and verification steps to be sequenced, versus unordered in Gherkin. The details are beyond the scope of this document, but an example instance is provided below.

Example AIT:

```
# Demo AIT Test Definition
Test Name: Remove Beanie Baby from item from cart
  Description: Make sure we can remove an item from the shopping cart.
  Tags: cart, remove
  Step: Search for Beanie Baby
```

```
    Context: SCREENNAME "Search"
    Input: ACTION SEARCH "Beanie Babies"
  Step: Add Item
  #Step: Add Item Any item will do.
    Context: SCREENNAME "Product" and HASWORD "Beanie Baby"
    Input: ACTION ADDTOCART
  Step: Remove Item
    Context: Cart and HASWORD "Beanie Baby"
    Input: Remove Item
  Step: Verify Item Removed
    Context: SCREENNAME Cart and NOTHASWORD "Beanie Baby"
```

The aspects to note are that this test format allows for repeatable app- and data-specific test input and validation are possible. The value of the AIT format is that it focused on the Abstract Intent of the Test Case, and all I/O is based not on exact steps or sequences in the application, rather they are notes to the execution of the ML testing bots that they need to 'find' a given labeled app state, interact with that screen's labeled element with a specific action.

This label-based approach to test case definition avoids one of the most common sources of test case maintenance pain--changes in the application UI or flow. Traditional frameworks are sensitive to changes in the DOM structure and flow of an app as each test step must be executed in exact sequence and it must find each element for each steps interaction based specific element search criteria. With ML testing bots, the burden of finding the app state and input elements is left to the bot's ML classifiers from the label training above. If the application's flow changes, the bots will still search the statespace of the app to find the new, correctly label state for data entry. In the case that an element for input has changed its location, size, color, parent-child relationship in the DOM, etc., the bots have been trained on thousands of applications and can still identify the correct element for input despite severe morphing.

4.7 ML Test Architecture

Here a reference Architecture for an ML-based test generation and execution system is shown.

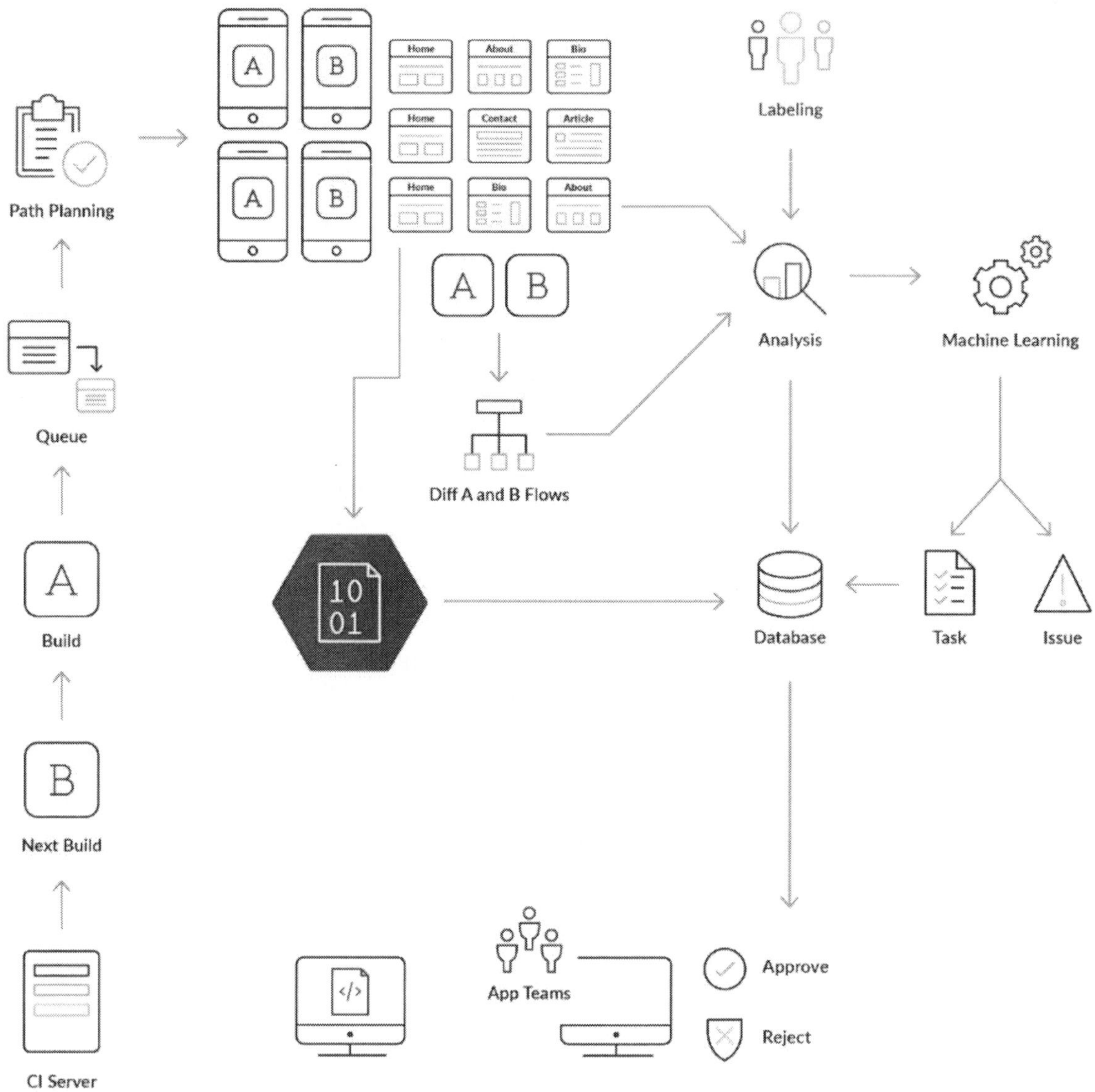

5 Testing AI Products and Features

Many applications and services are incorporating machine learning. In the current AI renaissance, there is an almost irrational rush to re-design old features with AI/ML, and add new features only possible with the advent of modern AI/ML and cloud compute. Often, this is done with little thought of how to test these new systems.

Versus classically coded functional features, AI/ML apps introduce a new set of software quality and testing challenges:

1. Feature Computation
2. Sampling Quality
3. Outlier Tolerance
4. Labeling Quality
5. Quality Drift
6. Traceability

5.1 Feature Computation

As we have seen for the ML testing methods above, all ML systems need input data for training and during execution. This is generally called Feature Engineering. In the above diagrams, this logic is built into the 'Application Driver'. Feature engineering is the work of transforming real world application or signals into a form that ML can understand. Generally speaking, ML systems can only understand inputs of floating point numbers between zero and one.

An example of feature computation is converting the number of buttons on a given application page, to a value useful for training networks.. The code for this 'feature', asks the platform driver for a list of all elements in the current application DOM, counts how many buttons appear in the DOM and then normalizes this count to a number between zero and one. This feature engineering is often traditional procedural code that needs traditional testing. There are often hundreds of features similar built for every ML system implementation. Each of these needs to be tested carefully because if the data used in the training or runtime is incorrect, the output of the AI feature or product will also be incorrect.

Beyond testing the functional quality of these 'features', it is important to note that the normalization is done correctly. In the example above, if the count of buttons in practice never exceeds 100 per page, if the normalization divides the the number of buttons by 50, some granularity will be lost in the training as pages with more than 50 buttons will be missed. Also, if the normalization includes a division by 1000, most every app will appear to the network to have very few buttons as the input values will always be in the range of [0, .1], leaving 9/10's of the possible values in the range [0, 1] unused.

Feature engineering and selection is an art, but it must be directly tested and questioned.

It is also important to note that the features into the ML are also likely related to the desired output, ideally correlated with the outputs if that is known. Irrelevant features mean the ML training time is more expensive as the ML learns to ignore that signal, might cause spurious outputs, and often results in lower quality ML execution as the ML could often have used the part of it's brain to suppress that bad signal, and used it to better differentiate other aspects of the input.

5.2 Sampling Quality

An often overlooked aspect of ML quality is the sampling of the training data. If the training set has a bad sampling of data, the ML system will appear to function well in test conditions, but in real world inputs it will behave poorly, or even dangerously.

AI-Powered web search can help illustrate this problem. The process of taking the top 50 results returned by the core search index and ranking system, then optimizing the results based on the actual query, who is issuing the query, where the query was issued from, etc. This last 'dynamic ranking' step helps put the right blue links at the top and is critical for web search relevance.

What do we need for training data? Lots of queries. We can't possibly train on all possible search queries, there are too many, and in fact new unique queries never seen before are issued every second. A lazy approach might be to just a random sample of 5,000 search queries from the 100M search logs from yesterday. That sounds reasonable but if we trained the web search ranker on this data:

1. If the training sample was taken from logs on a Wednesday, it likely doesn't contain, or adequately represent queries that happen on weekends--people are often searching for very different things based on time of day, week, and year.
2. Is the sample size correct? Is 5,000 enough? Probably not. Queries are made up of things like people's names, places, objects, shopping intent, UPS Shipping Codes, etc. How likely is it that your sample contains enough examples of each subtype of query? If 1 in 10000 queries is a UPS Shipping Code, it is likely your sample doesn't even have a UPS Shipping Code and the ML training won't even have a single example to train on.
3. Consider whether the sample represent the targeted or business motivated sample? If you work on a search engine that isn't the market leader, with a predominantly older and non-technical demographic, your search sample means the search engine you create will great at queries for these folks, not do well on technical, or queries typical of a younger demographic, meaning younger users will find your product subpar and not switch over.
4. Consider whether the sample is too broad? If you have an international, multi-lingual audience and you sample includes all of these languages, the ML can be easily confused, or you need enormous amounts of training data and compute to let the ML sort it all out. Or, you can build a classifier to determine the language of the query, and then route that query to an ML system that trained only on one language with a far smaller language-specific query sample.

In practice, for a production web search ranker, the training and test samples often include queries from all of the last month and year and significant holidays., 30,000 samples turned out to be a good balance between sampling breadth and training time, and yes, one team never realized they were training on demographically-based data.

5.3 Outlier Tolerance

Often, ML systems will perform very poorly outside the range of input they were trained on. When ML systems are deployed into real world environments, the input data can involve very odd outlier inputs to the system. Especially with ML systems, it is important to test for inputs that you cannot predict.

In the web search example, imagine Beyonce's next child's is named "UniverseOfAllThingsAmazingChild". Or, Facebook engineers create a chatbot that says: "balls have a ball to me to me to me to me to me to me to me". Though that might never happen, the internet may start searching for this unusual and nonsensical phrase.

To test the robustness of a system, it is often not enough to sample from the real world for test and training data. Testing should often include generated, deliberate outlier inputs to see how the trained system performs in strange situations.

5.4 Labeling Quality

As we saw above, a key aspect of training ML to behave intelligently (like humans) is to have human-labeled data which which to train on. The process of labeling is critical to the quality of the resulting ML system.

As with sampling training data, care should be taken when selecting the humans used to label your data. Labels are human-opinions and judgments and can have a strong impact on how the ML learns to behave. In the web search example, human labelers used to rate queries -> result matches. They look at the search query and rate the possible result links on relevance--based on their opinion. So, if a search engine used inexpensive humans and paid them all $10/hour, and that data is used to train the search engine, the resulting ML search ranker will sort results like $10 an hour worker. How intelligently do you think people willing to work for $10/hour will rate the results for a query on the topic of 'Artificial Intelligence'? What if the labelers were 90% women? Ensuring labelers and the labeling activity matches your desired application can be very important and is often overlooked.

It may not be obvious, but disagreement in labeling is common. People just think and see things differently. If you have only one person label each item, the labeling process will miss any disagreement. High quality labeling systems and processes ensure there is overlap in the ratings, meaning more than one person labels each artifact. In the web search example, if a labeler sees the query 'Bush', they will label the result for President Bush high if they are over 30 years of age or well educated. If the labeler is a farmer, or didn't grow up in the United States, they may label the result for tiny trees much higher. The labeling system must have overlap, and allow for disagreement in the labeling or risk having lopsided training data.

A well-known production web search engine once paid every labeler about $10/hour, and when labelers disagreed with the consensus vote of other labelers--they were fired. Avoid these actions in your own labeling activities to ensure a high quality ML training system.

5.5 Quality Drift

One of the most overlooked quality issues with ML systems is that each new version is a completely new implementation. In classically coded products, only a few lines of code change between each build and the next. Often, the means the regression testing can even rely on this and reduce the number of test (aka Test Selection).to only regress the areas of the app likely impacted those few lines of code.

Most every ML system has a completely differently implemented system after each training session. ML systems often start by randomizing their internal networks--yes, they randomize themselves to start with and that is a fundamental aspect of how they learn. Any small changes not just in the test data, but even the ordering of the training data, or if the training rand function isn't seeded, or even different training times or threshold configurations of the training system will often result in completely different implementations.

In the web search example, we measure the relevance of the system based on how well the results per query are ordered by the machine, compared to the human labeled suggestions of correct order. 100 would be a perfect search engine--it matches all the human labels. Perfect search engines don't exist, in fact that sit around 70% correct by most measures today. So, if we have a build from yesterday and it scored a 70, and a new build today also scores a 70, that only means that *on average*, the two builds have the same relevance/quality measure. In practice the two engines might perform very similarly and do well on the same queries and poorly on the same queries. It is often the case though , that any small tweak to the training data, feature set, or because of random initialization in the training process, the two engines do well on completely different subsets of queries, and poorly on another set of subqueries. They are very different search engines with the same average value. The first build may be great at people searches but suffer on technical queries. The reverse could be true of the second build of the engine. If we shipped a new build of the engine every day, searches for 'Britney Spears' will be amazing today and be of poor quality tomorrow. This is quality drift.

To ensure your ML product doesn't suffer from drift, or to at least track it, you must have separate measures of quality for each subset, or subcategory of test input, and track those quality measures separately and decide in the drift build to build is acceptable for your application.

5.6 Opacity and Traceability

I described ML as a black box above--that's not just true for the context of this paper, but in all practicality it is true for almost every ML-based product. Imagine not being able to debug your code, not having meaningful logs--that is the state of deployed ML. ML systems often have hundreds or thousands of nodes, each with seemingly random weights. Much like the human brain, it is difficult to understand why any given brain made a decision--its just did.

This means many classic approaches to quality such as log monitoring, stepping through code, and code-coverage analysis tools; are all useless in this new world of ML-based application logic.

Generally, the problem of testing and debugging this new wave of AI-based products and features is incredibly difficult. Not only is the problem difficult, but the consequences are grave as these AI systems are embedded in fast-moving vehicles on the road, controlling supply chains, and soon deciding where and when to fire a missile from autonomous drones.

DARPA (the Defence Advanced Research Projects Agency) has deemed this lack of visibility and traceability in modern AI systems to be a DARPA-hard problem as there is no obvious solution, or enough folks working on this problem today and it's consequences are worth of national security interest. DARPA has defined the XAI project and is starting to fund research in this area.

6 Summary

Artificial Intelligence (AI) and Machine Learning (ML) have the potential to dramatically improve the ability to test software applications. Realizing that ML-training systems and software testing are very similar implies that general ML solutions should readily apply to software testing tasks. The generality of ML-based testing systems that can execute on many different apps without customization greatly improves the re-use of test development efforts. This generality will speed up development of test cases, and improve quality by generating far more coverage through re-use.. ML-based testing solutions has the promise to both disrupt and help the world of traditional software testing.

The sudden increase of application software written using these very same AI and ML techniques will create even more difficult software quality and testing problems. ML-based products are often re-trained from scratch with each new version, difficult to debug, and their relevance and predictive ability is limited to the availability of training data. These issues indicate that quality will suffer relative to simpler, procedural-based applications. These new ML-based products create the need for standardization in the toolsets and best practices for testing such systems.

AI and ML will radically change the nature of software testing and quality in the coming years--far more radically than most expect.

References

Wikipedia contributors, "Machine learning," *Wikipedia, The Free Encyclopedia,* https://en.wikipedia.org/w/index.php?title=Machine_learning&oldid=796373868 (accessed August 20, 2017).

Wikipedia contributors, "Selenium (software)," *Wikipedia, The Free Encyclopedia,* https://en.wikipedia.org/w/index.php?title=Selenium_(software)&oldid=795945653 (accessed August 20, 2017).

Wikipedia contributors, "Test-driven development," *Wikipedia, The Free Encyclopedia,* https://en.wikipedia.org/w/index.php?title=Test-driven_development&oldid=790275486(accessed August 20, 2017).

Wikipedia contributors, "AlphaGo," *Wikipedia, The Free Encyclopedia,* https://en.wikipedia.org/w/index.php?title=AlphaGo&oldid=795373355 (accessed August 20, 2017).

Wikipedia contributors, "DeepMind," Wikipedia, The Free Encyclopedia, https://en.wikipedia.org/w/index.php?title=DeepMind&oldid=795218131 (accessed August 20, 2017).

KIF, "kif-framework/KIF: Keep It Functional - An iOS Functional Testing Framework", https://github.com/kif-framework/KIF (accessed August 20, 2017).

ESPRESSO, "Espresso | Android Developers", https://developer.android.com/training/testing/espresso/index.html (accessed August 20, 2017).

DARPA XAI Project, "Explainable Artificial Intelligence", https://www.darpa.mil/program/explainable-artificial-intelligence (accessed August 20, 2017).

Wikipedia contributors, "Cucumber (software)," *Wikipedia, The Free Encyclopedia,* https://en.wikipedia.org/w/index.php?title=Cucumber_(software)&oldid=794655871 (accessed August 20, 2017).

XCUITest, "User Interface Testing", https://developer.apple.com/library/content/documentation/DeveloperTools/Conceptual/testing_with_xcode/chapters/09-ui_testing.html (accessed August 20, 2017).

Thanks to the following people for their help editing this paper: Tariq King, Rick D. Anderson, and Chris Navrides.

Pre-Mortems

Keeping your project off the autopsy slab

Christopher Cowell
SDET, HealthSparq

What is a pre-mortem?

Formal risk identification and mitigation process

Why do a pre-mortem?

To decrease the chances of your project failing

Pre-mortem in 3 vague steps

Imagine that the project has failed

Imagine why it failed

Figure out what to do *now* to address those reasons

What does “risk” mean?

Anything that could reduce a project’s success

Catastrophic failure is not the only kind of failure

What does “risk” mean?

Anything that could reduce a project’s success

Catastrophic failure is not the only kind of failure

What does “anything” mean?

- Attitude
  - low morale, skepticism
- Event
  - server catching on fire
- Person
  - incompetence, negativity
- Constraint
  - not enough time
- Technology
  - unproven 3rd-party library

```
SParse1
# handle numeric address spec
R$* < @ [ $+ ] > $*    $: $>98 $1 < @ [ $2 ] > $3  numeric internet spec
R$* < @ [ $+ ] > $*    $#esmtp $@ [$2] $: $1 < @ [$2] > $3    still numeric: send

# handle virtual users
R$+ < @ $=w . >  $: < $(virtuser $1 @ $2 $@ $1 $: @ $) > $1 < @ $2 . >
R<@> $+ + $* < @ $* . >
                 $: < $(virtuser $1 + * @ $3 $@ $1 $: @ $) > $1 + $2 < @ $3 . >
R<@> $+ + $* < @ $* . >
                 $: < $(virtuser $1 @ $3 $@ $1 $: @ $) > $1 + $2 < @ $3 . >
R<@> $+ < @ $+ . >     $: < $(virtuser @ $2 $@ $1 $: @ $) > $1 < @ $2 . >
R<@> $+                $: $1
R< error : $- $+ > $*       $#error $@ $(dequote $1 $) $: $2
R< $+ > $+ < @ $+ >    $: $>97 $1

R$=L < @ $=w . > $#local $: @ $1       special local names
R$+ < @ $=w . >        $#local $: $1              regular local name
```

```
SParse1
# handle numeric address spec
R$* < @ [ $+ ] > $*     $: $>98 $1 < @ [ $2 ] > $3  numeric internet spec
R$* < @ [ $+ ] > $*     $#esmtp $@ [$2] $: $1 < @ [$2] > $3    still numeric: send

# handle virtual users
R$+ < @ $=w . > $: < $(virtuser $1 @ $2 $@ $1 $: @ $) > $1 < @ $2 . >
R<@> $+ + $* < @ $* . >
                $: < $(virtuser $1 + * @ $3 $@ $1 $: @ $) > $1 + $2 < @ $3 . >
R<@> $+ + $* < @ $* . >
                $: < $(virtuser $1 @ $3 $@ $1 $: @ $) > $1 + $2 < @ $3 . >
R<@> $+ < @ $+ . >      $: < $(virtuser @ $2 $@ $1 $: @ $) > $1 < @ $2 . >
R<@> $+                 $: $1
R< error : $- $+ > $*        $#error $@ $(dequote $1 $) $: $2
R< $+ > $+ < @ $+ >     $: $>97 $1

R$=L < @ $=w . >$#local $: @ $1        special local names
R$+ < @ $=w . >         $#local $: $1              regular local name
```

What does “anything” mean?

- Lack of knowledge
  - known unknowns (fix by spiking)
  - unknown unknowns

What does "mitigate" mean?

Small expense now to avoid a big expense later

- car insurance
- umbrella

Not free, but worth it

What does "mitigate" mean?

What a weird word.

Why not use:

- reduce
- minimize
- lessen
- shrink
- alleviate

In conclusion: English is dumb

What does “is” mean?

“It depends upon what the meaning of the word ‘is’ is.”

Pre-mortem in 10 concrete steps

1. Prepare
   a. Whole project, part of project, QA part of project?
   b. Synchronous or asynchronous?
   c. Distribute instructions
2. Imagine failure. Consider all degrees of failure.
3. Brainstorm reasons, including ridiculous ones (*meteor!*)
4. De-duplicate and clarify
5. Move down: low-impact (*1 day PTO*) or low-control (*meteor!*)
6. Move up: repeats
7. Vote for top *n*
8. Reasons → Risks (backward-looking → forward-looking)
9. Action items for mitigating top *n* risks
10. Track action item progress

Trackable action items are the whole point!

Trackable action items are the whole point!

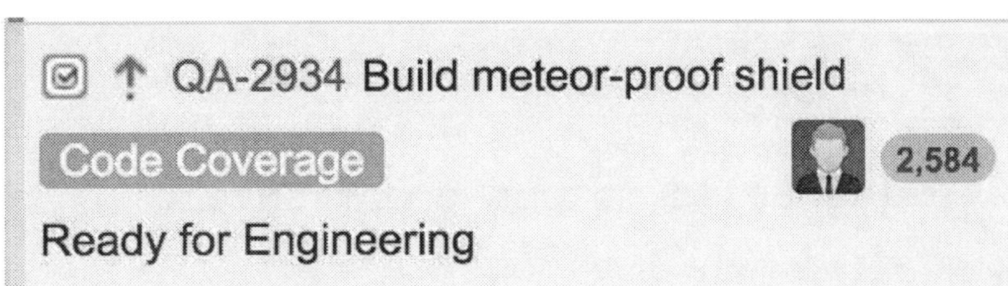

Trackable action items are the whole point!

Trackable action items are the whole point!

```
To Do

[ ] Build meteor-proof shield

```

Trackable action items are the whole point!

```
def build_meteor_proof_shield
  # TODO implement this
end
```

Trackable action items are the whole point!

To Do

build meteor-proof shield

Trackable action items are the whole point!

Who should NOT do pre-mortems?

When failure is an option

When success is hard to define (research spike?)

Using familiar process, familiar technology, familiar people

When team is huge (there are workarounds for this)

Example: Hafjell

3 people

Scoped to QA only

3 hours

There are no guarantees!

Pre-mortems can only shift the odds

Pre-mortems are not foolproof

Help Your Developers Help Themselves

Scott Stancil
@hoverduck

AUTOMATTIC

Challenges

The project I work on wasn't built with end-to-end testing in mind. Here are a few of the challenges we face:

- The tests live in a separate GitHub repo from the production code
- They run in a separate CI instance, making feedback to the code authors difficult
- The full test suite is only run autonomously against production *after* the code goes live for millions of users.

This means the only way to get early feedback on changes before merge is to run the tests manually. Historically this has only been done by a member of the QA team.

Complaints

As the project matures, we're trying to consolidate the automated tests into the development process, and get a common series of complaints and reasons why the development team can't run the tests themselves:

- The e2e test environment is too hard to set up
- Tests running in live browser windows interrupt their other work
- It isn't clear what set of changes are actually being tested
- The tests take too long

Developers ***love*** the feedback from a good suite of automated tests, but it's generally just easier for them to ping us to run them. And developers hate inefficiency.

Make It Convenient

Eliminate the roadblocks between your developers and the tests and you'll find them excited to run them earlier in the development process. The earlier bugs are found, the easier they are to fix.

- The e2e test environment is too hard to set up
  - Eliminate the setup by packaging up your test environment
- Tests running in live browser windows interrupt their other work
  - Hide the browser window in a virtual environment
- It isn't clear what set of changes are actually being tested
  - Run the tests against a local server hosting a specific code branch
- The tests take too long
  - Speed up your tests through increased parallelization

How Do We Do it?

docker

Docker is the magic that will enable you to make your developers' lives easier, which will in turn make your own lives easier 😀

Docker? DevOps?

The concepts of DevOps and Docker containers are often intimidating to folks. But if you're capable of writing a script to automate a web browser, you're capable of building a test infrastructure and sharing it with the world.

The Selenium open source project has made this incredibly easy with pre-built Docker images that address the first two of our developers' complaints:

- The e2e test environment is too hard to set up
- Tests running in live browser windows interrupt their other work

Docker Compose

Docker compose lets you easily consolidate your entire test environment in a single place, a file named `docker-compose.yml`. Let's review this simple example:

```
version: "3"
services:
  selenium:
    image:
selenium/standalone-chrome-debug:3.3.0
    ports:
      - "4444:4444"
      - "5902:5900"
    volumes:
     - /dev/shm:/dev/shm
```

Docker Compose Explained

```
version: "3"
services:
  selenium:
    image: selenium/standalone-chrome-debug:3.3.0
    ports:                              ^ the debug option enables VNC
      - "4444:4444" <- Selenium port
      - "5902:5900" <- VNC port
    volumes:
     - /dev/shm:/dev/shm
          ^ Ensures Chrome won't crash for lack of shared memory
```

How Does It Work?

- Just run `*docker-compose up*`, and Docker will launch a miniature Linux VM behind the scenes.
- Set the environment variable *SELENIUM_REMOTE_URL=http://localhost:4444/wd/hub*
- Run your tests as normal.

Problem Solved?

- The e2e test environment is too hard to set up
  - Not anymore 😀
- Tests running in live browser windows interrupt their other work
  - Nope, they're contained in a single VNC window

And as a bonus, you know now that every test run will be against the exact same version of Chrome, Chromedriver, etc. No more "it only works on my machine" 😀

The Second Half

The remaining issues on our list are a little more complicated.

- It isn't clear what set of changes are actually being tested
- The tests take too long

Let's start by looking at the last one and work our way back

Parallelization

Test runtime is by far the easiest metric to track, and it's also one of the easiest to address with the least technical effort.

In our project we cut our test execution time in half by using the *Magellan* test runner-runner to increase parallelization without needing any extra hardware.

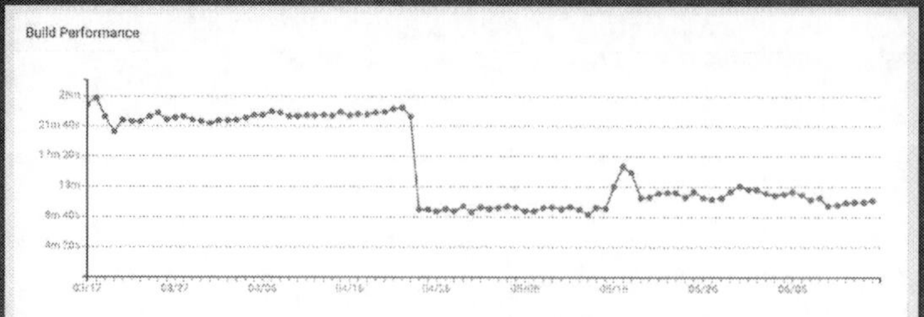

Testing Specific Changes

It's complicated, and highly dependent on your specific application. But Docker is extremely flexible.

Add your application server(s) to the docker-compose config. Now your tests and app will run on their own private network, and the app will be using the developer's own code base.

If your application isn't currently Dockerized, find the developer in your organization who's most enthusiastic about the idea and they'll help!

Loading the app in a container is also useful for general development work and manual testing.

Problem Solved!

- It isn't clear what set of changes are actually being tested
  - The developer can be sure that the code being tested is direct from his or her current branch
- The tests take too long
  - It's easier than you think to increase parallelization

With a Docker-enabled workflow for both testers and developers, everyone's job is easier in the long run.

Thanks

Scott Stancil
@hoverduck

AUTOMATTIC

How Golf Taught Me To Be A Better Software Professional

Alan Ark
Sr. QA Engineer - Duo Security
Pacific Northwest Software Quality Conference
October 2017

Credit: www.4gifs.com

Who am I?

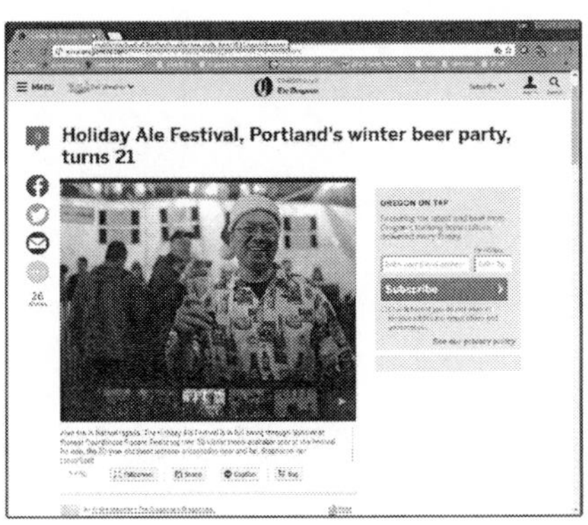

Who am I?

What to shoot for?

Blue Tees

Hole	1	2	3	4	5	6	7	8	9	Out
Yardage	357	423	180	372	465	376	181	371	504	3229
Par	4	4	3	4	5	4	3	4	5	36
Handicap	9	7	17	13	1	5	15	11	3	

Hole	10	11	12	13	14	15	16	17	18	In	Total
Yardage	381	215	420	536	396	191	414	527	391	3471	6700
Par	4	3	4	5	4	3	4	5	4	36	72
Handicap	12	16	8	4	14	18	6	2	10		

White Tees

Hole	1	2	3	4	5	6	7	8	9	Out
Yardage	346	414	166	353	454	367	171	360	493	3124
Par	4	4	3	4	5	4	3	4	5	36
Handicap	9	7	17	13	1	5	15	11	3	

Hole	10	11	12	13	14	15	16	17	18	In	Total
Yardage	354	210	393	498	375	162	404	489	384	3269	6393
Par	4	3	4	5	4	3	4	5	4	36	72
Handicap	12	16	8	4	14	18	6	2	10		

Red Tees

Hole	1	2	3	4	5	6	7	8	9	Out
Yardage	332	324	149	332	411	316	126	338	462	2790
Par	4	4	3	4	5	4	3	4	5	36
Handicap	9	11	15	5	1	3	17	7	3	

Hole	10	11	12	13	14	15	16	17	18	In	Total
Yardage	305	107	346	424	355	94	327	412	316	2686	5476
Par	4	3	4	5	4	3	4	5	4	36	72
Handicap	6	18	14	4	8	16	10	2	12		

Each one of these things increases your score (over par)

- Execution failure
- You land in a hazard
- Shoot yourself in the foot
  - You hit yourself with a golf ball - 2 strokes
- Swing and a miss? It's about intent. It counts

Each one of these things increases risk for your software

- Execution failure
- You land in a hazard - Bad requirements
- Shoot yourself in the foot
  - Question assumptions
    It happens to me all the time
- Swing and a miss? Build on your failures

Recognize when potential hazards are present

Use the right club

- Pick your targets well
- Take the hazards out of
  - Club up/down
  - Aim for a different

Credit: https://www.reddit.com/r/gifs/comments/605o7s/excuse_me_ill_go_play_golf_over_there

Recognize when potential hazards are present

Use the right resources

- Pick the right people/tools/processes
- Take the hazards out of play
  - Ask questions early and often
  - Aim for intermediate targets as checkpoints

Know your tools

Not the same for everyone....

- 150 yards – Driver (my wife)
- 150 yards – 6 iron (me)
- 150 yards – 9 iron (Sergio)

150 yard shot - 6 iron?

What are the conditions?

- Uphill - extra club
- Downhill - one less club
- What about the wind?
- Are you in the rough?

Practice doesn't make perfect....

Credit: www.afv.com

Practice the right things....

Practice the RIGHT things!!

- Work with Product
- Get actionable stories
- Define the expectations up-front
- Refine the backlog often

Credit: http://i.imgur.com/NToj4qY.gifv

Practice the RIGHT things!!

- Get to know the customer perspective
- Know why your work is important
- Celebrate wins often

Practice the RIGHT things!!

- Ask for help when you need it
- Collaborate with other engineers
- Get involved with code reviews
- Offer help to those in need
- Appreciate your co-workers

DUO

Practice the RIGHT things!!

- Automation can help
  - Use Continuous Integration
  - Use automated testing
  - Use build promotion
- Gain confidence in your build processes

DUO

Takeaway

- It's actually about people
  - Practice communication
  - Build trust
  - Truly work together as a team

Rock Creek Amateur - Team
Low Net
2016 - Alan Ark
Rock Creek

Rock Creek Amateur - Team
Low Net
Rock Creek Amateur - Team
Low Net
2017 - Alan Ark

APPLAUSE

BUILDING A CUSTOMER QUALITY DASHBOARD

John Ruberto
VP of Quality Engineering – Clover, a First Data Company

2

First, A story

4

9.86

5

6

What is 9.86?

Metric	First Negative Link in Google
Source Lines of Code	3
Cyclomatic Complexity	19
Function Points	11
Code Coverage	6
Defect Removal Efficiency	6
Defect Density	9
Bug Count	15

7

Principles for metrics

- Related to our goals
- Leading vs lagging indicators
- Process metrics vs outcome metrics
- Use the right technology to display

8

Related to our goals

9

Use the right technology to collect & display

10

Provides actionable insights

11

Goal-Questions-Metric

- GQM
- Victor Basili

- Align on a set of goals
- Ask questions about those goals
- Design & collect metrics to answer the questions

12

Why

- Setting goals, in alignment with the wider organization, gains acceptance
- Focus on what's most important to your stakeholders
- Provide "line of sight" from your metrics to your goals
- Build comprehensive view of your goals.

13

Example - Context

- Software as a service application
- > 500K active users
- Paying monthly subscription

14

Example

- Goal: Deliver better quality to our customers
- Questions:
  - How many defects do our customers report?
  - How are we trending on customer reported defects?
  - How quickly to we fix the defects?
  - What are the top causes of these defects?
  - Why aren't we catching these bugs before release?

15

Example –Delivered Quality

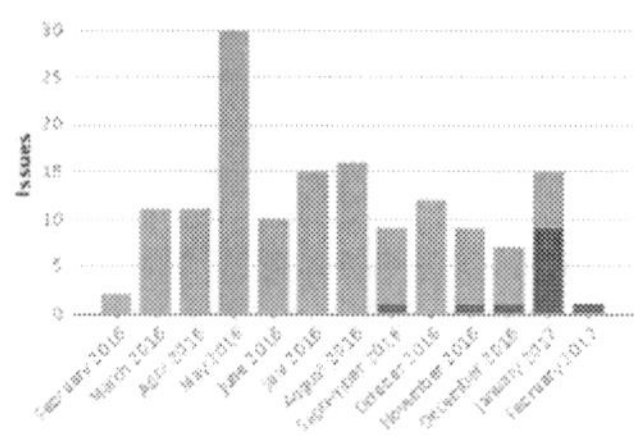

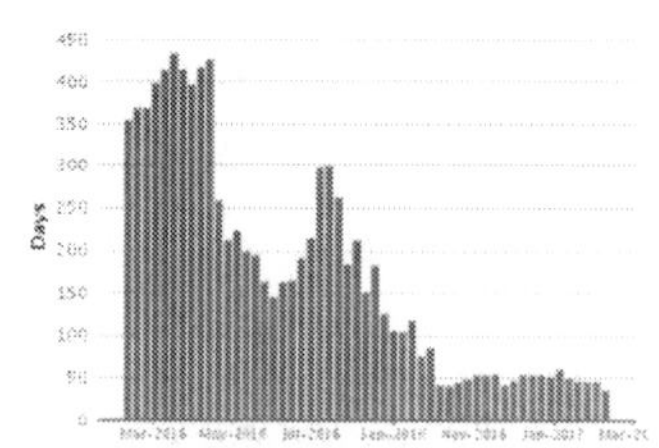

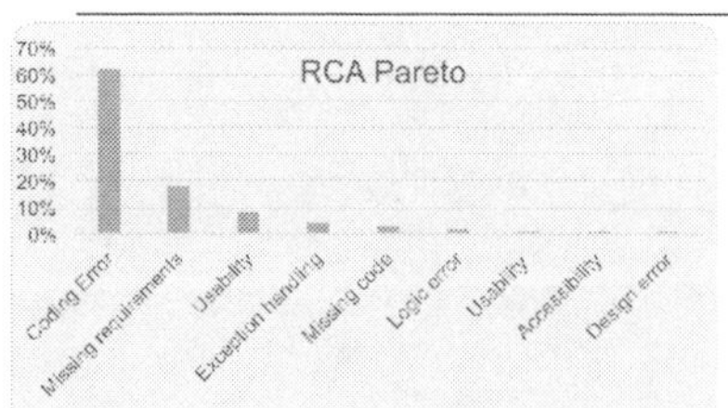

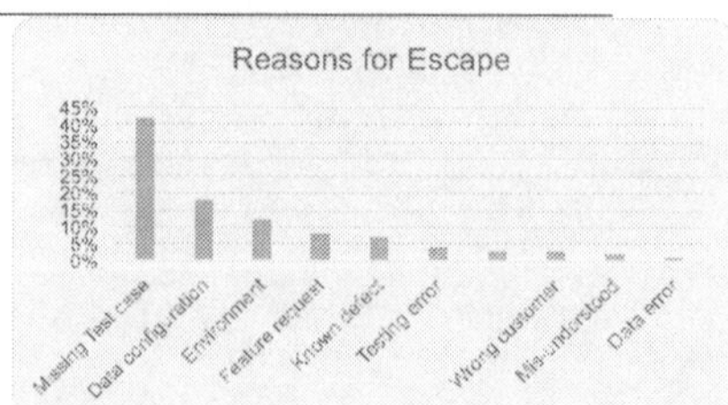

16

Characteristics to think about

- Process Metrics vs Outcomes
  - LOC / Review hour vs Defects found per review
- Leading Indicators vs Lagging Indicators
  - Code coverage vs delivered quality
- Median vs Average (Better yet: percentile)
  - Median page load vs Average page load
  - % fixes within SLA vs Average Age
  - 2012 average income in San Mateo County

17

Principles in using metrics

- Direct measures instead of derived
  - "quality score"
  - Apdex
- Actionable
  - Total crashes vs crash code pareto
- Live data is best data
  - No powerpoint...

18

Fallacies of Metrics - Gamification

- Goal: Improve Testing Efficiency
- Metric: Testing Efficiency: (fixed bugs / total submitted)

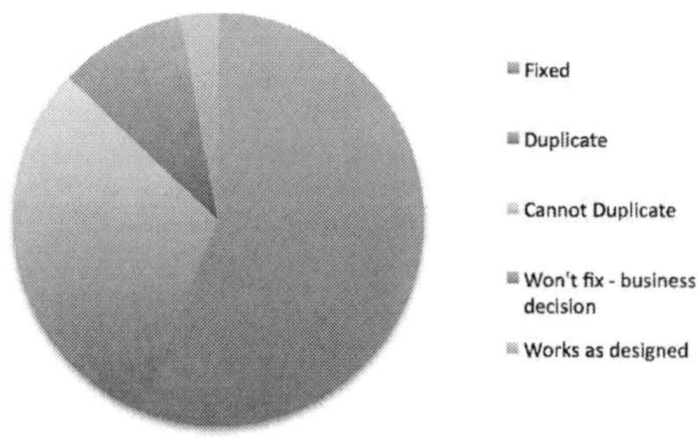

19

Fallacies of Metrics – Confirmation Bias

- Incoming bug rate improved dramatically – our quality must be outstanding!

Image Credit: By User:KAMiKAZOW (Transferred from en.wikipedia to Commons.) [Public domain], via Wikimedia Commons

20

Fallacies of Metrics – Survivor Bias

 21

Fallacies of Metrics – Survivor Bias

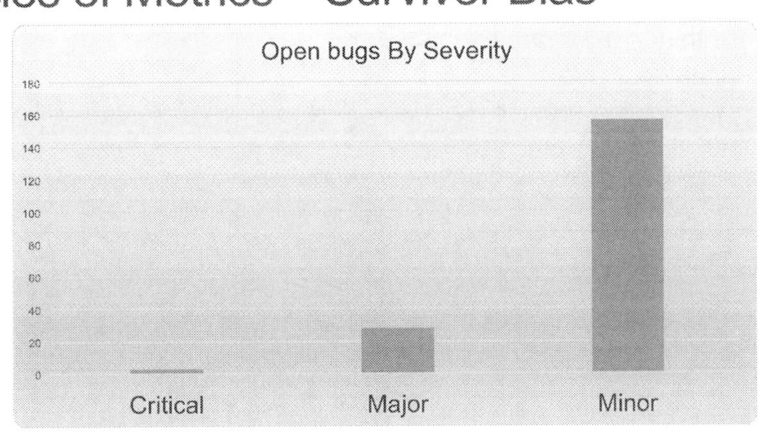

22

Measurement Bias

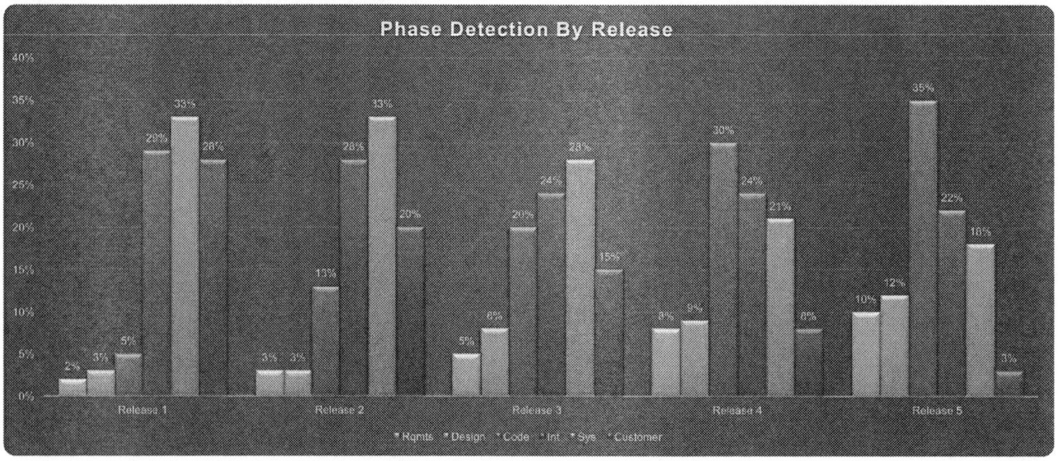

23

Vanity Metrics

- Don't measure things that matter
- Easily manipulated
- But, make us feel good

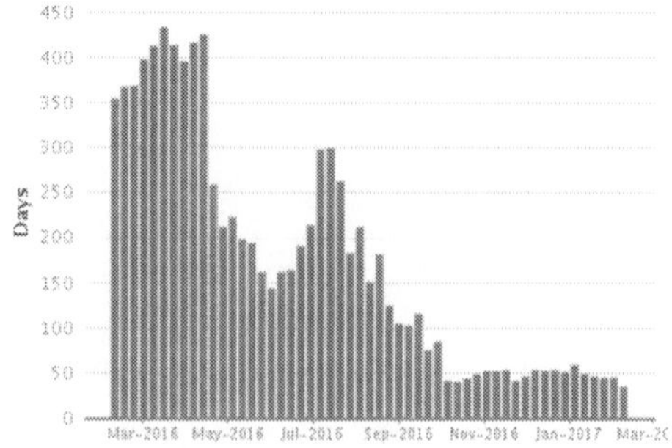

24

Keeping the gains

- Process Wrapper
  - Monitor & regulate
  - Automatic trigger
  - Wide distribution

25

- Questions?

- JohnRuberto@gmail.com
- @johnruberto
- http://linkedin.com/in/ruberto

26

Photo Credits

Nadia Comm: Ben Sutherland https://www.flickr.com/photos/bensutherland/
Bull: By Hollingsworth John and Karen, U.S. Fish and Wildlife Service [Public domain], via Wikimedia Commons
Cow: By Keith Weller/USDA (www.ars.usda.gov: Image Number K5176-3) [Public domain], via Wikimedia Commons

Data Quality?
Yes Please!

Bovard Doerschuk-Tiberi
PNSQC 2017

AKA "More Data Quality Please!"

What is Data Quality?

What is Data Quality?

There are many definitions of data quality but data is generally considered high quality if it is "fit for [its] intended uses in operations, decision making and planning."

- Wikipedia

Our Focus

Ensuring data quality in an event driven architecture

Our Focus

Ensuring data quality in an event driven architecture

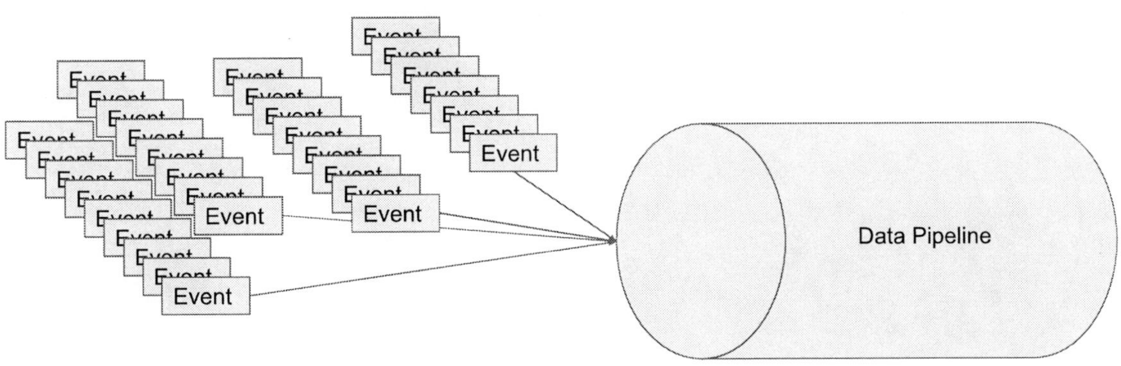

Common Issues

- Data Discoverability

Common Issues

- Data Discoverability

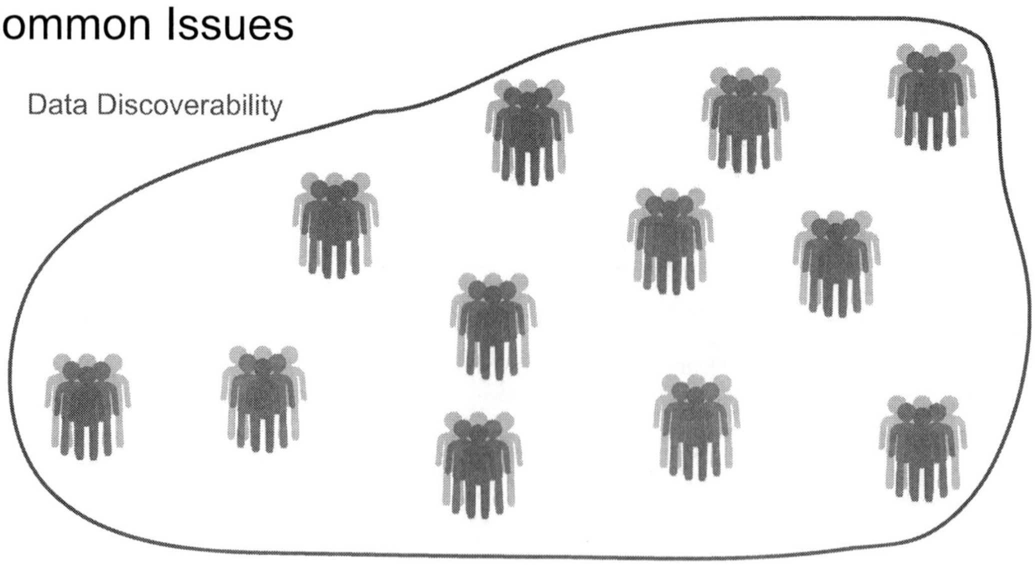

Common Issues

- Data Discoverability
- Data Standardization

Common Issues

- Data Discoverability
- Data Standardization

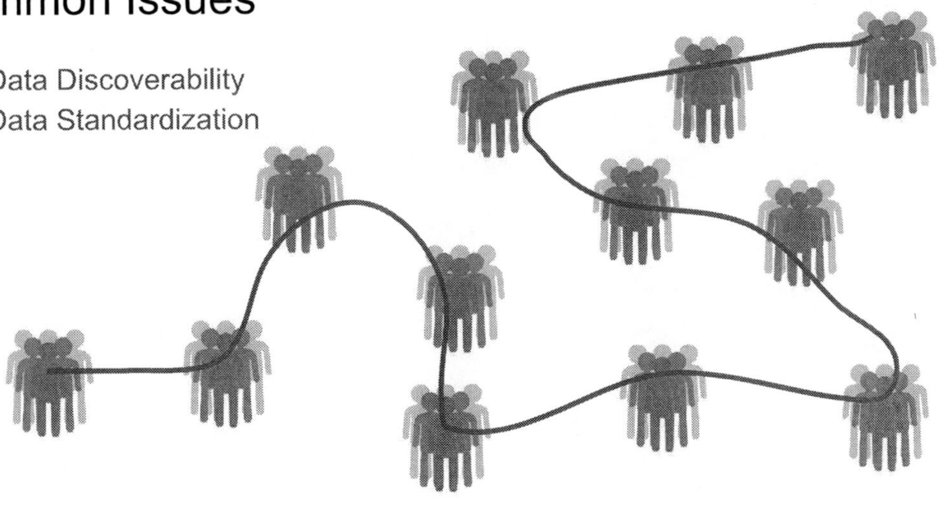

Common Issues

- Data Discoverability
- Data Standardization
- Data Completeness

Data Completeness

Complete

```
accout_id: 312353

user_id: 189678

document_id: 235789

timestamp: 1499486132

action: "save"
```

Not Complete

```
accout_id: null

user_id: "189678"

document_id: "TODO"

timestamp: -1499486132

action: ["save"]

extra_dimension: "lol!"
```

Common Issues

- Data Discoverability
- Data Standardization
- Data Completeness

Solution!

A central place…

Solution!

A central place…

with a list of all events...

Solution!

A central place…

with a list of all events…

a common set of dimensions...

Solution!

A central place…

with a list of all events…

a common set of dimensions…

and a well defined event definition...

Strongly `Typed` Data

Strongly `Typed` Data

(all aboard the strongly typed hype train!)

A central location for event schema

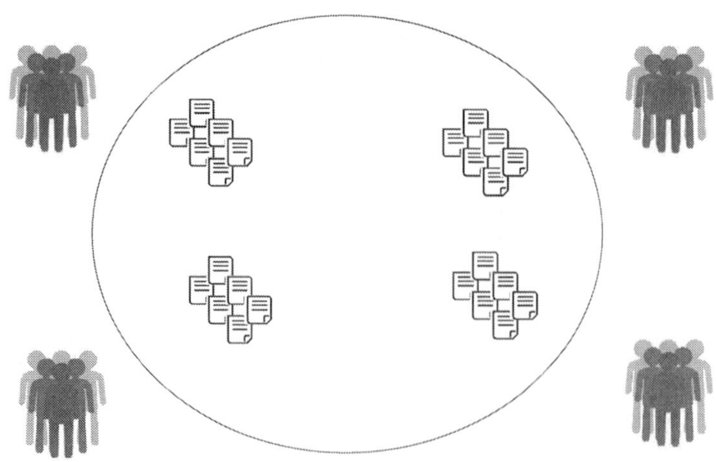

Event Schema

A list of dimension definitions

```
dimension: user_id
    type: string
    required: true
    description: id of the user
```

Event Schema

Event: Document Save

- **accout_id**: required, int
- **user_id**: required, int
- **document_id**: required, int
- **timestamp**: required, int

Event Schema Compilation

```
public DocumentSaveEvent(
    int account_id,
    int user_id,
    int timestamp,
    int doc_id
)
```

Sending Events

```
client.send(DocumentSaveEvent(
    account_id=689345,
    user_id=250983,
    timestamp=date.now(),
    doc_id=233584
))
```

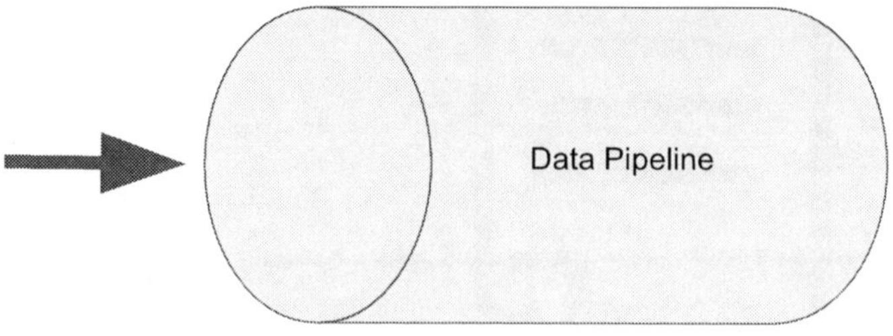

Sample and check

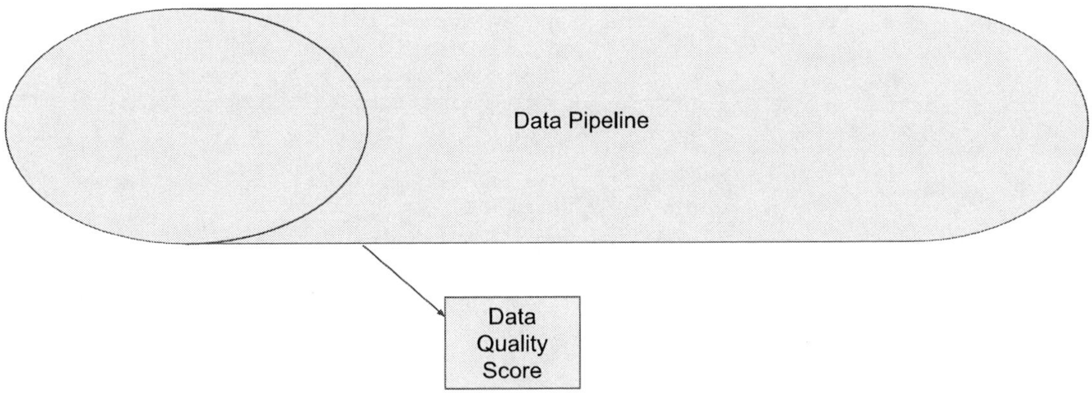

Sample and check

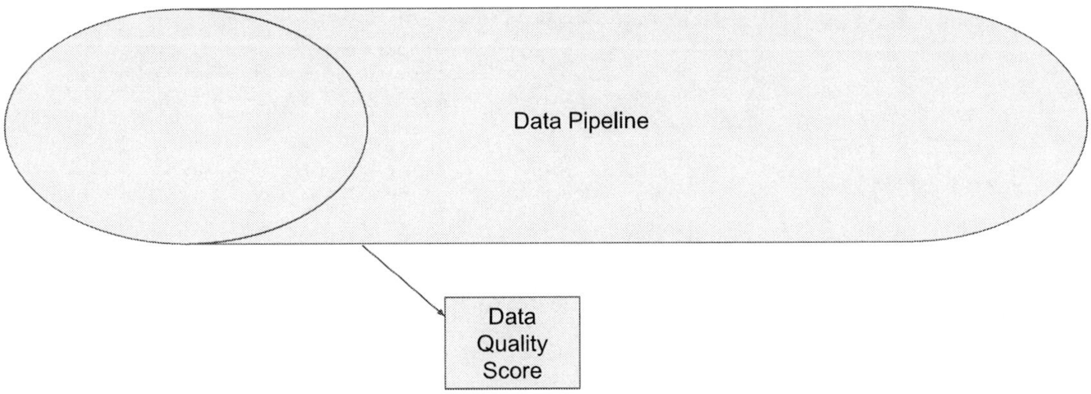

Data Quality Score

```
DocumentSaveEvent(
    account_id=689345,
    user_id=250983,
    timestamp=date.now(),
    doc_id=233584
)
```

Event: Document Save

- **accout_id**: required, int
- **user_id**: required, int
- **document_id**: required, int
- **timestamp**: required, int

Data Quality Score

```
DocumentSaveEvent(
    account_id=689345,
    user_id=250983,
    timestamp=date.now(),
    doc_id=233584
)
```

Event: Document Save

- **accout_id**: required, int
- **user_id**: required, int
- **document_id**: required, int
- **timestamp**: required, int

Data Quality Score

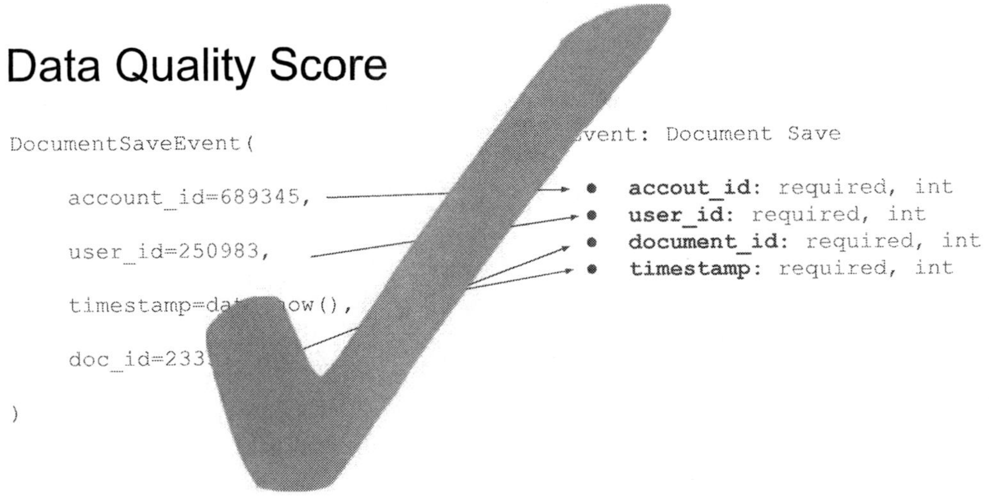

Track this score

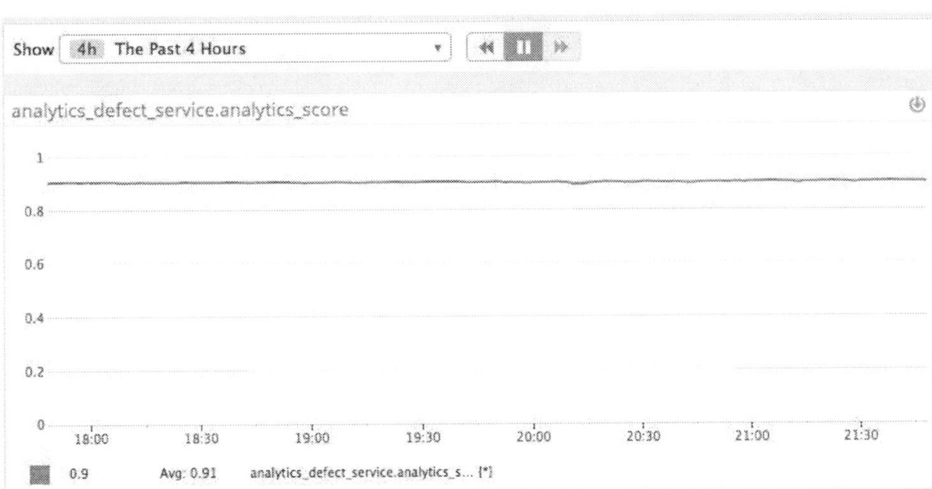

Alert on this score

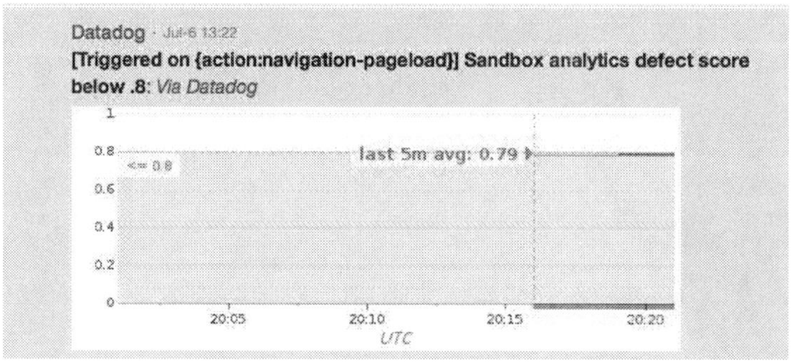

Schema Registry

- An accessible, central, searchable, versioned center of all analytics
- Schema's compile to class definitions
- Clients send these
- Check them for quality

Demo Time!

Time for a demo!

Quality in the Data Center: Data Collection and Analysis

Kingsum Chow, Chief Scientist
Alibaba System Software Hardware Co-Optimization

PNSQC 2017.10.07 3:45pm-5:20pm
Acknowledged: Chengdong Li and Wanyi Zhu

- 1996 – PhD University of Washington
- 1996 – 2016: Intel
  - 1996 – 1999 Intel CPU Performance Models
  - 1999 – 2001 Intel Online Services
  - 2001 – 2016 Assigned by Intel to optimize performance for Software Vendors
    - Appeal (JRockit) – acquired by BEA in 2002, then acquired by Oracle in 2008
    - Siebel (CRM) – acquired by Oracle in 2006
    - BEA (WebLogic) – acquired by Oracle in 2008
    - Sun (Hotspot JVM) – acquired by Oracle in 2010
    - Oracle Java and Cloud (2010-2016)

- 2016–now: Alibaba

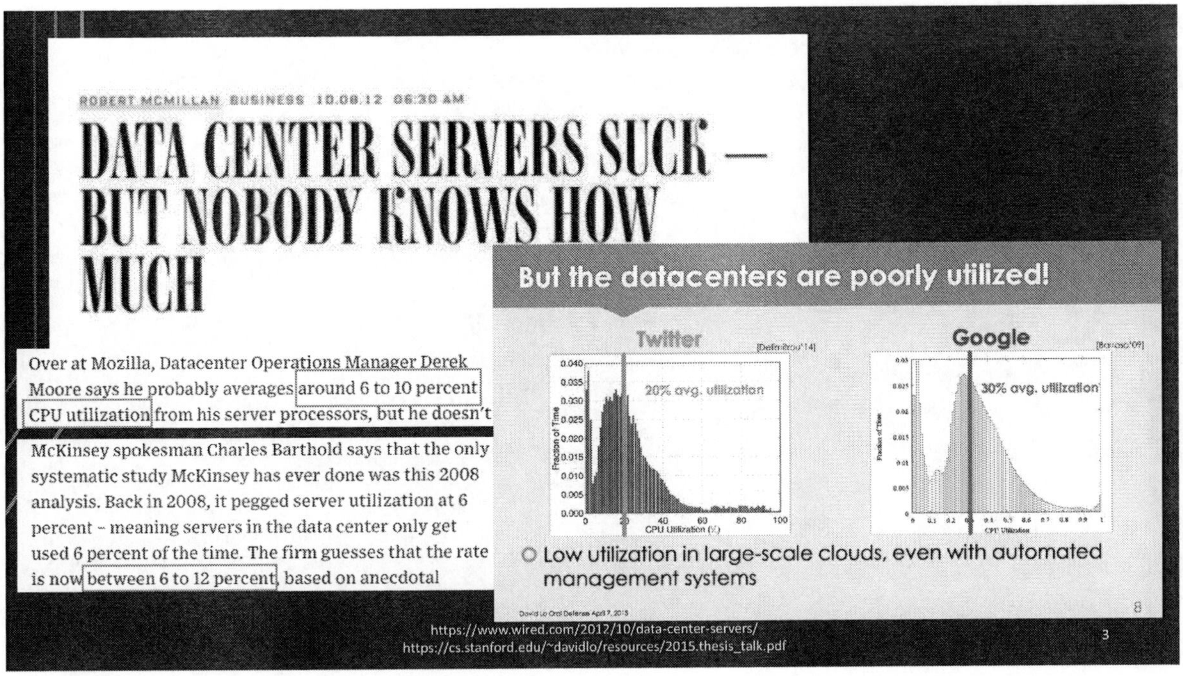
ROBERT MCMILLAN BUSINESS 10.08.12 06:30 AM
DATA CENTER SERVERS SUCK — BUT NOBODY KNOWS HOW MUCH
Over at Mozilla, Datacenter Operations Manager Derek Moore says he probably averages around 6 to 10 percent CPU utilization from his server processors, but he doesn't
McKinsey spokesman Charles Barthold says that the only systematic study McKinsey has ever done was this 2008 analysis. Back in 2008, it pegged server utilization at 6 percent – meaning servers in the data center only get used 6 percent of the time. The firm guesses that the rate is now between 6 to 12 percent, based on anecdotal
But the datacenters are poorly utilized!
Twitter
20% avg. utilization
Google
30% avg. utilization
Low utilization in large-scale clouds, even with automated management systems
8
https://www.wired.com/2012/10/data-center-servers/
https://cs.stanford.edu/~davidlo/resources/2015.thesis_talk.pdf
3

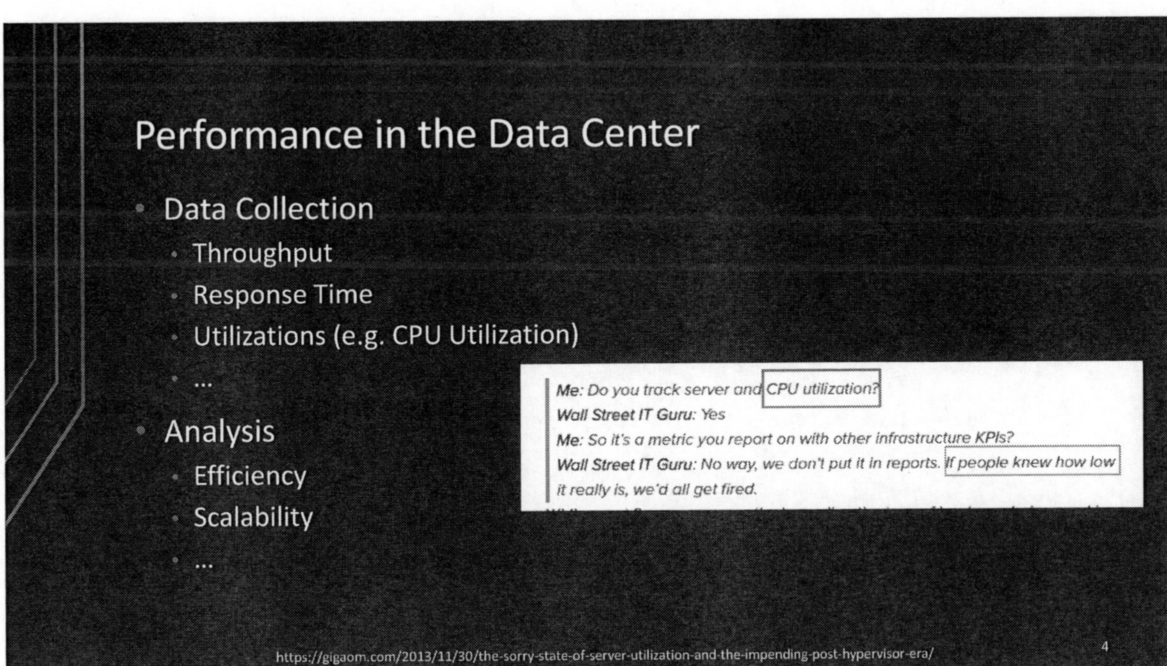
Performance in the Data Center
Data Collection
Throughput
Response Time
Utilizations (e.g. CPU Utilization)
…
Analysis
Efficiency
Scalability
…
Me: Do you track server and CPU utilization?
Wall Street IT Guru: Yes
Me: So it's a metric you report on with other infrastructure KPIs?
Wall Street IT Guru: No way, we don't put it in reports. If people knew how low it really is, we'd all get fired.
https://gigaom.com/2013/11/30/the-sorry-state-of-server-utilization-and-the-impending-post-hypervisor-era/
4

What is CPU Utilization?

- CPU utilization refers to a computer's usage of processing resources, or the amount of work handled by a CPU. Actual CPU utilization varies depending on the amount and type of managed computing tasks. Certain tasks require heavy CPU time, while others require less because of non-CPU resource requirements.
- It estimates the percentage of all the logical CPU cores in the system that is spent in your application -- without including the overhead introduced by the parallel runtime system. 100% utilization means that your application keeps all the logical CPU cores busy for the entire time that it runs.

https://www.techopedia.com/definition/28291/cpu-utilization
https://software.intel.com/en-us/node/638228

5

CPU Utilization

- Given: a data center that is 50% CPU utilized
- Assume: no software scaling and no interference problems
- Decide: reduce the number of servers by half

OOPS !!!

Did we misunderstand CPU Utilization?

6

Have you heard?

- Keep CPU utilizations low, or else bad things may happen.
- I optimized the bottlenecks of the software, but there is no improvement.
- Due to my smart code changes, my application now uses less CPU utilization.

7

Hardware Mechanisms of Intel HT Technology

Intel HT Technology allows one physical processor core to present two *logical* cores to the operating system, which allows it to support two threads at once. The key hardware mechanism underlying this capability is an extra *architectural state* supported by the hardware, as shown in Figure 1.

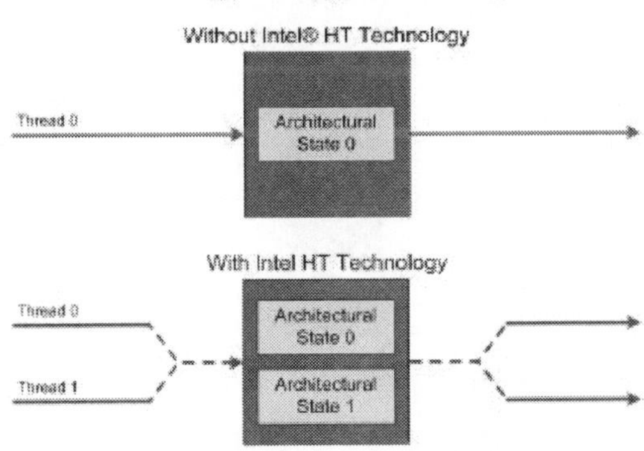

Figure 1. Intel® HT Technology enables a single processor core to maintain two architectural states, each of which can support its own thread. Many of the internal microarchitectural hardware resources are shared between the two threads.

Performance Insights to Intel® Hyper-Threading Technology
http://blog.csdn.net/sangyongjia/article/details/44426453

8

The block diagram of the Nehalem core-based processor in Figure 2 shows multiple cores, each of which has two threads when Intel HT Technology is enabled. Processors based on the Nehalem architecture exist with varying numbers of cores, as shown in the graphic.

Figure 2. The Intel® Core™ i7 processor and architecturally similar processors can have varying numbers of cores, each of which can support two threads when Intel® HT Technology is enabled.

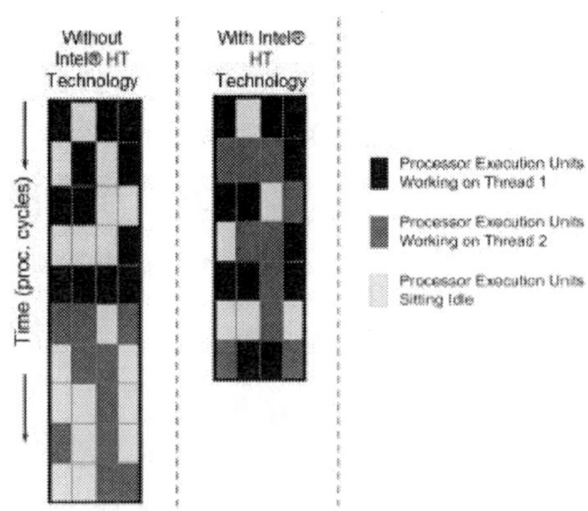

Figure 3. By giving the processor access to two threads in the same time slice, Intel® HT Technology reduces the level of idle hardware resources, which typically increases efficiency and throughput.

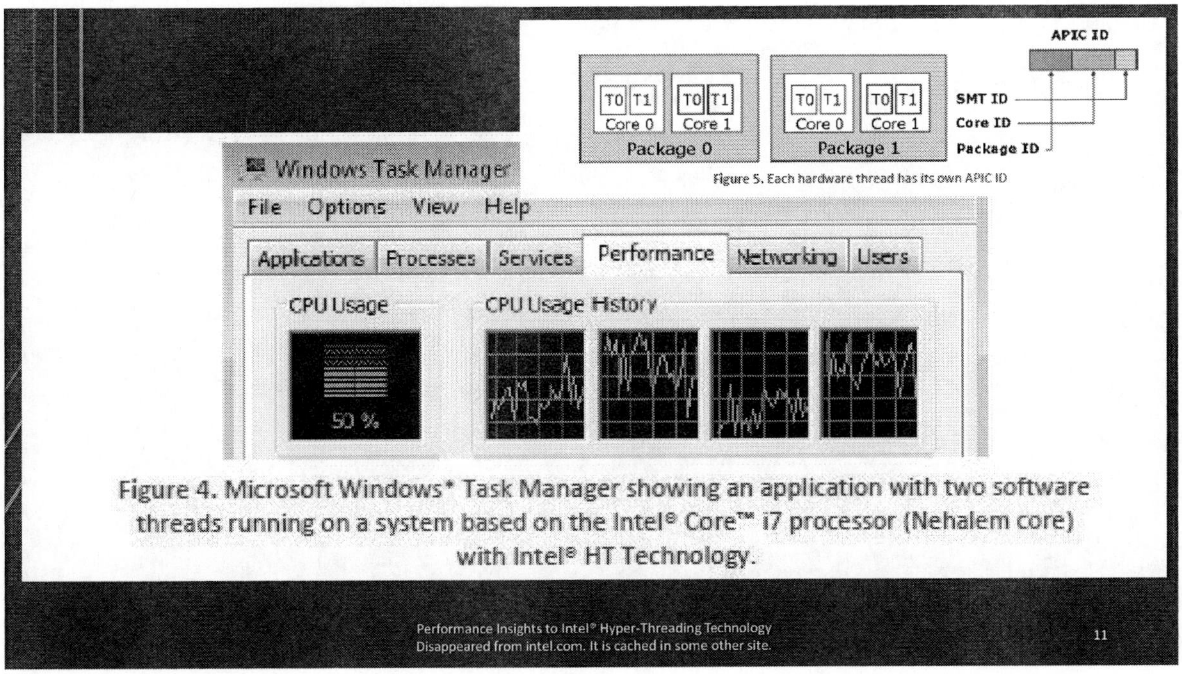
APIC ID
T0 T1
Core 0
T0 T1
Core 1
Package 0
T0 T1
Core 0
T0 T1
Core 1
Package 1
SMT ID
Core ID
Package ID
Figure 5. Each hardware thread has its own APIC ID
Windows Task Manager
File Options View Help
Applications Processes Services Performance Networking Users
CPU Usage
CPU Usage History
50 %
Figure 4. Microsoft Windows* Task Manager showing an application with two software threads running on a system based on the Intel® Core™ i7 processor (Nehalem core) with Intel® HT Technology.
Performance Insights to Intel® Hyper-Threading Technology
Disappeared from intel.com. It is cached in some other site.
11

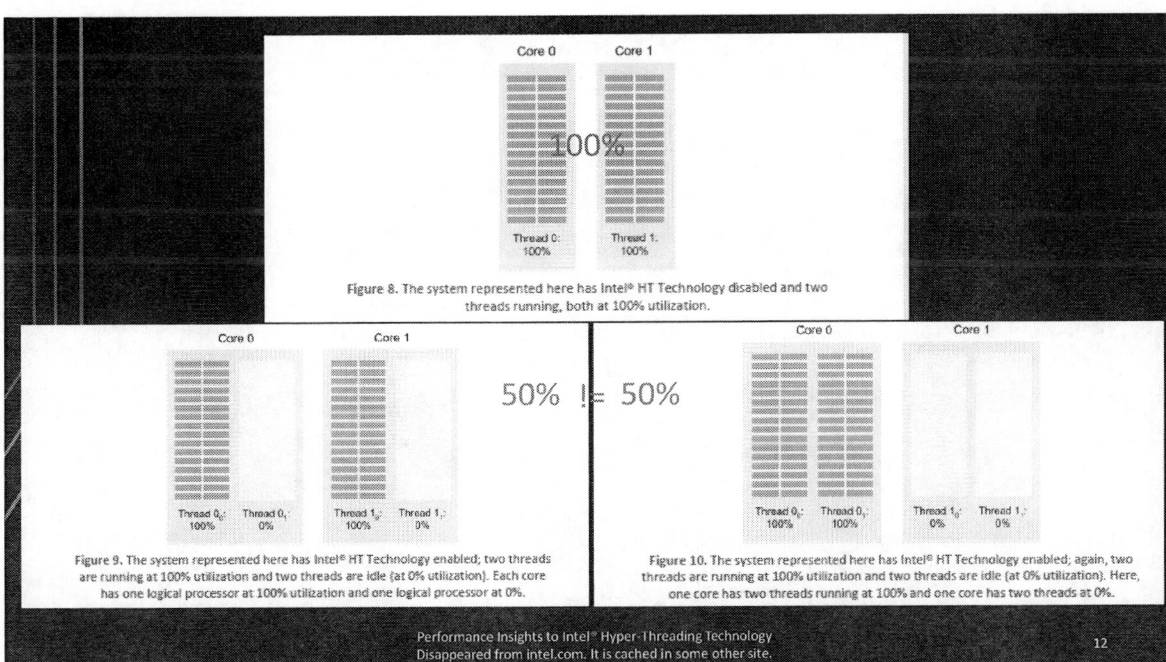
Core 0
Core 1
100%
Thread 0: 100%
Thread 1: 100%
Figure 8. The system represented here has Intel® HT Technology disabled and two threads running, both at 100% utilization.
50% != 50%
Figure 9. The system represented here has Intel® HT Technology enabled; two threads are running at 100% utilization and two threads are idle (at 0% utilization). Each core has one logical processor at 100% utilization and one logical processor at 0%.
Figure 10. The system represented here has Intel® HT Technology enabled; again, two threads are running at 100% utilization and two threads are idle (at 0% utilization). Here, one core has two threads running at 100% and one core has two threads at 0%.
Performance Insights to Intel® Hyper-Threading Technology
Disappeared from intel.com. It is cached in some other site.
12

Experiment: Misleading CPU Utilization

- Intel Xeon CPU, 2 sockets, 16 cores per socket, Hyper-threading turned on. Total 64 logical CPUs.
- SPECjbb2005 benchmark: each warehouse ran on one logical CPU.
- (1) 32 warehouses (half of all logical CPUs).
- (2) 64 warehouses (all logical CPUs).

13

Experiment Results

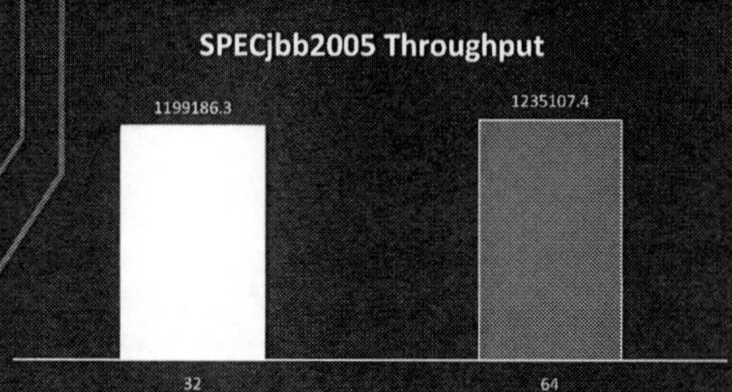

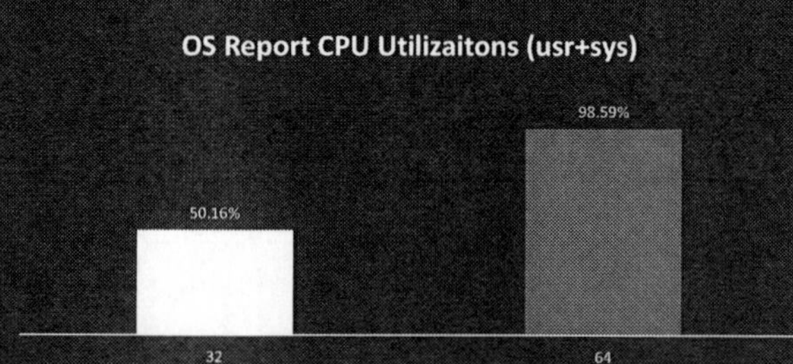

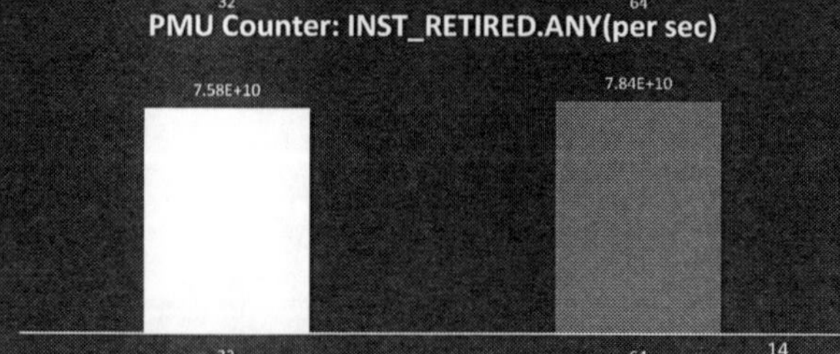

14

Quality in the Datacenter

- Data Collection
  - Tools
  - Data Quality
- Analysis
  - Outlier Detection
  - Performance Modeling

15

Google Cluster Data (2011)

- TraceVersion1
  - Time (int) - time in seconds since the start of data collection
  - JobID (int) - Unique identifier of the job to which this task belongs (may be called ParentID)
  - TaskID (int) - Unique identifier of the executing task
  - Job Type (0, 1, 2, 3) - class of job (a categorization of work)
  - Normalized Task Cores (float) - normalized value of the average number of cores used by the task
  - Normalized Task Memory (float) - normalized value of the average memory consumed by the task
- The clusterdata-2011-2 trace represents 29 day's worth of cell information from May 2011, on a cluster of about 12.5k machines.
  - task_usage tables. This new data is a randomly-picked 1 second sample of CPU usage from within the associated 5-minute usage-reporting period for that task.

https://github.com/google/cluster-data

16

Alibaba Cluster Data (2017)

- The trace data, ClusterData201708, contains cluster information of a production cluster in 24 hours period, and contains about 1.3k machines that run both online service and batch jobs.
  - timestamp
  - machineID
  - util:CPU
  - util:memory
  - util:disk
  - load1: linux cpu load average of 1 minute
  - load5: linux cpu load average of 5 minute
  - load15: linux cpu load average of 15 minute

https://github.com/alibaba/clusterdata

17

Outlier Detection

1. Background
2. Statistical Approach: Parametric method
3. Regression Approach: Linear vs. Non-Linear Regression
4. Multivariate Approach

18

1. Background

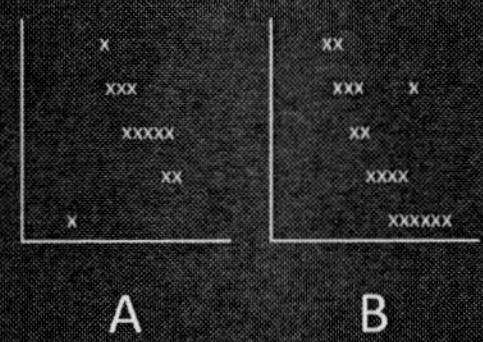

A: Outlier is extreme in both directions

B: Outlier is not extreme in any direction, extreme values are no outliers.

Outliers can't be detected visually:

- Detection would be restricted to low dimensionality
- Subjective
- Problems with large datasets
- > So detection should be fully automatic

19

1. Outlier

- Example: Below are the response time data of the same application collected from three servers

	Sample Size	Minimum	Maximum	Average	Median	Normal	Mode	95th Percentile	Standard Deviation
Data Set A	100	1	7	4	4	4	4	6	1.5
Data Set B	100	1	16	4	1	3	1	16	6.0
Data Set C	100	0	8	4	4	1	3	8	2.6

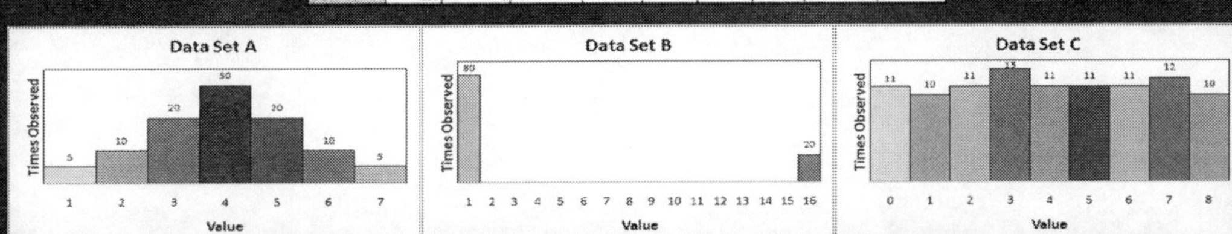

- Using mean estimate, there is no outlier in the three servers A,B,C
- Using the statistical distribution, the data from server B seems problematic

20

1. Outlier

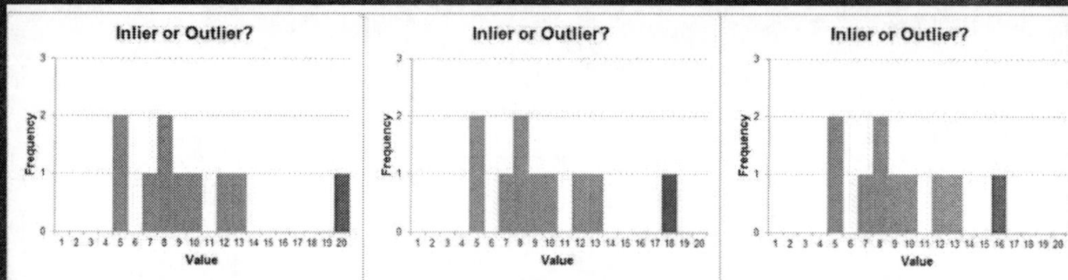

Outlier? Exclude it	Hmm, probably an Outlier! ... but shall we toss a coin?	Inlier? Keep it

21

2. Statistical Approaches

- Idea: learn a generative model fitting the given data set, and then identify the objects in low probability regions of the model as outliers
- Parametric method
  - Assumes that the normal data is generated by a parametric distribution with parameter θ
  - The probability density function of the parametric distribution *f*(*x*, *ϑ*) gives the probability that object *x* is generated by the distribution
  - The smaller this value, the more likely x is an outlier
- Non-parametric method
  - Not assume an a-priori statistical model and determine the model from the input data
  - Not completely parameter free but consider the number and nature of the parameters are flexible and not fixed in advance
  - Examples: histogram and kernel density estimation

22

2.1 Parametric Approach

For many applications, data distribution is unknown.

Solution: Distribution fitting.

Disadvantage:

- The distribution may not fit any of the standard distributions

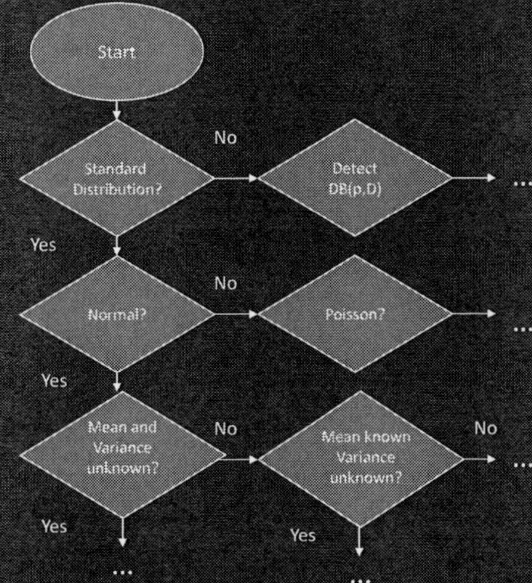

23

2.2 Parametric Approach

- If the values in the dataset follow some standard distribution, simply use the distribution to give concrete definitions of outliers. (Discordancy Test)
- For instance: normal distribution with mean μ and variance σ. Condition: a value is outlying if the value is not within the range of $\mu + 3\sigma$.

Advantages

-Clear indication of how strong an identified outlier is

-Can also identify a certain percentage of outliers in the data

Disadvantages

-Test are univariate: in most geographical data the dimensionality is high.

24

2.3 Distribution Threshold Definition

Gaussian/normal distribution assumed for data 68-95-99.7 rule

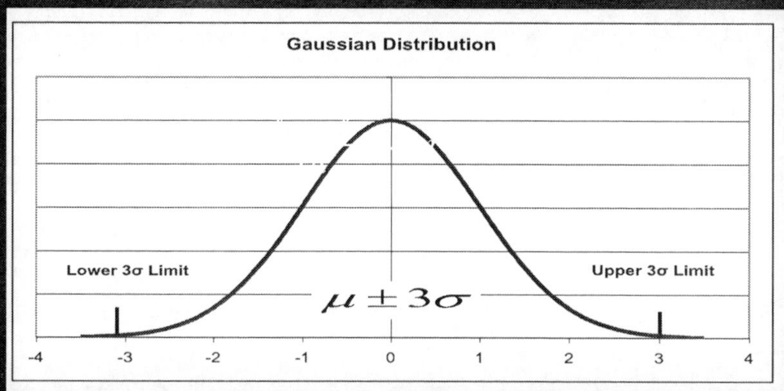

25

2.4 z-Scores

- The <u>*z*-score</u> is often called the standardized value.
- It denotes the number of standard deviations a data value x_i is from the mean.
- A data value equal to the sample mean will have a *z*-score of zero
- Z-scores that exceeds 3 in absolute value are generally considered as outliers

26

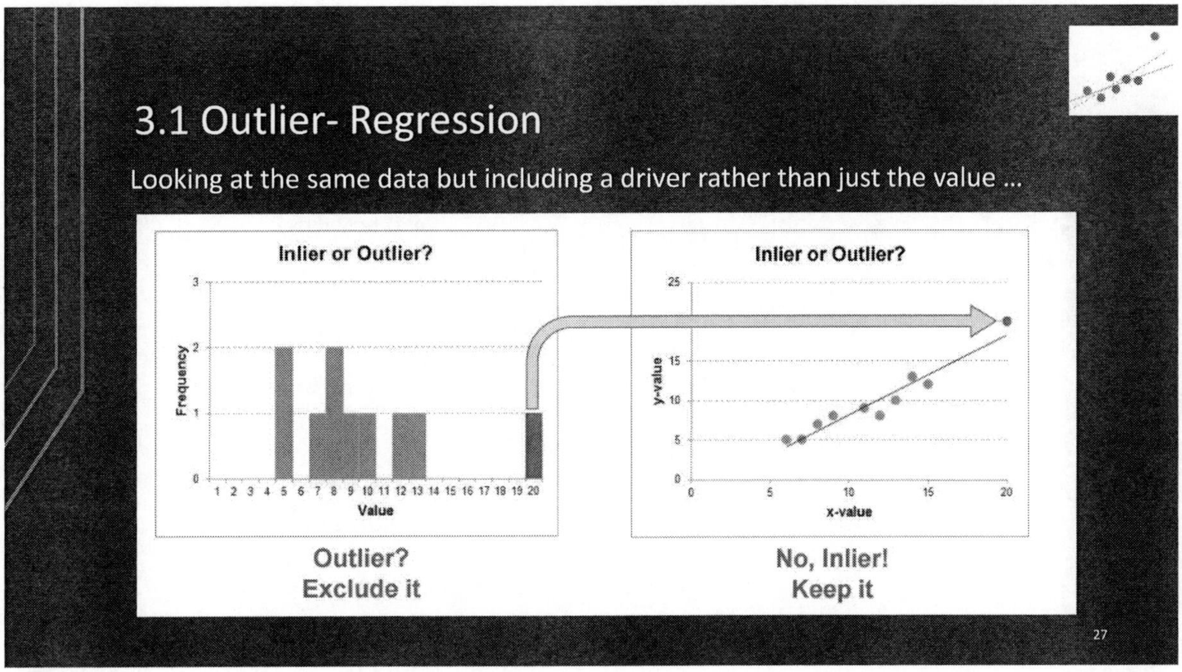
3.1 Outlier- Regression
Looking at the same data but including a driver rather than just the value …
Inlier or Outlier?
Frequency
Value
Inlier or Outlier?
y-value
x-value
Outlier?
Exclude it
No, Inlier!
Keep it
27

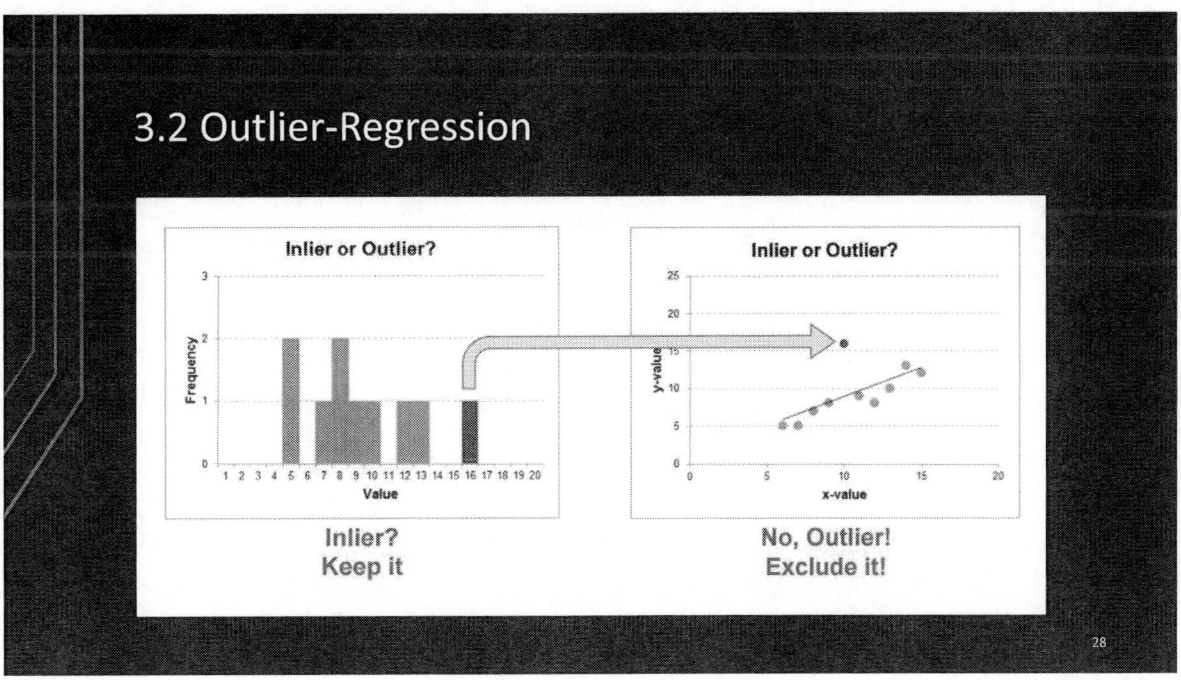
3.2 Outlier-Regression
Inlier or Outlier?
Frequency
Value
Inlier or Outlier?
y-value
x-value
Inlier?
Keep it
No, Outlier!
Exclude it!
28

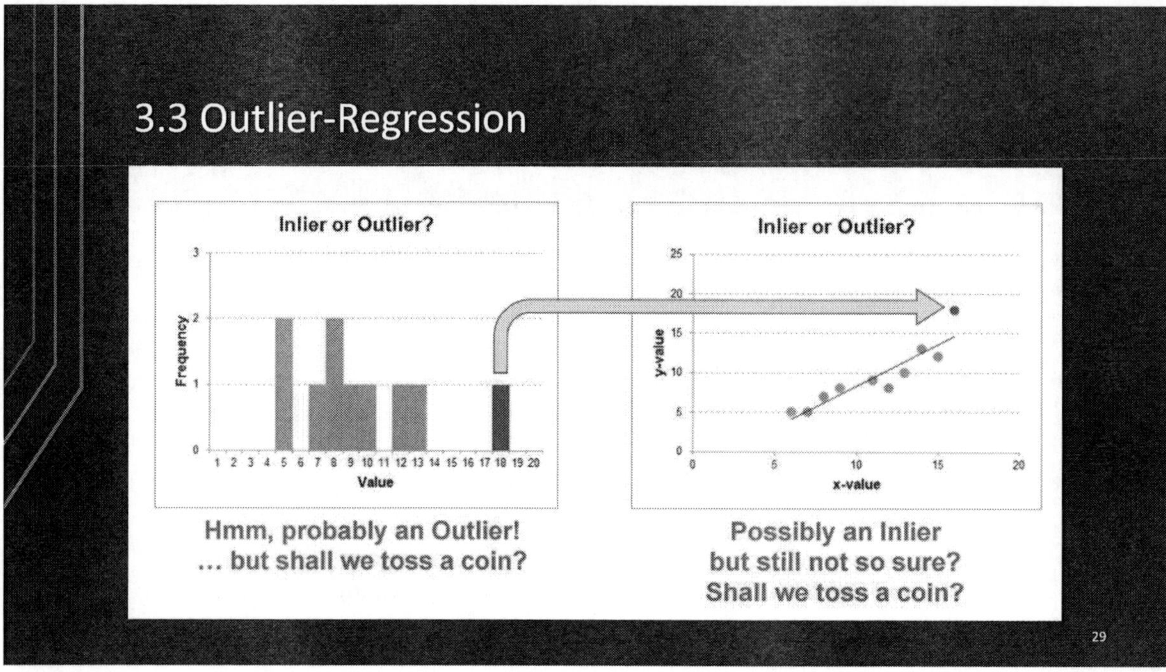
3.3 Outlier-Regression
Inlier or Outlier?
Frequency
Value
Inlier or Outlier?
y-value
x-value
Hmm, probably an Outlier!
… but shall we toss a coin?
Possibly an Inlier
but still not so sure?
Shall we toss a coin?
29

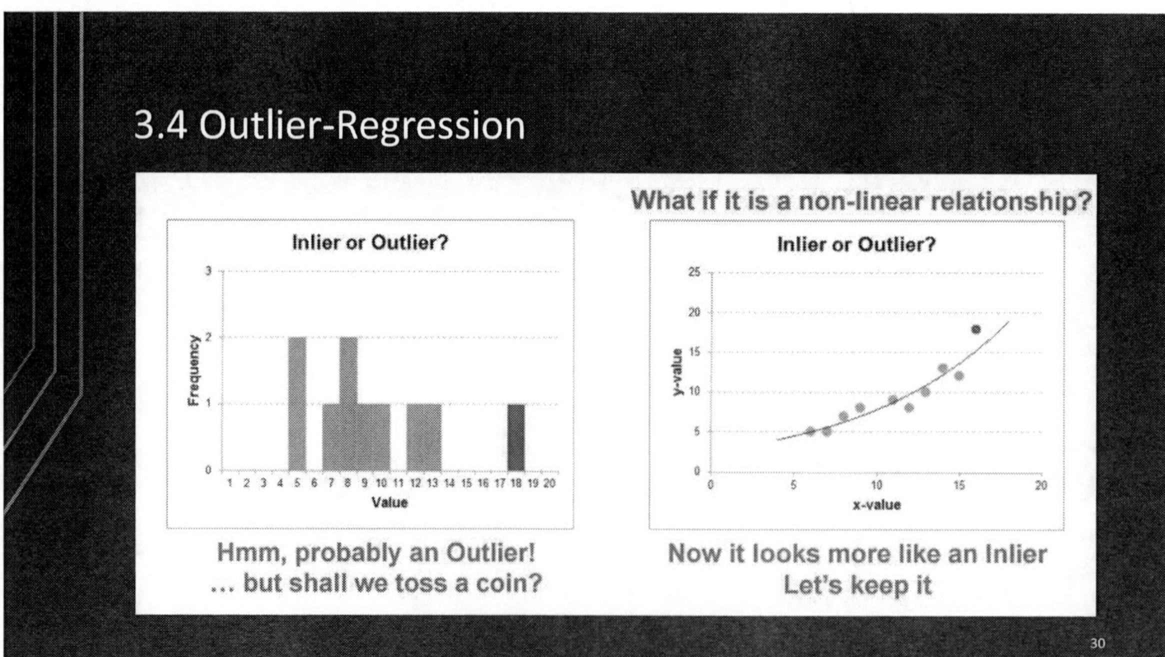
3.4 Outlier-Regression
What if it is a non-linear relationship?
Inlier or Outlier?
Frequency
Value
Inlier or Outlier?
y-value
x-value
Hmm, probably an Outlier!
… but shall we toss a coin?
Now it looks more like an Inlier
Let's keep it
30

4. Multivariate Analysis

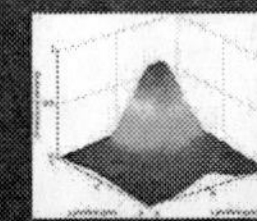

- Monitoring computers in data center:
- Computer features of machine
  - x1 = memory use
  - x2 = number of disk accesses/sec
  - x3 = CPU load
- In addition to the measurable features you can also define your own complex features
  - x4 = CPU load/network traffic
- If you see an anomalous machine
  - Maybe about to fail
  - Look at replacing bits from it

31

4.1 Multivariate Analysis- algorithm

- **1 – Choose features**
  - Chose independent features which describe the general properties
- **2 - Fit parameters**
  - Determine parameters for each feature μi and σi2
  - Use vectorized implementation rather than a loop probably
- **3 - Compute p(x)**
  - Use the formula for the Gaussian probability of a combination of independent features;
  - For the correlated features, use the covariance matrix to compute the p(x)
  - If the number is very small, very low chance of it being "normal"
- **4 - Determine ϵ**
  - ϵ is determined from the cross-validation set, and is typically selected as the value that provides the best F1 score
  -

$$F1 = \frac{2 * Precision * Recall}{Precision + Recall}$$

32

4.2 Multivariate Analysis- algorithm

1. Choose features x_i that you think might be indicative of anomalous examples.
2. Fit parameters $\mu_1, \ldots, \mu_n, \sigma_1^2, \ldots, \sigma_n^2$

$$\mu_j = \frac{1}{m}\sum_{i=1}^{m} x_j^{(i)}$$

$$\sigma_j^2 = \frac{1}{m}\sum_{i=1}^{m}(x_j^{(i)} - \mu_j)^2$$

3. Given new example x, compute $p(x)$:

$$p(x) = \prod_{j=1}^{n} p(x_j; \mu_j, \sigma_j^2) = \prod_{j=1}^{n} \frac{1}{\sqrt{2\pi}\sigma_j} \exp\left(-\frac{(x_j - \mu_j)^2}{2\sigma_j^2}\right)$$

Anomaly if $p(x) < \varepsilon$

$$p(x) = \frac{1}{(2\pi)^{\frac{n}{2}} (\det \Sigma)^{1/2}} e^{-\frac{1}{2}(x-\mu)^T \Sigma^{-1}(x-\mu)}$$

33

4.3 Multivariate Analysis- case study

- Two performance variables collected:

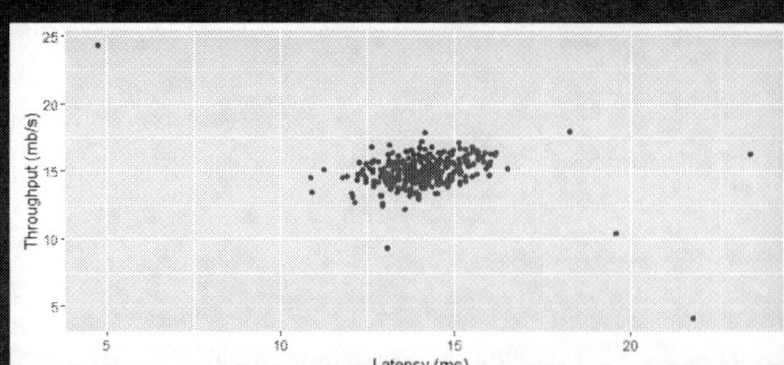

34

4.4 Multivariate Analysis- case study

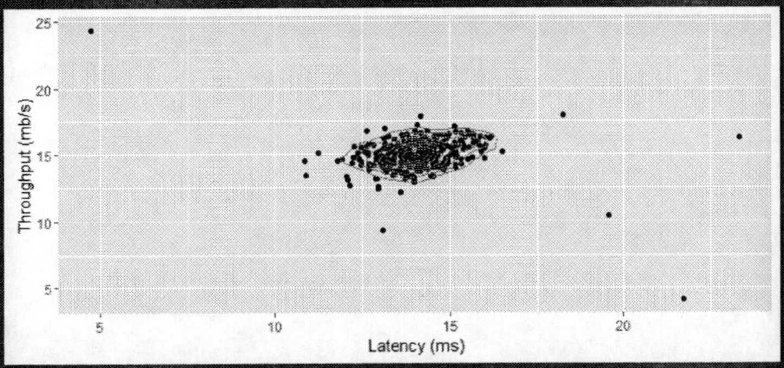

35

4.5 Multivariate Analysis- case study

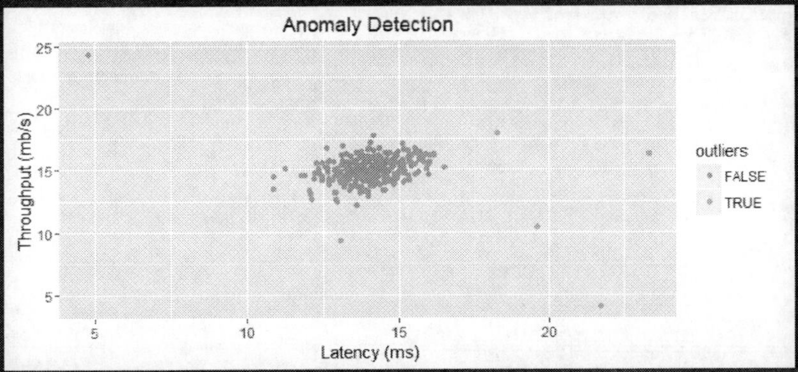

36

Summary

- The emergence of large-scale software deployments in the data center has led to several challenges in software performance analysis.
- Don't be mislead by these two data center quality problems
  - CPU utilizations
  - Outliers

37

Workshops

Wed 8:30am

- W7: Scaling Software Performance

Wed 1:30pm

- W8: Software Performance in the Cloud

Knowledge is a treasure, but practice is the key to it. - Lao Tzu

38

End to End Quality
with the
Sonar Ecosystem
and the
Water Leak Metaphor

G. Ann Campbell

@GAnnCampbell | ann.campbell@SonarSource.com
@SonarLint | @SonarQube | @SonarSource

sonarsource

SonarLint
Leak Period
Quality Gate

sonarsource

20+ Languages

Java
T-SQL C
C++
Objective-C HTML XML ABAP
C#
COBOL
RPG
Swift PHP
JavaScript Python VB.NET
PL/SQL
PL/I
TypeScript

sonarsource

The <3 of the ecosystem

Static Analysis

sonarsource

What is Static Analysis?

Analyzing code,
without executing it!

sonarsource

A Means to an End

Detecting Bugs, Vulnerabilities,
and Code Smells

sonarsource

Why use Static Analysis

Catch new problems ASAP

- the longer it takes to catch a bug, the more it costs
- no one writes perfect code *every time*
- rule description and precise issue location cut research time

sonarsource

Why use Static Analysis

Changing A might have added bugs in B

- peer review misses new issues in untouched code
- static analysis is machine-assisted code review; it looks at every file every time

sonarsource

Why use Static Analysis

Provide coaching

- language best practices
- team coding style

sonarsource

SonarSource's Toolbox

sonarsource

Lexical Analysis

Only two things are infinite, the universe and human stupidity, and I am not sure about the former.

sonarsource

Syntactic Analysis

Only two things are infinite, the universe and human stupidity, and I am not sure about the former.

Subjects

Verbs

Albert E.

sonarsource

Semantic Analysis

Only two things are infinite, the universe and human stupidity, and I am not sure about the former.

Albert E.

sonarsource

Semantic Analysis

Only two things are infinite, the universe and human stupidity, and I am not sure about the former.

Albert E.

sonarsource

Beyond Semantic: Symbolic Execution

```
Object myObject = new Object();


if(a) {  myObject = null; }
...
if( !a ) { ... }
else { myObject.toString(); }
```

sonarsource

Beyond Semantic: Symbolic Execution

```
Object myObject = new Object();


if(a) {  myObject = null; }
...
if( !a ) { ... }
else { myObject.toString(); } //NPE
```

sonarsource

Beyond Semantic: Symbolic Execution

```
Object myObject = new Object();
```

Program State#0
myObject != null

```
if(a) {  myObject = null; }
...
if( !a ) { ... }
else { myObject.toString(); } //NPE
```

sonarsource

Beyond Semantic: Symbolic Execution

```
Object myObject = new Object();
```

Program State#0
myObject != null

Program State#2
myObject = null
a = true

```
if(a) {  myObject = null; }
```

Program State#1
myObject != null
a = false

```
...
if( !a ) { ... }
else { myObject.toString(); } //NPE
```

sonarsource

Beyond Semantic: Symbolic Execution

Program State#1
myObject != null
a = false

Program State#2
myObject = null
a = true

```
...
if( !a ) {
   ...
} else {

   myObject.toString(); // NPE
}
```

sonarsource

Beyond Semantic: Symbolic Execution

Program State#1
myObject != null
a = false

Program State#2
myObject = null
a = true

```
...
if( !a ) {
   ... ✕
} else {

   myObject.toString(); // NPE
}
```

sonarsource

Beyond Semantic: Symbolic Execution

Program State#1
myObject != null
a = false

Program State#2
myObject = null
a = true

```
...
if( !a ) {
   ...  ✗
} else {
```

Program State#4
myObject = null
a = true

```
   myObject.toString(); // NPE
}
```

sonarsource

SonarAnalyzer for Java and JavaScript

Cross-Procedural Analysis

Java JS

sonarsource

What is Static Analysis ?

Analyzing code,

without executing it.

by (symbolically) executing

all possible paths!

sonarsource

Symbolic Execution Almost Everywhere

- SonarAnalyzers for C#, C/C++, Java, and JS
  - Dereferences of Null Pointers
  - Unconditionally True/False (sub)conditions
  - Division by zero
  - Resource leaks
    - Unclosed resources (Java)
    - Unreleased memory (C/C++)
  - Double free (C/C++)

sonarsource

Fewer slides, more code!

sonarsource

Full Cycle

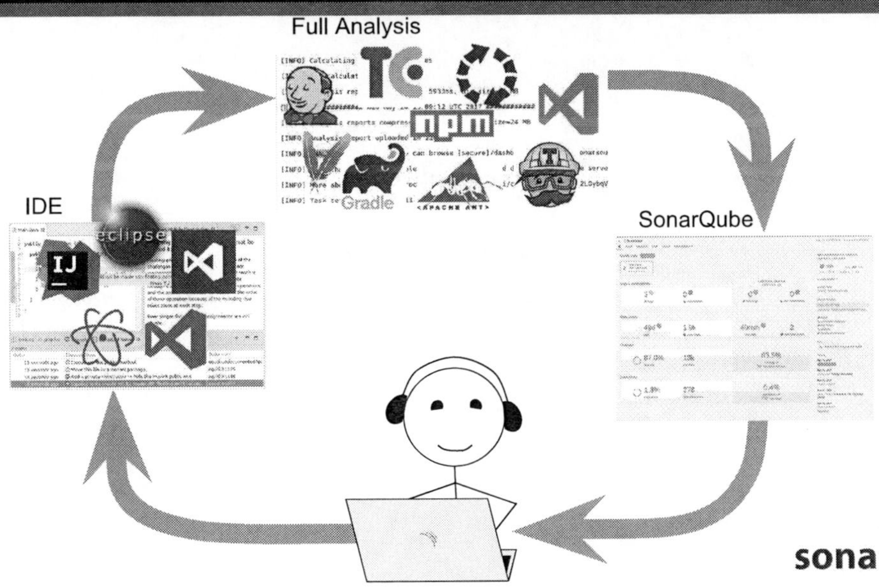

sonarsource

Full Cycle

sonarsource

Fix the Leak

✓ SonarLint
Leak Period
Quality Gate

sonarsource

Reimbursing the Debt

sonarsource

This is Hard

- Total amount of Technical Debt can be depressing
- How to get a budget to fix old Technical Debt?
- Risk of injecting functional regression
- This is not fun!

sonarsource

Project Homepage

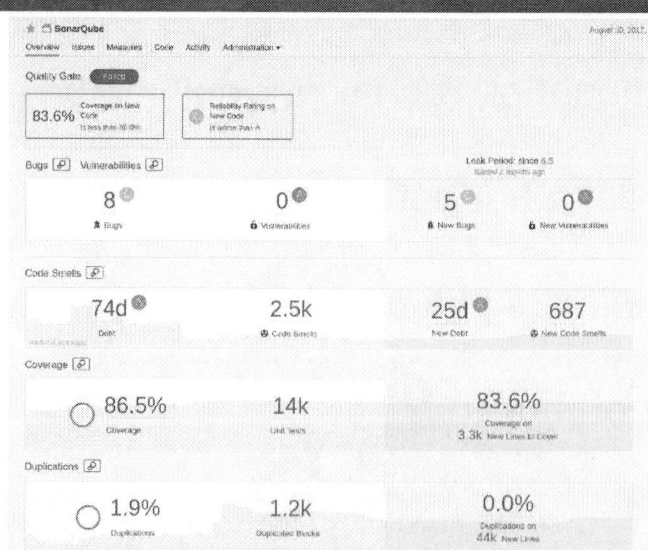

sonarsource

Project Homepage: Leak Period

sonarsource

Fix the Leak

- ✓ SonarLint
- ✓ Leak Period
- Quality Gate

sonarsource

Quality Gate

SonarQube way

Conditions

Only project measures are checked against thresholds. Sub-projects, directories and files are ignored. More

Metric	Over Leak Period	Operator	Warning	Error
Coverage on New Code	Always	is less than		80.0%
Maintainability Rating on New Code	Always	is worse than		A
Reliability Rating on New Code	Always	is worse than		A
Security Rating on New Code	Always	is worse than		A

sonarsource

Project Homepage: Quality Gate

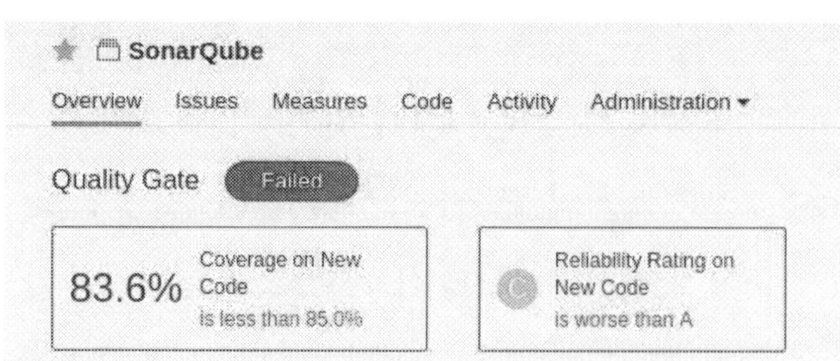

sonarsource

Quality Gate

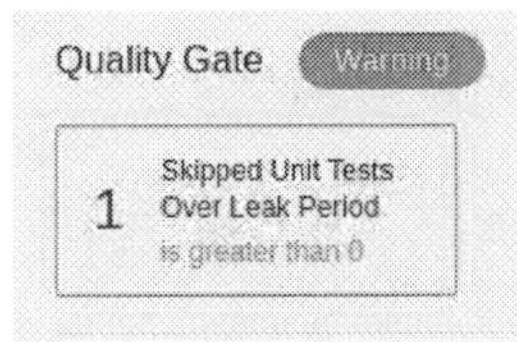

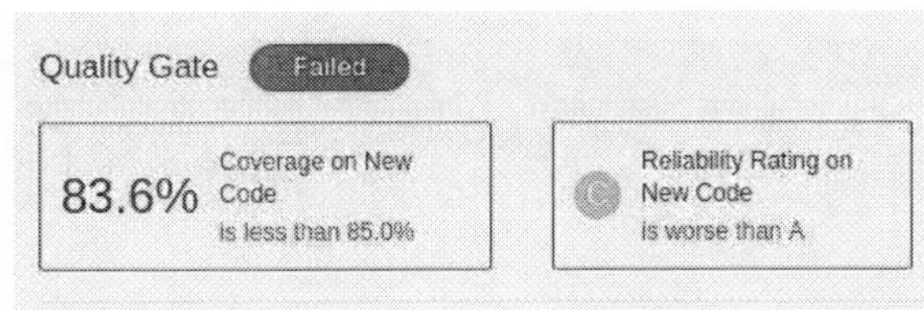

sonarsource

Fix the Leak

✓ SonarLint
✓ Leak Period
✓ Quality Gate

sonarsource

Thanks!

G. Ann Campbell

@GAnnCampbell | ann.campbell@SonarSource.com
@SonarLint | @SonarQube | @SonarSource

sonarsource

How Does Pervasive Leadership Improve Agility?

Jean Richardson

jean@azuregate.net

Abstract

Agile team members and those who embody the organizational infrastructure around them have, by and large, been raised in a culture that has taught them to follow and ask permission rather than lead and take the risks inherent in leadership. Every pause for permission is a delay that impacts decision latency. Organizational leaders have been enculturated to direct rather than coach which often leaves them in the position of making more decisions than necessary. This impedes important decisions due lack of access to them as deciders or due to allowing decisions to be made by default, which impacts decision quality. Pervasive leadership has been designed to address both decision latency and decision quality by focusing leadership at the locus of the most appropriate decision point.

Pervasive leadership is based on the following three principles:

- Change your mental model of I and Thou.
- Act locally; think holistically.
- Enact empathetic stewardship.

This paper discusses the details of pervasive leadership, expanding upon the author's January 2015 InfoQ article. The paper examines two short case studies wherein introducing pervasive leadership immediately improved an organization's ability to execute and addresses why this approach to leadership has the outcome of improved agility.

Biography

Jean Richardson is an Agile coach and process consultant and a consulting project and program manager. She also provides individual development and leadership coaching. She has been an instructor or adjunct professor at Oregon Graduate Institute, Portland State University, and Marylhurst University. She contributes to the community in her roles as Vice President of Professional Development for the Portland Chapter of the Project Management Institute, member of the Agile Alliance user group AgilePDX, and for the last 17 years as a mediator in the Multnomah County Court Mediation program. She is immediate past vice president of professional development for the Portland Chapter of the Project Management Institute and past president of the Portland Chapter of the Society for Technical Communication.

1 Introduction

I have been developing pervasive leadership since the early 2000's when I started researching the thesis I published in 2012, *In Your Own Hands: The Individual's Experience of Work Life*. Since then I have tried and tested it with clients, presented it for theoretical interrogation in 2014 at the Association for Graduate Liberal Studies Symposium, and presented it to various audiences including a door-busting Project Management Institute Audience in December of 2015. I am the innovator of this leadership approach. What is presented is evolved based on my experience, experiments, and thinking. It's greatest contribution to is address the limitations of servant leadership, which has been the dominant model in the agile community to date.

I noticed the challenges to agility in the servant leadership paradigm early in my Agile coaching career. While I valued the model, it was clear to me that it still limited individual ability to grow and lead from wherever you are in the organization, and, most importantly, it was still a power-over model while agility requires power-with models.[1] So, I developed and started experimenting with pervasive leadership and found that it has value almost immediately wherever I am able to expose the concepts. The key value delivered is in waking people up to their own ability and accountability to lead and waking leaders up to the value of having those they think of as follower, or "the led," lead.

2 Where Pervasive Leadership Sits Among Agility-Supporting Models

Pervasive leadership is among the newest agility-supporting models. It is an embodied leadership model and draws on the presence and character of the leader. It is presented as an alternative to servant leadership, the most-often recommended model for agilists because of the problems with and limitations of servant leadership I and others have noted.[2]

In the last several years, I have presented the pervasive leadership model at an Association of Gradual Liberal Studies conference where it was praised by social workers and labor organizers alike for its value to both organizations and the workforce; I have published an article on InfoQ to allow industry feedback; I have published several blog posts on the topic; I have presented the model to a gathering of over 200 project managers and received very positive feedback, and I have success in formally introducing it into two very challenged software organizations. In both cases where the model was formally introduced and taught to both teams and managers, the value of the model was sustained in my absence and after my departure.

2.1 Problems with Servant Leadership

More and more is being written about the problems with servant leadership, a model created by Robert K. Greenleaf in the middle of the 20th Century. Some people believe that the notion of the "servant" disempowers the leader. Mitch McCrimmon in "Why Servant Leadership is a Bad Idea" asserts that servant leadership is paternalistic and gets in the way of employee engagement. Neil Kokemuller in "Problems with the Servant Leadership Model" echoes much of what McCrimmon says but also raises concerns about what he regards as the special role of the manager in creating vision. Minnis and

---

[1] Power-over is a relationship between two people or groups of people where one has or exerts power over the other. This is a characteristic of competitive interactions and authoritarian relationships. Power-with is a relationship between two or more people or groups of people where power is not only balanced but typically used for mutual benefit. This is a characteristic of collaboration and facilitative relationships.

[2] http://www.management-issues.com/opinion/6015/why-servant-leadership-is-a-bad-idea/, http://smallbusiness.chron.com/problems-servant-leadership-model-50586.html, http://www.ufhrd.co.uk/wordpress/wp-content/uploads/2010/08/8_4.pdf

Callahan, in their paper "Servant Leadership in Question: A Critical Review of Power within Servant Leadership," claim that the model has been "defined through engendered language and a Judeo-Christian lens which implies certain values and leaves little space for questioning the theory."

My concern has to do with the power-over implementation of servant leadership which is far too common. In technology environments, I have observed that servant leadership has often been implemented as a form of doing for and to others what is best for them. Many self-identified servant leaders are completely unaware of the philosophical basis of the model and are also unaware of the "best test" that Greenleaf himself created to determine the presence of a servant leader. It is:

> Do those served grow as persons? Do they, while being served, become healthier, wiser, freer, more autonomous, more likely themselves to become servants? And, what is the effect on the least privileged in society? Will they benefit or at least not be further deprived?[3]

This test indicates to me that no one can self-identify as a servant leader, though many do. And, the typical implementation of servant leadership is to, in the eyes of the servant leader, kindly do what the leader thinks is best for the led. As I often say, I see more Soylent Green than Greenleaf in most servant leadership implementations.[4]

3 Purpose of Pervasive Leadership

Pervasive leadership is designed to decrease decision latency and increase decision quality through emphasizing the responsibility of everyone in the organization to lead from where they are and actualizing principle-based relationships that foster individual leadership at all levels. For instance, when a team member makes a local leadership decision based on his or her best judgement at the time and the outcome is not as effective as the management system would have liked, the focus is completely on validating that the individual took the best action they knew how to and on harvesting learning to ensure a higher quality decision next time.

In alternative medicine, healers have a notion of a "shadow heart" that pumps the lymph through the body, thereby keeping the immune system in good order while the physical heart pumps the blood. In the context of pervasive leadership, the management system is the shadow heart always on the alert to compassionately share its expertise and support the product teams as they focus on pushing the highest quality product out the best way they know how.

3.1 A Dialogic Stance

Pervasive leadership depends very much on a dialogic stance. When I refer to "stance" I am referring to how the leader orients to others both internally and externally.

A dialogic stance is not simply two-way communication or open communication. Dialogue is a form of conversation that is best contrasted with debate in terms of its premise, goal, attitude, focus, listening, inquiring and advocating behaviors; as well as the perceived role of the speaker. This is more specifically described in Table 1 below.

---

[3] Robert K. Greenleaf; Larry C. Spears. Servant Leadership: A Journey into the Nature of Legitimate Power and Greatness 25th Anniversary Edition (Kindle Locations 352-354). Kindle Edition.

[4] Soylent Green is a dystopian science fiction film and is also the name of a type of food made by a corporation depicted in the film. At the end of the film we learn that Soylent Green is made of human beings.

	Debate	Dialogue
Premise	One right answer, usually mine.	Many right answers; mine may be one.
Goal	To win, be right, sell, persuade, or convince.	To understand the other person from their point of view.
Attitude	Evaluating and critical	Curious and open
Focus	"What's wrong with this picture?"	"What's new? Of value? What can I learn?"
Behaviors	Listening	
	• Accept nothing at face value. • Hear advocacy as a challenge to be met. • Listen judgmentally. • Listen for errors and flaws. • Plan your rebuttal • Talk more than listen.	• Accept what is said at face value as true for the giver. • Hear advocacy as an opportunity to deepen understanding. • Listen for their story and without judgment. • Listen more than you talk. • Reflect instead of react.
	Inquiring	
	• Interrogate the other person. • Ask questions that support your perspective and challenge the other person's view.	• Ask questions in order to clarify and deepen your understanding and understand what another's ideas mean to them. • Explore taken-for-granted assumptions.
	Advocating	
	• Assert your own position. • Describe flaws in other perspectives. • Justify your position. • Defend your assumptions as truth.	• Offer your ideas as yours only. • Explore alternative points of view.
Role of Speaker	Devil's Advocate or Truth Sayer	Walk in Another's Shoes

Table 1. Debate Compared to Dialogue[5]

4 Pervasive Leadership's Guiding Principles

Pervasive leadership is based on three principles:

- Change your mental model of I and Thou.
- Act locally; think holistically.

[5] This table is a summary of Flick's work. See reference list at the end of this paper.

- Enact empathetic stewardship.

4.1 Change your mental model of I and Thou.

Pervasive Leaders see themselves as being in a dialogue with everyone in their work group, or, if the organization is small enough, everyone in their organization. They have something to learn and something of value to offer. Where they are granted power-over authority, they use it extremely rarely. They have learned to function in a way that makes that kind of authority largely unnecessary.

4.2 Act locally; think holistically.

Pervasive Leaders realize that patterns and problems they see in their immediate work group are also likely arising elsewhere in the organization. They solve them locally and offer the solution to the larger organization. They also seek solutions elsewhere because someone else may have spotted and solved the problem first. Their objective is always to help the organization move forward and fulfill its stated purpose as fully as possible as quickly as possible.

4.3 Enact empathetic stewardship.

Pervasive Leaders realize the importance of empathy and the risks of compassion fatigue. They realize also that, while each individual is uniquely valuable, the organization as a whole is the ship we all travel in, so they are careful to advocate for the needs of the organization in balance with the needs of the individual.

5 Appropriate Application of Pervasive Leadership

As I have developed and worked with this theory over the years, I have begun to consider the question of where pervasive leadership should and should not be used. My career spans thirty years in technology, primarily software development. Most of my engagements have been turnaround engagements where either the project or the team was in need of support and improvement. Many of these engagements have been red project turnarounds. Red projects are projects where the key indicators, usually schedule, cost, and quality, indicate that the project is highly likely to fail; extreme measures are typically required to get these projects back on track. For example, indicators on red projects may include such things as a project with a forecasted delivery date that moves out consistently week-over-week or month-over-month while the budget burn rate remains the same or a multi-phase project where customer satisfaction was extremely low in phase one but those quality indicators have no plans for remediation in succeeding phases.

Clearly, in a red project situation, it is frequently important to, after as brief as possible an analysis phase, propose and enact a get-well plan. I use a modified Delphi method (Kerzner, p. 724) heavily in the analysis phase and prefer that the team be involved in evolving the get-well plan. However, under extreme situations, a directive leadership style is at least briefly often necessary. This period should be as brief as possible and to the greatest degree possible, the turnaround leader should be "working out loud" so that knowledge transfer is happening during the turnaround. Other than such turnaround situations and critical failure threat remediation, I have not identified a time when pervasive leadership would be contra-indicated in most organizations. Given the state of the world today, it is clear that the society-healing benefits are of value and critically needed. Just as we all have a responsibility to lead in our organizations, we have a responsibility to lead in the broader world.

6 Two Pervasive Leadership Cases

The following two cases come from my own consulting practice and illustrate the value and use of pervasive leadership.

6.1 A Team with Heart, Music, and Dogs

One team that comes to mind is a more recent example. When I joined the effort the team was supposedly using agile methods, Scrum specifically. My first day with them was a day-long immersion interview. I watched while the technical lead berated the team, and some individuals, mercilessly. They had just hired a trained and experienced Scrum Master, and their Product Owner was in the process of leaving. The backlog was a stack of defects. The team had been sequestered on site with the co-development partner by their customer because their delivery reliability had been so poor. The customer's response was to monitor and task them at a lower and lower level.

This, of course, wasn't working.

In short order, and to the relief of everyone but his manager, the berating technical lead resigned. We talked among ourselves and the team decided they wanted to take their destiny back into their own hands.

The team decided to build a fort to keep themselves safe in the face of a tremendously challenging project:

- Focus
- Openness
- Respect
- Trust

Their FORT would be their protection as they started their recovery.

Together we looked at our inability to generate testable builds, and applauded ourselves for the great team dynamics we had even in the face of the kind of ill treatment and disrespect we had experienced. After proving we could deliver and did care about the customer's integration deadlines, we escaped from the client site where we were housed under very uncomfortable conditions and returned to our own offices where the team could have their dogs and their music, and where they could speak freely.

I remember being impressed with the team's eagerness to learn. Their Scrum Master was dedicated to teaching them "Scrum by the book," so they could get a taste of that before they started embroidering it with what they *thought* Scrum was. A new Technical Product Owner was hired, and the true state of the backlog was made clear, as was the state of the skills on the team. The team was under-skilled for the challenge in front of them.

The team was eager to learn, so management negotiated with their business partner to loan us their technical practices coach. One day of technical practices coaching had a lightning rod effect on the team. Suddenly they realized more about where they were in comparison with where they wanted to be. This both sobered and excited them. Then they started working together more closely and working more strategically. They wanted to understand how cross-functional communication could bring them a bigger payoff. They learned about pervasive leadership, which woke them up to their own value as leaders and the imperative of their assuming leadership. And, they took ownership of the project.

Impediments that would have stopped them in their tracks previously, such as running out of tasks or difficulties in scheduling, were easily moved by the team themselves. When things went wrong, such as a broken build, they called for help from other team members and went to work on the problem, whereas before, they would have wasted cycles in unproductive fretting rather than productive problem solving. Management stood back in frank surprise.

Everyone learned that there are technical practices in Extreme Programming that are vital to keeping a Scrum Team building good software. Everyone learned about pervasive leadership, which woke them up to their own power and responsibility to lead. In a matter of days, they were solving problems, helping each other, focused on the customer, and beginning to understand how to lead the project as well or better than the managers they were looking to for leadership in all things previously.

For example, the relationship between the team's organization and their business partner's organization was very rough. This was affecting interorganizational team dynamics and wasting time in getting the work done. The team could see this for themselves and raised a number of things they wished they had done sooner, for instance, integrating the two organization's (the client and the vendor) teams for troubleshooting.

The team reached out directly to their colleagues at the team level in the partner organization and invited them to come onsite on an as-needed basis where they could work as an integrated team in a dedicated team room. The team made the decision to do this and did almost all of the negotiation themselves as well as scheduling the visits. They only escalated when managers on the business partner's organization blocked their requests, which they did, at first. As part of this co-working arrangement, the team worked hard to repair the relationship between the two companies while appropriately retaining confidentiality for their employer.

Quickly the team demonstrated eagerness to participate in strategic decisions that would directly impact them, and they provided valuable feedback to management about proposed courses of action. They were particularly concerned about, and took action, to heal the relationship with their business partner.

6.2 The Teams That Were Coached Backwards

Another group of three teams had developed an increasing pattern of failing over a three-year period. They were working on re-coding and enhancing their already successful flagship product on another technical stack. They were "using Scrum," and had been coached by someone who "taught us the philosophy and then told us to go figure it out." The company had shrunk fifty percent through voluntary and involuntary terminations during the time they were "doing Scrum" based on this person's coaching. The pattern of forcing work into the team had become so routine that, when I led the first thorough retrospective some team members were shocked to learn that they were supposed to understand the work they were taking in before they committed to it.

I suggested everyone read the Agile Manifesto and Principles and that at least the Scrum Masters, but preferably everyone, read the Scrum Guide. They learned that they were missing a role and the entire review meeting as well as most of the intent of the retrospective. They learned that there was such a thing as Scrum Theory. They learned that there were strategies and tactics for turning around a failing sprint; they didn't have to just submit to imminent failure and disappointment again.

They decided to make some big changes, and we started inserting targeted learning and coaching opportunities into their sprints and looking for opportunities to bring learning from the last sprint into the current sprint. The management team learned that, while the team is the engine of the organization, the heart that pumps the blood, the management team is the shadow heart that pumps the lymph fluid through the body of the organization and keeps the immune system in good order so the team can thrive as it pursues agility.

Specifically, the management team learned to stop over-helping but, instead, to focus on clear high level requirements and being approachable for assistance. They learned to expect transparency, ask for it, and facilitate it. Transparency helped them step back and stop hovering over the team which behavior had the additional outcome of causing them to jump in to direct ad correct more often than was necessary, both for learning and for a good outcome. They learned to ask coaching questions to support growth. Learned that rescuing would only result in more rescuing in the future. They learned also to focus on creating a work context for good work outcomes and to expect those good outcomes rather than to fear poor outcomes.

As part of a series of short "pop-up" trainings, I formally introduced to engineering and product management organizations to pervasive leadership's purpose and principles, which I had been coaching senior members of the management team on in separate sessions. The feedback from the management team was that the introduction of these ideas to the teams rapidly changed the nature of the conversations they were having and highlighted for everyone the potential of their ability to execute and certain key organizational impediments.

7 Theoretical Underpinnings of Pervasive Leadership

Pervasive leadership combines aspects of servant leadership, chaordic[6] leadership, existentialism, facilitative leadership and personal leadership. This is an embodied leadership model, which means that it engages through the character and affect, or embodied presence, of the practitioner. It is operationalized through tools and techniques drawn from the facilitation, mediation, and agile software development communities as well as conversational models in existentialist practices, specifically, Peter Block's stewardship model. It assumes that "leader" does not presume follower in the traditional sense, and that true followers cannot be forced to follow. It also recognizes everyone in the organization has leadership potential and responsibility. Pervasive leadership draws from and distinguishes itself from the following existing models:

- Servant leadership, drawing the desire to support the evolution of the follower but has a greater emphasis on power-with.
- Personal leadership, drawing in the emphasis on individual accountability and integrity.
- Chaordic leadership, aligning with the notion that a true leader cannot be bound to lead. A true follower cannot be bound to follow.
- Facilitative leadership, emphasizing a facilitative stance and a broad range of facilitation tools to operationalize the philosophical orientation toward others and objectives

8 Apparent Efficacy of the Model

We have known for some years that managers in most contexts can no longer know the work as well or better than those they lead. This is especially true of those that rely on cross-functional teams as modern software development does. However, effective managers have been trained and have learned through experience how their organizations work and what tends to generate high quality output. Given the pace of the work and geographical distribution of team members as well as the thousands of micro-decisions line-level workers need to make today, it is extremely important that decisions are made at the time and location that the need for them emerges. Waiting for advice and permission wastes precious time. Frequently, there is not so much a "right" answer as there is a "best" answer based on what we know at the time.

Pervasive leadership encourages leadership at the locus of the need for decision and action while working to distribute power and knowledge across all levels in the organization to improve business outcomes. Managers distribute vision, policy, and "how we get things done here" information while line workers in teams distribute technical expertise, feasibility of vision implementation, and progress to outcome information. The communication loop must always be open, and it is to the benefit of all stakeholders to learn and practice a dialogic stance as well as to find way to effortlessly collect data about the work and the business context and make it transparently available to all stakeholders as well as to

---

[6] The term "chaordic" was created by Dee Hock, who led the creation of the Visa card and created the chaordic leadership model. The term refers to order which arises from chaos and has characteristics of both.

take point-in-time measures for the purposes of tuning and adjusting work processes and further developing relationships.

9 Opportunities for Further Development

Pervasive leadership has developed to the point where additional testing and development by others is important. If I am the only person testing the model, the tests prove only marginal durability of the model. It could be asserted that the model is specific to my individual practice. I am seeking a greater durability for this leadership model. Testing is also important because data persuades executive stakeholders, and this model should be spread not just for the sake of business but for the sake of society.

Pervasive leadership has the potential to create a better world. We are present in the world as our work teaches us to be. To create a better world, we must increase our awareness and noticing skills and reflect on how our presence also participates in creating our context. Our work processes effect everyone involved and those effects are carried out into the broader world.

9.1 Case work

It's important to develop a body of cases which show that other people can adopt the model to their and their organization's benefit. If you adopt the model, I'm interested in posting your brief case descriptions to my web site and, if it's mutually beneficial, helping you write the cases and find forums for discussing them. Cases can be as brief as a few paragraphs in this paper, more extended cases that describe metrics tracked while the case was evolving would also be welcome.

9.2 Methods/techniques

Currently, most of the methods and techniques that a pervasive leader might use come from the facilitation, mediation, and agile communities. They have only been briefly assembled in a set of leadership cards I have drafted and am trying to bring to prototype form. These cards need to be tested and possibly expanded through practice and guide providing background on them should be developed as a teaching tool. A prototype of the cards will be available at the presentation of this paper.

10 Conclusion

Pervasive leadership is a model offered as an alternative to servant leadership. It provides benefits that servant leadership cannot because it works to dismantle the power structure that can arise in the practice of servant leadership and which is resident in most organizational leadership roles today. It is an embodied power-sharing and power-with model designed to nurture leadership at all levels.

Having been scrutinized by scholars in the Association for Graduate Liberal Studies and introduced to a large number of project managers and two software development organizations, it is important that the theory be evolved and tested more broadly by more practitioners.

Pervasive leadership appears to apply booster rockets to agile adoptions by waking up everyone in the organization to their responsibility to participate in the leadership of the organization, by emphasizing that we are all born empowered, by inspiring individuals to take action and the management team to reorganize around its principles such individuals are not disciplined for leading from where they are but are coached to lead such that decision latency is minimized and decision quality is maximized.

References

Bens, I. (2006) *Facilitating to Lead! Leadership strategies for a networked world.* San Francisco: John Wiley & Sons, Inc.

Dreher, D., & Laozi. (1996). *The Tao of Personal Leadership.* New York: HarperBusiness.

Flick, D. Ph.D. (1998). Moving from Debate to Dialogue: Using the Understanding Process to Transform Our Conversations. Boulder: Orchid Publications.

Greenleaf, R. K. (1991). *Servant Leadership: A Journey into the Nature of Legitimate Power and Greatness.* Mahwah, NJ: Paulist Press.

Hock, D. (2000a). The Art of Chaordic Leadership. *Leader to Leader, 2000*(15), 20-26. Retrieved from Business Source Complete database.

Hock, D. (2000b). Birth of the Chaordic Age. *Executive Excellence, 17*(6), 6. Retrieved from MasterFILE Premier database.

Kerzner, H. (2006). Project Management: A Systems Approach to Planning, Scheduling, and Controlling. Hoboken: John Wiley & Sons, Inc.

Koestenbaum, P. and Block, P. (2001) *Freedom and accountability at work: Applying philosophic insight to the real world.* San Francisco: Jossey-Bass/Pfeiffer.

Macy, J. (1991) *Mutual causality in Buddhism and general systems theory: The dharma of natural systems.* Albany, NY: State University of New York Press.

Richardson, J. (2015) "We Need No Less Than Pervasive Leadership." Infoq.com: https://www.infoq.com/articles/need-pervasive-leadership Retrieved 9/1/17.

Reilly, S. (1996). *Facilitative leadership: Managing performance without controlling people.* Seattle: Peanut Butter Publishing.

Supporting Continuous Integration in Embedded Software

Andrew T. Graham

Tektronix, Inc. | andrew.graham@tektronix.com

Abstract

Applying continuous integration practices to embedded software development is an endeavor filled with challenges unique to a hardware-centric ecosphere. One such challenge, imperative to software quality, is overcoming a pure development mindset. In a hardware project, the ability to use a project's automation infrastructure to test a customer experience ahead of a traditional test phase is invaluable.

Continuous integration practices for an embedded software application enables: abstract and modular test pipelines, greater coverage over possible customer-facing permutations, and a flexible yet maintainable infrastructure.

This paper covers three key concepts that are core to continuous integration in embedded software: minimum accessibility, abstract communication, and dynamically reconfigurable hardware.

Biography

Andrew Graham is a Junior Software Engineer at Tektronix. His current work emphasizes improvement of build deployment and continuous integration architecture. In 2014, he graduated from Portland State University with a Bachelor's of Science in Computer Science and a double minor in Mathematics and Philosophy.

1 Introduction

Development of embedded software is heavily influenced by the hardware. Key project milestones often describe the progress of hardware. Software milestones, in this situation, can be mapped to those already defined by hardware. This leads to a situation where software can feel like it's in an unnatural gait. The demand for continuous integration practices and systems to ease these pressures is high, but, often it is challenging to begin implementation.

Continuous integration is a software development paradigm that encourages the frequent integration of code into a common repository. This simple action is frequently coupled with automated sequences that build, test, and qualify code with the goal of reducing risk (Duvall, Matyas, & Glover, 2007). Continuous integration systems need to include the hardware for embedded software. In embedded software, risk is reduced by verifying quality and behavior on the hardware it was intended to be distributed on.

This paper introduces three concepts that can be used to help begin continuous integration efforts in the field of embedded software. Those three concepts can be summarized as:

1. Minimum Accessibility
2. Abstract Communication
3. Dynamically Reconfigurable Hardware

In a typical software development scenario, there are many tools and best practices that are used to generate dynamic and flexible pipelines in continuous integration systems. Being able to use container images for just-in-time testing of small applications makes sense; however, measuring the quality of the software when physical hardware is involved adds complexity. We must test as closely to the physical end-user configuration as possible. That means, at minimum, testing the software on the hardware. In the best case, it means testing the software and hardware in conjunction while the product is in a customer facing state. As much testing as is possible should be:

1. On actual hardware (with the hardware optimally in an as-delivered state)
2. A component of an automated continuous integration pipeline

Software should be tested on prototype hardware as soon as it is available. Hardware, especially when proprietary, has an added challenge of being difficult to abstract into nice, organized containers or virtual machines. Even if concepts such as containers or virtual machines are used for simulating the hardware there is still a wide gap for testing the complete customer-facing package. This gap reinforces the need to test on the actual devices being developed. It also underscores the concept that the hardware needs to be accessible to the continuous integration infrastructure. The product and its interfaces spend time in infancy while being developed. The interfaces that will used to automate and test may not exist during the initial stages of development. When they are developed it's likely that they have never been automated before. Implementing continuous integration onto embedded software on developing hardware is not usually trivial. Initially, it can be a complicated form of parallel development, vying to take advantage of functionality as it becomes available.

When the number of possible customer configurations is high, integrating hardware with an automated build and test system becomes increasingly difficult. Often, each new physical product requires custom work to integrate into an automated system. It can be difficult to re-use automated functionality from product to product since much of it can be sensitive to the physical device itself. The significant cost of producing many prototypes to support development must be considered. Ideally, automation should be able to:

1. Accept an arbitrary physical device
2. Deploy applicable embedded software to the device
3. Execute relevant tests
4. Re-configure the device in preparation for the next iteration without the need for manual intervention

1.1 Example Infrastructure

The principles outlined in this paper may not be applicable to all embedded software applications. To demonstrate why some of the techniques work, it is first necessary to describe the supporting stack used during the evolution of these ideas.

This paper attempts to generalize as much as reasonable. Past this introductory section, reference to these specific tools will be limited unless it is necessary in the illustration of the core concepts.

The following applications comprise the continuous integration system referenced in this paper:

1. Jenkins (Cloud Bees, Inc., 2017)
2. Bitbucket (Atlassian, Inc., 2017)
3. VSphere (VMware, 2017)
4. Vagrant (HashiCorp, 2017)
5. Chef (Chef Software, Inc., 2017)

The automation server that will be referenced in this paper is Jenkins.

Bitbucket is used for version control, though that is a small aspect of the specific topics covered by this paper.

Virtual Machines were used extensively. The VSphere hypervisor was used to contain the virtual machines in conjunction with Vagrant for controlling availability and Chef defining the configuration of the Virtual Machines.

1.2 Testing the Software on the Hardware

Before getting into the three techniques that are the focus of this paper, a moment should be taken to emphasize the importance of testing on actual hardware when developing embedded software.

There are many techniques for simulating or sandboxing software applications in various containers, abstractions, and virtual machines. These methods work when you need to quickly verify the behavior of software that runs within the confines of other software. Embedded software, on the other hand, is meant to run in the confines of the hardware it's being written for. Mock interfaces and pure development environments should be used for quick prototyping. Gaining confidence in the quality of the software as a customer is supposed to receive it, however, requires a concerted effort in testing on the hardware it was intended to run on.

We gain in two critical areas with this approach: test coverage of the real hardware interfaces and confidence in the complete end-user package.

Mock interfaces are good for verifying ideal and logical behavior of software on hardware. They are not so good at identifying physical issues (timing for instance) that manifest when integrating the software with the hardware.

It should also be understood that development confidence in the customer facing solution is greatly enhanced by testing the salable product.

2 Minimum Accessibility

A typical product has a few existing customer-facing interfaces. Where possible, automated testing should use these interfaces. There are times it is not possible for automation to use the existing interfaces and special ones must be created for accessibility to functionality of the embedded software. The addition of these special interfaces is what constitutes minimum accessibility.

Minimum accessibility is the amount of additional access, on top of customer-facing interfaces, to the physical product that is tolerable to accommodate continuous integration of the embedded software on hardware.

Accessibility exceptions must be made, but, to the smallest extent necessary. Utilizing customer-facing interfaces is essential to gaining broad confidence in the quality of functionality in the embedded software. Abstracting those connections in automation is imperative. In an ideal world, we would always test the exact configuration a customer is going to buy. There would not be any of the assumptions, shortcuts, or band-aids that are often applied in a development environment.

Creating exceptions for accessibility is the pragmatic solution in the development of embedded software with continuous integration. Engineers should not be hindered any more than necessary in their pursuit of finding and fixing issues in a continuous integration system. If engineers are going to quickly and accurately debug an issue then they need more than the polite prompt or warning dialogue a customer might see. They are going to want access to consoles, logs, and the underlying system.

Minimum accessibility is practical because it means that the difference between a salable environment and an environment intended for testing is minimum, by definition. Given some customer-facing device then only explicit exceptions should be made available for continuous integration. Any exceptions should be well known and understood by the development team.

2.1 Deciding on Minimum Accessibility

The spectrum of embedded projects is vast and there is no one-size-fits-all rule for the correct amount of minimum accessibility in continuous integration testing. Making accessibility exceptions should be a matter of determining acceptable risk. Any modification to a customer-facing device introduces some risk. That risk should be well understood before committing to any sort of accessibility exceptions. Once the risks have been assessed, then the next step is determining how much accessibility is necessary and reasonable.

Minimum accessibility is achieved by starting at a strict customer state and then adding explicit exceptions for the continuous integration system. The system should collect applicable logs and gather as much information as is requested by the development team. This should not expand into a full debug environment. It may be the case that your customer-facing functionality already provides an adequate interface for automation.

We used the following questions can be used to determine what level of accessibility is necessary:

1. What interfaces are available to a customer? How expressive are they?
   a. Graphical User Interface
   b. Physical buttons/Display
   c. Programmatic Interface
2. What cannot be achieved through an existing customer interface? Is it accessible through a backdoor (think customer service/repair technician access)? Can automation access the device this way? Is that okay?
   a. Collecting or viewing logs
   b. Analyzing hardware state/internal diagnostics
   c. Testing manufacturing steps
3. What things cannot be acquired through a backdoor or interface (think engineering/development debug access)? Can external mechanisms simulate the action?
   a. Debug console
   b. Error case simulation
   c. Power operations (i.e. physically pressing the power button to turn the instrument on/off)
   d. Connecting/Disconnecting external media
   e. Connecting/Disconnecting fixtures, accessories, attachments

The amount of access that automation requires will depend on the breadth and depth of testing being done and the amount of information the software engineering team needs to be successful in development.

2.2 The Tradeoffs of Testing a Minimally Accessible System

When talking about testing software there is often a weighing of the pros and cons of release versus debug builds. Embedded software is no different apart from being embedded on some device. In fact, the same arguments can be made in the embedded world for testing both with and without some accessibility exceptions.

Some potential risks testing embedded software with minimal accessibility, depending on the exception, are:

1. Timing issues
2. Unintended reliance on debug mechanisms that should not exist in the release product
3. Access to functionality that does not accurately represent scenarios customers could find themselves in
4. Unintended security loopholes that become undetectable when special interfaces are enabled

On the other hand, testing embedded software with minimal accessibility has its upsides as well:

1. Access for debugging
2. Quick prototyping
3. Tolerant environment

3 Abstract Communication

Continuous integration systems have many positive qualities for workload and task balancing. Ideally, we would be able to have our hardware take advantage of those capabilities. When doing so, we have to be careful to respect minimum accessibility. Finding the compromise between the benefits of the continuous integration system and maintaining minimum accessibility brings us to abstract communication.

Abstract communication is how a continuous integration system communicates with a device under test while respecting minimum accessibility. This is achieved through intermediary applications, virtual machines, and/or containers that act as representatives to the continuous integration system for the hardware.

For Jenkins, there is the concept of slaves or nodes. These are the assets available to the continuous integration system for jobs to accomplish various tasks on. A traditional example of a node would be a build server. It is often possible to add the hardware that's being developed as a node in a continuous integration system. At face value, this has some benefits:

1. Streamlined build deployment
2. Easy to manage testing
3. Leverage the power of a continuous integration system

However, adding hardware as nodes in the system has the drawback of potentially over-exposing interfaces. This directly violates minimum accessibility and is undesirable. There is a compromise in abstracting the communication between the continuous integration system and the hardware.

Continuous integration systems are already decent at load balancing and managing pipelines. Given those positive qualities, the appeal of using the instruments as nodes for testing is highly desirable. The catch is that it is very undesirable to have Jenkins infrastructure installed on the customer-facing physical devices. If the salable product is not going to be enabled for use as a node in an arbitrary continuous integration server, then it does not make sense to allow for any of it to be present.

Yet, if the instruments are not nodes then it becomes an awkward balancing act. Jenkins already balances workload and testing in a transparent and sensible way. It is possible to reconcile the usage of customer-facing devices as test nodes, while practicing minimum accessibility principles by using abstract communication.

An abstract and modular pipeline is essential when deploying software builds to a dynamic range of hardware. Abstracted communication enables flexible pipelines to be created between the physical device and the automation infrastructure. Abstract communication is all about leveraging the inherent abilities of a continuous integration system while simulating physical instruments as testing nodes

3.1 Rationalizing Abstraction

Our first attempts at integrating instruments into continuous integration was to put the client code on the instrument. This created a scenario where the instrument itself was a node of automation. At face value, this achieved the basic benefits outlined earlier in this section, but it had the distinct disadvantage of not being in a customer-facing configuration. The modifications that were made to make the device a node made it difficult to maintain good minimum accessibility. This posed an unacceptable risk. For example, if the instrument crashed then it also crashed as a node. The situation required much manual intervention that was untenable in the long term.

Abstracting the relationship with a virtual machine, container, or other device achieves the same perceived benefits as directly using the product as a node without exacerbating the minimum accessibility problem. In fact, abstracting the communication demonstrates good discipline when assessing what is required to be minimally accessible by automation.

By abstracting communication additional testable events can be enabled that provide insight and coverage into various customer-facing interactions, such as:

1. Being able to install a new application on the instrument
2. Being able to perform power operations on the instrument (i.e. reboot, power off)
3. Being able to verify physical test configurations (i.e. check cables, sources, probes)

If the device were configured as a node on the continuous integration system then there is additional complexity added to the pipeline if a node needs to power-cycle. This would break the communication between the continuous integration system and the node until it came back alive. When the automation system communicates with an abstraction, then pipeline can be implemented in a transparent and straightforward way. For example, if the device needs to be reset then a test could be written to reset the device. The test will pass or fail depending on whether the device successfully reset and the continuous integration system gets test results from that operation.

Additional testable events and appropriate naming of the abstractions so they look like the actual devices to the automation system provide a marked advantage toward the appearance of a rational development pipeline. The idea of abstract communication can be expanded to more than the literal connection pathway between the device and the continuous integration system. Abstracted communication can also manifest itself as a bridge between developers and the testing of embedded software on some devices; For example, a developer might see the following sequence of events:

1. Build A triggers from a code change in version control
2. Build A deploys to some set of instruments in the test pool device(s)
3. Tests are executed against the device(s) running the embedded software
4. The test results are collected, analyzed, and the build is promoted (or not)

The reality of what is occurring behind the scenes is much more complicated:

1. Build A triggers from a code change in version control
2. Build A deploys to some set of instruments in the test pool; The abstract representation of each of these instruments:

    a. Executes diagnostic tests (Ensure the physical device is responsive and in a ready state for Build A)
    b. Executes an installation test
3. Tests are executed against the devices running the embedded software by the set of abstract representations of said devices
4. The abstract representations aggregate the test results and report back
5. The test results are analyzed and the build is promoted (or not)

This segues very well into changing the conversation about the automation lab, continuous integration, and the discrete instruments. Being able to remotely trigger events on an instrument in a customer facing configuration force developers to think about how a customer would perform actions all throughout the development cycle. This is especially poignant when some operation is expected that requires manual interaction with the physical instrument (i.e. plugging in a thumb drive or pressing the power button to turn on the instrument).

3.2 Abstracting Communication

We solved the problem of abstract communication with virtual machines (VM's). These machines were configured as lightweight headless VM's, whose sole purpose was to act as an intermediary between the physical instrument and the continuous integration system. We then acquired the ability to:

1. Abstract the VM's name in such a way that it appears to be a specific instrument when viewed in Jenkins (i.e. Oscilloscope-1234)
2. Utilize the VMs as a testing environment (The test VM executes applicable tests against a target device)
3. Use tools like Chef and Vagrant to manage a fleet of VMs; as opposed to having to configure many discrete instruments (this is especially ideal to ensure a consistent test environment)
4. Use Jenkins to manage workload and test coverage

Continuous integration systems already perform so many important tasks that it's very convenient to leverage that power against an abstracted test pool of discrete instruments. These abstractions can be configured to present the appearance that the actual device is connected to the build system as a node. They can also be used to convey information about the physical state of a device, which, in turn, can be used to facilitate test coverage over the various device configurations.

4 Dynamically Reconfiguring Hardware

Complex devices have many potential setups. It is not always possible to execute test iterations on all configurations. It should be, however, easy for a continuous integration system to accommodate devices that swap their physical state to some other setup.

Dynamically reconfiguring hardware means taking a device and altering its physical state into another valid configuration. The continuous integration system should tolerate these changes without manual intervention. The testing that the system performs should automatically adjust itself to appropriately test the new structure.

The ideal project, embedded or not, has a small set of finite testable configurations. Given a small enough set, it is reasonable to test all possible configurations. For embedded applications, the benefit is transparent in the cost of prototypes. Each device permutation adds additional cost to a project such that the budget required to test all permutations can quickly become unfeasible. Being able to dynamically reconfigure a smaller pool of resources helps to increase coverage while saving money and materials.

Given thousands of possible option permutations, it is prudent to test only a subset of configurations that represent typical customer usage. These likely customer permutations are known as high-value configurations. These are the configurations that have been identified as the common use cases or most likely applications.

Dynamic configurations are achieved in a two-factor approach. Since the tested item is a physical device, then it may be the case that it needs to be physically reconfigured. Once the device is in a new state then that change needs to be conveyed to the tests and automation. There are not many ways to automatically rewire a sufficiently complex device so, for today, this is largely a manual task. On the other hand, providing updated configuration information to the tests is much more receptive to programmatic methods.

The following is a brief example outlining reconfiguration steps:

1. Create a new test chain that executes the special test(s)
2. Physically re-configure instrument(s)
3. Update configuration settings (this could be a matter of a simple variable that conveys some physical state to the test frameworks)
4. Execute testing at desired interval/intensity

When the special test iteration has garnered enough information then the instrument is converted back into its default high-value state.

4.1 Use Case: Accommodating 'Edge Case' Issues

Even accepting the smaller pool of high-value test configurations it is still a desirable position to be able to reconfigure some, or all, of the lab into other permutations. This is especially the case during a test cycle that begins looking at special configurations or features (for example, characterizing a specific instrument configuration with intermittent failure(s)). These setups are known as edge cases. Even though they may be pointing out a practical and realistic application, it may be the case that they simply are not as likely to be used as other setups.

For example, it may be desirable to verify that certain features behave appropriately when used in stressed conditions. The likelihood of a customer achieving a similar state may be extremely low; therefore, the benefit of maintaining a test configuration that observes this interaction is not considered high-value.

Once the edge case or special test iteration is completed, it should be simple to revert the lab back into its default high-value state.

4.2 Use Case: Experimental Development

Developing a discrete product involves many disciplines including software, electrical and mechanical engineering, industrial design, and manufacturing. On top of software there is electrical, mechanical, industrial design, manufacturing, and many others. Each of these specialized groups approaches problems and tests their implementations in unique ways. Although the continuous integration system is tightly associated with software there are many instances when automation can bridge a gap and help another discipline exercise testing.

Take the example of powering the instrument. Software can have a role in the customer's experience of turning on and off the instrument, but, it's the electrical engineering team who are the key developers of the underlying behavior and design. The implementation can be tested through special configurations and tests that cycle power on the instruments at a high frequency, across many instruments, automatically – all through the comfort and familiar realm of the dynamically configurable lab.

5 Closing Remarks

Deploying continuous integration ideology and infrastructure into the world of embedded software has unique challenges. It is critical for continuous integration to be able to:

1. Make the minimum exceptions needed to adequately access and test the device

2. Communicate in an abstract way that honors minimum accessibility
3. Allow for physical reconfiguration of the discrete product with minimal disruption or refactoring

Those three concepts enable a project in embedded software to be developed using continuous integration workflows much like other non-embedded applications. To see success, there must be a combined effort from the multi-disciplinary teams it takes to produce an embedded application to practice continuous integration. Hardware simply adds an additional, though manageable, challenge that can be overcome by a dedicated and disciplined team.

6 References

Atlassian, Inc. (2017, June 17). *Bitbucket Server Documentation*. Retrieved from Confluence.atlassian.com: https://confluence.atlassian.com/bitbucket-server.documentation-776639749.html

Chef Software, Inc. (2017, June 17). *Learn Chef*. Retrieved from Chef Docs: https://docs.chef.io

Cloud Bees, Inc. (2017, June 17). *Jenkins*. Retrieved from Jenkins Documentation: https://jenkins.io/doc/

Duvall, P. M., Matyas, S., & Glover, A. (2007). *Continuous Integration: Improving Quality and Reducing Risk*. Pearson Education.

HashiCorp. (2017, June 17). *Vagrant by HashiCorp*. Retrieved from Documentation: https://www.vagrantup.com/docs/index.html

VMware. (2017, June 17). *VMware vSphere 6 Documentation*. Retrieved from VMware vSphere Documentation: https://www.vmware.com/support/pubs/vsphere-esxi-vcenter-server-6-pubs.html

Testing Lessons from Lean Startups

Lee Copeland

TechWell Corp.

lee@techwell.com

Abstract

The statistics are dismal. Even though magazines, newspapers, blogs, and even movies tell stories of successful entrepreneurs, most startups fail. Eric Ries was an entrepreneur with a history of startup failures under his belt. However, he learned many truths about managing startups and in 2011, he published *The Lean Startup* and revolutionized the way startups operate. Ries formulated the lean startup method, which has these cornerstones: Build-Measure-Learn loop, Minimum Viable Product, Validated Learning, Customer Development, and The One Metric that Matters. Lee Copeland has found lessons for testers in this lean startup approach. First, the minimum viable product suggests that we should consider a minimal set of tests, not striving for "completeness" at the beginning. This helps us implement the Build-Measure-Learn loop, which is similar to the Test Design-Test Execution-Learning loop of exploratory testing. The idea of customer development suggests that we should identify the different "customers" for our testing to determine what services they would actually like performed. Finally, the One Metric That Matters replaces the dozens of vanity metrics we gather now that don't really measure either the quality of our product or of our testing.

Biography

Lee Copeland has over forty years experience as an information systems professional. He has held a number of technical and managerial positions with commercial and non-profit organizations in the areas of applications development, software testing, and software development process improvement. As a consultant with TechWell Corp., Lee has developed and taught numerous training courses focusing on software development and testing based on his extensive experience. He is a well-known and highly regarded speaker at software conferences both in the United States and internationally. He currently serves as Program Chair for the STAR testing conferences, and the combined Better Software, Agile Development, and DevOps conferences. Lee is the author of A Practitioner's Guide to Software Test Design, *a compendium of the most effective methods of test case design.*

1 Introduction

Our story starts, as do all good stories, with "Once Upon a Time." Once upon a time I was vacationing on Phú Quốc Island in Vietnam. I was teaching on the weekends, and resting during the week. As I was walking along the beach, I saw a young woman reading a book. As I walked closer to check out her … book … I saw it was *The Lean Startup* by Eric Ries. I'd heard about it, but had never read it. Later, I bought a copy, and found it precepts very useful in software testing.

2 Topics

In the book, Ries describes the dismal record that starups have, a little about himself and his experience with startups, and the foundations of the lean startup philosophy. I then applied his basic ideas to software testing.

3 The Lean Startup Methodology

3.1 The Dismal Record of Startups

Ries defines a startup as "an organization created to deliver a new product or service under conditions of extreme uncertainty." Shikhar Ghosh of the Harvard Business School reports that 95% of all startups will fall short of their financial projections, 80% will fail to meet their projected return on investment, and 40% will cease operations with their investors losing everything." Not a pretty picture.

The Number One cause of failures in startups is that there is no market for their product of service. It may be a great idea – but no one wants to buy it.

3.2 Eric Ries

Eric Ries was an entrepreneur with an impressive track record – impressive for failures, that is. He created a product that connected students with … wait for it … employers, that failed miserably. (If he had only invented a product that connected people with people). Next he invented a product that allowed people to play in a 3D virtual world. It also failed.

Ries discovered that under conditions of extreme uncertainty, classical management methods do not bring success, in fact, they stifle it.

- When we lack knowledge – we gather more information
- When we lack alignment – we give more detailed instructions
- When outcomes are not what we expected – we impose more detailed controls

Each of these classical methods takes us farther away from success. They send us off in directions that are ultimately counterproductive.

So, Ries formulated the Lean Startup method based on his and other's experiences. In 2011 he published *The Lean Startup* which I discovered on the beach in 2014.

3.3 Foundations of the Lean Startup method

In his book, Ries describes the five key foundations of the Lean Startup method:

1. Customer Development
2. Build-Measure-Learn (BML) Loop
3. Minimum Viable Product (MVP)
4. Validated Learning

5. One Metric That Matters (OMTM)

3.3.1 Customer Development

Customer Development consists of learning and discovering who an organization's initial customers will be, and what markets they are in. This is a separate, distinct, and parallel process from classic Product Development.

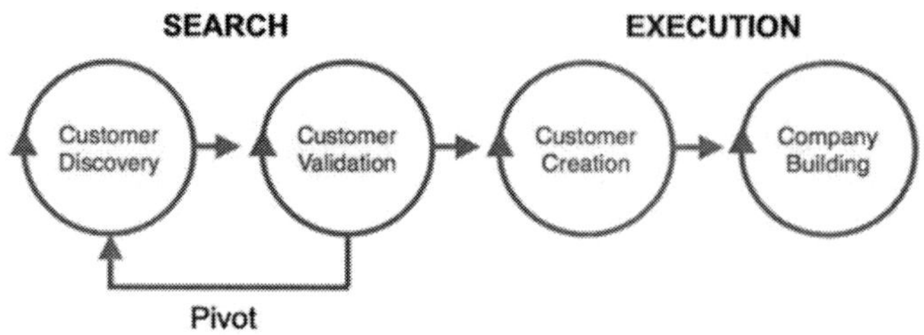

Ries incorporated this idea from Steve Blank who described it in his book *The Four Steps to the Epiphany.*

3.3.2 Build-Measure-Learn Loop

The Build-Measure-Learn Loop is a fundamental foundation of the Lean Startup method.

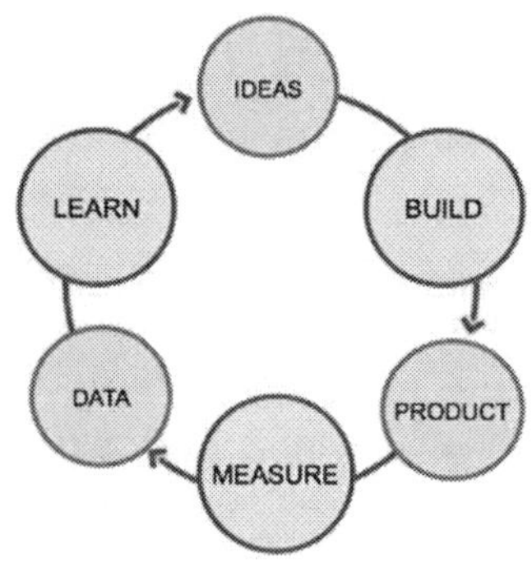

We start with a new idea, build a product that realizes that idea, measure the desirability of that product with data, and learn from this data to refine our ideas. We do this in rapid iterations to increase our learning at a minimal time and cost.

3.3.3 Minimum Viable Product (MVP)

In the Lean Startup method, our goal is to learn what the customers really want, not what they say they want or what we think they should want. We do this by creating a Minimum Viable Product (MVP). This is a version of the product that enables a full turn of the Build-Measure-Learn loop with the minimum amount of effort and the least amount of development time.

The minimum viable product will lack many of the features that may prove essential later on – and that's OK. We are trying to learn what will entice the customer, not what will satisfy every one of their needs.

3.3.4 Validated Learning

Validated learning is "the process of demonstrating empirically that the team has discovered valuable truths about the present and future business prospects." As Kurt Vonnegut wrote, "New knowledge is the most valuable commodity on earth. The more truth we have to work with, the richer we become."

3.3.5 One Metric That Matters (OTTM)

Most metrics that organizations gather are "vanity metrics." They make us feel good (or look good) but don't really show progress toward our goal. For example, "number of customers" might make us feel good, but if "cost to obtain each new customer" is too high, we may be headed in the wrong direction.

The One Metric That Matters measures the one most important thing at the present state of the startup.

4 The Value for Software Testers

As software testers, we are rarely part of an entrepreneurial startup team. In our role as software testers, are there valuable lessons we could learn and apply from the Lean Startup method?

4.1 Customer Development

The ideas in Steve Blank's book, *The Four Steps to the Epiphany,* can be applied to software testing. We should ask:

- Who are our customers?
- What are their problems that our testing services solve?
- Do our customers perceive these problems as important?
- Are they willing to pay for our testing services?

The idea of Customer Development suggests that we should identify the "customers" of our testing services – developers, users, managers – and serve them, NOT our testing process.

Otherwise we may find ourselves out of business. Remember WebVan, the largest dot-com flop in history. They were going to deliver groceries to our door – but no one wanted their services.

4.2 Build-Measure-Learn Loop

The BML loop is equivalent to the well-known Exploratory Testing Loop that we are familiar with.

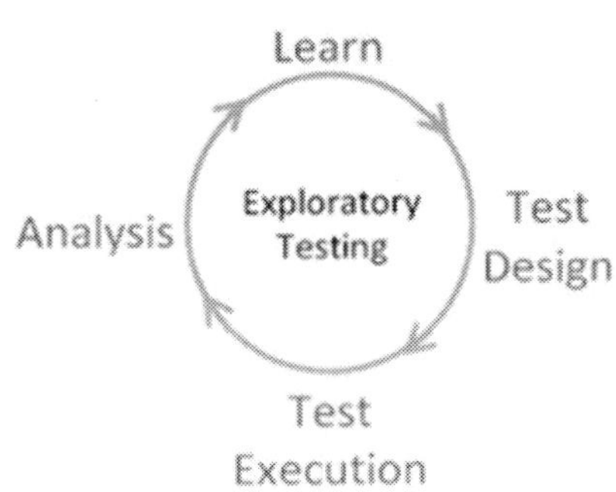

4.3 Minimum Viable Product (MVP)

The Lean Startup idea of a Minimum Viable Product suggest we could begin our testing with a minimum viable set of test cases. We don't need to strive for "completeness" from the very beginning. We can add additional tests as they become apparent and warranted.

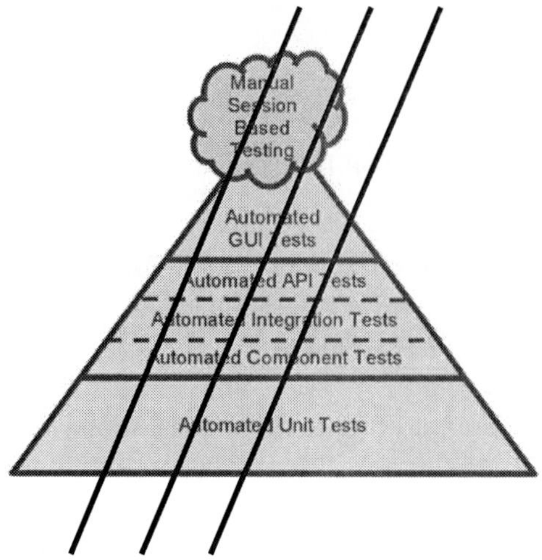

4.4 Validated Learning

Will Rogers, the famed American humorist, once said. “It isn’t what we don’t know that gives us trouble, it’s what we know that ain’t so.” The Lean Startup method suggests running frequent experiments to determine customer response. As testers, we can fun frequent tests to determine both system capabilities and customer satisfaction.

4.5 One Metric That Matters (OTTM)

Actor Fernando Lamas is rumored to have said, “It is better to look good than to feel good.” Many of our metrics are examples of “success theatre.” They make us look good, even if we aren’t doing good. Examples of typical testing vanity metrics are:

- Test cases planned
- Test cases implemented
- Test cases executed
- Test cases passed
- Test cases failed

While these may be useful, often the most important metric – one truly indicative of the quality or our product or the quality of our testing – is not defined, collected, or reported. Ivory Madison, in her talk, “Bonfire of the Vanity Metrics” asks these questions – Do your metrics:

- Measure your success at improving quality?
- Directly relate to your product’s success?
- Tie to real customers of your service?
- Help you determine what to do next?

If not, they are probably just vanity metrics.

5 Conclusion

The Lean Startup method has many insights to offer software testers. You can become familiar with its precepts and adopt its ideas for your testing.

6 References

Ries, Eric. *The Lean Startup: How Today's Entrepreneurs Use Continuous Innovation to Create Radically Successful Businesses*. 2011.

Hard Conversations: Project Quality & Sponsorship

Payson Hall

payson@catalysisgroup.com

Abstract

Managing the expectations of executive sponsors with regard to product quality is essential from the start, but often overlooked until the end of a project when expectations have hardened. This presentation describes the need to have early and ongoing conversations about product quality and schedule performance with executive sponsors, and provides examples and techniques for the discussions.

Biography

Payson Hall has experience building, managing, and reviewing large software development and systems integration projects. Formally trained as a computer scientist, Payson has worked on commercial software development and custom systems integration projects during his 35 years in data systems development. He has been engaged as a consultant by a variety of public and private sector projects throughout North America and Europe to assist them with project definition, planning, risk assessment, project reviews, and rehabilitation. In addition to his active consulting activities, Payson has authored a number of articles on project management and technical topics, written a book on project sponsorship, developed and taught seminars in practical project management, and been a featured speaker on project management topics at numerous professional conferences.

1 Introduction

Negotiations about product quality usually occur at the worst possible time – when a project is late, over budget, executive tempers are short, and the team is exhausted. These conversations are usually painful for all involved and the ugly-but-necessary trade-offs agreed to frequently provoke the recrimination, "If we'd had this conversation months ago, we wouldn't be in this dismal situation now."

In the real world, cost/time/quality trade-offs are a fact of life. On many projects, though – discussing quality trade-offs is the "third rail" of project management – a subject avoided whenever possible.

Delaying a discussion of project quality until the situation is dire is a disservice to everyone involved in the project: the sponsors, the product consumers, and the development team.

The goal of this paper/presentation is to offer constructive ways to engage project sponsors and teams in early conversations about project quality and sustain those conversations throughout product development to minimize surprise and disappointment in a project's final days.

2 Defining "Quality"

The luminaries of quality have developed surprisingly diverse definitions of the term over the past 80 years.

- Ishikawa & Deming – "Quality and customer satisfaction are the same thing."
- Juran – "Quality is meeting or exceeding customer expectations."
- Crosby – "Quality is conformance to requirements."
- Weinberg – "Quality is value to some person."

My favorites are Crosby – because if I can get agreements about requirements then I have a clear target, and Weinberg because it reminds me that humans are involved and that there is uncertainty.

Crosby famously said, "If a Cadillac conforms to all the requirements of a Cadillac, then it is a quality car. If a Pinto conforms to all the requirements of a pinto, then it is a quality car."

Weinberg famously cautioned, "This assumes the requirements are correct."

If requirements correctly capture what is important to the wrong people, that is a failure.

If requirements incorrectly or incompletely capture what is important to the right people, that is a failure.

For the purposes of this conversation, I'm going to define "project quality" as "conformance to requirements, where conformance represents value to some person (including the project's sponsors)."

My reframing is not intended to be arrogant (these luminaries are all smarter than I am), but to put a heavy project focus on the definition of quality for purposes of our discussion. Recall that all of the luminaries above (except Weinberg) were talking about product and process quality in a manufacturing sense.

3 The Holy Trinity of Project Management

A "Project" is a temporary effort undertaken to accomplish a defined objective within specified limits of schedule and resources - this broad definition encompasses a variety of business undertakings. Key words in this definition are:

- Temporary - a project must have a beginning and an end
- Defined objective - there must be an outcome that can be evaluated at some point in the future as "successful" or "unsuccessful"
- Schedule limits – there is a desired or required time target for completion of the project
- Resource limits - there are identified constraints on what an organization is willing and able to invest to achieve the desired outcome

Ideas for projects come from a variety of sources. When projects are proposed, an organization must decide whether it fits among the projects the organization chooses to pursue with its limited resources. This involves judgments based on the anticipated return on investment, the risk of failure, the risk or penalty of not doing the project, the size of the investment required, and the duration of the project. The initial decision to pursue a project is usually based upon preliminary assumptions of project cost, time to complete, and the resulting value of a successful project.

Projects are traditionally defined in three dimensions:

- Scope – What the project will produce to what quality standards, and constraints on how it will be produced
- Schedule – When the project will occur
- Resources – What people, equipment, facilities, materials, and finances will be invested to perform project work.

Some project management texts quibble and attempt to add quality as a fourth dimension, but this is needlessly complex. Project scope and project quality are inseparable concepts – how can we talk about what a project creates without specifying applicable quality standards?

Projects are defined in terms of scope, schedule, and resources. They are planned in terms of scope, schedule, and resources. Project tracking and status reporting should address scope, schedule, and resources. Scope… and QUALITY are an integral part of project management.

4 Sponsorship Defined

Projects are started with the best of intentions to solve a business problem, implement a change or develop a new product or service. The initial business case may be sound, but it is based upon limited information. The project starts with the assumption that it is doable, can be achieved within a prescribed or reasonable time frame, and that the results will be worth the investment and worth the risk. Most organizations have a selection process that tries to assure that projects look "reasonable" or worth the risk before they are begun. After a quick sanity check, and perhaps prioritization among the other projects in the current portfolio, they assign a project manager and team, give them marching orders, and wait for the vision to become reality.

When a candidate idea is advanced from "project proposal" (*"Here's an interesting idea..."*) to "approved project proposal" (*"Let's spend time and money exploring this..."*), it means that one or more leaders within the organization believe the project is a worthwhile investment. The individuals who decide to invest organizational resources in a project are called the project's "sponsors". Sponsors play a critical project role. Sponsors represent the organizational needs that initiated the project and communicate those needs to the project manager and the team. Sponsors are the organization's voice when answering the question "How will we know this project has been successful?"

Sponsors choose to sponsor a project because of two fundamental assumptions they hold about the effort:

1. The project can be completed successfully within specified schedule, scope and resource bounds
2. The value of the successful project is worth the investment and the risk of failure

Sponsors are expected to be organizational champions for the project as long as the project goals remain aligned with the goals of the business. Sponsors control resources within the organization and have the ability to commit those resources to the project's goal. Sponsors should have the authority to cancel or redefine projects that are subsequently revealed to be poor investments.

Sponsors are the ultimate arbiters of project scope, and therefore the quality of the work products that the project will create.

5 Initiating Conversations: Project Definition

One of the most important meetings in the life of a project should happen at the project's inception. I call it the "Cheeseburger Talk."

Anyone who has engaged in marketing that involved schmoozy clients lunches knows the business lunch rule: Never order messy food. No ribs, no spaghetti, no drippy cheeseburgers. The reason? It's difficult to maintain an aura of dignity and propriety when you have ketchup on your chin. The cheeseburger talk is specifically designed to break this rule and capitalize on the consequences.

An important discussion must occur at the start of a project between the project's sponsor and project manager. To be effective, this discussion needs to be relaxed and candid. Getting the sponsor away from the workplace, away from the trappings of his or her office (the credenza, secretary, and that BIG desk) to engage in one-on-one dialog is essential. If the executive gets sauce on his or her hands or face, you get extra credit.

The relationship between the project manager and the sponsor is unique. The sponsor has a business problem to solve and controls the priorities and resources of the organization. The project manager's job is to work with the sponsor to define a project that addresses the business problem and then look for a credible way to perform the project within the sponsor's schedule and resource targets. The project manager is there to support the sponsor's decision making as well as to define, plan and manage the project. To do this well the project manager must understand the sponsor's goals. The best way to discover what someone wants is to ask.

Some questions that must be asked may be perceived as insubordinate or challenging of the sponsor's authority or wisdom… so they shouldn't be asked in a public forum, by e-mail, or in an environment that encourages the sponsor to wear their "boss" hat. The intention of the cheeseburger and the cheeseburger talk is to help the project manager get to the heart of the sponsor's motivation and to lay a foundation for defining and running the project. I strongly recommend approaching these questions the first time in a casual setting.

Scope

- What do you want?
- Why is our organization interested in doing this?
- What would a successful project produce?
- How will we know we are done and successful?
- What is the successful project worth to our organization?

Resources

- What resources are you willing to commit to the project (people, equipment, materials, facilities, $$$)?
- How did you come to believe that these resources were sufficient for the project?

Schedule

- When do you want it?
- Why then?
- What is the business impact of delivery a day or a week or a month later than your target?
- What would early delivery be worth?

History

- How did we come to be here?
- Why haven't we done this sooner?
- Has this project (or anything like it) been attempted before? What happened?

Relationships

- As the project progresses, what status information would you like to receive?
- How often do you want to receive regular status?
- How shall I contact you if I have questions or issues with the project?
- Who is authorized to change the schedule, scope and resource bounds of the project once we have agreed to a written project definition?
- If at any time, I develop concerns about the project's viability, when do you want to know?

The last question is key. You will always get the same answer, "I would want to know right away.", but the question underscores the relationship between the project manager and the sponsor. The project manager is the sponsor's eye and ears. If new information suggests the project goals are in trouble, it is the project manager's obligation to notify the sponsor promptly. This question reminds both parties of that duty.

These questions make a great agenda for lunch. They can be covered in casual conversation to provide the project context and history as well as the schedule, scope and resource boundaries. They may look simple, but it is surprising how many project managers cannot answer these "simple" questions for projects that have been underway for months.

The cheeseburger talk sets a tone for the project. It establishes a foundation for the project manager prior to project definition and it reinforces the sponsor/project manager relationship. A perfect ice-breaker, this conversation helps establish the project manager/sponsor relationship at the start of the project, or any time there is a personnel change in the project manager or sponsor role.

This provides a foundation for later discussions about project quality.

6 Initiating Conversations: Project Priorities

A sign on a print shop wall read:

People want their projects *good*, *fast*, and *cheap*.

We say, "Pick two."

A lot of wisdom in twelve words. Getting priority information on your projects can be challenging, but the idea is similar. We must understand sponsor priorities among schedule, scope, and resources.

As a project proceeds, there are always adjustments and tradeoffs from a project's original goals to better match changing realities both on the project and in its sponsoring organization. The tradeoffs may be subtle, but there are ALWAYS tradeoffs. If you choose to work a weekend to make a delivery date, you have increased resources to defend schedule. If you choose to defer a function from release 1 to release 2, you have deferred scope to preserve schedule. Elect to slip a schedule two weeks to allow time to correct defects before you ship, you are allocating additional time and resource to preserve scope (quality).

Trade offs are a natural. Becoming good at identifying tradeoffs is a good career skill. Being able to explore and understand your sponsor's priorities so that you offer the right tradeoffs is essential.

On my projects, I use a tool called an RSS Matrix to discuss priorities with a sponsor (see figure). I try to discuss priorities early in the project as the initial scope, schedule, and resource goals emerge. The rules of the matrix are simple,

1. One "X" per row,
2. One "X" per column, and
3. The sponsor must choose.

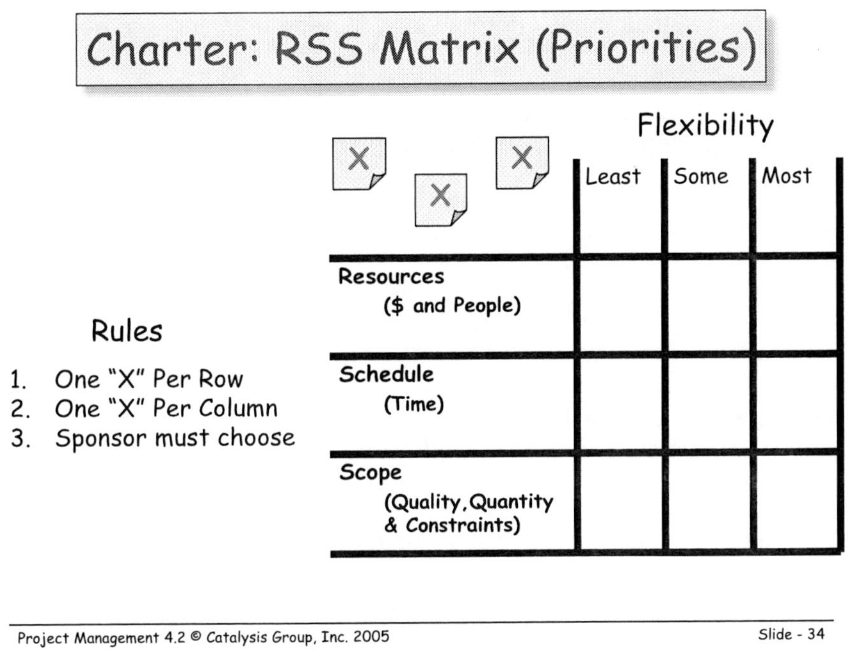

I build an empty matrix and put "X" post-its in the "least flexible" column for all three variables (an illegal matrix) to begin. Then I walk a sponsor through the sorting, asking a series of hypothetical questions that make pair-wise comparisons of scope and schedule, schedule and resources, resources and scope.

Although it takes a bit of practice, the result is worth it. Some suggestions as you start:

- Assure the sponsor that they are not committing to ANYTHING in advance. This tool only helps identify potential tradeoffs consistent with the sponsor's priorities. He or she will have a chance to approve any specific tradeoffs before they are made via your change management process (or some similar consultation).
- Be patient with new sponsors – some will think you are looking for wiggle room. You are trying to understand their priorities to better support their business decisions.
- Don't try to read the sponsor's mind – This is a vital discussion to have with the sponsor explicitly. Don't make an inference based upon the business case or corporate culture. You will usually learn something about the project as part of the discussion. Make the sponsor choose.
- This is a crude tool – actual priorities may vary over time. This general guideline is helpful to support your problem solving. If the reaction you get to specific proposals consistently digresses from the RSS Matrix guide, you might want to check with the sponsor to see if priorities have changed.

- No ties – There are ALWAYS priorities. If the project were going to be a day late or a dollar over budget, which would the sponsor choose if making a choice was unavoidable?

The RSS Matrix accomplishes three important things:

1. It reminds the sponsor that tradeoffs might be necessary
2. It captures their thinking at a specific moment in time
3. It serves as a guide for problem solving and a starting point for negotiation

7 Planning and Negotiating for Quality

Once the project is well defined and the sponsor's priorities among schedule, scope and resources have been established, the project manager has information to support planning and negotiating for project quality.

If the schedule is particularly aggressive or resources are constrained, effective planning will involve seeking sponsor concurrence on prioritizing and potentially deferring scope or negotiating quality standards early in the project.

Practical considerations include:

- Is there a particular requirement straining the project that could eliminated or negotiated to a later phase?
- How might scope be reduced without compromising project objectives?
- Can quantity be negotiated?
- Can throughput/performance be negotiated?
- Helpful changes to rules/constraints/assumptions?
- Are quality standards appropriate? Are they negotiable?

These conversations are difficult, but much easier to have at the beginning of a project if a good relationship has been established with the project sponsor and priorities are clear. They have the added advantage of helping to keep the team oriented to the sponsor's goals from the beginning of the project.

8 As the Project Unfolds

If project scope, schedule, and resource consumption is being consistently and effectively tracked against project plans and expectations this can be the basis for an ongoing conversation (often called "status reporting") to the project sponsors to alert them of surprises encountered along the way.

Early detection of schedule, resource, or scope pressure facilitates revisiting project boundaries and discussions of project scope when small course corrections might be sufficient to accomplish project goals – again by looking for tradeoffs among schedule, resources, and scope/quality.

9 Summary

Discussions of project quality are painful if they are deferred until late in project implementation. Although the conversations can be challenging, establishing rapport with project sponsors and getting information about their desires and priorities facilitates early and thoughtful conversations about project scope and quality tradeoffs when they are necessary.

Farm Credit Services of America

AGRICULTURE WORKS HERE.

Farm Credit Services of America, based in Omaha, Nebraska, is dedicated to serving the agricultural credit, risk management and financial needs of farmers and ranchers in Iowa, Nebraska, South Dakota and Wyoming.

https://www.fcsamerica.com/

www.farmcredit.com

Agenda

1. Enterprise Quality Vision
2. Strategy
3. Jenkins Demo
4. Questions

Why Enterprise Quality?

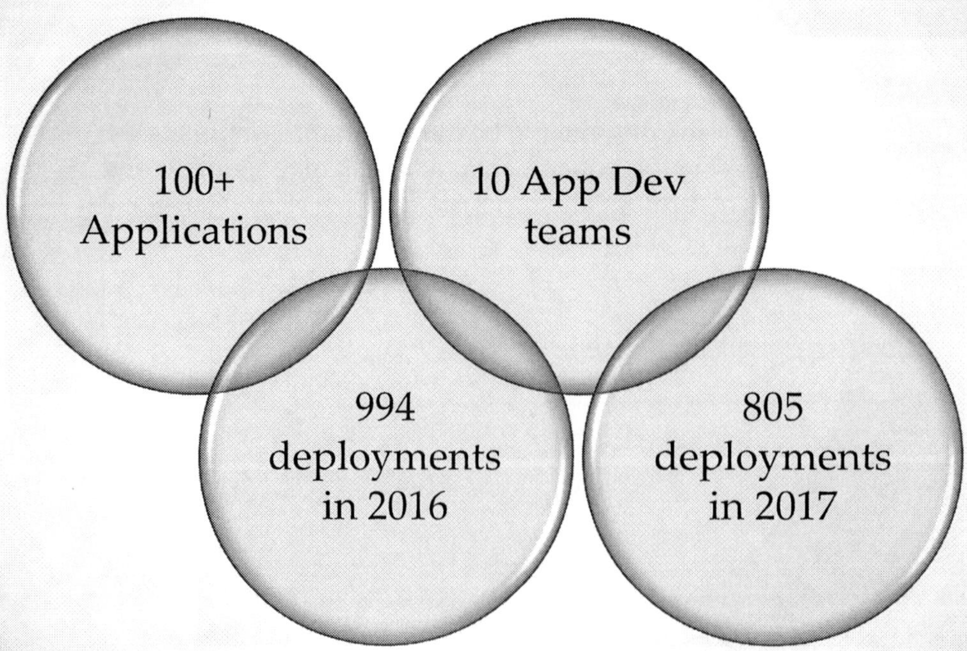

Why Enterprise Quality?

My Role

As an EA my primary focus is to bring visibility and consistency to our process

Strategy

1. People / Roles
2. Process
3. Tools

1. QAE (job description)

Quality Assurance Engineer

Strategy and Planning:

- Lead development of test strategies in accordance with project scope and project plan
- Ensure test environment documentation and testing strategy documentation per project
- Review project test coverage to avoid redundancy

Testing:

- Manage the design, implementation, and maintenance of automated testing solutions to ensure the software meets the business requirements
- Provide guidance and mentoring to other team members as it relates to the quality of software delivery
- Collaborate with the team to create testing scenarios to validate story requirements
- Oversee creation and maintenance of test data
- Lead creation and maintenance of test environments to meet all project testing needs (servers, virtuals, software, repositories)
- Work with the team to verify product functionality after a deployment
- Manage scheduled and manual test execution
- Facilitate defect identification, documentation, and resolution

System Health Analysis

- Communicate test results of active projects (automation, integration, fitness, unit, performance, load)
- Collect and analyze data to identify project quality trends and suggest improvement areas
- Communicate issues in relevant environments for assigned projects
- Establish performance metrics and benchmarks for assigned projects
- Monitor and maintain regression suites of post projects based on priority
- Participate in root cause analysis of production defects and mitigation

Peer Group

- Participate in discussions pertaining to QA guidance, make recommendations for changes in the guidance, and follow agreed upon guidance
- Pair with other QA Engineers related to QA approach and how best to implement QA guidance
- Work with Enterprise Architect on QA team initiatives
- Cultivate and share knowledge of QA guidance and evolution of QA best practices
- Share topics at QA team meetings, on QA blog, and present at relevant meetings
- Evaluate and recommend software testing tools

1. Mindset

- Let developers test and verify their own code
- Let product/business owners test and validate the product
- Quality experts who understand software testing as well as everything else that goes into producing and delivering quality software

2. Process

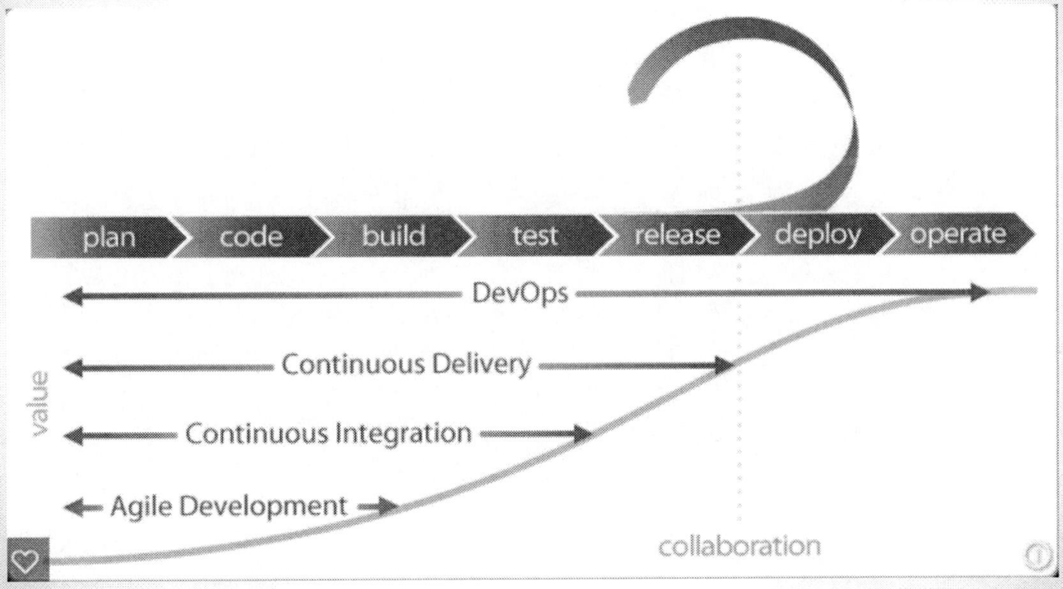

2. Process

- **Automation** is our new bacon
- Continuous Delivery with **Smarter Testing**

git

Source Control

- Use version control as the single source of truth for Automation Scripts.

Dev

- VSTS
- Visual Studio
- GIT
- Common lib
- Project Repo

QA

- VSTS
- Visual Studio
- GIT (sourcetree)
- QA
- QA Repo

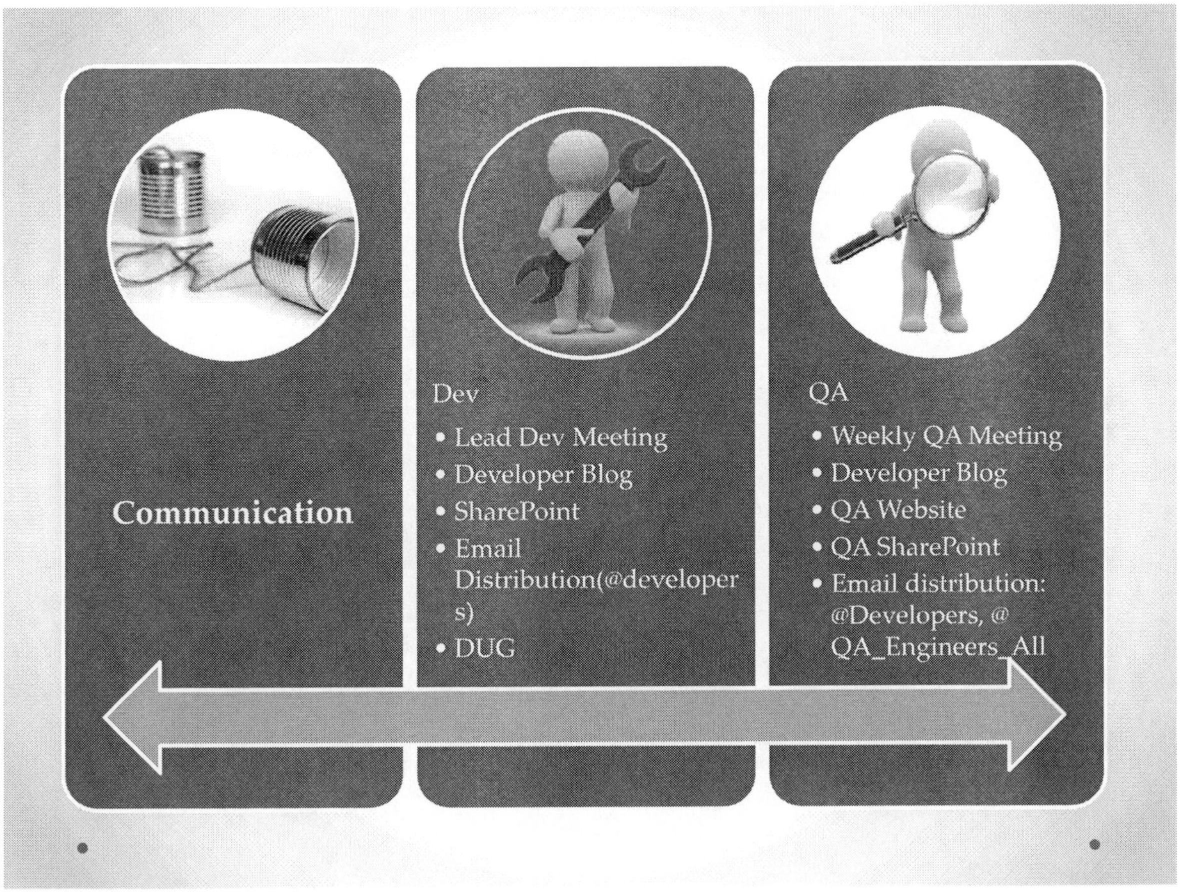
Communication
Dev
• Lead Dev Meeting
• Developer Blog
• SharePoint
• Email Distribution(@developers)
• DUG
QA
• Weekly QA Meeting
• Developer Blog
• QA Website
• QA SharePoint
• Email distribution: @Developers, @QA_Engineers_All

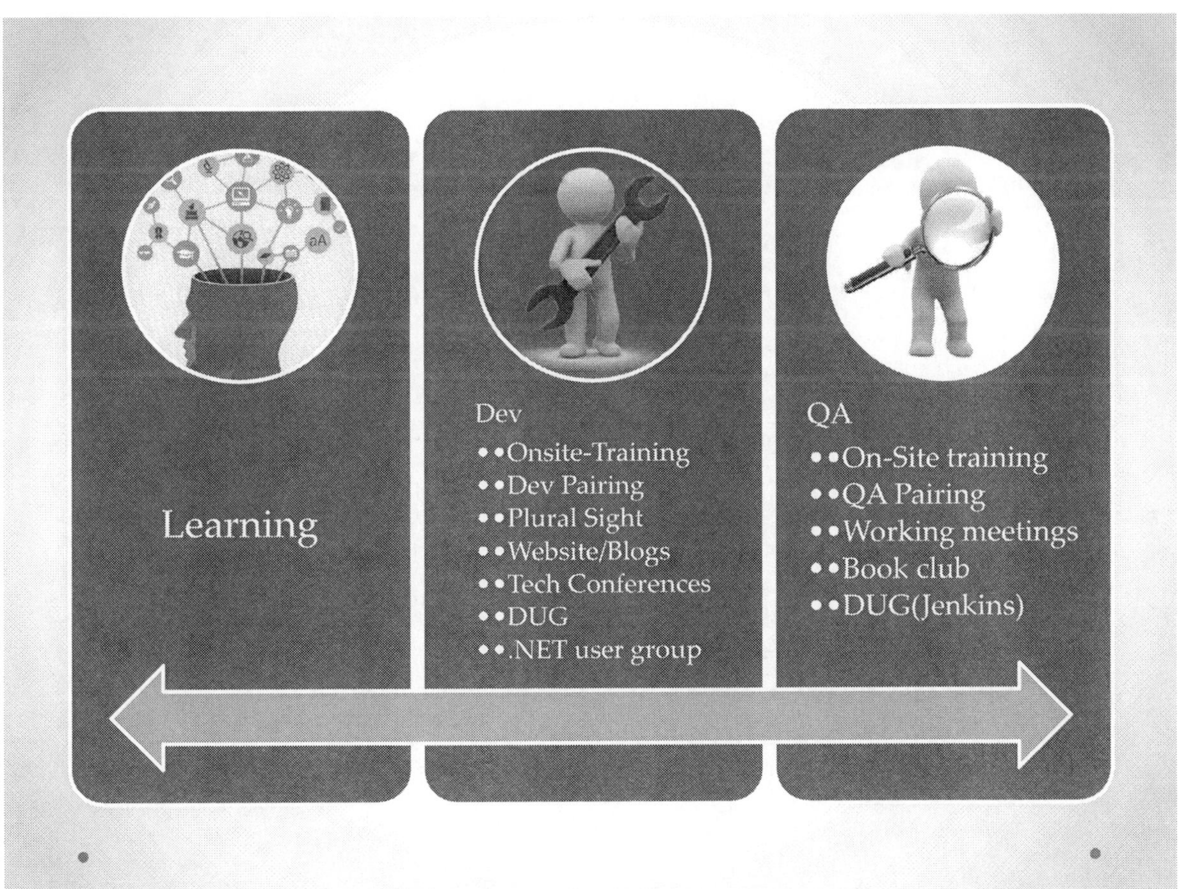
Learning
Dev
••Onsite-Training
••Dev Pairing
••Plural Sight
••Website/Blogs
••Tech Conferences
••DUG
••.NET user group
QA
••On-Site training
••QA Pairing
••Working meetings
••Book club
••DUG(Jenkins)

3. Tools

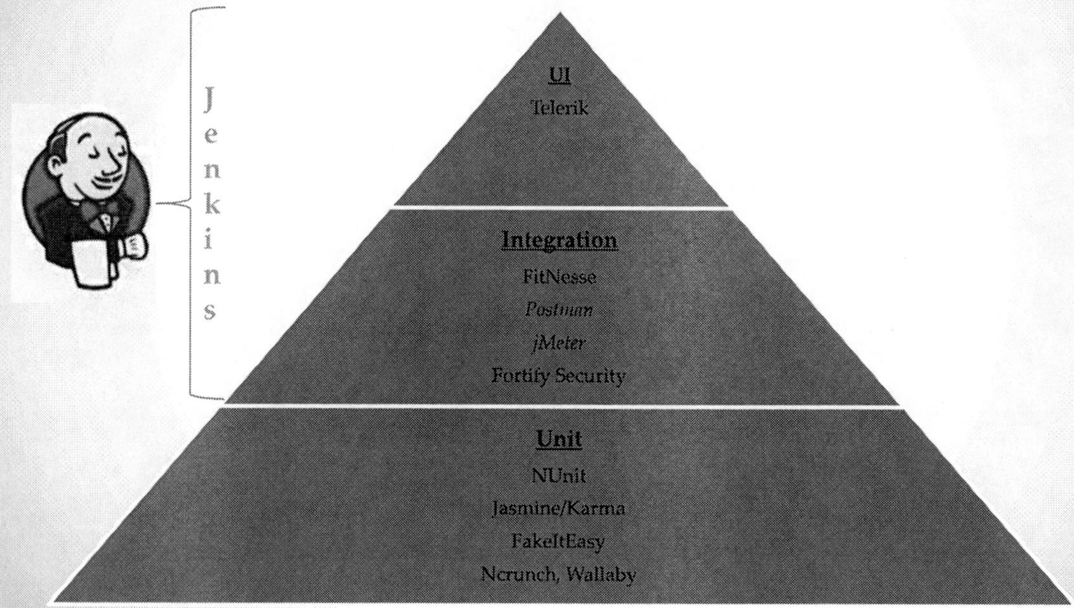

Jenkins CI Server

Why Jenkins?

Flexibility ! Jenkins is a highly configurable system by itself.

- Single Platform
- Automate the build and test
- Get Source code from repository
- Dashboard - everyone can see what's happening
- Generate report and notify stakeholders of build status
- Plug-in extensibility: Unit test coverage, last success and failure, Build trend.

Jenkin's Demo

- Main Page
- Project Status

QA Infrastructure

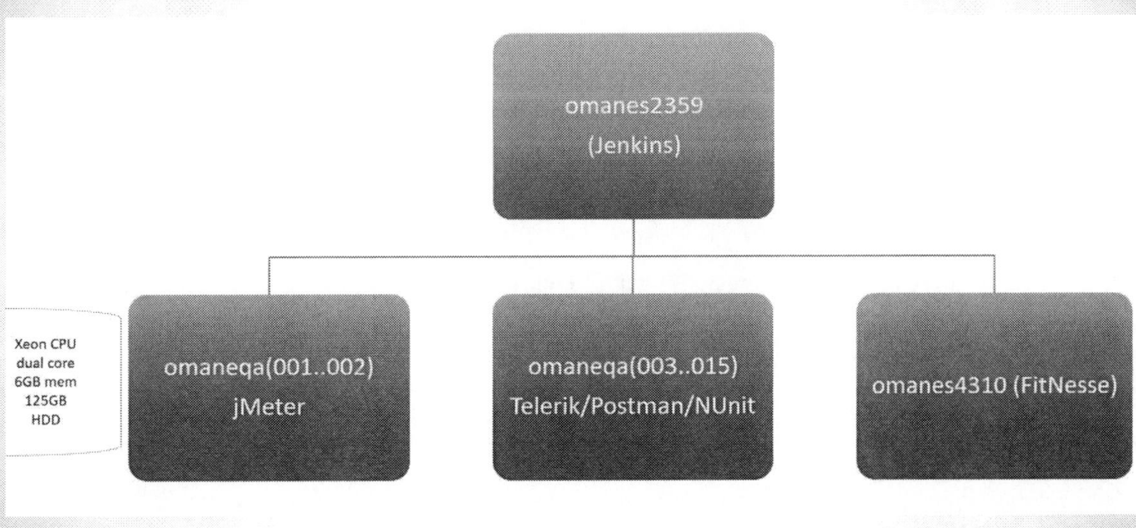

QA Image

Target Install

- Telerik Runtime/ Chrome Plugin
- Postman(Node/Newman)
- jMeter
- NUnit

Common Software

- GIT
- Jenkins
- Beyond Compare
- Notepad++

QA Group Policies

- TesterM AutoLogin, Disable Screen Lock, UAC
- Browser Settings, Screen Resolution

Base Win 10 FCSA Image

- Includes (Java, Nuance PDF)

Summary

- **The problem**: There was no unified approach in our Quality Practices(tooling and process) across our 10 AppDev teams. We were good at Continuous Integration but inefficient at Continuous Delivery.

  Solution:
  - Implemented the Testing Pyramid Strategy
  - Testing Architecture using Jenkins(Test Farm, Tool Standardization)
  - Increased collaboration and communication between QA and Devs.

  Impact:
  Any friction leads to lower adoption rate. We were able to automate 2300 tests suites per day from 400 per day. Increased our expertize by standardizing the toolset and collaboration across teams. Our confidence is delivering software in increasing everyday.

#teamwork

What's next ?

- Enterprise Health
- Test Data
- Testing Community

Never Stop Testing…

Thank you !!!

An Empirical Analysis of Java Performance Quality

Simon Chow

simonichow15@gmail.com

Abstract

Computer scientists have consistently searched for ways to optimize and improve Java performance utilizing a variety of methods. Methods including the just-in-time compilation, the garbage collection system, and adaptive optimizing have increased Java performance by reclaiming unneeded memory and optimizing areas of frequently executed code. Although many people have repeatedly improved the performance of their Java programs by modifying the code to make it more concise and efficient, Java performance can be upgraded without touching the original code at all. Adding additional RAM and computer cores can increase Java performance, along with reconfiguring VM and storage allocations, upgrading solid-state disks and using distinct disks for various types of files. This paper will cover how we can make Java performance even more efficient without changing the code of the Java program. After running these programs, we will experiment to find the most efficient methods and changes that can be made to the computer to maximize the Java performance. Without the need to change a single bit of code, we can optimize the Java performance in computers without going through every line of the Java program and figuring out which sections of the program should be modified to increase its efficiency. Thus, the user has the benefit of not having to understand how the program works to optimize the Java performance.

Biography

Simon Chow is a junior at Lincoln High School. He has participated in FIRST Robotics Challenges since 2007. Since 2014, he has participated in the high school branch of FIRST Robotics: FIRST Tech Challenge (FTC). In FTC, students program their Android phones using the Java language to navigate their self-designed robots around the FTC field, completing missions and attempting to outscore their opponents. Besides participating in FTC, Simon has also learned the fundamentals and main data structures of Java programming in Lincoln High School. Simon has also been part of a previous FTC team that has published the PNSQC paper "Brewing Quality in Android Robots" and presented it at the PNSQC conference in 2015.

1 Introduction

Many people are familiar with improving Java programs or applications by changing the Java code directly. However, we are writing this paper to show how the Java performance can be improved by tuning Java benchmark parameters rather than modifying the code.

Related Work

So far, a lot of work has been done to creating SPECjvm benchmarks. Experiments haev also been conducted comparing the newer SPECjvm2008 version with other, older SPECjvm versions and observing the improvements over time. Ultimately, this paper is unique as it focuses on tuning Java parameters such as memory heap size and garbage collection to see its effect on improving Java performance.

2 SPECjvm2008 and Benchmarks

SPECjvm2008 is a benchmark suite that measures the performance of a computer system through its Java Runtime Environment (JRE). SPECjvm utilizes ten major benchmarks: Compiler, Compress, Crypto, Derby, MPEGaudio, Scimark, Serial, Startup, Sunflow and XML.

The compiler benchmark compiles a set of java files and can deal with memory using its own FileManager, rather than relying on a physical disk.

The compress benchmark compresses data using Lemep-Ziv-Welch (LZW) method, substituting common substrings with variable size code.

Crypto has 3 different subsections: Aes, rsa, and signverify. The Crypto benchmark encrypts and decrypts using their respective protocols.

The Derby benchmark focuses on BigDecimal computations and database logic.

The MPEGaudio benchmark is floating point heavy and tests mp3 decoding.

Another floating point benchmark is the Scimark benchmark. There are large dataset and small dataset versions of this test, with the large data set being connected to memory systems and the small dataset connected to the JVM.

The Serial benchmark transforms data structures into storable formats or vice versa. The Serial benchmark deals with primitives and objects.

The Startup benchmark start each benchmark's first operation.

The Sunflow benchmark tests graphics visualization using an open source rendering system.

The XML benchmark has 2 sub-benchmarks: transform and validation. Transform applies style sheets to XML documents. Validation processes style sheets.

When running a benchmark, there will be a warmup phase (120 seconds), followed by an iteration phase (240 seconds). The warmup period will allow the computer to perform some initial, brief testing of the benchmark, but the results from the tests do not go into the actual benchmark results. However, the iteration phase does produce the benchmark performance results[1].

Running SPECjvm2008

We used Windows Command Prompt to run the SPECjvm benchmarks that we downloaded. In order to run SPECjvm, we had to point the JAVA_HOME variable to where the Java Virtual Machine (JVM) is being held in our computer.

Tuning the Parameters

There are many parameters. Two of them are -Xmx (the maximum heap memory size) and -Xms (the minimum heap memory size). When experimenting with the parameters, we decided to test the maximum memory allocation with 1GB, 2GB and then finally with 3GB (the parameters would then be -Xmx1g, -Xmx2g and -XMx3g respectively). To test the effects of changing these parameters on the specJVM runs, we changed the maximum memory heap size (-Xmx#g) in our run-SPECJVM file. From here, we can observe how changing the allocation of memory can affect how many operations the computer can perform. For the experiments in this paper, we will be testing with the Serial, Derby and Sunflow benchmarks.

Java Garbage Collection

Garbage collection is a process in programming languages in which the computer identifies all the objects that are being used in the program as well as the ones that are not. After identifying the dead objects, the computer will locate the dead objects and remove them, and rearrange the "living" objects in order to free up space and allow the program to run more efficiently[2].

We will be tuning garbage collection parameters in these SPECjvm experiments as well.

In addition to tuning the memory heap size parameters, we also tuned several parameters related to garbage collecting. We specifically experimented with G1, MarkSweep and Parallel garbage collection systems[3]. Here are the additional parameters for each of the garbage collection types.

- set JAVA_OPTS="-XX:+UseG1GC"
- set JAVA_OPTS="-XX:+UseConcMarkSweepGC"
- set JAVA_OPTS="-XX:+UseParallelGC"

3 Experiments

For our experiments, we chose to perform SPECjvm runs of the Serial, Derby and Sunflow benchmarks.

Serial

	Performance (op/min)		
Java Parameter	Trial 1	Trial 2	Trial 3
None	86.51	87.37	94.46
"-Xmx1g"	85.82	98.74	79.45
"-Xmx2g	83.7	97.67	75.86
"-Xmx3g	86.06	96.94	95.67

Derby

	Performance (op/min)	
Java Parameter	Trial 1	Trial 2
None	267.99	257.27
"-Xmx1g"	230.48	265.54
"-Xmx2g	225.02	241.62
"-Xmx3g	210.65	260.13

Sunflow

	Performance (op/min)
Java Parameter	Trial 1
None	45.17
"-Xmx1g"	44.73
"-Xmx2g	46.28
"-Xmx3g	45.82

Garbage Collection Data

Serial	Performance (op/min)		
Java Parameter	Trial 1	Trial 2	Trial 3
None	94.31	96.20	91.49
G1	94.18	87.69	96.59
MarkSweep	90.00	96.28	94.73
Parallel	96.26	98.52	94.66

Derby	Performance (op/min)		
Java Parameter	Trial 1	Trial 2	Trial 3
None	282.95	299.14	284.41
G1	303.54	298.83	312.73
MarkSweep	285.29	259.12	275.20
Parallel	253.10	284.79	275.78

Sunflow	Performance (op/min)		
Java Parameter	Trial 1	Trial 2	Trial 3
None	46.76	47.73	46.93
G1	47.19	49.93	51.09
MarkSweep	50.05	46.99	43.16
Parallel	44.31	41.80	43.33

4 Analysis

Performance Monitor

In order to see why our SPECjvm runs all came out roughly the same despite the change in the maximum memory heap size, we the performance monitor application to detect any changes in our computer's processing during the SPECjvm Serial runs, especially focusing on the CPU performance[4].

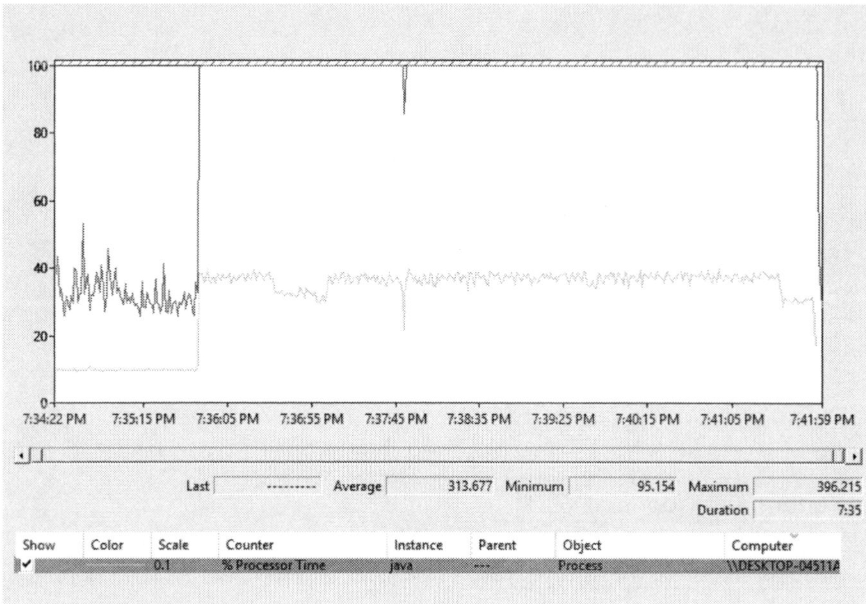

Figure 1: Graph of the data collected by Performance Monitor. The red line represents the total % processing time while the green line represents the Java % processing time.

While running Performance Monitor, we tested for both the total processing time percentage (red) and just the java processing (green). We found the green to peak at around 390 (as Figure 1 depicts the Java Percentage multiplied by 0.1), while red maxes out at 100. We believe the green goers above 100% as the computer has 4 logical processors, thus actually having a max at 400%, whereas the total processing (red) takes all 4 logical processors into account beforehand and thus caps at 100%.

Performing Data Analysis

We saved the data from Performance Monitor as an Excel .csv file. By saving the data as an Excel file, we were able to read, process and analyze the data using RStudio[4].

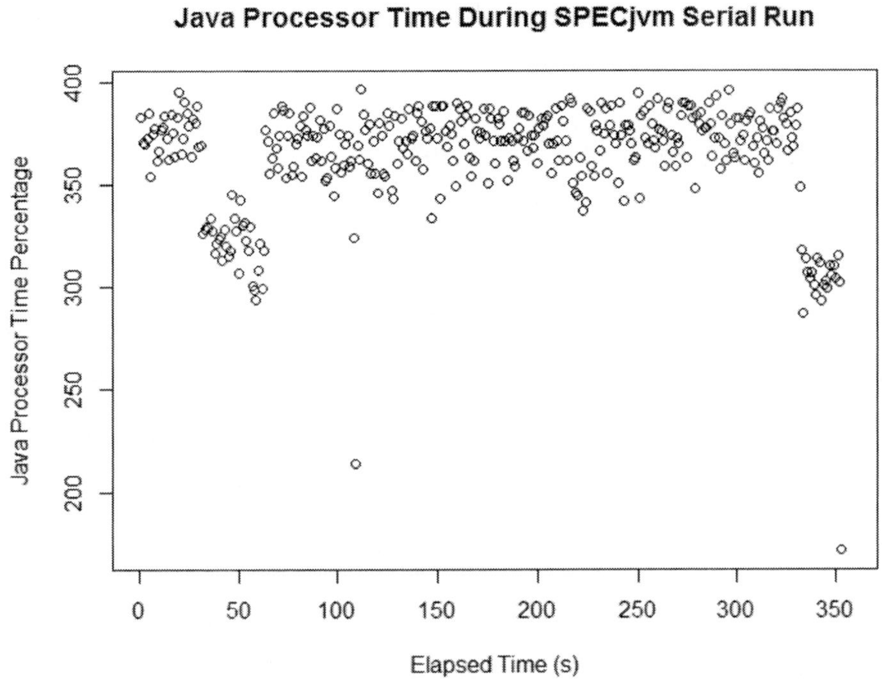

Figure 2: Java performance graph during a SPECjvm run of the Serial benchmark

When the Serial benchmark begins running, the Java % processing time increases up to nearly 400%. There is a lot of fluctuation between 350% and 400%. This fluctuation is normal as it means that each logical processor is on average using between 90% and 100% of their total processing power, due to the various applications running on the computer. Slightly after 100 seconds into the run, there is a significant drop as the Serial benchmark switches from its warm-up run to its iteration run. The significant drop at the end after 350 seconds signifies the end of the Serial benchmark run.

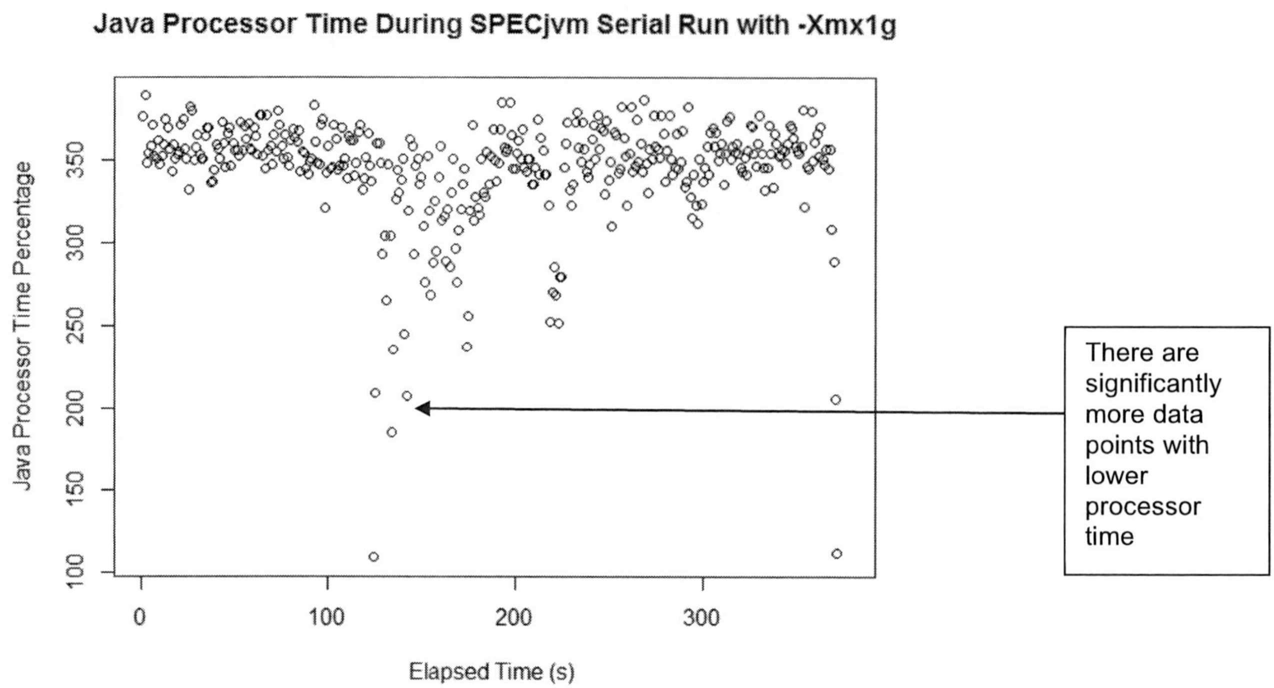

\

Figure 3: Java performance graph during a Serial benchmark run with modified memory heap size

This graph illustrates a Serial benchmark run, but with a modification to the memory heap size. By setting Java memory heap size parameter to -Xmx1g, the Java performance of the computer can be affected. When comparing this graph to the unmodified JAVA_OPTS graph, we notice that the data points on this graph are more scattered and on average lower, than the original graph.

Derby Graphs

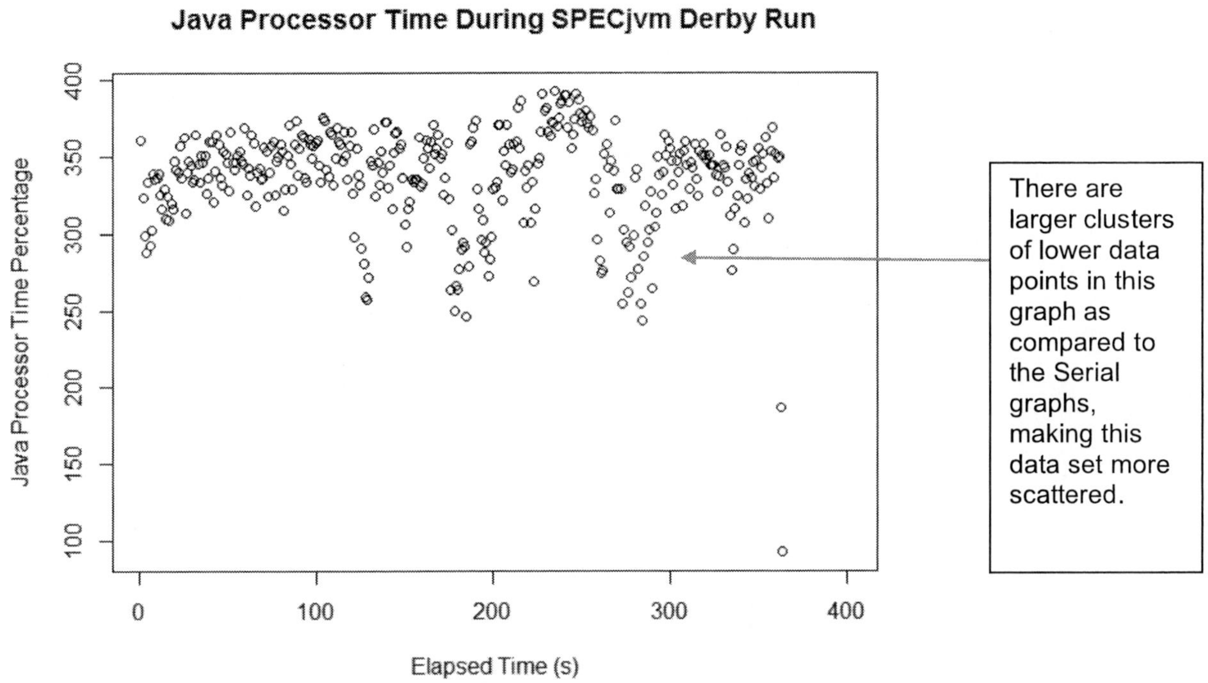

Figure 4: Java performance graph with Derby benchmark

The graph of the Derby benchmark appears to be more scattered than the respective Serial benchmark graph, fluctuating from 250% to 400%, instead of 350% to 400%. Consequently, most of the data points are near the 350% or 340% line whereas the original Serial benchmark graph clustered at the 375% line.

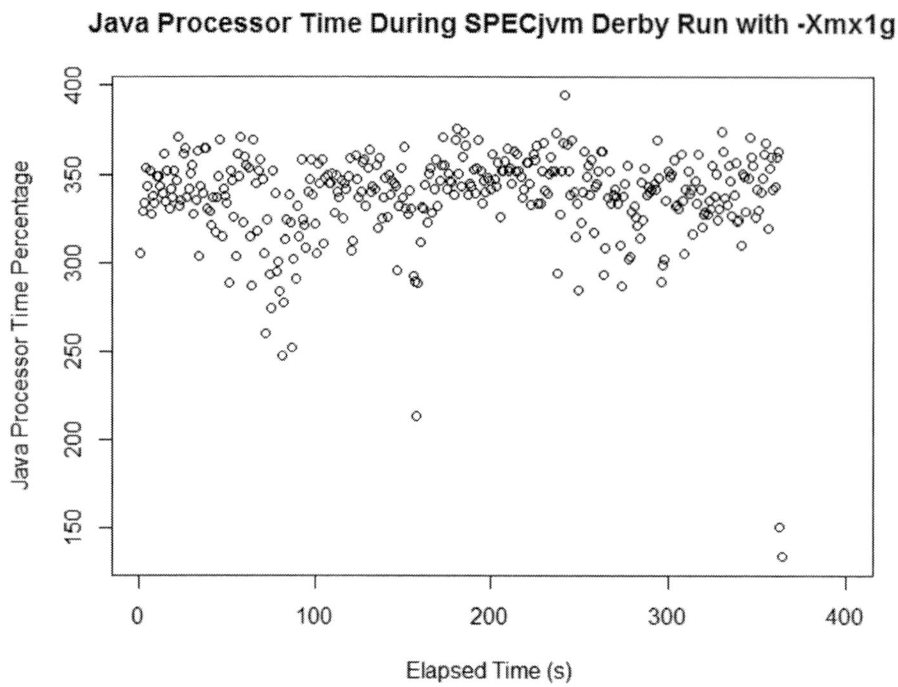

Figure 5: Java performance graph with Derby benchmark and modified memory heap size

After modifying the memory heap size, the data and graph appear roughly the same. It is possible that fluctuation caused this graph to look like the original Derby graph even though it should be different. Thus, the memory heap size does not seem to affect the performance, at least not significantly. A possible explanation of this is that the computer already has more than enough memory to run the SPECjvm experiments and therefore, additional memory will have little to no effect on the computer's performance or processing.

5 Conclusion

Modifying the memory heap size parameter seems to have little to no effect on the Java performance of our computer during the experiments. We believe the reasoning for this to be because the memory heap size is already more than sufficient at 1GB and thus adding in any more gigabytes of memory should have theoretically no effect on the performance. Thus, a sensible next step for these experiments is to try running the java benchmarks with lower maximum heap memory sizes, such as 500MB.

For the garbage collection options, it appears that the G1 garbage collection is faster in performance than the parallel and MarkSweep performance while it is unclear whether the parallel, or the MarkSweep garbage collection options is the slowest of the three.

Experimental Errors and Other Factors

The SPECjvm experiments were done on different days and thus different application on the computer were opened and running, varying the performance results. Another unexpected variable in our experiments was that we tested our SPECjvm runs on two different computers as our first computer broke partway through the tests. Thus, the slight differences in memory or processing across these computers may have played a role in our SPECjvm results. To remedy these errors, only the applications necessary for the experiments should have been open and the same computer should have been used the whole time.

The contributions of this paper are:

- 1) Understand the trade-offs between Java configurable parameters and the performance of Java workloads
- (2) Design experiments for different Java programs, and also non-Java programs to understand performance trade-offs
- (3) Conduct performance analysis without modifying the code of the Java programs

Acknowledgments

The author wishes to express their gratitude to his reviewers Suresh Chandra Bose and Moss Drake, whose assistance and feedback have been invaluable.

References

[1] "Standard Performance Evaluation Corporation." *SPEC - Standard Performance Evaluation Corporation*, Standard Performance Evaluation Corporation, spec.org/.

[2] Morgan, Johnny. "An Overview of Garbage Collection in Java - DZone Java." *Dzone.com*, DZone, 27 June 2017, dzone.com/articles/an-overview-of-garbage-collection-in-java.

[3] Lee, Sangmin. "Understanding Java Garbage Collection | CUBRID Blog." *Open Source Database*, CUBRID, 31 May 2017, www.cubrid.org/blog/understanding-java-garbage-collection/.

[4] "Windows 7 Performance Monitoring Tools." *SearchITChannel*, TechTarget, searchitchannel.techtarget.com/feature/Windows-7-performance-monitoring-tools.

[5] *RStudio Team (2015). RStudio: Integrated Development for R. RStudio, Inc., Boston, MA URL http://www.rstudio.com/.*

Unit Level "Secure by Design" Approach

Authors: Vasantharaju MS & Joshua Cajetan Rebelo

Vasantharaju_MS@McAfee.com Joshua.Rebelo@Siemens.com

Abstract

With cyber-attacks on the rise and high-profile breaches becoming the new normal, being on top of the current trends in cyber threats is a key to improve your cyber security posture. Organizations span the spectrum when it comes to the maturity around creating secured products. Overall, organizations should have a well-defined security software development lifecycle (SDL) process which embeds security in each SDLC process instead of considering security as a feature.

Any change to the application or environment, changes the attack surface. If you don't have a "secure by design" strategy at every stage - from product development to product deployment, addressing security can become very intimidating and challenging. Security findings found late in the release cycle or post release, can ask for architecture redesigning, which can be expensive.

The current scenario is that Unit test design and coverage in most cases covers the functionality and not the security aspect of the product. Security mostly gets addressed later in the SDL cycle, and the product team will rely on the penetration test results.

In this paper, we present a Unit level "secure by design" approach which will help in early security defect finding. This approach will help to address multiple layered security testing i.e. address security at Unit level. Many times, penetration test, and security test might not be able to penetrate deep into the product. This is where Unit level test will help to address security. Unit testing platform supports mocking and accessing private members which can be leveraged to ensure security at different abstraction layers of software. As more organizations are adopting Test Driven development (TDD), Unit level security testing will enforce security by design, thus, addressing security early in the SDL cycle.

Biography

Vasantharaju M.S. is a Senior Software Development Engineer at McAfee Software with over 9 years of experience in developing enterprise-class software. His past experiences include; designing and implementing back-office solution to address a Dodd-Frank clause, enhancing web crawler and vulnerability detection in SaaS based vulnerability scanner and executing multiple Proof-of-Concepts for enhancing SaaS based security management platform. He has a keen interest in application security and secure coding.

Joshua Cajetan Rebelo is a Security Researcher at Siemens with 13 years of experience in the security domain. He ensures that the products are under continuous development to incorporate the highest Security Software Development Lifecycle (SDL) standards and adheres to the Product Security Maturity Model (PSMM). He has vast experience in conducting security code reviews, evaluating software architecture for potential risk. He has expertise in Application security, System security, Cloud security, and Industrial Control System security. He is a mentor on product security to many teams. He also brings innovation with new ideas and has three patents issued to his credit.

Intended Audience

The target audience for this paper includes program managers, project managers, developers, quality assurance engineers, and IT professional who are familiar with the software security literature. This paper is also meant for people who are passionate about security and want to integrate security into their standard software development lifecycle (SDL) processes to enhance the product security maturity model to stay secured.

1 Introduction

In a typical SDLC approach, unit test is always written to ensure that the unit is functional. These functional unit tests take precedence over secure architecture design. These unit tests which include standard unit testing terminology will not be exhaustive enough to test all possible negative and attack scenarios. These gaps of unexplored code path are of interest to the cyber attackers. These gaps need to be considered, reviewed and addressed.

This paper ensures that

- The unit is secure
- Security is embedded at different abstraction layers of software.
- Unit test penetrate deeper into the application and increase the code coverage.
- Product teams write secure software at early stage of product development.

2 What is Secure Software?

Secure software exhibits the following characteristics:

- Takes care of implementation errors with exploitable effects
- Contains security features which cannot be bypassed
- Is self-protective
- Minimizes the consequence of successful attack ("fail well")

The multi-layered security can be achieved by adopting the STRIDE Threat-Model approach.

Spoofing identity

Tampering with data

Repudiation

Information disclosure

Denial of service

Elevation of privilege

This paper will help in writing unit test using this STRIDE model to get maximum security coverage, thus helping developers adopt a "Secure by Design" Approach at unit level.

Before we dive deep into the paper, let us understand what Test-driven development is and how we can use it in making the unit level security tests efficient in building multi-layered security.

Test-driven development is a software development process that relies on the repetition of a very short development cycle: first the developer writes an (initially failing) automated test case that defines a desired improvement or new function, then produces the minimum amount of code to pass that test, and finally refractors the new code to acceptable standards.

For the sake of this paper, the examples shown are for java development, but can be adopted in any other technology.

3 Test-driven development (TDD) life-cycle

1. Write the test
2. Run the test (there is no implementation code, test does not pass)
3. Write enough implementation code to make the test pass
4. Run all tests (tests pass)
5. Refractor
6. Repeat

Let us consider the requirement from product management of an application with logon functionality integrated to a database through the data access object layer (DAO).

Let us consider the following example of an insecure login application which didn't follow secure coding or design practices or TDD approach.

This example of login application is vulnerable to attacks like SQL injection, Sensitive Information disclosure, repudiation attacks, spoofing, tampering and privilege escalation etc

```
public boolean authenticate(String userName, String password)
{
    logger.trace("Authenticating the user="+userName+" with password="+password);
    String sql = "SELECT * from USERS where USERNAME ='"+userName+"' and PASSWORD='"+password+"'";
    try ( PreparedStatement stmt = connection.prepareStatement(sql);)
    {
        ResultSet rs = stmt.executeQuery(sql);

        if(rs.next())
            return true;
        else
            return false;

    }
    catch(SQLException sqlException)
    {
        logger.error(sqlException);
    }
    return false;
}
```

Figure 1: Insecure Login Application

If the unit test design and coverage was focused only on covering the functionality of the module and not the security aspect, then the unit test would be as follows.

```
public void testNullUser() {
    try {
        login.authenticate(null, "password");
    } catch (Exception e) {
        assertEquals(true, e instanceof FailedLoginException);
        assertEquals("Login failed due to username or password is null", e.getMessage());
    }
}

public void testEmptyUser() {

    try {
        login.authenticate("", "password");
    } catch (Exception e) {
        assertEquals(true, e instanceof FailedLoginException);
        assertEquals("Login failed due to username or password is null", e.getMessage());
    }
}


public void testValidUser()
{
    try {
        boolean bool = login.authenticate("Alpha","Alph@1");
        assertTrue(bool);
    } catch (Exception e) {

    }
}
```

Figure 2: Unit Test of insecure login Application

As seen in figure 2, the unit tests don't cover attacks like spoofing, tampering, repudiation, information disclosure, denial of service and privilege escalation as defined by the STRIDE model. In the next section we shall see how secure test-driven development approach addresses this problem.

4 Secure Test-Driven development

The following would be the approach of secure test-driven development to build secure software with multi-layered security:

1) Start Design discussion
2) Create Data flow diagram for all functionalities and work flows
3) Identification of mocking module
4) Threat Identification using STRIDE Threat Model
5) Unit test designing to detects identified threats
6) Run the test (there is no implementation code, test does not pass)
7) Write enough implementation code to make the test pass
8) Run all tests (tests pass)

Let us see how this Secure Test-Driven development can help transform the insecure login application seen in figure 1, into a secure application having multi-layered security in-built.

4.1 Identification of Mocking Modules

It is critical to identify the applicable mocking modules, since mocks are prerequisites for fast execution of tests and ability to concentrate on a single unit of functionality. By mocking dependencies external to the method that is being tested, developer can focus on the task at hand without spending time to set them up. Execution of tests without mocks tends to be slow. Good candidates for mocks are databases and scripting engines.

Following are some of the mocking module which can be leverage in writing unit test.

a) HSQLDB - to mock the database to test SQL injection attack and error / exception handling.
b) MOCKITO - to mock interfaces so that a dummy functionality can be added to a mock interface that can be used in unit testing.

4.1.1 Hyper SQL Database (HSQLDB)

Each database will have different dialects like hint or comment, add-on features like server-side executable and limitations. As seen below, we will be using hsqldb which will help to mock the DB for faster execution and to remove the external dependencies.

```
public void setUp() throws Exception {
    login = new ApplicationLogin();

    // Load HSQLDB Driver

    Class.forName("org.hsqldb.jdbc.JDBCDriver");

    // Clean up the public Schema
    destroy();

    //Set the connection object for login object
    ((ApplicationLogin) login).setConnection(getConnection());


    try (Connection connection = getConnection(); Statement statement = connection.createStatement();) {
        statement.execute("CREATE TABLE USERS ("
                + "ID INT NOT NULL, "
                + "USERNAME VARCHAR(50) NOT NULL,  "
                + "PASSWORD VARCHAR(50) NOT NULL)");
        connection.commit();

        statement.executeUpdate(
                "INSERT INTO USERS VALUES (1001,'Alpha', 'A1ph@!')");
        statement.executeUpdate("INSERT INTO USERS VALUES (1002,'Beta', 'BeT@!')");
        connection.commit();

    } catch (SQLException e) {
        e.printStackTrace();
    }

}
```

Figure 3: Using HSQLDB to create database for sample login application for Unit testing

Similarly other mocking modules like Mockito, PowerMock etc can be evaluated for applicability.

4.2 Threat Identification using STRIDE Model

For the logon functionality application (figure 1), following are some of the threats identified using the STRIDE Model.

What if:

- User tries to login with invalid username and password combination **(Spoofing, Tampering)**
- User tries to login with non-existing user **(Spoofing, Tampering)**
- DB connectivity lost due to injection attack. **(Information Disclosure, Denial of Service)**
- Long string inputs for username and password **(Denial of Service)**
- SQL exception is encountered **(Information Disclosure)**
- Unhandled or handled exception occurs **(Information Disclosure)**
- Sensitive data is been logged **(Repudiation, Information Disclosure)**
- Attackers tries Injection attacks **(Tampering, Spoofing)**
- Because of inadequate logging, malicious attacks go undetected **(Repudiation)**

4.3 Security Unit Test Designing

Once the threats and attack vectors are identified, the next step is to design security unit test for the identified threats and attack vectors.

4.3.1 Security Unit Test: STRIDE - Information Disclosure

Information disclosure threats involve the exposure of information to individuals who are not supposed to have access to it. Users are rightfully wary of submitting private details to a system. If it is possible for an attacker to publicly reveal user data at large, whether anonymously or as an authorized user, there will be an immediate loss of confidence and a substantial period of reputation loss.

An important aspect of secure application development is to design a robust error and exception handling module. Error messages give an attacker great insight into the inner working of an application. Error handling code assures the application fails safely under all possible error conditions, expected and unexpected. This diminishes the chance of any uncaught errors "Bubbling up" to the front end of an application.

A piece of application code will have different layers of abstraction. A good approach to error handling and exception handling is to assert for specific exception at different layers of abstraction. Thus, ensuring a defense-in-depth architecture is in place.

Following are examples of Error and Exception handling unit tests to address information disclosure vulnerabilities.

```java
@SuppressWarnings("serial")
class FailedLoginException extends Exception
{
    private String reason ;

    public FailedLoginException(String reason) {
        this.reason = reason;
    }

    @Override
    public String getMessage() {
        return "Login failed due to "+reason;
    }
}
```

Figure 4: Custom Exception Handler Class

```java
public void testNullUser() {
    try {
        login.authenticate(null, "password");
    } catch (Exception e) {
        assertEquals(true, e instanceof FailedLoginException);
        assertEquals("Login failed due to username or password is null", e.getMessage());
    }
}

public void testEmptyUser() {

    try {
        login.authenticate("", "password");
    } catch (Exception e) {
        assertEquals(true, e instanceof FailedLoginException);
        assertEquals("Login failed due to username or password is null", e.getMessage());
    }
}

public void testNullPassword() {
    try {
        login.authenticate("user", null );
    } catch (Exception e) {
        assertEquals(true, e instanceof FailedLoginException);
        assertEquals("Login failed due to username or password is null", e.getMessage());
    }
}

public void testEmptyPassword() {

    try {
        login.authenticate("user", "");
    } catch (Exception e) {
        assertEquals(true, e instanceof FailedLoginException);
        assertEquals("Login failed due to username or password is null", e.getMessage());
    }
}

public void testEmptyUserAndPassword() {

    try {
        login.authenticate("", "");
    } catch (Exception e) {
        assertEquals(true, e instanceof FailedLoginException);
        assertEquals("Login failed due to username or password is null", e.getMessage());
    }
}

public void testNullUserAndPassword() {
    try {
        login.authenticate(null, null);
    } catch (Exception e) {
        assertEquals(true, e instanceof FailedLoginException);
        assertEquals("Login failed due to username or password is null", e.getMessage());
    }
}
```

Figure 5: Unit tests for detecting "Information Disclosure Vulnerabilities"

As seen in figure 4 ad figure 5, the security unit test are designed to handle all negative scenarios to detect and prevent information disclosure vulnerabilities and tampering attacks by ensuring that appropriate exceptions with messages are thrown and handled.

4.3.2 Security Unit Test: STRIDE - Tampering

Injection Attacks are examples of tampering attacks. Injection attacks refer to a broad class of attack vectors that allow an attacker to supply untrusted input to a program, which gets processed by an interpreter as part of a command or query which changes the course of execution of that program.

Details of injection attack can be foundhere.

In the next section, we shall see how different web attacks (injection attacks) can be detected using Unit test

4.3.2.1 Unit test to detect "SQL Injection" attack

```
public void testSQLInjectionSimpleSQLInjectionWithoutKnowingUsernameorPassword()
{
    try {
        boolean bool = login.authenticate("SQLInjection' or 1=1--","unknown");
        assertEquals(false,bool);
    } catch (Exception e) {
        e.printStackTrace();
        assertEquals(true, e instanceof FailedLoginException);
        assertEquals("Login failed due to username or password is not bound", e.getMessage());
    }
}

public void testSQLInjectionUNIONAuthenticateUserWithoutKnowingPassword()
{
    try {
        boolean bool = login.authenticate("Beta' UNION SELECT * from USERS where USERNAME='Beta","BeT@");
        assertEquals(false,bool);
    } catch (Exception e) {
        e.printStackTrace();
        assertEquals(true, e instanceof FailedLoginException);
        assertEquals("Login failed due to username or password is not bound", e.getMessage());
    }
}

public void testSQLInjectionCOMMENTAuthenticateUserWithoutKnowingPassword()
{
    try {
        boolean bool = login.authenticate("Beta' -- # /*","BeT@ */");
        assertEquals(false,bool);
    } catch (Exception e) {
        e.printStackTrace();
        assertEquals(true, e instanceof FailedLoginException);
        assertEquals("Login failed due to username or password is not bound", e.getMessage());
    }
}

public void testSQLInjectionImpersonateAsRandomUser()
{
    try {
        boolean bool = login.authenticate("unknown' OR USERNAME is not null UNION SELECT * from USERS where USERNAME='Beta","BeT@");
        assertEquals(false,bool);
    } catch (Exception e) {
        e.printStackTrace();
        assertEquals(true, e instanceof FailedLoginException);
        assertEquals("Login failed due to username or password is not bound", e.getMessage());
    }
}
```

Figure 6: Unit tests to detect different type of "SQL Injections"

4.3.2.2 Unit test to detect "Stored Cross-Site Scripting" attack

Cross-Site Scripting (XSS) attack is an injection attack where an attacker uses a web application to send malicious code to a different end user. Flaws that allow these attacks to succeed are widespread and occur anywhere a web application uses input from a user within the output it generates without validating or output encoding it. While performing output encoding, it is important to understand the different potential contexts related to XSS and how the context-specific filtering is done.

In this paper, we shall talk only about stored XSS attack. Reflective and DOM based XSS attacks are out-of-scope of unit test.

Let's assume that a successful injection is possible in username parameter. As seen below, we shall save the injected XSS string into the database as part of Setup.

```
try (Connection connection = getConnection(); Statement statement = connection.createStatement();) {
    statement.execute("CREATE TABLE USERS ("
            + "ID INT NOT NULL, "
            + "USERNAME VARCHAR(50) NOT NULL,  "
            + "EMAIL VARCHAR(50) NOT NULL,  "
            + "PASSWORD VARCHAR(50) NOT NULL)");
    connection.commit();

    statement.executeUpdate("INSERT INTO USERS VALUES (1001, 'xX<<XxX>>Xx' , 'alpha@pnsqc.com' , 'A1ph@!')");
    statement.executeUpdate("INSERT INTO USERS VALUES (1002, '\" onload=alert(1)'  , 'beta@pnsqc.com'  , 'BeT@!')");
    statement.executeUpdate("INSERT INTO USERS VALUES (1003, '<script>alert(1)</alert>' , 'gamma@pnsqc.com' , 'Gamm@!')");
    connection.commit();

} catch (SQLException e) {
    e.printStackTrace();
}
```

Figure 7: Setup creation - Database table with the injection in username field

```
public void testIfStoredXSSPossibleWithHTMLInjection() throws SQLException, ServletException, IOException   {
    HttpServletRequest hsreq = Mockito.mock(HttpServletRequest.class);
    when(hsreq.getParameter("userId")).thenReturn("1003");

    HttpServletResponse hsres = Mockito.mock(HttpServletResponse.class);
    StringWriter sw = new StringWriter();
    PrintWriter pw = new PrintWriter(sw);
    when(hsres.getWriter()).thenReturn(pw);

    UserDao ud = new UserDao();
    ud.setConnection(getConnection());
    UserServlet us = new UserServlet();
    us.setUdao(ud);
    us.doGet(hsreq, hsres);
    pw.flush();

    assertFalse( sw.toString().contains("<script>alert(1)</alert>"));

}

public void testIfStoredXSSPossibleWithIntrusiveHTMLInjection() throws SQLException, ServletException, IOException  {
    HttpServletRequest hsreq = Mockito.mock(HttpServletRequest.class);
    when(hsreq.getParameter("userId")).thenReturn("1001");

    HttpServletResponse hsres = Mockito.mock(HttpServletResponse.class);
    StringWriter sw = new StringWriter();
    PrintWriter pw = new PrintWriter(sw);
    when(hsres.getWriter()).thenReturn(pw);

    UserDao ud = new UserDao();
    ud.setConnection(getConnection());
    UserServlet us = new UserServlet();
    us.setUdao(ud);
    us.doGet(hsreq, hsres);
    pw.flush();

    assertFalse( sw.toString().contains("xX<<XxX>>Xx"));

}
```

Figure 8: Unit test to detect "Stored Cross-Site Scripting" attack

As seen in figure 8, a successful stored XSS attack is detect in unit test 'testIfStoredXSSPossibleWithHTMLInjection'

4.3.2.3 Unit test to detect "Directory Traversal" attack

Directory traversal is a web exploit which allows attackers to access restricted directories and execute commands outside of the web server's root directory

Let us consider an example of application which allows a user to upload a logo.

```
import java.io.File;
import java.io.IOException;

import org.apache.commons.lang3.StringUtils;
import org.apache.log4j.Logger;

public class UserLogo {

    private String basePath = "";
    private File baseDir = new File(basePath);
    private static Logger log = Logger.getLogger(UserLogo.class);

    public File getUserLogoPath(User user) throws IOException
    {
        if( user==null || StringUtils.isBlank(user.getName()) )
            throw new NullPointerException();

        File path = new File (baseDir , user.getName());

        if( ! path.getAbsolutePath().equals(path.getCanonicalPath()))
        {
            log.error("Possible Directory traversal");
            throw new IOException("Directory traversal");
        }

        return path;
    }
}
```

Figure 9: Examples of userLogo application

```
public void testPathTraversal() throws SQLException
{
    User user = new User("../../1","sample@pnsqc.com");
    userLogo = new UserLogo();

    try
    {
        userLogo.getUserLogoPath(user);
    }
    catch(IOException ioe)
    {
        assertEquals("Directory traversal", ioe.getMessage());
    }
}

public void testValidPath() throws SQLException, IOException
{
    User user = new User("1","sample@pnsqc.com");
    userLogo = new UserLogo();

    File path = userLogo.getUserLogoPath(user);
    assertEquals("C:\\1", path.getAbsolutePath());
}

public void testNull() throws SQLException, IOException
{
    User user = new User("","sample@pnsqc.com");
    userLogo = new UserLogo();

    try
    {
        userLogo.getUserLogoPath(user);
    }
    catch(NullPointerException npe)
    {
        assertTrue(npe instanceof NullPointerException);
    }
}
```

Figure 10: Unit test to detect "Directory Traversal" Attack

As seen in the figure 10, the unit test detects directory traversal attack and also the null point exception thrown for negative scenario like NULL path.

4.3.3 Security Unit Test: STRIDE - Repudiation

Repudiation threats are associated with users who deny performing an action without other parties having any way to prove otherwise due to insufficient auditing or recordkeeping of their activity. For example, a user performs an illegal operation in a system that lacks the ability to trace the prohibited operations.

Following are examples of unit test which takes care of these repudiation attacks.

```
@PrepareForTest(LogManager.class)
public void testPasswordIsNotLoogedInSucessfulLogin() throws SQLException
{
    PowerMockito.mockStatic(LogManager.class);

    MockLogger ml = new MockLogger(Login.class.toString());
    when(LogManager.getLogger(Login.class)).thenReturn(ml);

    login = new ApplicationLogin();

    //Set the connection object for login object
    ((ApplicationLogin) login).setConnection(getConnection());

    try
    {
        boolean bool = login.authenticate("Alpha", "A1ph@!");
        assertEquals("Make sure Succeful login", true,  bool );
        assertEquals("Make sure Password is not logged", false,  ml.sb.toString().contains("A1pha!"));

    }
    catch(Exception e)
    {

    }
}
```

Figure 11: Unit Test to detect "Information Disclosure" for successful login

```
@PrepareForTest(LogManager.class)
public void testPasswordIsNotLoogedInFailedLogin() throws SQLException
{
    PowerMockito.mockStatic(LogManager.class);

    MockLogger ml = new MockLogger(Login.class.toString());
    when(LogManager.getLogger(Login.class)).thenReturn(ml);

    login = new ApplicationLogin();

    //Set the connection object for login object
    ((ApplicationLogin) login).setConnection(getConnection());

    try
    {
        boolean bool = login.authenticate("alpha", "a1");
        assertEquals("Make sure UnSuccessful login", false,  bool );
    }
    catch(Exception e)
    {
        assertEquals("Make sure Password is not logged", false,  ml.sb.toString().contains("a1"));
    }
}
```

Figure 12: Unit Test to detect "Information Disclosure" for unsuccessful login

As seen in figure 11 & 12, enough data is logged into logs for all successful and unsuccessful logins. And at the same time the unit test detect if any sensitive PII data like username & password is logged in logs.

```
@PrepareForTest(LogManager.class)
public void testLengthyUsernameIsNotLoggedInFailedLogin() throws SQLException
{
    PowerMockito.mockStatic(LogManager.class);

    MockLogger ml = new MockLogger(Login.class.toString());
    ml.setLevel(Level.ERROR);
    when(LogManager.getLogger(Login.class)).thenReturn(ml);

    login = new ApplicationLogin();

    //Set the connection object for login object
    ((ApplicationLogin) login).setConnection(getConnection());

    try
    {
        boolean bool = login.authenticate("123456789012345678901234567890123456789012345678901234567890", "a1");

    }
    catch(Exception e)
    {
        assertEquals("Make sure FailedLoginException is thrown" , true ,( e instanceof FailedLoginException ));
        assertEquals("Make sure Username is not logged", false,   ml.sb.toString().contains("123456789012345678901234567890123456789012345678901234567890"));
        assertEquals("Make sure exception message is logged", true,   ml.sb.toString().contains("username or password is not bound"));
    }
}
```

Figure 13: Unit test detects that enough data is logged with proper exception for negative scenarios

```
@PrepareForTest(LogManager.class)
public void testExceptionMessageLoggedInFailedLogin() throws SQLException
{
    PowerMockito.mockStatic(LogManager.class);

    MockLogger ml = new MockLogger(Login.class.toString());
    ml.setLevel(Level.ERROR);
    when(LogManager.getLogger(Login.class)).thenReturn(ml);

    login = new ApplicationLogin();

    //Set the connection object for login object
    ((ApplicationLogin) login).setConnection(getConnection());

    try
    {
        boolean bool = login.authenticate(null, "blank");

    }
    catch(Exception e)
    {
        assertEquals("Make sure FailedLoginException is thrown" , true , e instanceof FailedLoginException );
        assertEquals("Make sure Password is not logged", false,  ml.sb.toString().contains("blank"));
        assertEquals("Make sure exception message is logged", true,   ml.sb.toString().contains("username or password is null"));
    }
}
```

Figure 14: Unit test to detect that accurate exception is logged

As seen in all of the unit tests above, accurate and adequate data is logged for different types of exception. This is very important to detect repudiation attack.

4.4 Secure Application

Using the above mentioned unit test for secure test-driven development a secure application can now be developed.

Following is an example of secure login application

4.4.1 Secure login application – Defends against Injection and repudiation attacks.

```
@Override
public boolean authenticate(String userName, String password) throws FailedLoginException
{

    if ( StringUtils.isBlank(userName) || StringUtils.isBlank(password))
    {
        logger.info("username or password is null for attempting user = <<"+userName+">>");
        throw new FailedLoginException("username or password is null");
    }

    if ( userName.length() > 50 || password.length() > 50) // 128 is derived from length of varchar in USERS table
    {
        logger.info("username or password is not bound");  // Possible DoS Attack >> Intentionally not Loggin the username or password
        throw new FailedLoginException("username or password is not bound");
    }

    if ( ! checkComplexity( password))
    {
        logger.info("username or password complexity is not met for attempting user = <<"+userName+">>");
        throw new FailedLoginException("username or password complexity is not met");
    }

    logger.debug("Authenticating the user="+userName);

    try ( PreparedStatement stmt = connection.prepareStatement("SELECT * from USERS where USERNAME=? and PASSWORD=? ");)
    {
        stmt.setString(1, userName);
        stmt.setString(2, hashPassword(password));
        ResultSet rs = stmt.executeQuery();

        if(rs.next())
            return true;
        else
            return false;

    }
    catch(SQLException sqlException)
    {
        logger.error("Authentication for user="+userName+" failed due to"+sqlException);
        throw new FailedLoginException(sqlException.getMessage());
    }
    catch(Throwable t)
    {
        logger.error("Authentication for user="+userName+" failed due to"+t);
    }
    return false;
}
```

Figure 15: Secure Login Application

As seen, this login application protects against repudiation attacks and injection attack like SQL Injection.

4.4.2 Secure application - Defends against Stored Cross-Site Scripting attack

```
    public void doGet(HttpServletRequest request, HttpServletResponse response)
       throws ServletException, IOException {


       Long userId= new Long(request.getParameter("userId"));
       User user = udao.getUserById(userId);
       // Set response content type
       response.setContentType("text/html");

       // Actual logic goes here.
       PrintWriter out = response.getWriter();
       out.println("<h1>" + StringEscapeUtils.escapeHtml4( user.getName() ) + "</h1>");
       out.println("<h2>" + StringEscapeUtils.escapeHtml4( user.getName() ) + "</h2>");
       out.println("<img src=\"" + EscapeUtils.escapeHTMLAttribute( user.getName() ) + ".jpg\"/>");


    }

    public void destroy() {
       // do nothing.
    }


}

class EscapeUtils
{
    public static String escapeHTMLAttribute(String str)
    {

        return str.replace("\"", "\\\"");
    }

    public static String escapeJavascript(String str)
    {
        return str.replace("'", "\'");
    }
}
```

4.4.3 Secure application - Defends against Directory Traversal attack

```
import java.io.File;
import java.io.IOException;

import org.apache.commons.lang3.StringUtils;
import org.apache.log4j.Logger;

public class UserLogo {

    private String basePath = "";
    private File baseDir = new File(basePath);
    private static Logger log = Logger.getLogger(UserLogo.class);

    public File getUserLogoPath(User user) throws IOException
    {
        if( user==null || StringUtils.isBlank(user.getName()) )
            throw new NullPointerException();

        File path = new File (baseDir , user.getName());

        if( ! path.getAbsolutePath().equals(path.getCanonicalPath()))
        {
            log.error("Possible Directory traversal");
            throw new IOException("Directory traversal");
        }

        return path;
    }
}
```

5 Conclusion

As demonstrated in this paper, we see that secure test-driven development will help to build secure software with multi-layered security using the Unit Level "Secure By Design" Approach. The developed secure robust software can handle many of the attacks defined by the STRIDE model. With all security controls in place, the attack surface will be reduced to a minimum thus improving the security posture. This change of settings the mindset for secure development is crucial in addressing security.

6 References

[1] Unit Testing : https://en.wikipedia.org/wiki/Unit_testing

[2] Mockito: http://site.mockito.org/

[3] HSQLDB : http://hsqldb.org/

[4] STRIDE : https://msdn.microsoft.com/en-us/library/ee823878(v=cs.20).aspx

[5] TDD : https://en.wikipedia.org/wiki/Test-driven_development

[6] OWASP: https://www.owasp.org/index.php

What's next for traditional Functional QA Managers?

Author: Jim Trentadue

Email Address: Jim.Trentadue@outlook.com

Abstract

With the rapid implementation of Agile development in most IT environments, the traditional roles of functional QA managers are changing. Testing is now the responsibility of the product owner; day-to-day testing tasks and accountabilities are largely owned by the product team and defect status is discussed on a quick daily meeting. But yet all of the testing personnel report into the QA Manager from an organizational viewpoint. What are the new responsibilities of the QA Manager if they are not responsible for any of the above?

There are avenues for the traditional, functional QA manager and they involve owning the quality, the release management principles, the technical solutions, a smaller testing operational team and advancement of new testing areas within the Agile lifecycle.

This is different from how QA Managers have functioned before, but it is a transformation of their career putting them right in the middle, and even ahead of the curve in some cases, as opposed to being left behind.

Biography

Jim Trentadue has more than eighteen years of experience as a leader in the software testing field. Jim has focused on test execution, automation, management, environment management, standards deployment, and test tool implementation. Jim is a regular speaker at software testing events, like STAR, BS/AD, STP and QAI Conferences.

Recently, Jim has worked on the vendor side for test automation solution companies engaging customer and prospects. Currently, Jim has started his own Test Automation Foundations & Principles workshop aimed at helping manual testers get started with automation as well as working as a consultant to restart stalled automation efforts.

1 Introduction

For traditional QA Managers, we continue to see the world dramatically change all around us. With the advent of Agile, it's said that the product teams own the quality, not just the QA team as we once knew. This has been a game changer for us. If we think of the traditional roles from Waterfall with Project Managers, Business Analysts, Developers, Quality Assurance and Test Analysts, there were managers that typically supported each one of the functions.

Each team owned their specialty for their project and to their craft. But how has this changed for testing within Agile projects? Consider this transformation, typical in most organizations:

Role	Waterfall Role	Agile Role	Agile Testing role
Project Manager / Project Coordinator	Project Manager, owner of the scope, time & cost for project	Many have converted to Scrum Masters	Contributes to the testing scope definition
Business Analysts / BA Managers	Business Analyst, owner of the requirements definition for project	Many have converted to Scrum Masters or Product Owners; define the epics and stories	Contributes to the testing scope definition
Developers / Development Managers	Development, owner of the development delivery for project	Developers & Dev Managers still own the technologies used; define development activities for project	Contributes to the testing scope definition
Testers / Testing Managers	Testing, owner of the testing and quality assurance definition & delivery for project	Varies, but role is very different. Some managers have gone the way of Scrum Masters, others still own quality, but not readily enforceable	Contributes to the testing scope definition

It seems as if the full Agile team wants to contribute to what is being tested and to have input to the testing scope – what QA / Testing Managers used to do. This does not appear to be as prevalent on the Product Owner side, Scrum Master or Development side. Sure, the team contributes to this, but in my experience, I have not witnessed team members being as influential as they are to what they believe is the right approach to testing. This is a great approach to testing collaboration, sorely needed to increase the quality.

There has no mention yet for those associates & managers that were always a step behind in the project lifecycle, such as: Database Administrators & Managers, System Administrators and Infrastructure Managers. The inception of DevOps changed the world for them for the better and the IT industry continues to forge ahead strongly in this direction.

Where does this leave traditional QA Managers? I've heard some crazy transitions, even one change where the QA Manager at a previous employer transitioned to being HR Manager for IT! There is hope, and excitement ahead for QA Leaders, being creative and innovative.

2 High-Level focused areas

Here are some areas I have seen QA Leaders morph into and some that are still untapped by and large within the industry. Consider the options below. I have broken the roles into more process-oriented roles and technical-oriented roles:

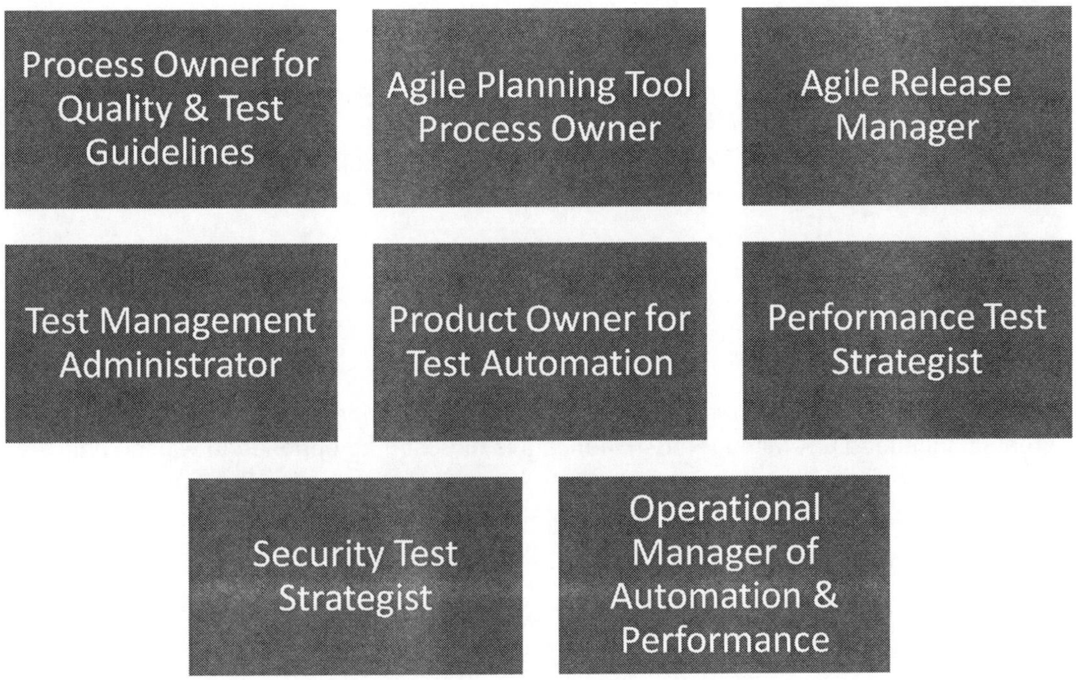

Here is a brief description of each and will be elaborated on more in the upcoming sections:

<u>Process-Oriented</u>

Process Owner for Quality & Test Guidelines:

Helping set the standard of what each test should have included minimally, factoring in regression, negative, boundary, equivalized class testing just to name a few testing types.

Agile Planning Tool Process Owner:

Great for process-oriented QA Managers focusing on the overall quality of the Agile process. Quality reviews for how epics, stories, defects and test results are written and reported.

Agile Release Manager:

Bringing good release management practices back into the fold to ensure all criteria has been satisfied for a successful deployment to each promotion stage.

Technical-Oriented

Test Management Administrator:

By owning the administration of the test management solution, the QA Manager can ensure releases are on schedule and the defect burn is trending the right way to list two simple metrics.

Product Owner for Test Automation:

As some test automation specialists are used to fulfill operational requests and not dedicated to the specified product team, the QA Manager is the product owner for overall products requests.

Performance Test Strategist:

Incorporating performance testing into each sprint is more theory than practice currently, but a great chance for a QA Manager to influence this direction as opposed to waiting until the end.

Security Test Strategist:

Similar to that of performance test strategist, fusing security testing into each sprint is rarely done in most cases. Another great opportunity for a QA Manager to include these into the culture.

Operational Manager for Automation & Performance:

With automation & performance specialists deployed on to product teams, there should be a good balance for operational personnel as well looking at the maintenance of the solution(s).

These eight areas may or may not be a full-time role in and of itself, but two or three collectively are certainly secure ways where QA Managers can ensure they are embedded not only to each of the Agile teams, but also to the overall Agile process.

QA Managers have shown skillset in some of the following areas: holding to the quality process, negotiating on testing breath vs. depth, collaborating with other stakeholders, coordinating with peers, investigating new testing approaches, implementing testing solutions. The definition in each of these areas maps very well to the skillset most QA Managers already possess.

3 Section breakout

Process-Oriented

Process Owner for Quality & Test Guidelines:

QA Managers have long been known to be the owners of quality in the IT industry. In this section, we'll examine the make-up of quality of tests vs. the test types used. This is where QA / Test Management can shine and has great potential to do so. This responsibility would require with getting more intimate with the test cases (primarily manual test cases for now), than might have been done previously.

What are components of high-quality test cases? Here are some criteria the industry has thrown around for quite some time:

- ✓ Tests must be written with clear starting and end points
- ✓ Tests need to be written in such a manner that anyone can execute them
- ✓ Tests must be written using a modular approach (even if grouped in one test case). Automation specialists will be able to automate this much easier if so
- ✓ Test author provides an appendix spelling out any and all acronyms used in test case
- ✓ Test data is not hard-coded. New tests are not generated just for testing a different set of data with the same steps and procedures

That's a good enough checklist to start for QA / Test Management to use for all tests across product teams. Lean criteria verification makes this Agile-friendly to Product Owners, but compliant for those working in regulatory environment or have to undergo audits.

With regards to the test types used, QA Management can help define the structure within the test management solution (regardless of how formal or not formal a solution is for this). As testers are creating tests for the assigned stories, it's in my experience that the test follows the straight path primarily. I won't refer to just the "happy path", but many are not expanding to the various test types that are recognized by the testing community.

There is opportunity to define each test type that should be included within each story, with the understanding that the scope of the testing type is resident with that story only. The testing types can be any or all of the combination below to give a sample listing:

Negative	Boundary
Equivalent Class	Security
Component	Exploratory

Notice that regression testing was not listed. That is imperative for every release and may or may not be included within the sprint. Product teams are dedicating sprints for regression testing, making the testing type listing above even more critical to ensure the tests are of high-caliber.

Agile Tool(s) Process Owner:

There is a growing trend among the QA / Test Management community and that's pursuing their Scrum Master certification. This is not typically where the skillset lies for test leadership, but they are broadening their horizons, as well as going for their PMP (Project Management Professional) certification to increase their marketability.

The Agile planning tool is at the heart of Agile development, but it certainly does not stop there. Let's examine this a little deeper:

Epic	What is the criteria that needs to be said about the quality of this high-level requirement in essence? Who regulates and governs that for the rest of the team? The Product Owners own this yes, but quality leaders can assist greatly.
Stories	Are there defined guidelines that state how a story should be written and what details need to be included within this? Is there anyone measuring the story-effectiveness? For example: When a story has been given initially to the development and testing team, how many times does this have to go back and forth? How many hours or days were impacted because of this. Granted this is a key principle of Agile, but the goal is not just to accumulate technical debt right out of the gate. It would be nice if there someone was helping measure this across teams to identify training gaps and areas of improvement of the overall Agile process.
Defects	This should not have changed greatly, but is anyone doing a quality-defect review for defects reported? The report should ensure the defect is addressing a singular point, clearly states the problem, lists the software build and environment tested, and finally, sequentially states the step-by-step details to reproduce. By having base criteria documented and knowing these are under review from QA Management for adherence, the developer is better equipped to analyze / fix the issue quickly, the tester (original or new tester) to retest with a solid understanding of the problem and fix, and for the Product Owner to accept the story as complete because of the quality put in throughout the process.
Test Results	Much like the defect portion of this section, the standards for reporting test results should not have varied much at all. Depending on what you need from the execution run, you may have to capture a bit more or less. For example, do you need accompanying screen shots for the validation points in your test or do you need to show a pass / fail on each corresponding step? This part is well drawn out for QA Leadership to assist and consult each of the Product Owners during the testing time of the sprint.

Agile Release Manager:

Following along the lines of ensuring the quality of tests and the test types used, QA Managers are in a strong position to help govern the acceptance criteria process for the overall release. Each sprint should account for this, but who is watching the overall release plan for adherence to the agreements made? Test Leadership can be the Product Owner's best friend in this capacity.

The key Agile solution to govern is the Continuous Integration process. Most IT organizations are utilizing a Continuous Integration (CI) solution for integrating the builds with the speed of the Agile process. Becoming an administrator for this can help ensure the right pieces are going into the right build, with the right adherence followed.

With this type of solution being used in almost every Agile development process, there may be struggles to find one person take ownership of the solution itself and the guidelines that all should follow. Another great opportunity for QA Leadership to manage and own.

Technical-Oriented

Test Management Administrator:

Of all areas that are the best fit for QA Leadership, this should be the most natural. There may be managers that need to learn the technical aspect of making configuration changes within the solution or how to integrate into other systems, but here are system elements that need to be defined, configured and connected into your Test Management or Application Lifecycle System.

Defined	Configured	Connected
Requirement records	Requirement → Test Case workflow	Agile Planning
Test Plan entities	Test Case → Defect workflow	Continuous Integration
Test Design template	Defect → Test Case workflow	Test Automation
Test Case forms	Test Case → Requirement workflow	Performance Test
Test Execution records	Defect → Requirement workflow	Configuration Management
Defect forms		
Defect reports		

If all of these elements are defined properly, this can be a very smooth & streamline process that allows for QA management oversight to ensure proper testing regardless of the SDLC used.

Testing leadership is in a strong position with Product Owners & Testers to ensure the right amount of information is listed within the story. Ideally this would be tracking at the scenario-level as the detailed information is in the Test Management solution itself.

QA Managers are the best to facilitate this process by first implementing the technical constructs as listed above.

Product Owner for Test Automation:

Many of the items listed until this point are not full-time positions themselves. A collection of a few of the areas of interest for QA Leadership will add value to the organization. However, this area would be a full-time role being a Product Owner for Test Automation.

Test Automation could encompass both Functional Test Automation and Performance Testing. Not that this needs the extra work for prioritizing Performance Tests because Functional Test Automation is enough! The focus should be on component-level automation that can apply for any type of testing. This also applies for API / Web Service Testing as much as UI automation.

Think of the responsibilities that Product Owners have & see how an automation team functions:

Solution — Ownership of the Automation solution

- Stays on top of product updates, upgrades, new libraries, licensing and solution alignment with the systems being tested

Program — Total ownership of the program

- Defines the vision of what automation will test and what it will not, manages the backlog and implements in sprint or regression cycles, and prioritizes all items often and as appropriate

Stories — Writes the epic or story

- After the epic is defined, drafts each automation story, understanding the technical dependency on how each outweigh the manual testing effort

Acceptance — Define criteria

- The automation module should execute without failure, work with the module that flows before and after logically, and meet the standards of the overall framework

If Test Leadership follows this guideline, this can be a great position as they are responsible for the success of automation, and ultimately test success. More organizations are leveraging automation as a service & the QA Manager is in prime position to be the Product Owner for this.

The area of caution here is not to attempt to replace all testing with automation. If working in a service capacity, the criteria of how the request comes in is just as critical. It will be QA / Test Leadership to negotiate and work with the requestor as to what they need to have defined and documented prior to a story making it into the queue.

The good news is that this expands beyond just the QA world. This applies for anyone who has an automation request, not just a functional test automation request from the QA team. This will be new for QA Management, but exciting nonetheless.

Performance Test Strategist:

Performance testing has been organized as a separate team and has been done typically at the end of the release cycles regardless of SDLC used in many organizations. There is a large push to integrate performance testing into sprints, but that has proven to be more theory than practice. This is still an unknown entity on how to loop this in for each sprint.

A hands-on QA Manager can help define the performance testing objectives per sprint and for the overall release. This person would also be the owner & champion of the solution being used. Having a test strategist apply this approach early, here is what can be achieved and how the role can be positioned to stakeholders:

- ✓ Bottlenecks identified and remediated early
- ✓ Continuous performance tests run like functional automated tests
- ✓ Additional infrastructure needs identified
- ✓ Code modifications made early as opposed to the very end, usually crashing schedules

Coupled within the process, QA Leaders can integrate this strategy nicely with a Product Owner.

Security Test Strategist:

Security testing can get even more ambiguous on defining what to do than performance testing. These are two of the biggest elements of non-functional testing and have gone largely unapplied into the actual Agile sprint cycles. This goes well beyond penetration testing that the security, infrastructure or network team may do. A QA Manager may not know all of the security tests to run immediately, but can work closely with the teams mentioned for penetration testing to form a solid test strategy. It may be an array of tests that get run per sprint or determines at which sprint it's best to be run in. Solid technical testing knowledge required, but also coordinating with others.

Operational Manager for Automation & Performance:

This is another area that lines up closely with the Product Owner role of Test Automation. Assuming the QA Manager is the Product Owner for this team, the work that is being done is usually part of an operational team. This means non-sprints, no dedicated resource to a product team if you are part of the operational team. Functional automation as part of the sprints is truly an effective team member, but let's paint the following scenario:

- ➢ Sprint 1 has automation work and is completed in sprint 1
- ➢ Sprint 2 has automation work built on sprint 1 and is completed in sprint 2
- ➢ Sprint 3 has automation work built on sprints 1 & 2 and is completed in sprint 3

- ➢ Sprint 4 has automation work built on sprints 1-3, but is broken due to an element change

This can either accumulate as technical debt or given to the operational team to help repair and get the sprint teams back on pace. Managing an Operational Test Automation team will not only get this resolved, but will also manage and grow the overall automation regression strategy.

4 Conclusion

The Agile world seems to have one of the largest impacts on the role and function of the traditional QA & Test Manager. As the Product Teams own the day-to-day direction of testing and the quality of the release, QA Leadership is not always included in this mix. But we know there is value add for them in the organization, but where is the right fit?

It's time for QA Leaders to redefine themselves and jump into areas of focus. Leaders will gravitate either towards the process-oriented path, or the technical-oriented path. Both are needed. The sections outlined in this paper will get managers back on the career path they have chosen, and most likely, with more enthusiasm as they can expand in areas of interest.

This will be evident to the individual and to the organization, which should lead to a successful and stable future ahead!

Kolibri

Feeling like a fake

- The Impostor Syndrome

Berglind Ósk Bergsdóttir
PNSQC 2017

What is the Impostor Syndrome?

What is the Impostor Syndrome?

Feeling like a fake

- Perfectionism
- Unrealistic expectations
- Self-doubt
- Dismissal of compliments
- People pleaser

What is the Impostor Syndrome?

Feeling like a fake

- Stress
- Anxiety
- Overworking
- Burnout
- Depression

What is the Impostor Syndrome?

Feeling like a fake

Feeling like a fake

How to overcome it?

How to overcome it?

Feeling like a fake

Break patterns

How to overcome it?

Feeling like a fake

Recognise your success

How to overcome it?

Feeling like a fake

Recognise your strengths

(and weaknesses)

How to overcome it?

Feeling like a fake

Ask for help

How to overcome it?

Feeling like a fake

Be authentic

How to overcome it?

Feeling like a fake

Break the downward spiral

Feeling like a fake

Work culture

Work culture

Feeling like a fake

Agile

Work culture

Feeling like a fake

Pair programming

Work culture

Feeling like a fake

Feedback

Work culture

Feeling like a fake

Social rules

Work culture

Feeling like a fake

Working agreement

Work culture

Kolibri working agreement

Feeling like a fake

- Practice open and constructive communication
- Ask for help and work in teams, especially in difficult situations
- Assume the best in people.
- Engage when present.
- Listen more than we speak.
- We are biased toward action.

Work culture

Kolibri working agreement

Feeling like a fake

- Practice open and constructive communication
- Ask for help and work in teams, especially in difficult situations
- Assume the best in people.
- Engage when present.
- Listen more than we speak.
- We are biased toward action.

Feeling like a fake

Post Impostor

In my experience there's no such thing as luck

Kolibri

Thanks!

Berglind Ósk Bergsdóttir
@berglind0sk
berglind@kolibri.is

How a Technology Client became 1st in North America to be TMMi Level 3

Suresh Chandra Bose, Ganesh Bose

SureshChandra.GaneshBose@cognizant.com

Abstract

As a QA professional, I am sure you must have grappled with the following questions at some point in your career:

- Can testing practices/processes be benchmarked by industry standards?
- Can organizations improve effectiveness of testing?
- Can test maturity be sustained?
- What should the implementation plan include to improve testing processes?

As an Accredited TMMi Lead Assessor, I will provide an exhaustive approach in response to the above questions. This paper is about how we (Cognizant) enabled a Technology Client in their TMMi journey to become North America's first organization to be TMMi Level 3 certified.
We started supporting the client's adoption of TMMi as a reference framework for driving process improvement by conducting an initial assessment of the current testing processes, and identified areas of improvement and recommended a roadmap including Process Standardization, Training, Piloting and Institutionalization of the TMMi practices across the organization.
We performed a phase-wise iterative approach, with a focus on quality of deliverables and effective test practices. The underlying objective was to reduce cost of rework by improving quality through better maturity on testing practices, in accordance with TMMi Level 3. The 'one-size-fits-all' approach proved ineffective here, and hence came the need to highlight various elements of Organizational Change Management, instrumental in process roll-out after new QA processes, guidelines and checklists are defined. This was a huge initiative that helped the client transition to a higher maturity in overall testing - instilling scalable, measurable and predictive capabilities.

Biography

Suresh Chandra Bose, Ganesh Bose *is a Manager - Consulting at Cognizant Business Consulting practice. Suresh is an accredited Lead Assessor from TMMi Foundation and has been in the IT Industry for more than 18 years with vast consulting experience in various industries. He has executed strategic initiatives for many Fortune 100 companies in the areas of PMO, PPM, Process Consulting, Program Management, TMMi Assessment/Implementation, Organization Strategy, Test Consulting and CIO/Governance Dashboard/Metrics across the globe.*

Suresh holds 18 International certifications in IT and speaks at numerous international conferences, such as the American Software Testing Qualifications Board (ASTQB) and the Pacific Northwest Software Quality Conference (PNSQC).

1 Background

One of the key strategic goals for the large Technology Organization (will be referred to as "the Client" in this paper) is to improve the Testing maturity of their policies, practices, processes and capabilities in order to achieve Level 3 Maturity Certification from the Test Maturity Model Integration (TMMi) Foundation which will provide a higher degree of confidence in their capabilities to their customers, both internal and external. They also wanted to improve the Testing efficiency and effectiveness. The Client is primarily focused on Storage, Server and Hardware. They were spread across USA, India and Taiwan with team size of 400.

It was during 2014, the Client had a need to assess their current Testing processes against TMMi Level 3 Maturity and also receive recommendations on ways to implement the fixes for TMMi Level 3 (L3). Their initial level was level 1 and wanted to achieve level 3.

To determine the extent of gaps between the current state and their desired future state of TMMi Level 3, Client engaged Process and Quality Consulting (PQC) within Cognizant Business Consulting during 2014 to conduct an informal TMMi assessment. The PQC team conducted initial TMMi assessment of Client's current Testing processes, and identified areas of improvement along with a Recommendations roadmap and Improvement approach.

2 TMMi Maturity Levels

There are five levels of maturity in TMMi: starting from a level of being ad hoc and unmanaged, to improving in maturity to one which is managed, then defined, measured, and finally optimized. The process areas for each TMMi maturity level are shown below in Figure 1.

- Level 1 - Initial: There are no defined process areas to be considered level 1. This means any organization regardless of whether they have any testing process can be considered at level 1. The actual maturity rating starts from level 2 upwards.
- Level 2 - Managed: This level has five process areas starting from Test policy and Strategy. The process here is considered stable and can repeat the tasks at the project level.
- Level 3 - Defined: Level 3 is standardization of processes at the organization level and also has five process areas.
- Level 4 – Measured: This level is quantitatively managed with focus on measurement, product quality, and advanced peer reviews.
- Level 5 – Optimized: The organization is capable of continually improving its processes based on a quantitative understanding of statistically controlled processes. The testing techniques are optimized with continuous focus on fine tuning and process improvement.

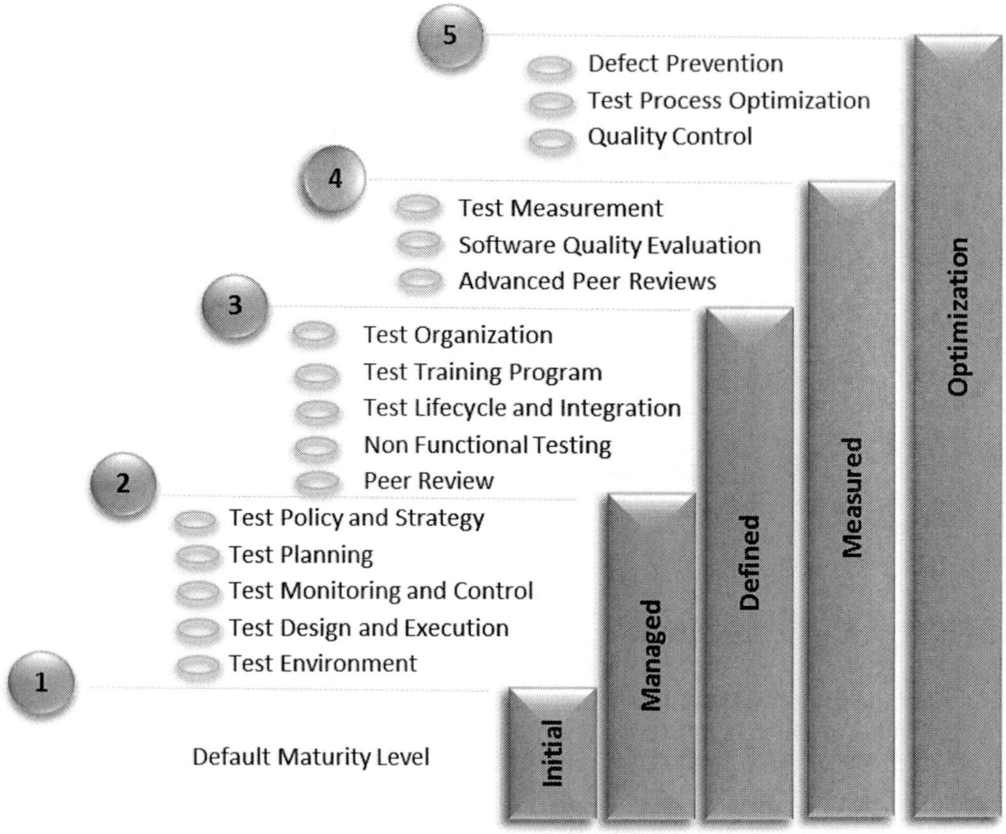

Figure 1: TMMi Maturity Levels

3 Approach

We used the following five different phases to approach the need of the Client.

- Informal Assessment
- Implementation
- Ongoing Audits
- Readiness
- Formal Assessment and Certification

3.1 Informal Assessment

Informal Assessment is the first step in benchmarking the progress in test process improvement with three main phases as shown in Figure 2.

As part of the planning phase, we (refer to my team as "we" since it may not be done by a single person) understand the scope of the assessment with focus on the business units, geographical locations, sample projects representing the organization getting assessed covering all lifecycle methodologies and project size.

Once the interviews are scheduled, we talk to the various stakeholders (which includes Test Engineers, Test Managers, Test Leads, Development team and the Senior Management) to understand the current landscape of the organization. We also perform documentary evidence reviews. The interviews are to ensure adequate coverage of the generic and specific goals and practices across various process areas of TMMi. Timelines change based on the maturity assessment level chosen by the organization to be assessed.

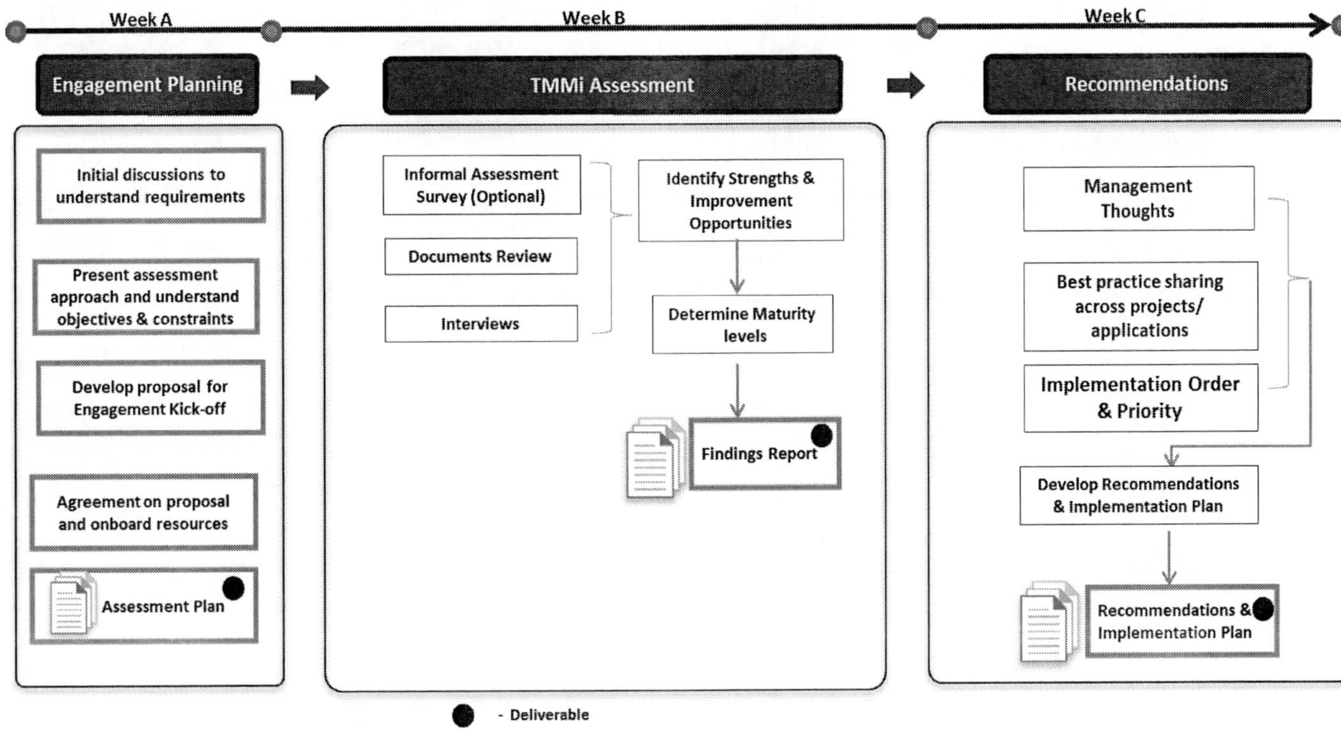

Figure 2: Informal Assessment Phases

Based on the outcome of the findings report, recommendations are developed for every gap identified and they are prioritized based on the inputs from the organization. A detailed Implementation roadmap is finally developed with timelines for all the prioritized recommendations.

3.1.1 TMMi Assessment Maturity Rating Methodology

The rating process strictly adheres to what is laid out in TMMi Assessment Method Application Requirements (TAMAR) which defines the requirements considered essential to Assessment methods intended for use with the TMMi framework.

There are 16 process areas, 77 goals and 345 practices including the specific and generic practices from level 2 to level 5. The interviews and document evidence are rated for all the specific and generic practices which are rolled up to the goals, then to process area, and finally to the maturity level. See Figure 3 for an overview of the TMMi Rating Mechanism.

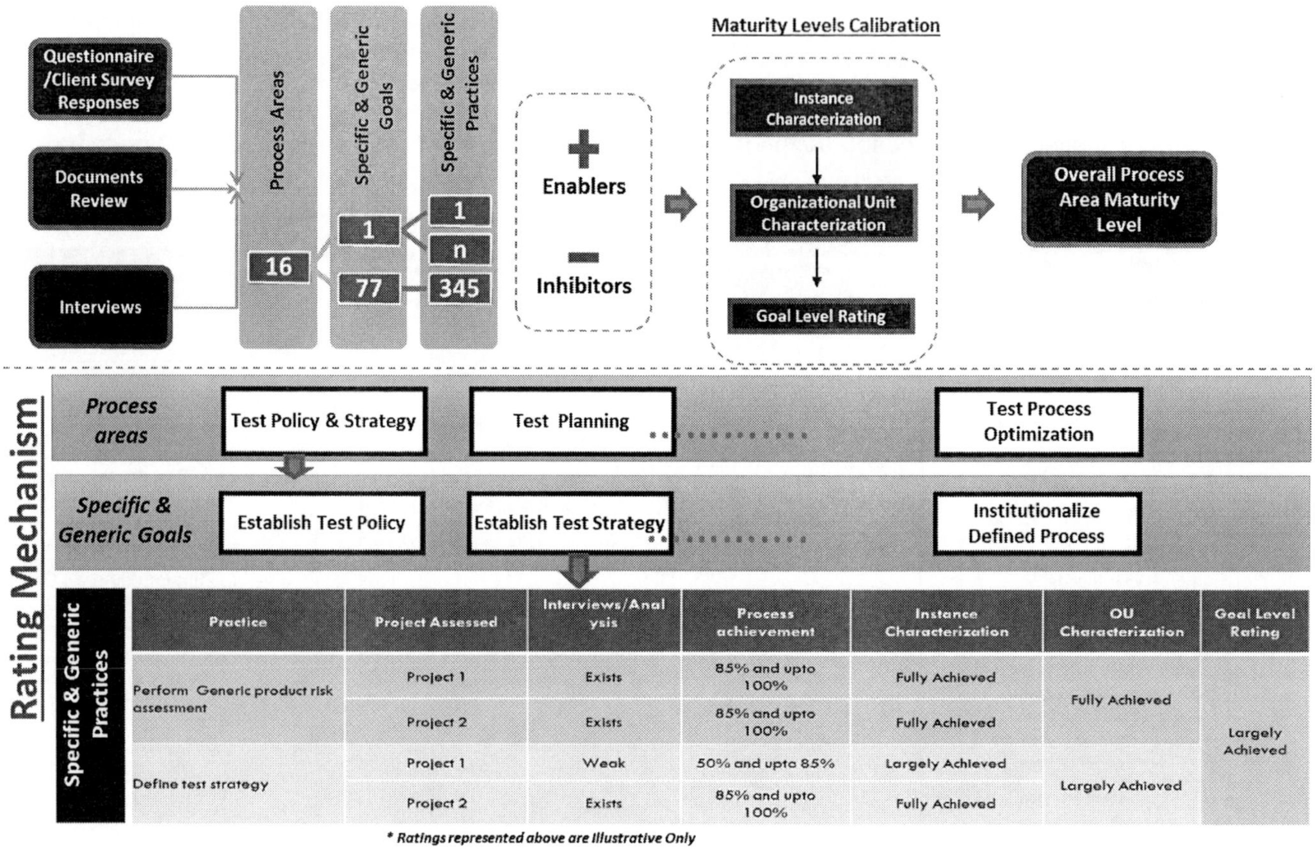

Figure 3: TMMi Rating Mechanism

3.1.2 TMMi Maturity Level Calibration Guidelines

Process Areas are designated the appropriate maturity levels based on the following guidelines:

Rating	Description
Fully Achieved	• Convincing evidence of process compliance • Systematic and widespread implementation of process • No obvious weakness in distribution, application and results of this process exists • Process achievement is between 85% and up to 100%
Largely Achieved	• Significant evidence of process compliance • Minor weakness in distribution, application and results of this process exists • Process achievement is between 50% and up to 85%
Partially Achieved	• Some evidence of process found • Process exhibits significant weaknesses, is incomplete, not widespread, or inconsistent in application or results. • Process achievement is between 15% and up to 50%
Not Achieved	• Little or no evidence of process • Process achievement is between 0% and up to 15%

Not Rated	• Any supporting goal that cannot be rated based on the current phase of the project must be "Not Rated"
Not Applicable	• The process area is considered not to be in the scope of the assessment or applicable to the organizational unit by the Lead Assessor

3.2 Implementation

PQC worked on the complete Implementation of the prioritized recommendations from the informal assessment which included **Process Standardization, Training, Piloting and Institutionalization** (see Figure 4) of the TMMi practices across the entire Organization within Enterprise Validation. PQC performed a phase-wise iterative approach for the implementation with a focus on quality of deliverables and effective Test practices. The approach empowered Client's underlying objective to reduce the cost of rework by improving quality through better maturity on testing practices in accordance with TMMi Level 3.

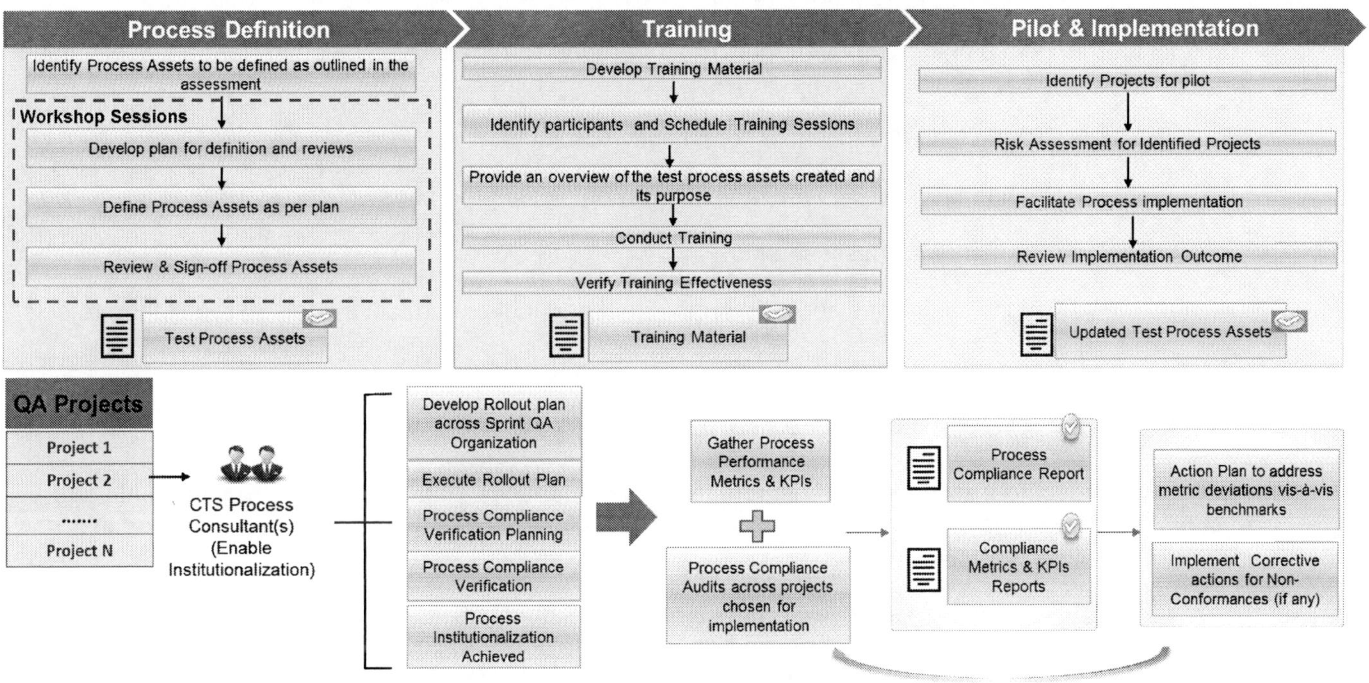

Figure 4: TMMi Implementation

- Restructured the testing organization focusing on consistent processes, cross trained testers and key support functions
- Identified 14 key improvement areas and implementation priorities based on existing landscape to achieve TMMi maturity level 3
- Provided a 12 month implementation roadmap to define, setup, train and rollout processes for 400+ team including full-time employees and contractors
- Refined existing processes based on audit feedback, trained project teams and prepared implementation inventory over a period of 8 months for formal certification readiness

3.3 Ongoing Audits

We formed Audit Champion to oversee the audits for all current projects in multiple geographies. The Audit Champion is a single person but will have internal auditors in each region to conduct audits. An Audit plan was developed to conduct spot checks and audits to assess effectiveness of testing organization against instituted processes. Based on the outcome of the audit findings, we analyzed the Organizational level gaps (Non-Compliance) and trends and took preventive actions and ensured all gaps are closed in a timely fashion.

3.4 Readiness

The objective of Assessment Readiness phase is an attempt to build confidence among the Client's Enterprise Validation team, just before taking up the Formal Assessment. This is done by understanding the positive compliances and the gaps (Non-compliances and Opportunity for improvements) both at project level and at Organizational level with respect to TMMi practice implementation and then derive a plan and action to fix the gaps to ensure readiness towards Formal assessment.

The goal for this Phase of the engagement is to prepare the Enterprise Validation for formal assessment through the following means:

- Closing Non-Compliances for all active projects
- Provide facilitation to the project team on closing the gaps
- Conduct mock assessments
- Collate sufficient evidences (both direct and indirect artifact evidence) for all the projects

3.5 Formal Assessment and Certification

Finally we conducted a six week engagement to gather evidences, data submission requirements and document final findings for formal certification. The following activities were performed as part of this Formal TMMi Level 3 Assessment:

- Conduct interviews with identified stakeholders
- Document Analysis and review for the selected projects
- Follow-up interview/discussion with the stakeholders
- Completion of all Interviews and Document review
- OU (Organizational Unit) level findings
- Goal Ratings
- Process Area Ratings
- Recommendations on how to address weaknesses
- Final Assessment Report (Formal Assessment)
- Data Submission Requirements to TMMi Foundation

4 Summary

Cognizant conducted the formal assessment using TMMi approved model "**Cognizant TMMi Assessment Method 1.2"** which was led by the TMMi Accredited Lead Assessor Suresh Chandra Bose Ganesh Bose from Cognizant's PQC. Suresh Chandra Bose, the only TMMi Accredited Lead Assessor from North America, using similar approach successfully transformed the technology giant to become the first organization in the United States to be formally certified at TMMi Level 3. This was a huge initiative that helped the client transition to a higher maturity in overall testing - instilling scalable, measurable and predictive capabilities with improved Testing effectiveness, efficiency and productivity. Currently there is only one company in North America at Level 3 and would like to see more companies reach that maturity level and higher.

5 References

Journal Articles:

Suresh Chandra Bose, Ganesh Bose. Chart a Roadmap for Test Maturity with TMMi, 2017
https://www.linkedin.com/pulse/chart-roadmap-test-maturity-TMMi-suresh-chandra-bose-g-pmp

Web Sites:

Cognizant TMMi Capabilities & Success Case Study, 2016
https://www.TMMi.org/wp-content/uploads/2016/08/Cognizant-TMMi-Success-Case-Study.pdf

Journal Articles:

Suresh Chandra Bose, Ganesh Bose. "How to Take Organizations to Higher Testing Maturity" ASTQB Conference, 2015
https://www.astqb.org/certified-tester-resources/astqb-software-testing-conference/conference-agenda/how-to-take-organizations-to-higher-testing-maturity/

Book:

TMMi Foundation. TMMi Reference Model (Release 1.0), 2012
http://www.TMMi.org/pdf/TMMi.Framework.pdf

Web Sites:

"Dell Enterprise Validation First in North America to achieve TMMi Certification", 2016

http://en.community.dell.com/dell-blogs/dell4enterprise/b/dell4enterprise/archive/2016/04/26/dell-enterprise-validation-first-in-north-america-to-achieve-TMMi-certification

How to become Agile in Enterprise

- Align organizational attention to achieve global optimization

Optimization at different levels

- We all know Agile is hard in big enterprise – because Agile in R&D is a local optimization
- Every organization optimizes for its own benefit
  - Developers optimize around development process, technology, etc.
  - QA optimizes around testability, automation, etc.
  - Finance optimizes around spend, cost, capitalization, etc.
  - Support optimizes around response time, call volume, etc.
- Because of this, organizational alignment is difficult to achieve
  - Different processes are created to specifically optimize each o
  - From the outside, everyone looks like headless chicken

Headless chicken?

- Time – 2014
- Location – a giant conference room in a giant retail company
- What happened – red-faced project managers and scrum masters were performing an incredible political dance to defend their budget request through dozens of spreadsheets and hundreds of line items. They were desperately trying to please a group of senior leaders who control budget.
- Why they were headless chickens? The entire spreadsheet and the requested budget were simply …

Introducing organizational attention

- Organizational attention is defined as the socially structured pattern of attention evidenced by decision makers within the organization (Ocasio, 1997)
- Organizational attention has the following characteristics
  - Can be treated as a currency
  - Limited – like true currency, it's not only limited but can rise and fall with time
  - Commands focus and effort – attention translates directly into time of focus and effort spent on any particular issues, risks, projects, etc.
  - Costs can be lowered through either controlled or automated process
- Local optimization relies on processes to increase its own organizational attention, often at the cost of global optimization

Examples of organizational attentions through local optimization

- Tradition Software Development
- Agile Software Development
- Finance
- Hosting

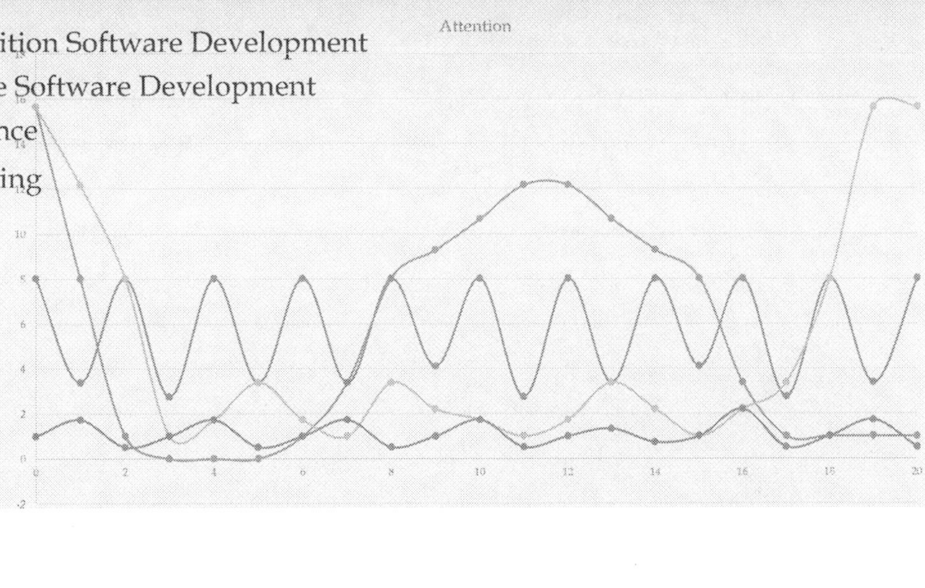

Aligning attention for sympathetic vibration

- Enterprise level Agility can only be achieved through global optimization
- Align organizational attention at global level can ensure Agile implementation's success (think sympathetic vibration)
- What does this do to each of the organizations?
  - Engineering - develop gated feature release on top of frequent releases
  - QA - revolutionize both process and tooling
  - Product management - segment features through thin slice of features
  - Finance - align spend, timesheet entry, create "permanent" team
  - Hosting - align with development through use of DevOps
  - Support - align support through controlled release process
  - Marketing - retool marketing methods, capabilities, build-in feature toggle for gated go-to market strategy

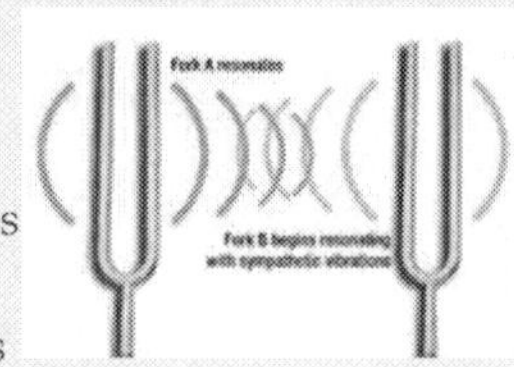

Examples of globally optimized model - MatrixCare

- Agile Software Development
- Finance - why there's a lag in synchronization? (timesheet cycle)
- Hosting - what makes hosting to synch up with development? (DevOps)

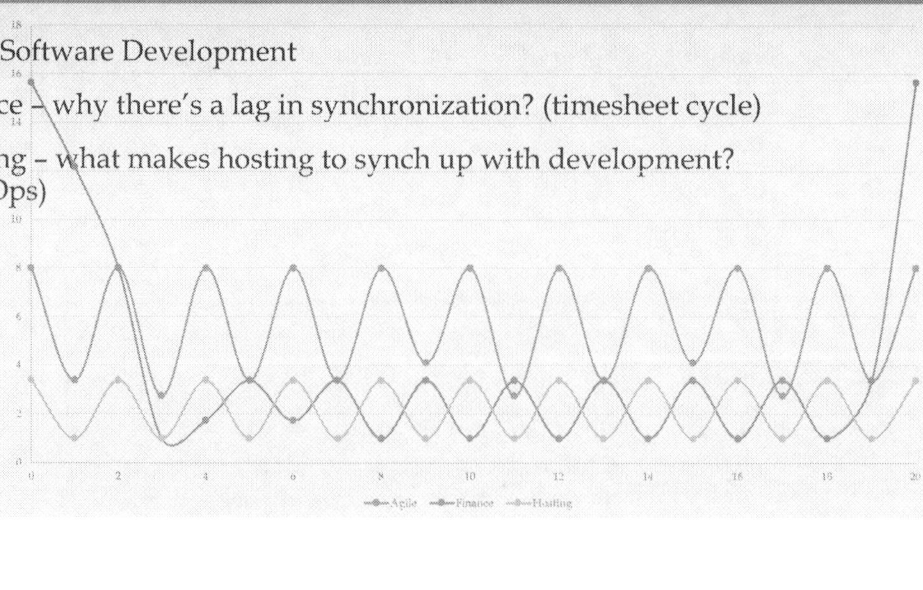

Results

- When you can align organizational attention to focus on global optimization, amazing results can happen
  - Level 1 – everyone gives up something to achieve something greater
  - Level 2 – everyone works on a synergized set of processes to achieve clarity
  - Level 3 – everyone feeds off the synergy to achieve something far greater.
- At MatrixCare, we have aligned organizational attention throughout almost all departments, and we have achieved…

MatrixCare Achieves Record KLAS Score in the Long-Term Care Category, Rated #1 for 2017.

Providers Give MatrixCare Highest Category Leader Score Ever in Long-Term Care Category.

Questions?

How do you measure success rate of large scale agile process?

[BHAGEERATHI BAI]

About me..

Bhageerathi Bai*, Software Quality Engineer at* ***Intel India Pvt Ltd.***

Our teams

Quality reviews and releases

Challenges

Solution

Success Measure

Large Scale Agile Players...

- Internal — Hardware, Software, System teams
- Third party — Software and Hardware Teams
- Manufacturer — Component and Board Manufacturers
- Integration — Software and Hardware Integrators

A define/build/test component team

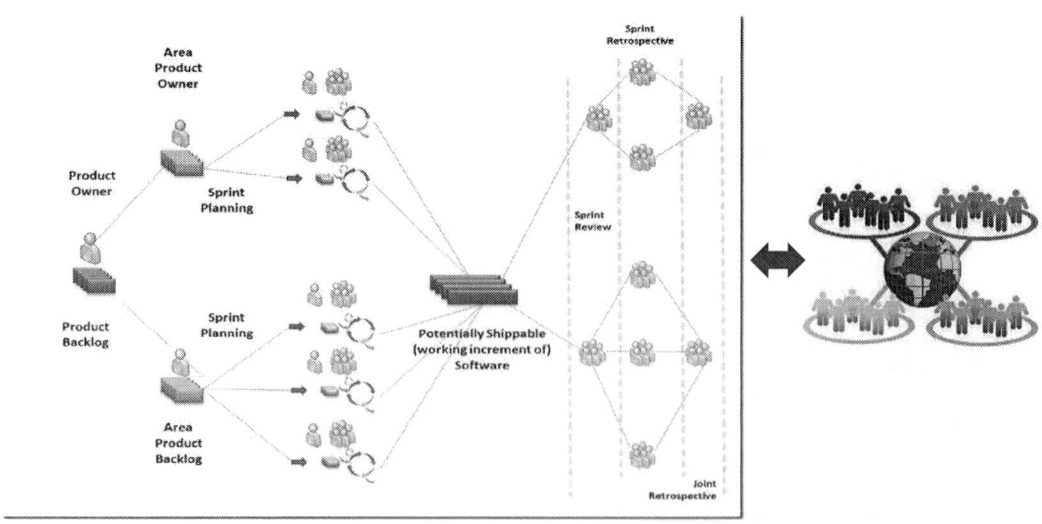

Large scale Agile teams distributed ...

Our teams
Quality reviews and releases
Challenges
Solution
Success Measure
intel
7

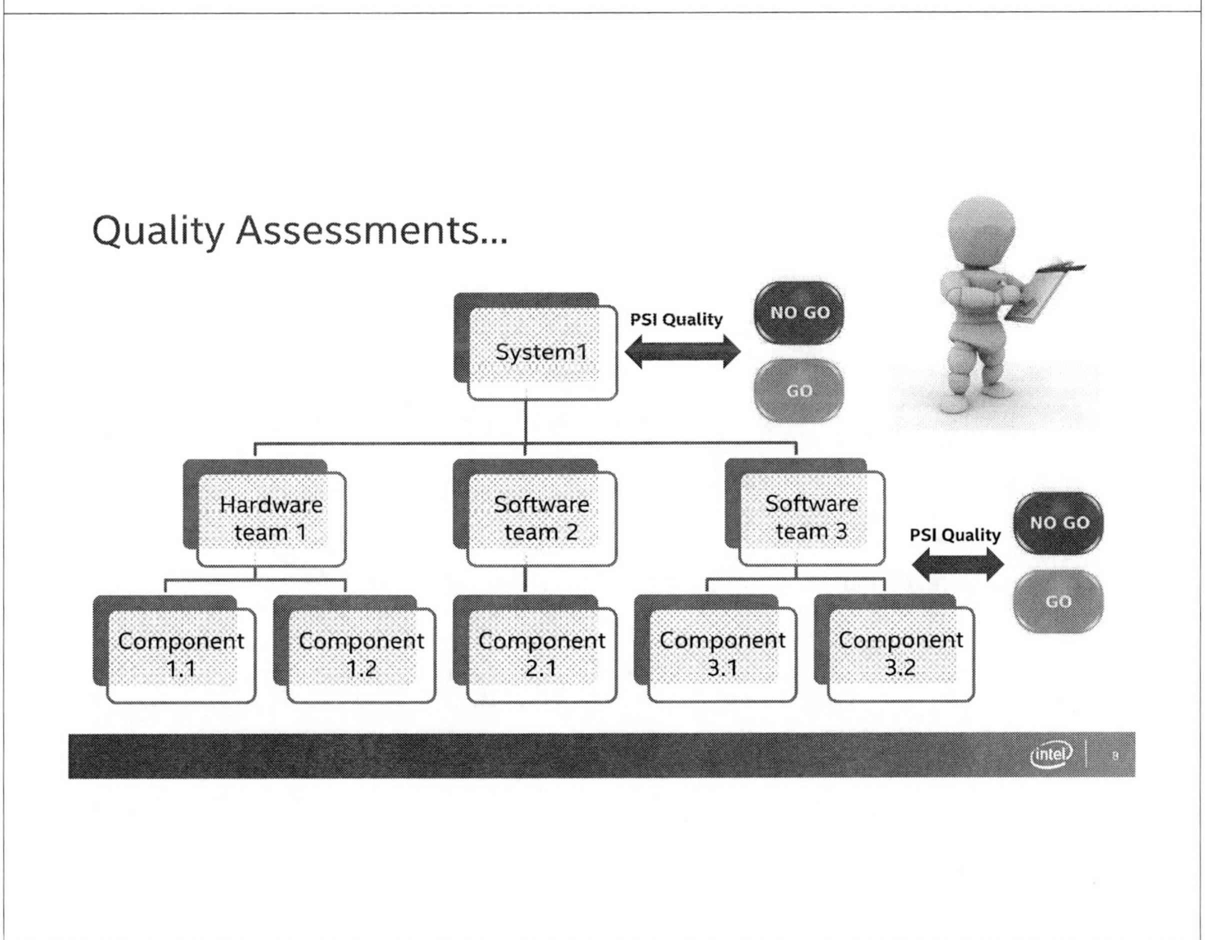
Quality Assessments...
System1
PSI Quality
NO GO
GO
Hardware team 1
Software team 2
Software team 3
PSI Quality
NO GO
GO
Component 1.1
Component 1.2
Component 2.1
Component 3.1
Component 3.2
intel
8

Go/No-Go meetings..

9

Quality Assessments of Components – Pre-requisites

Define Goals/Criteria

Collect Metrics

Generate Assessments

capture quality trends

10

Milestone Candidate Quality review process – CUSTOMIZED

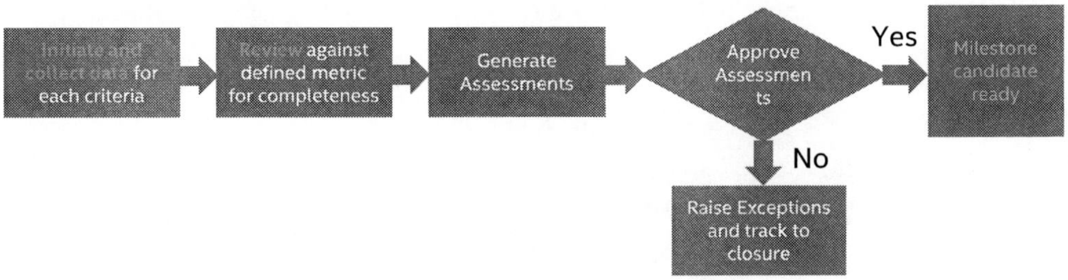

Milestones

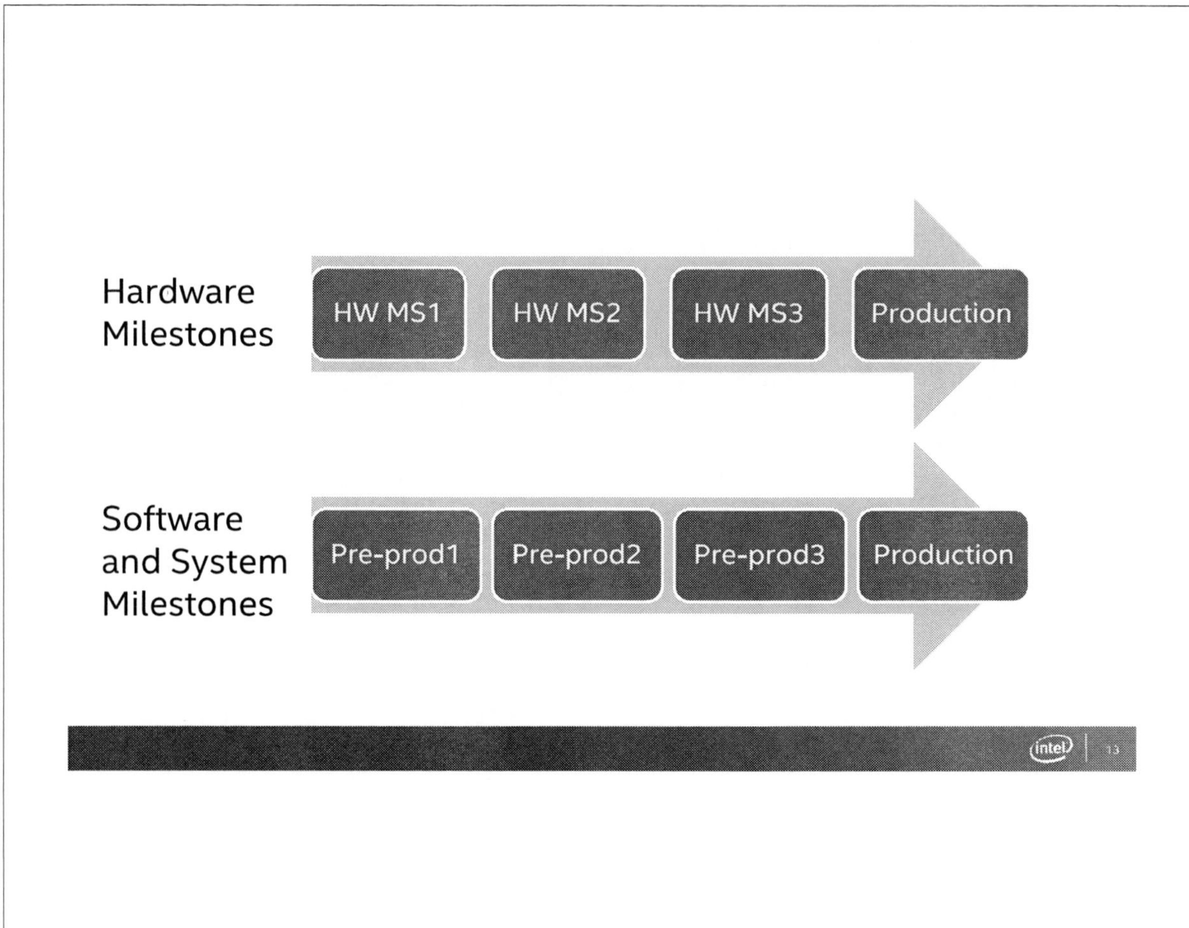
Hardware Milestones
HW MS1
HW MS2
HW MS3
Production
Software and System Milestones
Pre-prod1
Pre-prod2
Pre-prod3
Production
intel
13

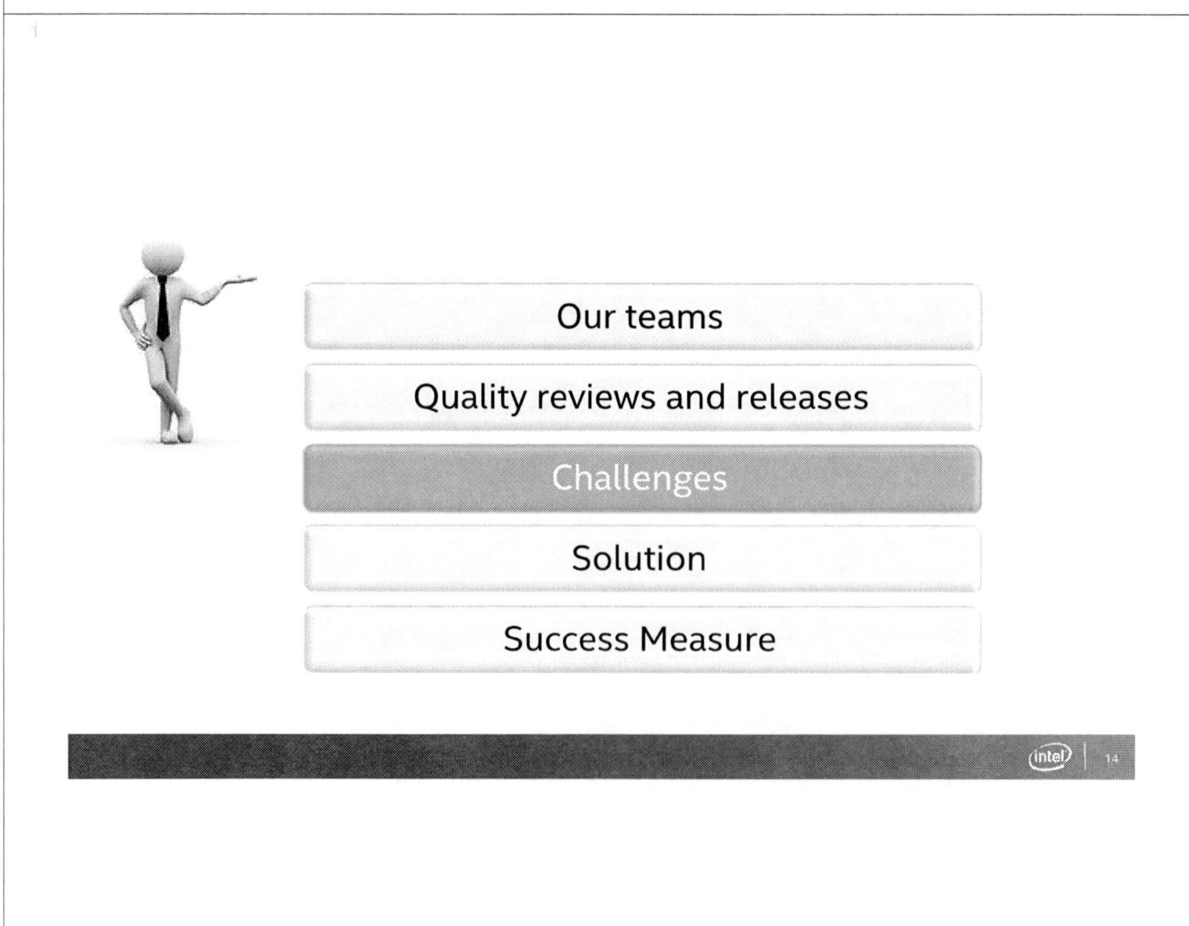
Our teams
Quality reviews and releases
Challenges
Solution
Success Measure
intel
14

- **Customized** Quality Assessments of Individual components

- **Unsynchronized** release cycles

- Component Deliverables to customers in **isolation**

Our teams

Quality reviews and releases

Challenges

Solution

Success Measure

17

Tailoring large scale Agile ...

Common Quality Framework

Synchronized Release cycles

Effective Exceptions Management

18

How did we implement!!

Establish **Common Quality language –** goals and challenging metrics

Roll out Organization wide **training plan**

Mandated Common **release review Process**

Ensured **Adoption** by all the teams

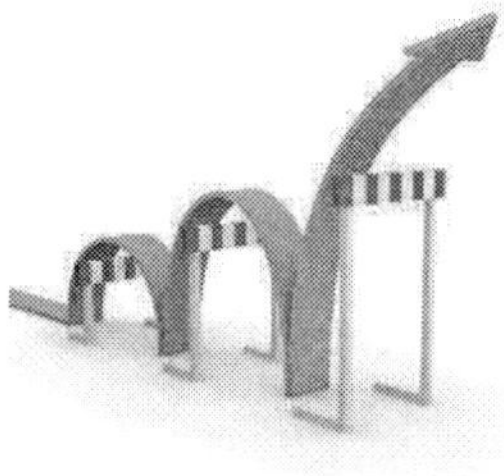

Common Quality Framework measured areas.. REVISED!!

- Requirements management
- Feature Development
- Defects and customer escalations
- Third party Compliance
- Manufacturing checks
- Compatibility tests
- Customer scenarios
- In-house Deployment Tests
- Documentation ... etc.

intel | 21

Product release review process..

intel | 22

What Changed?... HW/SW Milestone Candidate Quality review process

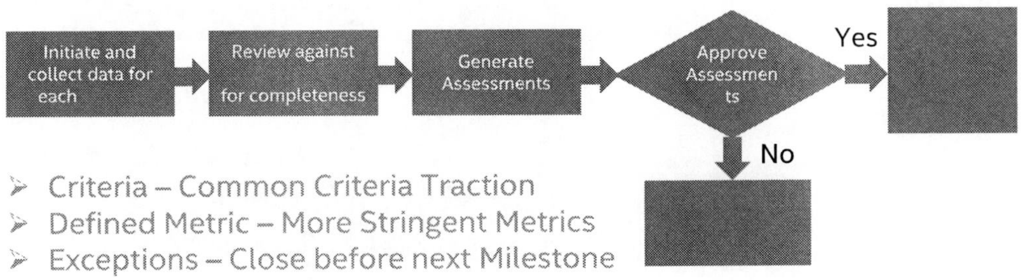

- Criteria – Common Criteria Traction
- Defined Metric – More Stringent Metrics
- Exceptions – Close before next Milestone
- Milestone candidate – New Integration Process to synchronize releases

Synchronize releases..

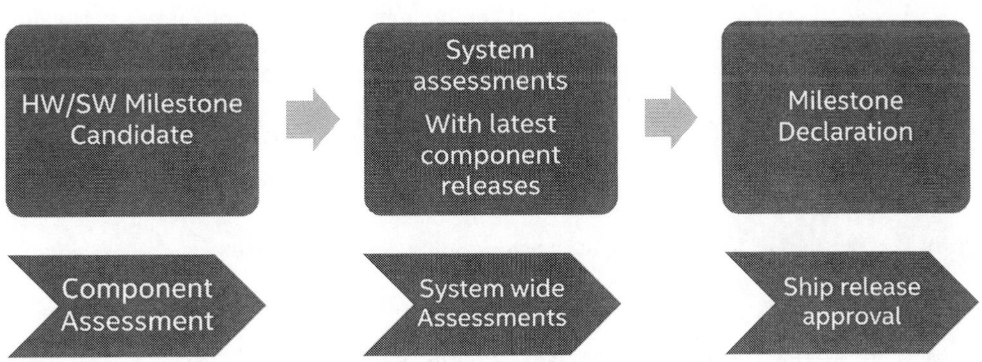

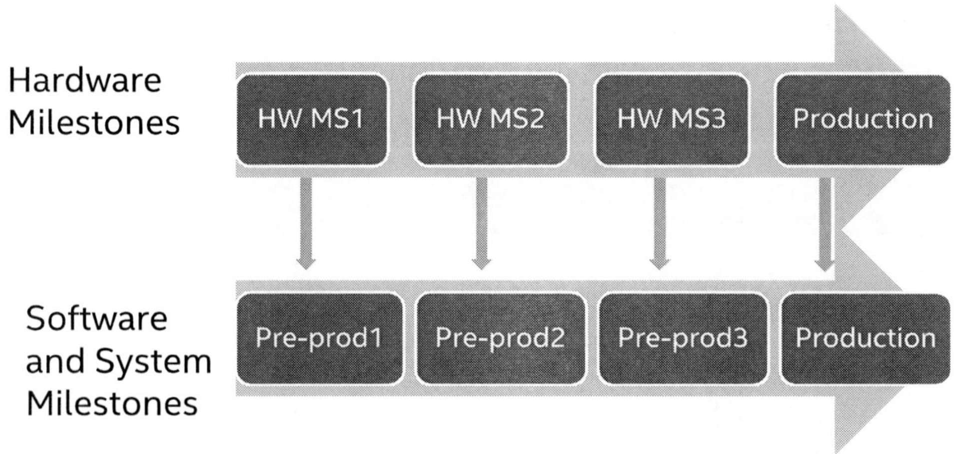

Dependencies were taken care...

25

Common Quality Framework ensures...

- Establish Common Quality standards across organization
- Prevent component team declaring release in isolation
- Help ask **"right"** questions during ship decisions
- Transparency across entire system
- Central change control process
- Consistency of business processes
- Manage quality and risk of the product
- Raise the quality bar to align with customer **expectations**

26

Our teams

Quality reviews and releases

Challenges

Solution

Success Measure

intel | 27

Results

- Stream line dependencies and Release schedules
- Team collaboration Improved
- Improvement in the Quality Processes
- Time to market was met as planned
- Plan future releases with horizon of Predictability
- Maintained zero critical exposure defects
- Associated Finance Risks were in control

intel | 28

Limitations!

One Size doesn't fit all

Resistance to Change

Conclusion

- Delivering what customer **wants**
- **Open Communication** with customer
- Being **trusted** by customer
- Synchronize Release cycles to show **working software** frequently

Questions ?

31

Building in Quality – Ten Years Later

Kathy Iberle
Iberle Consulting Group, Inc.

kiberle@kiberle.com

Abstract

We've all heard that it's better to "build in quality" than to test in quality. Have you ever wondered how exactly *is* quality built in?

Despite the quality shortfalls we often see, the steps to build in quality are not a complete mystery. Teams creating high-reliability software in fields such as aerospace, telecommunications, and medical applications have been building in quality for decades, and doing so for a very reasonable price. However, most of the methods for building in quality were originally designed for waterfall development.

In this talk, Kathy Iberle will revisit her 2007 perspective on building in quality and reflect on what's been learned through the agile movement. She'll update the methods, the approach, and the tools to fit today's agile projects.

Biography

Kathy Iberle is the Principal Consultant at Iberle Consulting Group, Inc., where she helps clients improve their productivity and quality. Her extensive background in process improvement and quality methods enable her to blend classic quality control with the best of current Lean thinking.

Kathy Iberle has been working with software quality and development process improvement in both agile and traditional teams for many years. After a long career at Hewlett-Packard as a programmer, quality engineer, and process improvement expert, she is now the principal consultant and owner of the Iberle Consulting Group. She has published regularly since 1997, served as co-chair of the Program Committee of the Pacific Northwest Software Quality Conference (PNSQC) in 2009, and participated in the invitation-only Software Test Managers Roundtable for five years.

Kathy has an M.S. in Computer Science from the University of Washington, and an excessive collection of degrees in Chemistry from the University of Washington and the University of Michigan. Visit her website at www.kiberle.com

1 Introduction

Ten years ago, I presented a paper at this conference named "Building Quality In". The paper described how software organizations in high-reliability fields achieved high quality levels at a reasonable cost. When a failure can kill people, relying mostly on testing is too risky and too expensive. While large business projects struggled with enormous defect backlogs and crushing design problems, teams in aerospace, medical, and telecommunications were quietly building systems that worked, usually at less expense.

The primary tools used in those high-reliability projects were designed for waterfall projects. Today, with a much more complex environment, are these methods still relevant? Still useful? And how do they fit into today's agile development?

Let's take a look at how quality was achieved back in the waterfall days of 2007 and before. Then we'll jump to the present and reflect on what to bring forward and what to leave behind.

2 Building in Quality – the Waterfall Era

2.1 How Defects are Created

Why do we have defects in the first place? Basically, because someone makes a mistake during the complex and lengthy process of building an application.

We start by collecting the users' wants and desires. During this activity, we can introduce defects by:

- Misunderstanding the needs and wants stated by the user.
- Assuming the user is able to tell the team what they need. (The user often cannot articulate it.)
- Failing to ask the user about certain topics.
- Misplacing or losing the users' wants and desires.

Then we turn the users' desires into a description of features and attributes which will meet those desires. Whether that description is a collection of user stories or a traditional Software Requirements Specification (SRS), we can introduce more defects by:

- Omitting some of the user's desires.
- Writing incomplete or confusing specifications.
- Misplacing or losing some of the specifications.

Then we design software which will deliver the planned features and attributes. What will the structure of the system be, what libraries shall we use, how do the components interact? We can introduce yet more defects during this activity by:

- Making logical design errors – omitting cases, writing a state machine with incorrect transitions, insufficiently specifying interfaces, and so forth.
- Failing to implement some of the features.
- Failing to cover *unstated* quality attributes. (Everyone knows it shouldn't crash when I do this…)
- Ignoring possible behaviors of the environment – operating system, network, etc.
- Incorporating libraries which won't perform well enough for your needs.

And then we turn the design into code. We can create defects by:

- Misinterpreting the design.
- Making logical coding errors. (Ran off the end of the array, did you?)
- Using the wrong versions or the wrong files.

We create similar errors during integration and installation by:

- Installing the wrong files.
- Putting the wrong values in the configuration files.

2.2 The Quality Plan

Teams building high-reliability software were very aware of all these opportunities for error. It wasn't (and isn't) possible to achieve truly high quality without a solid understanding of where defects come from. The organization would thoughtfully and explicitly build a series of defenses to prevent errors or detect them very early. Those defenses were often captured in a *quality plan*.[1] The quality plan may have been a separate document, or it might have been spread across several different documents and plans, but the planning was there.

A quality plan usually focused on two main topics:

- Detecting mistakes very early via *quality gates*.
- Preventing mistakes completely with *preventative measures* and (sometimes) a *product risk analysis*.

2.3 Quality Gates

After each activity, there was a quality gate intended to find and fix mistakes made during that activity before proceeding to the next activity. The quality gates for requirements, specifications, and designs consisted of reviews and inspections of the written documents resulting from those activities.

A typical quality gate for moving code into system integration on a 1990s medical instrument project:

- ❑ Compiles with no flags level 3 or above.
- ❑ Unit testing completed with 100% path coverage (ed. note: Yes, we really did that.)
- ❑ Passes all unit tests
- ❑ Integration test scripts written
- ❑ Code complexity at or below level 10
- ❑ Modules with complexity above 4 have been peer-reviewed
- ❑ Complies with coding standards

Figure 1: The V-Model
with Quality Gates

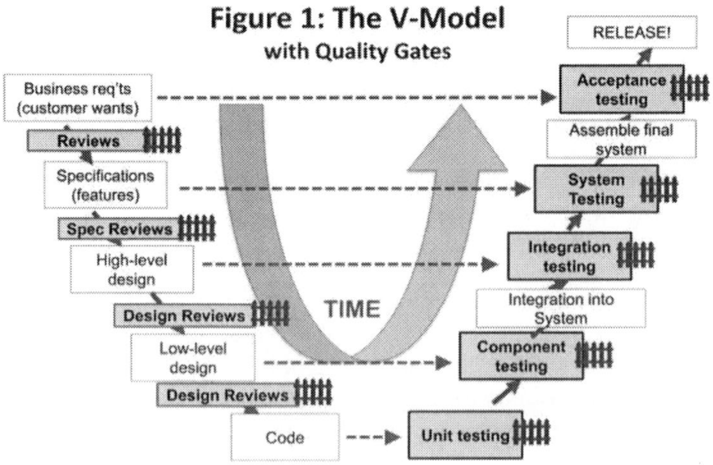

The reviews and inspections never caught anywhere near all the defects, so more quality gates were added, consisting of layer upon layer of testing.

This was popularly called the *V-model*. Mistakes made on one side of the V are found by testing on the other side of the V.

Each layer of testing was designed to find the mistakes from a particular activity, as shown by the dotted lines. For instance, unit testing is good at finding logical coding errors, but it's not effective at finding missing requirements, so you also need acceptance testing, which focuses on whether customer wants were met.

---

[1] To quote the American Society for Quality: "A quality plan is a document, or set of documents, which together specify quality standards, practices, resources, specifications, and the sequence of activities relevant to a particular product, service, project, or contract". (ASQ, 2017)

The final quality gate was known as *release criteria*. Since a waterfall project assumes all functionality is complete, the release criteria focused on assessing the impact of issues we already know about, and the likelihood of finding more problems later. Waterfall release criteria often looked like this list (Rothman, 2002).

- All code must compile and build for all platforms
- Zero high priority bugs open
- For all open bugs, documentation in release notes with workarounds
- All planned QA tests run, at least ninety percent pass
- Number of open defects decreasing for last three weeks

The quality gates dealt with the natural tendencies of humans to make mistakes in each activity, but they also dealt with problems caused by how the work was organized.

For instance, in some organizations making business software, each activity was performed by a specialized team, and the work then handed off to another specialized team. Different people wrote the specification, did the design, and did the coding. Each handoff was an opportunity for misunderstandings and lost information.

Some organizations responded by creating yet more quality gates requiring yet more detailed documentation. Businesses in high-reliability fields tried instead to prevent those handoff errors by creating cross-functional teams instead, where the same team was responsible for requirements, design, coding, integration, and testing. As a medical products developer, I didn't see a separate test team, let alone an entire department just for testing, until twelve years into my career.

In high-reliability fields, organizations typically used most or all of the quality gates shown in Figure 1. Outside high-reliability fields, it was pretty common to skip most of the quality gates and rely primarily on system testing, as shown to the right. Projects using this model were often known as "late".

Figure 2: The V-Model
with very few gates

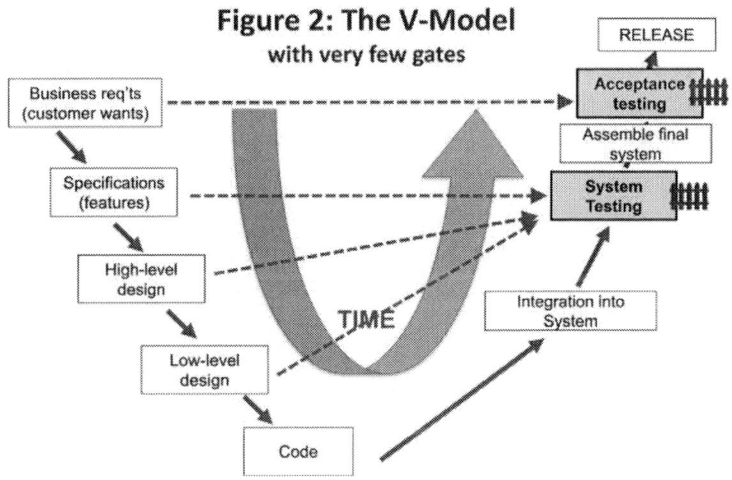

Because design reviews, unit testing, and the like had not been done, system testing typically found large numbers of defects late in the project. This required a lot of rework and made the project late. Requirements gaps were a particular problem, since they were often not spotted until near the end of the project. The final quality was often problematic, because system testing simply isn't very good at finding low-level coding errors.

2.4 Preventative Measures: Building in Quality

Along with a quality gate to exit from an activity, the quality plan also defined preventative practices to be used during the activity, such as coding standards, design methods, and so forth. These were intended to prevent the developers from creating defects in the first place.

Preventative measures usually used one or more of these strategies:

- **Make the structure & logic visible**. If you can't see the structure, you **will** make mistakes. For instance, the intent of most coding standards is to make the logic easily visible.
- **Maintain intellectual control.** If you think about too many things at once, you **will** lose track and make mistakes. About seven things will fit in your head at once, so if your code or design has more than seven, decompose into smaller pieces. Work in small, verifiable steps.
- **Know your domain**. If someone has explained how to use this API, or how this service works, or how to apply this design pattern, do acquire this knowledge! A decent education in the methods and technology prevents a lot of problems.
- **Mistake-proof the routine stuff.** Use, and if necessary build, tools which won't let you make certain mistakes. FORTRAN started out in 1957 as a way to translate math formulas into code more quickly and reliably than was ever possible using assembly language. (UM 1999). You can build your own tools to prevent your own mistakes. For instance, a wizard to write those pesky configuration files.
- **Design away the opportunity for error.** Sometimes a good design choice can eliminate a certain class of errors. An example from James Shore (Shore 2010): "if you have repeated problems with UI field lengths being inconsistent with database field lengths, change your design to base one value off of the other."

I'll describe a few of the broader preventative measures which were commonly used in the waterfall era.

2.4.1 Defining and Tracking Non-functional Requirements

Non-functional requirements or *quality attributes* are those requirements which state not what a product does, but how well it does what it does. For instance (Wiegers 2013 pp 269-273)

- The system shall protect against unauthorized addition, deletion, or modification of data.
- At least 98% of the time, the trading system shall update the transaction status display within 1 second after the completion of each trade.

Typical non-functional requirements are performance, security, availability, usability, and many other "ilities". If the developer doesn't know what is expected, she can't drive the design and code to meet the target. In high-reliability fields, we always defined our targets carefully so we'd have a fighting chance of hitting them. Practices to prevent missing or misunderstanding the non-functional requirements included checklists of quality attributes to consider defining, templates, and training on how to ask customers what they need in these areas without over-promising. We sometimes wrote system tests for the non-functional requirements quite early, because writing the tests helped clarify the requirements.

2.4.2 Quality Factoring

It's great to define your non-functional requirements, and write system tests to check against those requirements, but if that's all you do, your system will fail the tests. You've got to think about how to meet those requirements.

In high-reliability fields, we traced the non-functional requirements through the design. At each level, we noted both what needed to be done in order to achieve the goal, and what should be tested at that level to ensure we were on track. Martyn Ould calls this *quality factoring* (Ould, 183). For instance, when the instrument was expected to respond in 1 second, that requirement was linked to a *performance budget* in the design for the responsible subsystem. In the performance budget, each firmware component in the response chain was assigned a portion of that 1 second, and a corresponding test was added to that component's test suite. The owner of the component might factor this further by creating a performance budget for each module in the subsystem, and so on.

Some attributes were achieved by defining system-wide criteria which linked to system-wide practices. For instance, a security attribute might require all user data entry fields to screen for commands such as "DROP TABLE". In all cases, you were expected to work through a 3-step process and factor as needed:

1) What's the goal?
2) How will the system achieve the goal?
3) How will I verify the system has achieved the goal?

In my experience, quality factoring was commonly used but rarely taught in any systematic fashion. It didn't even have a consistent name. One of the better descriptions is in Martyn Ould's book (Ould 1999). Quality factoring was similar in some ways to today's a*cceptance-test driven design* (*ATDD)*. However, since the waterfall process forced us to deal with the entire system at once, rather than a small group of stories, the sheer volume of detail to track and the long feedback loops could overwhelm the process.

2.4.3 Product Risk Analysis

Another widely used preventative measure was the product risk analysis. Early in the project, the team was asked to list the ways in which the end product could fail terribly. What disastrous damage could this product do? How could it injure a user, destroy all their data, damage your company's reputation, bring down your state's electric power grid, alienate your users?

After identifying the most likely disasters, the team looked for ways to prevent those disasters by working backwards from the disaster to its potential root causes. The team would then strengthen the quality gates with more detection measures (reviews, inspections, testing) and/or add more preventative measures to the quality plan. Some preventative measures I've seen come out of a product risk analysis:

Product Risk	Preventative measures
Routines which call third-party library don't work, because we didn't fully understand the third-party library.	**Know your domain**. Send team member to training class. (It's surprising how often this is neglected.)
Installation instructions in the install poster and on-screen don't match.	**Design away the opportunity for error.** Don't put the instructions in both places. Put them only on-screen. That's where most people look.
Printers don't install correctly due to minor errors in their configuration files.	**Mistake-proof your process**. Automate the writing of the configuration files with a wizard to do all the tedious predictable steps.
Device control doesn't work correctly in all cases, due to errors in a long set of nested if-then-else statements.	**Know your domain**. Design and code a state machine instead of ad-hoc if-then-else statements.

Today, the most common place to find a product risk analysis is in testing books.[2] In my opinion, this is the wrong place. Development teams should do the product risk analysis, so they can reduce risk by reducing the potential to make those mistakes. All the test group can do is find them after they're made.

2.5 What Didn't Work – Slow Feedback

Over the years, many organizations built very reliable and robust systems using these methods and a waterfall lifecycle. However, the waterfall lifecycle had one enormous drawback. Feedback was extremely slow. Mistakes were made, and nobody knew about them until months later when the problems showed up in integration or system test. That made them expensive to fix.

---

[2] You can find a more detailed discussion of risk analysis in many books on testing, such as *Critical Test Processes* by Rex Black [Black 2004] and resources on quality planning such as Martyn Ould's *Managing Software Quality and Business Risk*. [Ould 1999].

The mistakes with the longest feedback time were those involving understanding what the user actually wanted. That's bad because there will almost certainly be gaps in that understanding. Users aren't always able to articulate what they need, and sometimes they simply don't know. By 1999, many organizations were using multiple forms of prototyping to elicit customer needs by showing them running software or mockups of running software.

The long feedback loop was a problem in design as well, since the results of a design decision are often not visible until the system is running. Many teams prototyped parts of the design before completing the design, despite their waterfall process saying they shouldn't. In essence, the team was performing an architectural spike to investigate some worrisome aspect of the design.

I first tried an iterative method in 1993, when we used staged delivery to design, code, and deliver a medical product. Despite not using many of today's tools such as cadence and user stories, we found that simply reducing our feedback loop from eighteen months to about six weeks was an enormous help in dealing with both requirements misunderstandings and designs that didn't work as expected.

3 Building in Quality – the Agile Era

What's changed in the last ten years? Well, defects are still created by making mistakes during activities. The core activities still involve gathering user requirements, deciding what features to build, designing the system, coding it, and integrating or installing it. The biggest change in software development practices over the last ten years has been the widespread adoption of agile practices. How does this affect building in quality?

3.1 You Can't Know Everything

One of the fundamental concepts of agile is that you can't know everything in advance. There will be "mistakes" of omission. You won't understand everything the user wants, the environment will change under your feet and affect your design, new security challenges will arise. Rather than trying to prevent these omissions with detailed documentation up front, an agile project assumes the omissions will happen and concentrates on finding them rapidly.

3.2 The Agile V: A Single Sprint

Figure 3: The Agile V

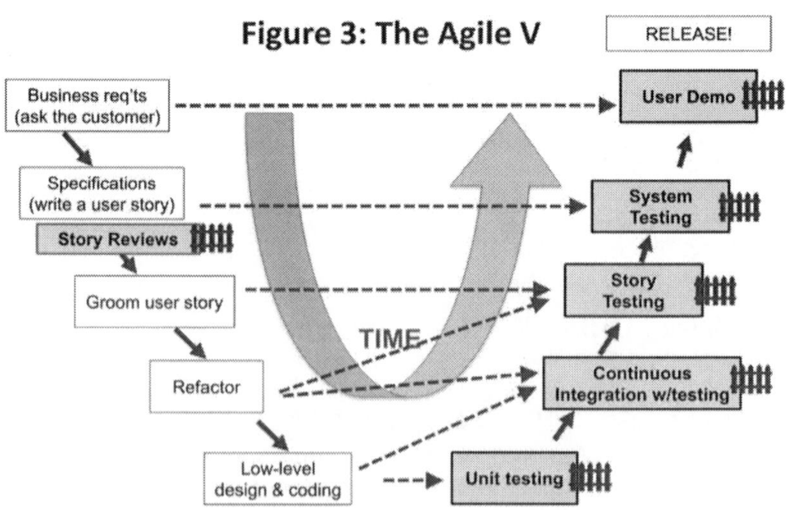

In an agile project, the entire "V" is performed in just a couple of weeks, instead of months or years. The "V" is repeated over and over on successive user stories.

As shown to the right, there's less distinction between design and coding activities. User stories capture requirements (what the user wants and why) and the specification is captured as acceptance tests.

The quality gates meant to find omitted requirements look very different in agile than in waterfall – and they're a lot more effective. There's two quality gates for requirements – a user story review and the sprint review. During the sprint review, the user sees the finished features and can provide feedback. The time between deciding what to make and getting customer feedback on your decisions is a couple of weeks instead of many months, so the inevitable misunderstandings are small and easy to fix.

Omissions in design are also detected rapidly, if the acceptance testing is sufficiently thorough. And finally, because the same team performs all the activities in quick succession, there are far fewer handoff errors than in a waterfall process with separate teams for each activity.

3.3 Quality Gates in Agile

During initial adoption of agile, many teams continued to struggle with mistakes made during design and coding, often causing the team to miss their sprint commitments. In my experience, this is often due to insufficient quality gates and preventative practices inside the sprint itself. For instance, they'd have the sprint review but not the earlier user story review, or they'd completely skip unit testing.

Some organizations were simply carrying over their poor waterfall practices into agile. They'd relied mostly on system testing to find defects in their waterfall days, rather than focusing on preventing them or finding them early. They did the same in their agile projects, spending the first half of the sprint coding and then discovering reams of defects as soon as they started testing.

Other organizations dropped all their internal quality gates when they switched to agile, believing that the gates weren't needed inside an agile sprint. This was particularly common in groups that adopted Scrum without any exposure to XP or earlier agile methods. The Agile methods prior to the Agile Manifesto included quality gates.[3] XP insisted on several very powerful quality practices and gates: test-driven design, pair programming, and extensive unit testing. (Beck, 2000). However, Scrum initially had little to say on the topic. Many people didn't understand that Scrum was a project management structure, not a full-featured engineering practice. They assumed that if Scrum didn't teach it, you didn't need it. This resulted in dropping quality gates inside the sprint, and not putting anything in their place.

3.3.1 Definition of Done

By 2005, Scrum training sessions had started restoring those quality gates as a "Definition of Done". (Agile Alliance 2017). A Definition of Done is the exit criterion for the entire sprint. It almost always includes quality gates for individual activities within the sprint, as you can see in this Definition of Done from James Shore's *Art of Agile Development*. (Shore, 2010)

This Definition of Done is a combination of all the internal quality gates and the release criteria in a typical waterfall process. There isn't much emphasis on meeting the quality gates in a specific order, but that doesn't matter much when all the activity takes place in a week or two. The small iterations actually make it easier to convince the developers to use ***more*** quality gates. Meeting each and every criterion apparently doesn't seem so daunting when you're looking at just a single story's worth of code.

Definition of Done: (Shore, 2010)

- ❑ Tested (all unit, integration, and customer tests finished)
- ❑ Coded (all code written)
- ❑ Designed (code refactored to the team's satisfaction)
- ❑ Integrated (the story works from end to end—typically, UI to database—and fits into the rest of the software)
- ❑ Builds (the build script includes any new modules)
- ❑ Installs (the build script includes the story in the automated installer)
- ❑ Migrates (the build script updates database schema if necessary; the installer migrates data when appropriate)
- ❑ Reviewed (customers have reviewed the story and confirmed that it meets their expectations)
- ❑ Fixed (all known bugs have been fixed or scheduled as their own stories)
- ❑ Accepted (customers agree that the story is finished)

---

[3] For instance, staged delivery (McConnell 1996) and evolutionary delivery (Gilb 1985)

Here's a more detailed Definition of Done from a medical products company using Agile. (Herman, 2016). Despite looking a bit waterfall-ish, this Definition of Done doesn't obligate the organization to perform design and coding sequentially. They just have to demonstrate that they did everything on the list by the time the sprint ends.

The author observes that the list deliberately calls out design and coding separately so it's clear to both themselves and regulatory agencies how they are preventing or finding problems in each activity.

It's also interesting (and admirable) that they're requiring a root cause analysis for each defect found in acceptance testing.

Definition of Done: Checklist for Technical Completeness for User Stories (Herman 2016)

Design:

- ❑ Design covers everything in the user story and acceptance criteria.
- ❑ Design reviewed by area experts and feedback is incorporated.
- ❑ User story has a link to the design.

Code:

- ❑ Code implements the design.
- ❑ Unit tests cover the design (includes use cases, API contracts).
- ❑ Code compiles and runs, on the build server, without errors, warnings, or unit test failures.
- ❑ Code and unit tests have been peer reviewed and adjustments made per comments.
- ❑ No new defects.

Acceptance Testing:

- ❑ Acceptance tests in a form listed below have been written and entered into project management system.
    - ❑ May include manual, automated, and unit or integration tests
    - ❑ Verification Procedure and/or SMART for high risk stories
    - ❑ SMART for stories with medium risk
    - ❑ Acceptance tests have been reviewed by a developer and feedback has been incorporated.
    - ❑ Acceptance tests pass on a branch or main build; unresolved issues found on main build have been logged into defect tracking system.
    - ❑ Executed results have been attached to project management system.

Defect Fixing:

- ❑ Minimal steps to reproduce are documented in the defect description.
- ❑ Root cause analysis is documented in the defect description.
- ❑ Fix approach is documented in the defect description.

3.3.2 More Than One Definition of Done

A single Definition of Done makes sense if there are no handoffs between teams inside the sprint, and each sprint results in releasable code. The process is a series of tiny V's with a quality gate at the end of each "V" or sprint.

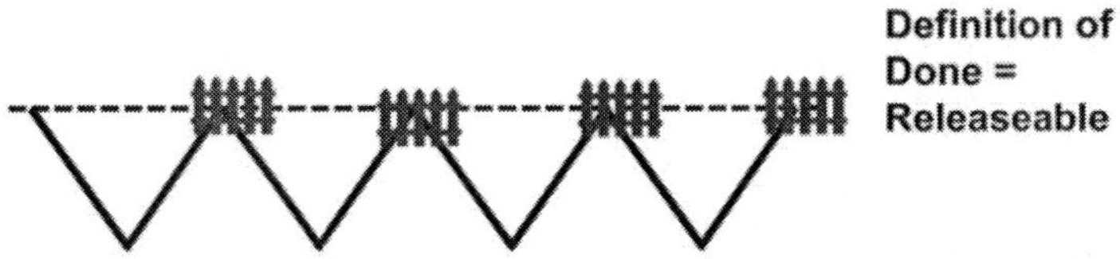

But what if your system doesn't reach releasable quality at the end of each sprint? Perhaps your organization has a hardening sprint, system testing, or localization after the sprint is over. That process might look more like this. The Definition of Done clearly is not the same as Releasable.

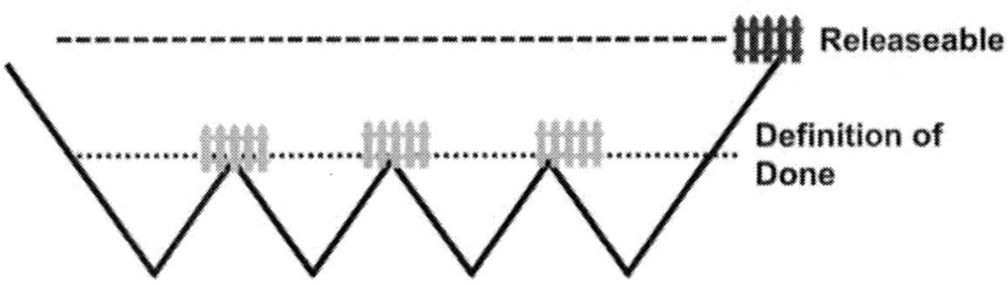

In this case, you'll need additional criteria prior to release. You might call it "done-done", or you might call it release criteria, or something else again. Whatever you call it, it's a second quality gate.

It's not unusual to see organizations define three levels of "Definition of Done", as shown to the right. In this case, multiple stories are individually completed to meet the Definition of Done for a story, and then the whole group of stories is integrated together and reviewed by the user to meet the Definition of Done for the Sprint. And then further work is done on the results of several sprints to meet a Definition of Done for release. That's three quality gates.

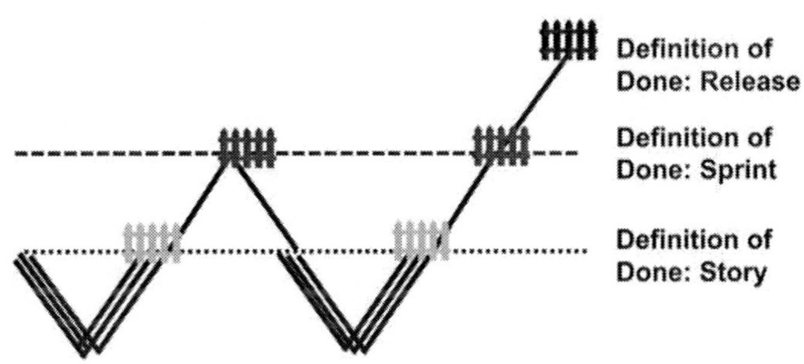

Joseph Ruskiewicz, in his paper "Establishing a Definition of Done in Complex Organizations" (Ruskiewicz 2015), reflected on what happens when a large organization with multiple interrelated teams and a semi-agile process passes work from one team to another. They concluded that they needed quality gates for handoffs from one team to another, and that the gates shouldn't all be identical. The gates are all named "Definition of Ready" rather than "Definition of Done", to avoid confusion over what "done" actually means. The practice seemed to be:

- All groups define a Definition of Ready to ensure a level of quality is met before passing their work to another group.
- The organization mandates a few basic criteria must appear in every Definition of Ready.
- Teams add their own specific criteria, specific to their technology and known risks.

You can certainly argue about whether this is or isn't an agile process, but whatever your point of view, the organization needs to control its quality within its current process. They need those quality gates. Different Definitions of Done for different purposes makes sense in this context.

3.3.3 Continuous Integration: A Special Quality Gate

Continuous integration (CI) is the practice of checking code into the shared repository frequently, where it is compiled and subjected to some automated testing. Continuous integration is intended to find certain types of defects, so it acts as a quality gate inside the sprint. Simply compiling all the code together will find certain types of coding conflicts, but the main goal is running automated tests to find design conflicts between different individuals' or teams' code. The code is sent through this gate as often as is practical, given the tools available and the amount of automated testing.

Back in the 1990s, system-wide integration daily or weekly was not unusual on smaller projects. On large projects, building the entire system from scratch more frequently than daily often wasn't practical with the available tools, and the lack of tools and machine speed often put severe limits on the amount of automated testing which could be done.

Today, continuous (or very frequent) integration is much more practical than it was ten or fifteen years ago. Just remember that the goal is to detect problems, not just to run builds. If your builds never fail, or the tests never report any errors, you aren't getting any benefit from this quality gate. Likewise, if the tests fail but there's not enough information to find the defects causing the failure, this quality gate isn't much use.

3.4 Preventative Measures: Building in Quality

XP and evolutionary delivery both placed a lot of emphasis on preventing developers from making mistakes, rather than finding the mistakes afterwards. This has carried over into the wider agile practice. Good practices from the past were incorporated and often transformed to fit the small increments of agile.

Some of the most popular and effective practices are

- design patterns
- test-driven development (TDD) and refactoring
- acceptance-test driven development (ATDD) and its cousin Behavior-driven development (BDD)
- pairing

3.4.1 Design Patterns

Design patterns originated in object-oriented programming as a way of capturing reusable concepts in object-oriented software design. Prior to that, reusable concepts were typically captured as algorithms (which are still used today, of course) and design rules in structured programming. The typical design pattern provides:

- A pattern name.
- A pattern intent or purpose. What problem is this pattern intended to solve?
- The pattern itself – an outline of the objects or classes and their basic behaviors.
- The pattern's consequences and side-effects which may affect whether it is an appropriate solution for a given problem.

Design patterns help a developer maintain **intellectual control** by providing an abstraction using the concepts of classes and inheritance. A pattern is a simpler way to look at a complicated bunch of code. And knowing a lot of design patterns relevant to your domain is **knowing your domain**. If somebody else already solved this, why solve it again? Books of algorithms serve much the same purpose as design patterns on a more detailed level.

3.4.2 Test-Driven Development and Refactoring

Test-driven development, or TDD, is very effective at preventing errors during coding and low-level design. In TDD, developers write the unit tests first, verify that the tests fail, and then write the code and verify that the tests pass. TDD forces you to maintain **intellectual control** by working in small, verifiable steps.

TDD can be used to great positive effect in waterfall projects as well as agile projects. Some people did practice TDD before Kent Beck wrote about it (Larman 2003), but it didn't have a name and wasn't widely known. Giving the practice a name and writing about how to do it made TDD much easier to adopt and therefore much more widespread. Today, TDD is a cornerstone of quality plans in many organizations.

Refactoring is a relative of TDD. To quote Martin Fowler, refactoring is "a change made to the internal structure of software to make it easier to understand and cheaper to modify without changing its observable behavior." Basically, a section of code is rewritten in small steps verified by tests. Again, we see the strategies of **maintaining intellectual control** and **making the logic visible**.

3.4.3 Acceptance-Test Driven Development

TDD prevents coding errors, but it doesn't do much to prevent missing requirements or misunderstanding the demands of the environment on the design.

An effective practice for capturing requirements and design constraints is acceptance-test-driven development, or ATDD. In ATDD, the agile team captures many of the requirements and design constraints for each story as *acceptance tests* for that story.

The old V-model actually recommended something very similar - write the requirements, and then write the acceptance tests for those requirements before beginning design. However, it wasn't as effective as today's ATDD because there wasn't as much user review of the tests (to ensure requirements were understood) and the whole practice tended to bog down under the sheer weight of trying to cover every aspect of the product at once.

3.4.4 Pairing and the Three Amigos

Pairing is another effective method for preventing defects. Two programmers might pair to write code, or install instructions, or any other deliverable. A tester and a developer might pair to write user stories. In all these cases, more than one set of eyes on the job prevents mistakes.

Johanna Rothman describes the advantages of multiple viewpoints during ATDD in *Create Your Successful Agile Project* (Rothman 2017). "When teams use the Three Amigos [to develop stories], they split into triads of one developer, one tester, and one product owner or BA. The idea is that each person has his or her unique perspective on the possible story:

- The developer thinks about how to implement the story.
- The tester thinks about what can go wrong.
- The business analyst thinks about what the customer or business wants to accomplish with this story.

… If they add acceptance criteria, especially in the form of Given-When-Then, the team is much more likely to understand the story."

3.4.5 Non-functional Requirements in Agile

Remember those non-functional requirements? The ones the customer hardly ever tells you about? When organizations stopped writing big requirements documents and started writing user stories, many of them left out the non-functional requirements. Then they were surprised when the end product didn't meet their unwritten non-functional requirements. Others realized that they needed to keep the non-functional requirements, but they weren't sure where or how.

Today, I see agile organizations handling their non-functional requirements in several different ways.

- Some groups define each non-functional requirement as a story or epic, such as "As a user, I expect all screens to respond within 1 second".
- Other groups add the non-functional requirements to the Definition of Done for all stories, often in the form of an acceptance test. E.g. "Each story must pass Test B which demonstrates that screen response time is still 1 second." This works well in concert with ATDD.
- SAFe treats the non-functional requirements as "constraints or restrictions on the design of the system across the different backlogs." http://www.scaledagileframework.com/non-functional-requirements/.

All of this assumes that someone actually defined the non-functional requirements, despite the users' usual vagueness on this topic. That's frequently a big hole. Johanna Rothman recommends getting users involved during initial stakeholder agreements by including the non-functional requirements in the project's Release Criteria. She gives some examples in her new book *Create Your Successful Agile Project* (Rothman 2017).

"*Performance*: For a given scenario (Describe it in some way), the query returns results in a minimum of two seconds.
Scalability: The system is able to build up to 20,000 simultaneous connections and scale down to under 1,000 connections."

4 Continuous Improvement

Even with all the quality gates and preventative practices, problems still do occur. The classic response was to monitor defects found in the field and use defect cause analysis to pinpoint areas where a stronger gate or a preventative practice would help. (Iberle, 2007)

This is still a very effective method for improving the development process. Unfortunately, it is often left out of sprint retrospectives, probably because the data isn't available until well after the sprint is over.

Any group that is really serious about improving their quality should master the art of defect cause analysis. Some hints:

- Developers, not testers, should determine the cause of the defect. The testers don't know, so don't ask them to do it.
- Developers need some training. Many initially think that all defects are coding mistakes. As we saw earlier in this paper, that's not the case.
- Pairing or teaming can be much more effective than working individually.

There's a longer description and references for defect cause analysis in my 2007 paper, which is available on my website as well as in the PNSQC archives. There's a link in the References.

Once you know where the problems are coming from, you'll want to fix that process. James Shore says it well: "The best way to fix your process is to make mistakes impossible. For example, if you have a problem with UI field lengths being inconsistent with database field lengths, you could change your design to base one value off of the other.

The next best solution is to find mistakes automatically. For example, you could write a test to check all UI and database fields for consistency and run that test as part of every build.

The least effective approach (but better than nothing!) is to add a manual step to your process. For example, you could add "check modified database/UI fields for length consistency" to your "done done" checklist." (Shore 2010)

5 What We Have Learned Since 2007

The key to building in quality is still prevention of defects, rather than finding and fixing them after the fact. The strategies for preventing defects haven't changed fundamentally, but we do have more and better practices to prevent defects due to both agile development and faster machines, while many of the older practices such as coding standards remain mainstays of the profession.

Better tools and faster machines have made continuous integration practical, and there's many more tools for automating unit and regression tests, which makes refactoring easier and safer. Agile and object-oriented programming have brought us some new practices, many of which are also applicable across agile and waterfall. Design patterns, pairing, and TDD can be effective on many types of projects.

Adoption of agile with its short iterations changes the quality game for the better in several ways:

- The user story format leads the developers to think more about why the customer wants the feature, capturing requirements which were often left out in the past.
- Cross-functional teams cut down on handoff errors and increase communication.
- The short iterations provide rapid feedback on whether user needs have been correctly understood and whether the design works.
- The short iterations with less documentation make rigorous quality practices (as captured in a Definition of Done) seem feasible rather than overwhelming.

However, adoption of agile can pose challenges to achieving high quality, especially if the adoption is done "by the book" without understanding why the ideas in the book work:

- Collapsing all your quality gates into a single Definition of Done can result in dropping useful quality criteria and letting defects escape. If you have additional steps between the end of the sprint and releasability, you need at least two quality gates.
- Not understanding how to manage non-functional requirements in agile can result in losing sight of important quality attributes and failing to implement them.
- An overly strict focus on delivering immediate user value in every single user story can make it very difficult to achieve some non-functional requirements. Some system-level design work is often necessary to identify the acceptance criteria which will eventually add up to the desired non-functional requirement.

Many organizations, both waterfall and agile, still don't use either product risk analysis or defect cause analysis to identify the defect prevention mechanisms which will be most effective for them.

6 Conclusion

If you only remember one thing from this paper, I hope it will be one of these strategies to prevent defects and build quality into your software from the start!

- Make the structure & logic visible.
- Maintain intellectual control.
- Know your domain.
- Mistake-proof the routine stuff.
- Design away the opportunity for error.

7 References

Agile Alliance. "Definition of Done", https://www.agilealliance.org/glossary/definition-of-done/ (accessed 7/20/2017).

American Society for Quality (ASQ). 2017. "Learn About Quality: Quality Plans". http://asq.org/learn-about-quality/quality-plans/ (accessed 7/20/2017).

Beck, Kent. 2000. *Extreme Programming Explained*. New York: Addison-Wesley.

Black, Rex. 2004. *Critical Testing Processes*. New York: Addison-Wesley.

Herman, Neal. 2016. "Implementing Agile in an FDA Regulated Environment". Agile Dev/Better Software DevOps West 2016. https://www.stickyminds.com/presentation/implementing-agile-fda-regulated-environment-0 (accessed 7/14/2017).

Iberle, Kathy. 2007. "Building in Quality". Proceedings of the Pacific Northwest Software Quality Conference 2007. Also available at http://kiberle.com/wp-content/uploads/2016/01/2007-BuildingQualityIn.pdf

Larman, Craig. 2003. Computer, June 2003 issue. Accessed at: http://www.craiglarman.com/wiki/downloads/misc/history-of-iterative-larman-and-basili-ieee-computer.pdf

McConnell, Steve. *Rapid Development.* Microsoft Press. 1996.

Poppendieck, Mary. Poppendieck, Tom. 2003. *Lean Software Development: An Agile Toolkit*. 2003. Addison-Wesley. Pp 142-143.

Ould, Martyn. *Managing Software Quality and Business Risk*. 1999.

Rothman, Johanna. 2002. "Release Criteria: Is This Software Done?" *STQE Magazine*, March/April 2002. https://www.jrothman.com/articles/2002/03/release-criteria-is-this-software-done/

Rothman, Johanna. 2007. *Manage It! Your Guide to Modern, Pragmatic Project Management*. The Pragmatic Programmers.

Rothman, Johanna, 2017. *Create Your Successful Agile Project*, Ch. 5. The Pragmatic Programmers.

Ruberto, John. 2017. "100 Percent Unit Test Coverage Is Not Enough.", Agile Connections by StickyMinds, entry posted 7/10/2017, https://www.stickyminds.com/article/100-percent-unit-test-coverage-not-enough/ (accessed 7/17/2017).

Ruskiewicz, J, 2015. "Definition of Done". Proceedings of the Pacific Northwest Software Quality Conference 2015.

Shore, James and Warden, Shane. 2007. *The Art of Agile Development.* O'Reilly.

Thibodeaux, Adrian. Pandya, Chintan. "End-to-End Quality Approach: 14 Levels of Testing". AgileDev/Better Software West 2016. https://www.slideshare.net/JosiahRenaudin/endtoend-quality-approach-14-levels-of-testing (accessed 7/14/2017).

University of Michigan 1999. http://groups.engin.umd.umich.edu/CIS/course.des/cis400/fortran/fortran.html (accessed 7/28/2017).

Embedding Security in Product Lifecycle

Arvind Srinivasa Babu, Deepti Chauhan

Arvind_Babu@McAfee.com, Deepti_Chauhan@McAfee.com

Abstract

A product goes through several processes before it is released into the market. An oversimplified process will involve a lot of planning, analysis, design, development, testing and marketing before a release. But how many products involve security in this lifecycle? During a product's lifecycle, a lot of new features, bug fixes and other development activities take place which essentially means that new code is being added. Though this code might stand up against good product test cases, what is the confidence level that this new code has not opened a backdoor or added a vulnerability that would allow an attacker to exploit, monitor or cause damage?

This paper will explain how some best security practices can be incorporated within a product lifecycle. We will also demonstrate why it is essential to maintain threat models up-to-date for every release which allows automation of security test cases as the product evolves. Automated security test cases allow us to add security as part of a Continuous Integration(CI)/Continuous Delivery(CD) pipeline. There are several open source tools that allow testing different aspects of security on a product, we will glance over some of these tools and the functionality they bring to security testing.

Biography

Arvind Srinivasa Babu is a Software Development Engineer and Product Security Champion at McAfee, with more than eight years of experience designing and implementing software. He has been performing the role of a scrum master and strives for continuous improvement in testing and development. His areas of interest span over security, network, user interface interaction, system programming, product security and mobile application development.

Deepti Chauhan is a Software Development Engineer at McAfee, with five years of experience in developing products. She has participated in various product life cycles and been a key contributor to various releases within McAfee. Her areas of interest span over system programming, network and mobile application development.

1 Introduction

Software Quality is gauged by a lot of different metrics like complexity, reliability, efficiency, security, maintainability, scalability and much more. We believe that a software's durability relies on triangular aspects of Security, Performance/Efficiency, and Quality. We define quality as an aspect that includes simplicity, maintainability, scalability and most important of all offers minimum or no disruption of customer business. Product lifecycles have evolved over the past couple decades from linear validation phases to validating software in a continuous manner. An engineering team depending on the life cycle they have adopted would have acceptance criteria, which would try to balance security, performance, and quality. A software that doesn't find the right balance between these aspects will lose business. For example, if we define a metric to measure the quality, security and performance of a software in broadly 5 levels (0-4) as shown in the below table,

Maturity Level	Quality (least disruptive)	Security	Performance
0	Frequent crashes	No security process in place to mitigate vulnerabilities caused by the product.	Consumes resources that cause maximum CPU usage
1	Major functional failures	High severity vulnerabilities reported from field for every release. Few security processes followed.	Causes slowdown of entire system
2	Minor functional failures	Medium or low severity vulnerabilities reported from field for every release. Few security processes followed.	Causes noticeable slowdown when performing certain tasks
3	Mostly Non-Functional or some functional failures with no impact to customer business. (logs, spelling mistakes etc.)	Most security defects addressed before release of product, partial adherence to security process within a product life cycle. Occasional reports of vulnerabilities from field.	No degradation of system resources only optimization required is with the algorithms employed within the software.
4	No failures after released	No vulnerabilities reported from field. Adherence of secure product lifecycle.	No impact on business and product is at max efficiency.

The following diagram measures different version of a software each representing different maturity levels in every aspect. While every team aims for a perfect product, budget cuts, process execution blunders and cutbacks lead to compromises which impacts any of the aspects mentioned.

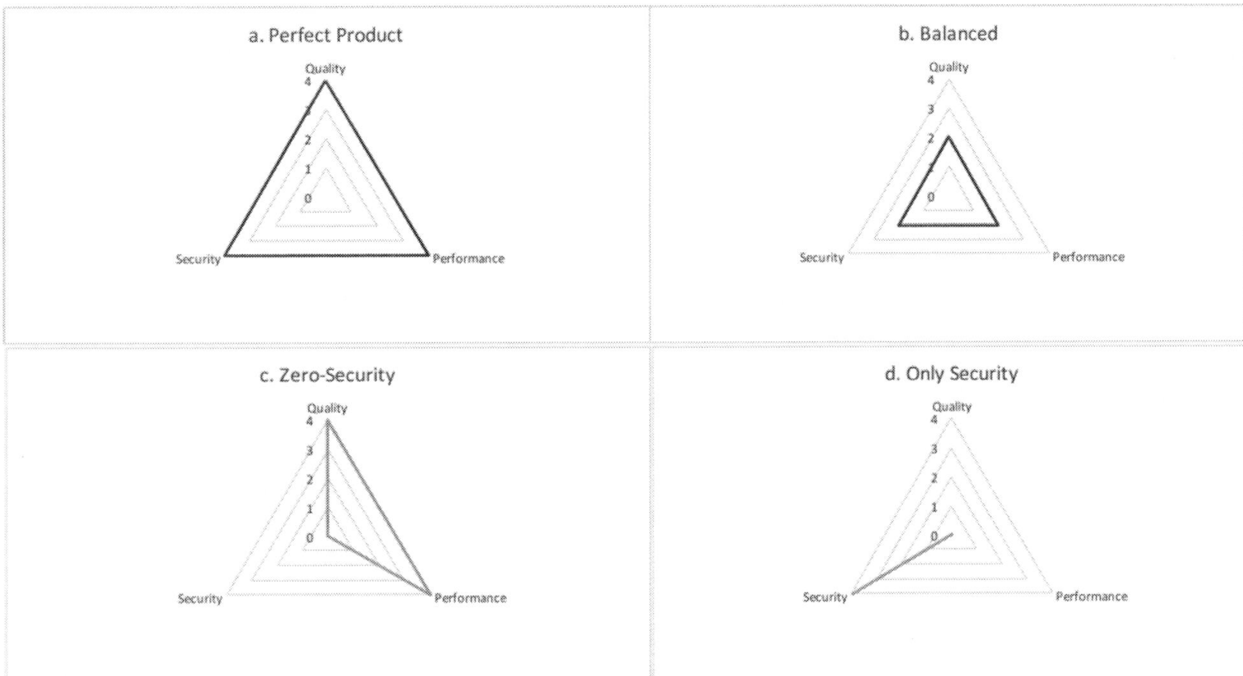

Figure 1 - Different charts that show the relationship triangular aspects of Quality, Performance and Security measured on their maturity levels.

In this paper, in the first section we will be talking about how typical product life cycles look with their activities, different methodologies, their philosophies and what are the advantages and disadvantages when executed well. The second section talks about differences between product defects and a vulnerability and how they need to be handled. The next section dwells on software security, the different activities involved when dealing with software security followed by a detailed section on how to embed these activities in different phases of a product lifecycle. The next section will provide an insight on what threat modelling is and why it is important to maintain threat models up-to-date during every release. We will finally have a glance on the functionalities provided by various tools that can help perform penetration testing on your products.

2 A Typical Product Life Cycle – Waterfall, Agile or DevOps

A textbook definition of a product life cycle is the progression of a product across multiple stages from inception, requirement gathering, design, development, validation, release and support. Over the past couple of decades, various teams have followed multiple product life cycles to improve their reliability in making releases in a stipulated time. A few largely popular lifecycle models are Waterfall, Agile Scrum, DevOps, most models are either a spin-off of the above or a hybrid among them. The key takeaway from comparing multiple product lifecycles is the improvement in the ability to assigning tasks in parallel and execute projects quicker.

Waterfall product lifecycle model [1], one of the oldest process models, focused on every stage in a sequential manner, this usually leads to software release taking up to a year or two.

An Agile product lifecycle model [2], allows a faster execution of a software release, by splitting products into features and minor incremental deliverables. These incremental deliverables are accumulated, validated and finally the product is released. Usually each sprint is a couple weeks for receiving minor product increments and product can be released every month, or quarter.

DevOps [3] is an evolving product lifecycle in its methodological stages that requires heavy collaboration between Product management, Engineering and Operations. It involves a collection of tools to help facilitate automated deployment or delivery of a product in a continuous fashion.

3 Product Defects vs Security Defects vs Product Vulnerability

The most popular terms used within engineering teams related to security are defects and vulnerabilities. While an engineering team might encounter such defects, and use of this terminology within their product lifecycle, it is important to understand the differences between these terms and the impact they have on the product, company and brand. We will focus on the differences between Product defects, Security defects and a Product vulnerability.

Product defects are those kinds of defects that typically affect the product's ability to fully function. This could be a result of poor design, poor algorithm, poor validation of functionalities that eventually lead to disruption of customer business thereby decreasing the quality of the product delivered. These are the kind of defects that are detected and corrected in a product life cycle's validation phase. There are multiple types of product defects that affect the performance, or functionality or provide poor integration with other components. These can either be detected early in the lifecycle or late. As the product moves along its lifecycle, it might not be feasible to address all product defects due to budget and time constrains eventually leading the defect to be deferred for a future release. Most low severity bugs that have least business disruption capabilities are picked up for deferrals.

Security defects are the kind of defects that arise from products that provide security features or controls like Confidentiality, Integrity and Availability or handle sensitive data like keys, passwords etc. but the security is compromised because of incorrect implementation of security controls that eventually leads the system to grant unprivileged user access rights to privileged information or denial of service. Security defects can range from incorrect memory handling (buffer overflows, incorrect de-initialization etc.), input validation errors, incorrect thread synchronization, incorrect authentication, or lack of privacy controls.

A **Product vulnerability** is the mechanism which exposes the weakness within a product that allows an attacker to exploit the system to gain entry and access confidential information or cause business disruptions. While a vulnerability is often confused with security defects, vulnerability is more focused on the methodology by which an attacker can gain access to the system. It requires a great deal of analysis to find vulnerabilities from a black box perspective. A security defect leaves an exploitable piece of code that may or may not remain discovered, vulnerability provides the mechanism to access the exploit and an attacker uses that to exploit a system.

Product defects, security defects and vulnerabilities are terminologies that are often interchanged and cross-referenced within product teams and customers. To a customer, the only terms they would be familiar with are "vulnerabilities" and "support cases". Vulnerabilities in products can send general alerts and panic within the customer's security team and would request the engineering team to provide a fix. A business disruption because of product defects on the customer side would lead to support case to be opened. To an engineering team, the operational term would be a "defect" or "bug". The details of these defects may never reach the customer view. When engineering team evaluates a vulnerability, the root cause analysis would point to a security defect which will be addressed within the lifecycle. A product that has a lot of vulnerabilities caused by undetected security defects within its lifecycle, would ultimately lead a customer to move to competitors who provide better security products with minimal or no vulnerabilities.

4 What is Software Security?

Software Security is the assurance that a product is provided free of vulnerabilities to its customers. Software security like Quality and Performance cannot be built into a system in a fixed timeframe, it's a continuously evolving process that needs to be properly executed and documented for future enhancement.

Software Security Process can be termed as a set of security activities that can be performed across various stages of a product life cycle to detect and correct security issues. As mentioned earlier, a product life cycle methodology focuses mainly on delivery of features and not on the set of life cycle activities. Following is the set of security activities that detects and addresses different security aspects for the product.

4.1 Security Activities

4.1.1 Architectural and Security Design Review

This activity will focus on architectural reviews and design reviews from a security standpoint. If there are no architectural changes, design reviews alone can be carried out for new features else both the activities can be combined as a single activity. Major focus areas in this activity would be to establish the trust, integrity and data handling of the product or feature in secure fashion. This activity would involve senior members of the product team like architects and senior leads who will brainstorm on implementing security from an architectural or design standpoint.

4.1.2 Threat Modelling

This activity involves having engineers who understand the product very well identify data flows within the product. Each data flow, and architectural input help the threat modeler to identify attack surfaces and threats that can compromise the system. This input can be taken into an architectural or design review to address any concerns on the threats and attack surfaces. Once a threat model is prepared, it will present a list of security requirements for the product to implement and provide security against identified threats. We will explore more on threat modelling in a later section.

4.1.3 Coding Standards and Manual Code Review

Every product development team follows a coding standard to keep the style of code in a readable format. Security engineers within a team are responsible to collect, collate and maintain a repository of secure coding standards that can be applied during development. This helps in building security right from the point where code is written. Each language used for development has its own secure coding standards and is responsibility of the engineer or team to monitor and update the repository as more standards are introduced.

We recommend making code reviews a mandatory activity that must be performed for every code commit to ensure that the product team is adhering to the defined coding standards. While most code reviews focus on functionality of the feature to catch early defects, it's important to monitor the security standards being properly followed. Every code review must at least include two or more senior engineers, ideally where one can focus the review on functionality/architectural correctness and the other can focus on the security standards adherence.

4.1.4 Static Analysis

Static Analysis is a practice where the code is examined without executing it for common programming errors when handling resources or memory handling etc. While there are multiple static code analyzers like Synopsis Coverity, Fortify, Clang, Visual Studio Code Analysis, while each of these analyzers have their strengths they also have a weakness in detecting false positives. We recommend running multiple static analyzers on the code for every commit or on regular intervals if analysis takes a lot of time. We recommend making this a mandatory practice that must be followed throughout the lifecycle. Static analysis is the second line of defense for products to detect memory leaks from analyzing code patterns. Although there are risk of false positives arising from an analyzer, running multiple analyzers to get a comprehensive summary of issues and addressing them will improve the products stability and security posture.

4.1.5 Dynamic Analysis

While static analyzers examine code without executing it, Dynamic analysis focuses on examining code as it executes data in real-time. This gives more accurate information on memory leaks, input validations and other types of privilege escalations. This activity becomes conditionally required if you are dealing with web applications and new features dealing with lot of memory management. Fuzzing is a methodology by which random data is supplied to input interfaces of the software to check for potential errors in handling unrecognized data. Smart fuzzing involves mimicking the data to be a valid input format with few alterations which presents much more detailed coverage into your system. Dumb fuzzing is simply supplying a random blob of data which has the potential to cause crashes due to incorrect format parsing etc. While each method of fuzzing has its advantages and disadvantages, it is up to the security tester to employ the fuzzing techniques suited for the product.

4.1.6 Security Testing Plan

It's important to charter a plan that would allow a team of quality assurance engineers to pick up security testing activities. This planning activity will be carried out every sprint and the test executions can be automated or performed manually single or multiple times in a release depending on the bandwidth availability of engineers and process lifecycle. Documenting the security plan for future use will help identify testing gaps when vulnerability slips through security testing.

4.1.7 Vulnerability Scanning

Vulnerability scans detect known vulnerabilities and exposures in a binary executable or in the environment where it is being deployed. This activity is conditionally required to be performed if there are new features that use system resources like opening socket connections or access new files etc. Mostly software implementation consumes third-party libraries, and these third-party libraries can be an older version with newly discovered vulnerabilities. Vulnerability scans can identify such libraries and provide information on the various vulnerabilities that have been directly or indirectly introduced in the software.

4.1.8 Privacy Reviews

Privacy should be the top most priority for any software product that handles Personally Identifiable Information (PII). A Personally Identifiable Information refers to any information that allows an attacker to identify a specific individual. This review process determines the storage access controls for PII that should be implemented. This is mandatory activity if you are accessing PII data anywhere in the system irrespective of the time the data is held within the product.

4.1.9 Penetration Testing

Penetration testing is a complex activity involving analysis of data collected from multiple tools to ethically break into a system and access privileged information. There are multiple types of testing performed, depending on the type of testing, platform, network, technology where the software is deployed. The level of penetration one can achieve in a system is entirely dependent on the skillset of the individual(s) performing the pen-testing so this activity should be performed whenever required either by discovery of vulnerabilities from the field or when there are significant architectural or design changes. There is a cost associated, since members with a specific skillset are required to perform pen-test activities.

5 Embedding Security Activities in Product Life Cycle

In the previous section, we had a glance at various security activities that handle various areas of security. Explaining what each product life cycle is beyond the scope of this paper and hence we will elaborate more on incorporating security activities in each type of model to maximize a product's security posture.

5.1 DevOps

DevOps is a combination of Development and Operations that facilitates a reliable delivery of software. This is more of a methodology rather than a product life cycle but is being adopted in many organizations in recent times as a product life cycle. The success of DevOps is complemented by Lean and Agile paradigms and adopts the best of both.

5.1.1 DevOps Overview

DevOps primarily has seven stages which involves the following activities:

5.1.1.1 Plan (Stakeholders planning)

- Collect Business requirements.
- Define metrics
- Architecture
- Infrastructure planning
- Release Scope and Planning

5.1.1.2 Code (Continuous Integration)

- Design feature and configuration
- Develop software features
- Build

5.1.1.3 Validate (Automation)

- Automated testing
- Acceptance testing
- Configuration testing

5.1.1.4 Staging (Packaging)

- Approvals
- Package Configuration
- Pre-release pods

5.1.1.5 Release (Continuous Delivery/Deployment)

- Deployment
- Fallbacks, Recovery

5.1.1.6 Configure (Infrastructure Orchestration)

- Storage
- Database
- Application Provisioning

5.1.1.7 Monitor (Telemetry)

- Production Metrics
- Performance

While DevOps is aimed at continuously delivering or deploying products, every feature and defect must pass through these stages. The amount of code being released could be as simple as few lines or code or could be multiple huge complicated components.

5.1.2 Embedding Security Activities in a DevOps Model

The key to providing security in a DevOps model where code is to be delivered as early as possible with highest quality, performance and security, would require a cultural change in an organization following agile scrum or any other product lifecycle, as well as heavy reliance on automation. There is also a fundamental change in how product is viewed in a DevOps environment. DevOps is usually implemented for solution containing multiple products. So, there are few key activities that need to be performed on an overall security perspective.

5.1.2.1 Plan

As mentioned, stakeholders include product managers, IT operations, Engineering team, security engineers and architects discuss on the architecture, infrastructure and requirements which defines the scope of a release. Security engineers from each product contribute in performing **Architecture reviews**, **Infrastructure reviews** (an activity that will review the security controls in place to mitigate threats from accessing the infrastructure e.g. Private Cloud solutions, Amazon Web Services (AWS), Microsoft Azure etc.), and **Threat Modelling** the infrastructure and architecture. A **Security Audit** of consumed third-party modules is also initiated eliminating weak third-party libraries. Third-party evaluation is a continuous process by itself and evaluated versions are taken up for audit to decide whether libraries are no longer applicable or whether it needs to be updated to newer versions. **Security Test Plan** is created

5.1.2.2 Code

The only manual activities in this phase is development, code review of the feature by the engineering team. **Continuous Integration(CI)** should be implemented to ensure unit-tests are in place, **Code reviews** will be used to promote the code into the CI branches [4] from feature branches. After which Static Analysis is performed on the code. Unit tests also contribute to a certain level of **Dynamic Analysis**.

5.1.2.3 Validate

Automation is the key for **Continuous Delivery (CD).** While automation will focus on functional testing, security engineers will focus on automating the Security Test Plan into the CD pipeline. **Dynamic Analysis** is performed by providing fuzzed data to the various inputs to check for any failure in input validations. Security engineers also review how Personal Identifiable Information (PII) is being accessed and handled and perform **Privacy Reviews** to ensure that proper access controls are in place. Threat models also needs to be updated if issues are found during security testing.

5.1.2.4 Staging

Once all issues are addressed, packaging is performed to ready for release. Cloud solution would prepare for release by deploying to a staging area like Beta Pods, or pre-release pods. **Vulnerability Scans** can be performed in this stage to review any known vulnerabilities that is accidently deployed in pre-production environments. Issues discovered would then be addressed before deploying onto a production environment.

5.1.2.5 Release

At this point, security checklists must be met. Static Analysis, Dynamic Analysis, Vulnerability Scans, Privacy Reviews, Threat Models being up to date, Code Review data must be artifacts for post-release reviews or for simple recordkeeping.

5.1.2.6 Configure

Once the release is deployed, appropriate storage, virtual machines, databases are provisioned or configured with the new version of the application. Deployment tests should include an automated security validation to scan for configuration errors like failing to apply necessary patches, or configuration to ensure appropriate access controls are in place for the infrastructure. Closing out Infrastructure reviews in adherence to the Infrastructure plan is crucial and needs to be worked upon by both security engineers and IT operations managing the production environment.

5.1.2.7 Monitor

This is mostly IT operations to monitor the stability of cloud after deployment of the solution, but security engineers can periodically monitor the infrastructure by deploying internal scanners to periodically scan for vulnerabilities or malwares.

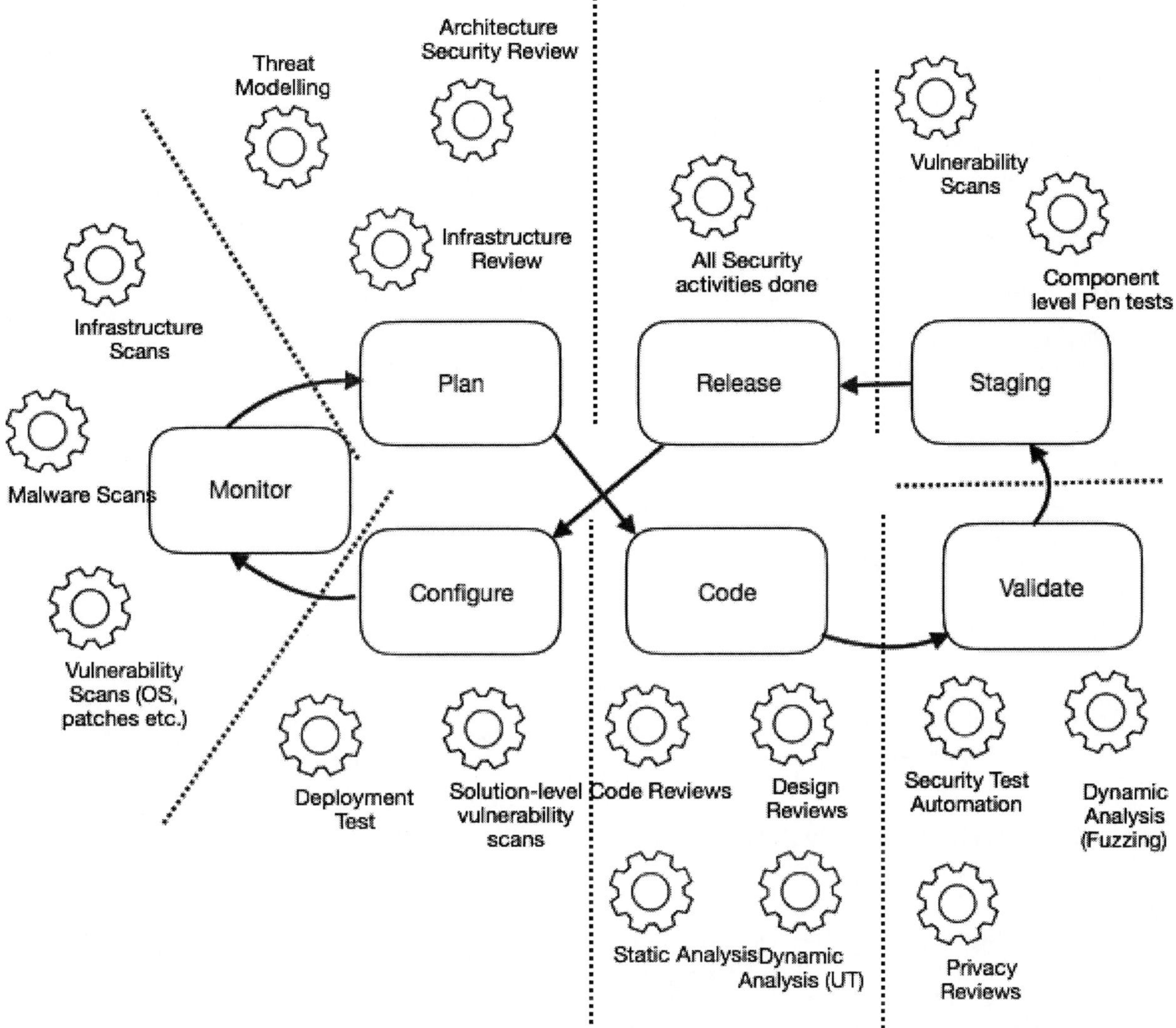

Figure 2 DevOps Lifecycle for every feature/bug.

5.2 Agile

5.2.1 Agile Overview

Agile product lifecycle is one of the most successful models in recent times, it is executed in a specific timeframe and is iterative to deliver the final product. The goal is to split the product into epics and user stories that can be delivered incrementally until the full product is developed. There are several methodologies within the agile philosophy and a few of which are worth mentioning is Kanban, Scrum, Extreme Programming, Lean Development etc. For the scope of this paper we will be embedding security within Scrum model.

An agile scrum model involves the following stages within which the following activities are followed

5.2.1.1 Release Planning

- Plan of Intent
- Product Backlog
- Epic creations
- Feature Prioritization

5.2.1.2 Sprint Planning

- Team backlog
- Story creations
- Task breakdown
- Story Estimation
- Prioritization
- Capacity planning

5.2.1.3 Sprint Tracking

- Design
- Daily Scrum
- Burndown
- Build
- Validation

5.2.1.4 Sprint Review

- Potentially shippable product
- Retrospective
- Reprioritization

5.2.1.5 Release

- Deployments
- Release to customers
- Documentation

5.2.2 Embedding Security in Agile Scrum

5.2.2.1 Release Planning

In this stage, security engineers are engaged early on to discuss on the requirements and defining the scope of changes for a planned release. **Privacy Reviews** are initiated and data gathering starts for all PII that is being handled. **Threat modelling** activity is initiated using architecture diagrams and **Architecture Reviews** are performed. Teams perform architecture within sprints or they do a complete architecture and break it into deliverable sprints. Either way, threat model needs to be updated accordingly as requirements keep changing every sprint and appropriate updates needs to be made.

5.2.2.2 Sprint Planning

In this stage, the architecture is broken into incremental deliverable modules. **Threat Modelling** activities are performed at this stage capturing the minor incremental code changes. **Security Test Plan** is created for the upcoming sprint and targets defined.

5.2.2.3 Sprint Tracking

Design of incremental deliverables are performed in each sprint and corresponding **Design Reviews** needs to take place. **Code Reviews** are performed for every code commit that is checked into the version control system. **Static Analyzers** are run on the codebase to identify issues for every build that is triggered. **Dynamic Analysis** can be scoped and performed on the incremental deliverables by performing fuzzing, detecting memory leaks etc. **Security Test Plan** execution is undertaken for every sprint and results updated accordingly. Automating these test cases wherever applicable allows faster execution of security tests. **Privacy Reviews** should be conducted regularly to ensure that proper security controls are being implemented when handling PII information in every sprint.

5.2.2.4 Sprint Review

Each sprint review will have a sprint checkpoint for security activities to meet a Definition of Done (DOD) where Sprint Security Test Plan is executed successfully, all issues addressed and fixed. Any defects that have low severity and moved into next sprint needs to be fixed by the next sprint and backlog is groomed to accommodate these bug fixes. This security checkpoint will also expect Static Analyzers and Dynamic Testing to be performed.

5.2.2.5 Release

All documentations and artifacts related to the security activities needs to be archived for future reference. Third party evaluations completed and updated to the product. **Privacy Review** must be completed. Security Test Plan execution must be completed and any issues arising from the same needs to be addressed. All issues that arise in the field both product and security defects enter into agile lifecycle as issues or stories and are picked up in the backlog of the new version during the release and sprint planning.

5.3 Waterfall

5.3.1 Overview

The waterfall model is one of the oldest product life cycles, it is a sequential execution of stages starting from inception, design, development & validation, release and support. The stages in waterfall model are self-explanatory. The inception stage involves lot of planning, identifying business requirements, once this is performed, design of the modules and architectural plan is formulated for the entire product and all the modules. Once the design and architecture has been finalized, the development team proceeds with implementation of the design and the product is given for validation. Once the product is validated it is released and post release support is provided. Though waterfall is the oldest and is phased out by most companies and product teams there are still some areas of the waterfall model which is still being followed as either a hybrid model like waterfall-agile etc. We will cover how security activities can be embedded within this model so that it can be applied on hybrid models.

5.3.2 Embedding Security Activities in Waterfall

5.3.2.1 Inception

During this phase, it is critical to include your product security engineers in the loop to ensure that they understand the impact of changes that is being planned for a release. Security engineers can use the opportunity to create a plan of security activities that can be achieved in each phase and execute it as they deem necessary. Security engineers can also use this phase to set up **Secure Coding Standards** database with list of all coding standards that will be applicable and developers needs to follow during the development phase.

5.3.2.2 Architecture & Design

During this phase, **Architecture and Design Security Reviews** can be performed. Security engineers should have a strong architectural review skills to identify basic security problems with an architecture or design. **Threat Modelling** should be performed here for the new architectural or design change and used in reviews. Identify all Personal Identifiable Information (PII) data that the product design is going to make use of and prepare for **Privacy Review**.

5.3.2.3 Development & Validation

Most activities performed here would be to run **Static Analysis** to detect problems with memory or resource management and fix them regularly. **Code Reviews** should include senior engineers and security engineers to ensure that the coding standards are adhered by the development team. Security engineers and Quality Assurance engineers should work together to formulate a **Security Test Plan** for the project. During validation, the security test plan should be executed alongside functional test plan. **Dynamic Analysis** can also be performed during this stage providing fuzzed data and detect memory leaks. **Privacy Review** must be performed to enforce secure handling and enforce appropriate access controls of PII data.

5.3.2.4 Release

Most of the product development would be complete at this point, with proper code reviews, static analysis, dynamic analysis, proper privacy access controls must be in place and complete security test plan executed. Any issues arising from these activities needs to be addressed within the release. An activity of **Penetration Testing** can be performed at this point which is entirely dependent on the skillset of engineer who is performing the pen-test and cost associated with it. With a final review of all PII data performed and reviewing all open source licensing agreements, the product can be ready to be released.

5.3.2.5 Post-Release and Support

With any product model, there are bound to be issues that can slip even in case of following above activities. There should be mechanism where external pen-testers or customers can report issues and you can address security issues through hotfixes or patches. In event of such cases, threat model should be updated with the new attack vector.

6 Threat Modelling

6.1 What is Threat Modelling?

Threat Modelling is a structured approach that involves identifying, accessing, quantifying and mitigating security issues. Threat Modelling is a defensive posture in security where the security engineer is the attacker and models the architecture in terms of identifying possible threat agents and attack surfaces and create a plan to address them as the software evolves through different stages of a product life cycle. With current technology standards, it is not possible to automate this activity and involves manual interaction and analysis.

6.2 Who can Threat Model?

Any engineer who has a sound product knowledge and understands what threats and attack surfaces are can come up with a threat model for their product or solution. Threat modelling is not a skill that can be learnt off the bookshelves and perform some diagrammatic representation of threat vectors and attack surfaces, it is about identifying all possible threats and this skill to identify threats from threat models improves by doing multiple threat models for smaller designs and multiple architectures.

6.3 Threat Modelling Guidelines and Vocabulary

6.3.1 Brook Schoenfield's: ATASM [18]

Brook's ATASM model focuses on the following

- **A**rchitecture
- **T**hreats
- **A**ttack **S**urfaces
- **M**itigation

A detail of this threat model is provided in Brook's book mentioned in the references section and conference presentations [17]. The goal is to arrive at security requirements that will be built to bring the system to the desired defensive posture.

6.3.2 Microsoft's STRIDE

Microsoft STRIDE model [5] is a threat classification model which focuses primarily on the following categories

- **S**poofing
  Any threats that allow an attacker to illegally access information using another user's authentication. In the threat model, all areas where such sensitive information is accessed or handled will be brought under the threat model and security test cases will be designed based on that.
- **T**ampering
  This category of threat deals with unauthorized access to modify persistent data like databases, files and data transmitted over network.
- **R**epudiation
  Repudiation deals with establishing trust information on the authenticity of the user. Audit logs, general product logs, purchase receipts, login credentials are all ways to establish actions performed by a user.
- **I**nformation Disclosure
  Information disclosure revolves around threats that provide access to users who are not authorized to read the data. Few examples would be to read a file without proper access controls etc. Personal Identifiable Information also falls under this category.
- **D**enial of Service
  Denial of Service attacks deny access to valid users by bombarding the system with too many negative authentication calls.
- **E**levation of privilege
  Elevation of privilege involves an unauthorized user penetrating into the trust level of the system. The level of escalation leads for untrusted entity to be part of the trusted system.

6.3.3 Process for Attack Simulation and Threat Analysis (P.A.S.T.A)

Process for Attack Simulation and Threat Analysis [6] is a Threat Modelling methodology which involves identifying the potential threats and risks assessment. The model involves identifying the Threats/Vulnerabilities from attacker's viewpoint. PASTA is a seven-step process. The process starts with identifying the business objectives and requirements along with the security requirements. Followed by decomposing the application using DFD and Use Case diagrams etc. It involves further Threats and Vulnerabilities analysis and using methods like Attack Trees and Attack Surface analysis for modelling the attacks. The process finally ends with Risk and Impact Analysis.

6.3.4 Vocabulary

Threat Model

A threat model is a diagrammatic representation of data flow diagrams in conjuncture with architectural components.

Asset

An asset is any device, data or component that is crucial for business continuity which generally requires an access privilege.

Attack Vector

An attack vector is a unilateral attempt or path by which an attacker can compromise a system

Attack Surface

Attack surface is the sum of all attack vectors which allows an attacker to gain access into the system

Attack Tree

It is a part of threat model that determines the flow of threat to target an asset.

Threat

A threat is a path by which an attack can traverse across boundaries in conjuncture with attack surface to compromise an asset.

Vulnerability

Vulnerability is the mechanism that allows an attacker to gain access to the system.

Exploit

Exploit is a tool or software that is designed to attack and take control of an asset using a vulnerability.

Boundary

A trust boundary is simply a representation of different access privileges a component has in a threat model.

6.4 Tools for Threat Modelling

There are various tools to perform threat modelling. It is dependent on comfort zone for an engineer to use the tool that represents all the attack surfaces and vectors. A few tools that can help are

- **Microsoft's Threat Modelling Tool** [7]
  This is a tool that heavily relies on representing components as processes data flow diagrams. It has all the data representation diagrams necessary to show how the data flows in the system traversing through various trust boundaries. Once the diagram is completed it allows a report generation based on the properties set for each data flow, process, boundaries etc. This is free to use tool.
- **Microsoft Visio**
  Visio is one of the best tools available for performing threat modelling as it is not restricted to Gane Sarson representation of Data flow diagrams. Users can freely mix architecture and threat modelling concepts to represent a model that allows them to express the product design and security workflows. It also has layers to hide specific components that allows deeper threat assessment on individual module.

There are various other free tools which users can use to perform threat model assessments on their products.

6.5 Frequency and Benefits of Threat Modelling

There is no hard-set standard or timeframe to the frequency of threat modelling. It takes time to understand different threats and how they affect your system. The idea to incorporate threat modelling within a product lifecycle is to gradually ramp up the threat modelling activity frequency. Security engineers or architects can gradually ramp up threat modelling as per release to per sprint. Keeping threat models up-to-date with attack vectors from externally reported vulnerabilities improves the overall security posture of the product. Threat modelling allows engineering to harden the product against various attacks thereby securing without compromising on quality or performance. Having a good documented threat model also allows engineering to catch early defects in design and architecture before code is even written thereby saving cost and time.

7 Security Standards and Tools

This section will provide a glance of various security tools and their usage and few coding standards.

7.1 Coding Standards

Coding standards is probably followed in every development team. Generally, there are different types of standards that every engineering team adopt when developing a product. They are not limited to code style, function prototyping, naming conventions etc. Secure Coding Standards are specifically guidelines that enable developers to make informed decision on to how to securely load sensitive data into variables and how data should be handled.

Every language has its own set of secure coding standards and discussing all the standards is beyond the scope of this paper. SEI CERT has a confluence website [8] set up where the standards are constantly updated and new ones being worked out. It is a good starting place to deep dive into secure coding standards.

In C or C++, Secure Coding standards can be very simple enforcement like initializing variables to a value to prevent garbage value interfering with application logic or can be very complex not limited to the programming language or platform like how passwords or keys should be handled in memory. SEI Cert has all the language specific standards covered.

When dealing with passwords or keys within memory, we must explore into native support on how memory regions can be protected so that debuggers don't attach themselves and start analysis memory for patterns like username etc. User authentication information should be encrypted for maximum amount of time even though they are stored in memory. A simple example would be how we would have a structure or class that stores username and password in an object. It might seem very plain and harmless, but when you take a memory dump either by attaching a debugger to the process or analyzing a full memory dump, all the attacker needs to look for is a username and start investigating the memory blocks around a username password to extract the password. It is impossible to protect secret keys and passwords as we will end up in a chicken and egg problem as to where to store the key for the memory encryption. The goal of security when dealing with secure information handling is to make it harder for an attacker to look for the information. Secure Zeroing the memory where such sensitive information also adds to the coding practice of securing the memory if it was reallocated to some other pointer.

7.2 Security Tools

There are a bunch of security tools that help with providing data and a collation of these data help penetrate a system. Detailing over each tool is not in the scope of the paper, we will mention some of the most popular tools and their uses and how they help with penetrating a software. For detailed documentation, you can refer to the respective tools website.

7.2.1 Network Tools

7.2.1.1 NMap [9]

NMap is a network scanner that is flexible, powerful, free and easy to use, to scan networks. It uses raw sockets to do a variety of discovery, protocols used, the ports open on a target machine and to a level identify applications running on the open ports.

7.2.1.2 WireShark [10]

Wireshark is a network sniffer tools that allows an attacker to monitor network traffic. Unsecured data over TCP or any protocol can be viewed using this tool.

7.2.2 System Tools

The list provided here are specific to Windows OS.

7.2.2.1 SysInternalSuite [11]

SysInternalSuite is a set of tools that is currently offered by Microsoft. It has a whole bunch of tools that allows monitoring, collect data or and launch programs with escalated privileges. All of the tools

7.2.2.2 ProcMon

Process Monitor is a tool within the SysInternalSuite that needs a special mention because of the trove of data that it collects on all process. Most system calls are captured and security attacks like DLL sideloading can be analyzed from such logs.

7.2.2.3 Dependency Walker

Dependency Walker is a tool that lists out all the DLL imports and the all the exports that a DLL makes. It is useful to analyze the DLL dependency tree.

7.2.2.4 Process Explorer

Process explorer is a tool within the SysInternalSuite that allows exploring all the process, the threads, the call stack in each thread, the resources opened by a process, DLL handles, Event handles, namedpipes etc.

7.2.3 Vulnerability Scanner

7.2.3.1 Nessus [12]

Nessus is one of the popular vulnerability scanners that is regularly updated with vulnerabilities and uses it to scan machines in a network for unpatched vulnerabilities.

7.2.3.2 Microsoft Baseline Security Analyzer [13]

Microsoft Baseline Security Analyzer provides a streamlined method to identify missing security updates and security misconfigurations.

7.2.3.3 NetSparker [15]

NetSparker is a web application security scanner, with support to detect vulnerabilities in web applications.

7.2.4 Exploit Tools

7.2.4.1 Metasploit [14]

Metasploit is an advanced open-source platform for developing, testing and using exploit code. It also provides a purposeful insecure linux environment to test metasploit and other tools.

7.2.5 Pentest Framework

7.2.5.1 Kali Linux [16]

Kali Linux is a debian based linux distribution aimed at advanced penetration testing and security auditing. It includes more than **600** penetration testing tools and is free.

8 Conclusion

In this paper, we went over the basics of what software security is, what are the fundamental differences between different lifecycle models and how security activities can be embedded in product lifecycle. One of the key takeaways is to breakaway the false notion of compromising quality or performance for security and vice versa and have a structured process to build in security right into a products lifecycle as it moves through different stages. We explored into the vocabulary of threat modelling and what threat modelling is all about with different methodologies and glanced through few of the tools that are commonly used to penetrate a system. The paper will provide a good starting platform for product teams to adopt security within their respective lifecycle for the first time or improve their existing methodologies.

9 References

1. Waterfall Model, https://en.wikipedia.org/wiki/Waterfall_model
2. Agile Model, https://en.wikipedia.org/wiki/Agile_software_development
3. DevOps Toolchain, https://en.wikipedia.org/wiki/DevOps_toolchain
4. Successful Git branching model, http://nvie.com/posts/a-successful-git-branching-model/
5. Microsoft STRIDE Threat model, https://msdn.microsoft.com/en-us/library/ee823878(v=cs.20).aspx
6. Process for Attack Simulation and Threat Analysis, https://www.owasp.org/images/a/aa/AppSecEU2012_PASTA.pdf
7. Microsoft Threat modelling tool, https://www.microsoft.com/en-in/download/details.aspx?id=49168
8. Secure Coding Standards for most high-level languages, https://www.securecoding.cert.org/confluence/display/seccode/SEI+CERT+Coding+Standards
9. NMap, https://nmap.org
10. Wireshark, https://www.wireshark.org
11. SysInternalSuite, https://docs.microsoft.com/en-us/sysinternals/downloads/sysinternals-suite
12. Nessus, https://www.tenable.com/products/nessus-vulnerability-scanner
13. MBSA, https://www.microsoft.com/en-in/download/details.aspx?id=7558
14. Metasploit, http://www.metasploit.com
15. Netsparker, https://www.netsparker.com
16. Kali Linux, https://www.kali.org
17. Brook's RSA Conference presentation, https://www.rsaconference.com/writable/presentations/file_upload/lab3-w04_threat-modeling-demystified.pdf
18. Brook Schoenfield's book, **Securing Systems: Applied Security Architecture and Threat Models**.

QA? Who Needs That?!

In depth look at absorbing the quality assurance position within an organization.

Konnor Willison

- 7 years quality assurance experience
- Worked for companies like Bluehost, Overstock, Vivint, and Salesforce
- Work mostly in management tracks with a strong focus on software quality
- Originally from Bay Area, moved here in 2010.
- Married with two kids and a doggo.
- Love Utah outdoors

Building in Quality

Building in Quality

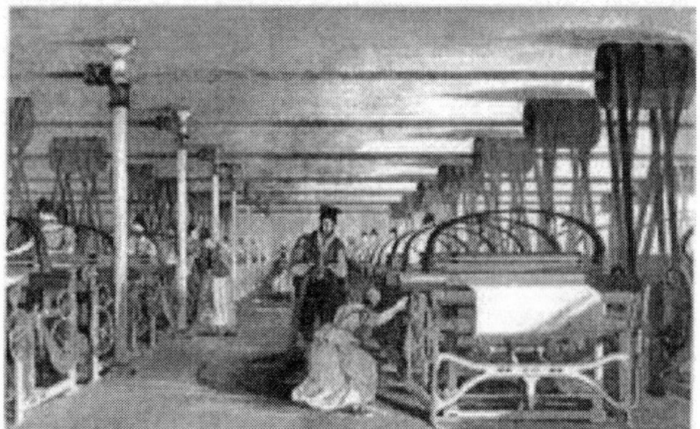

Building in Quality

What is the QA Role doing in Your Org?

- Are they at the end of the cycle?

- Are they assigned to each team?

- Are you improving the development life cycle with automation and CI/CD?

How is Your Org Set up?

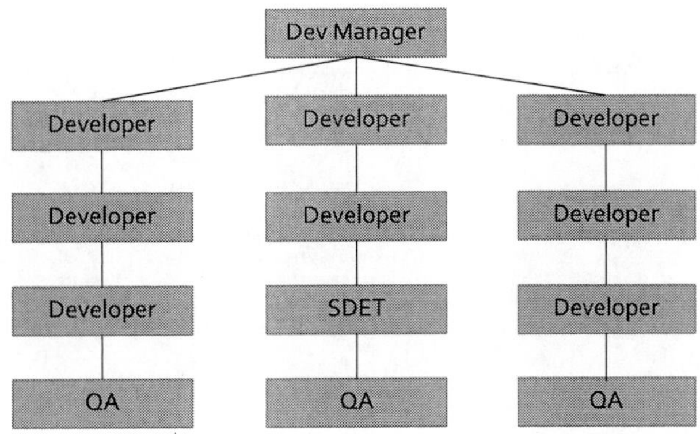

QA Manager

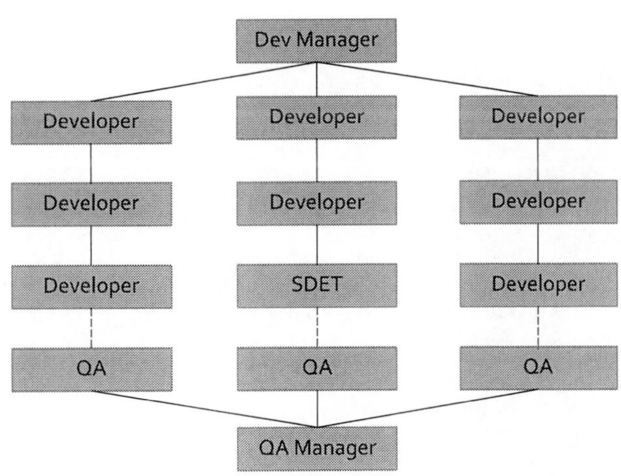

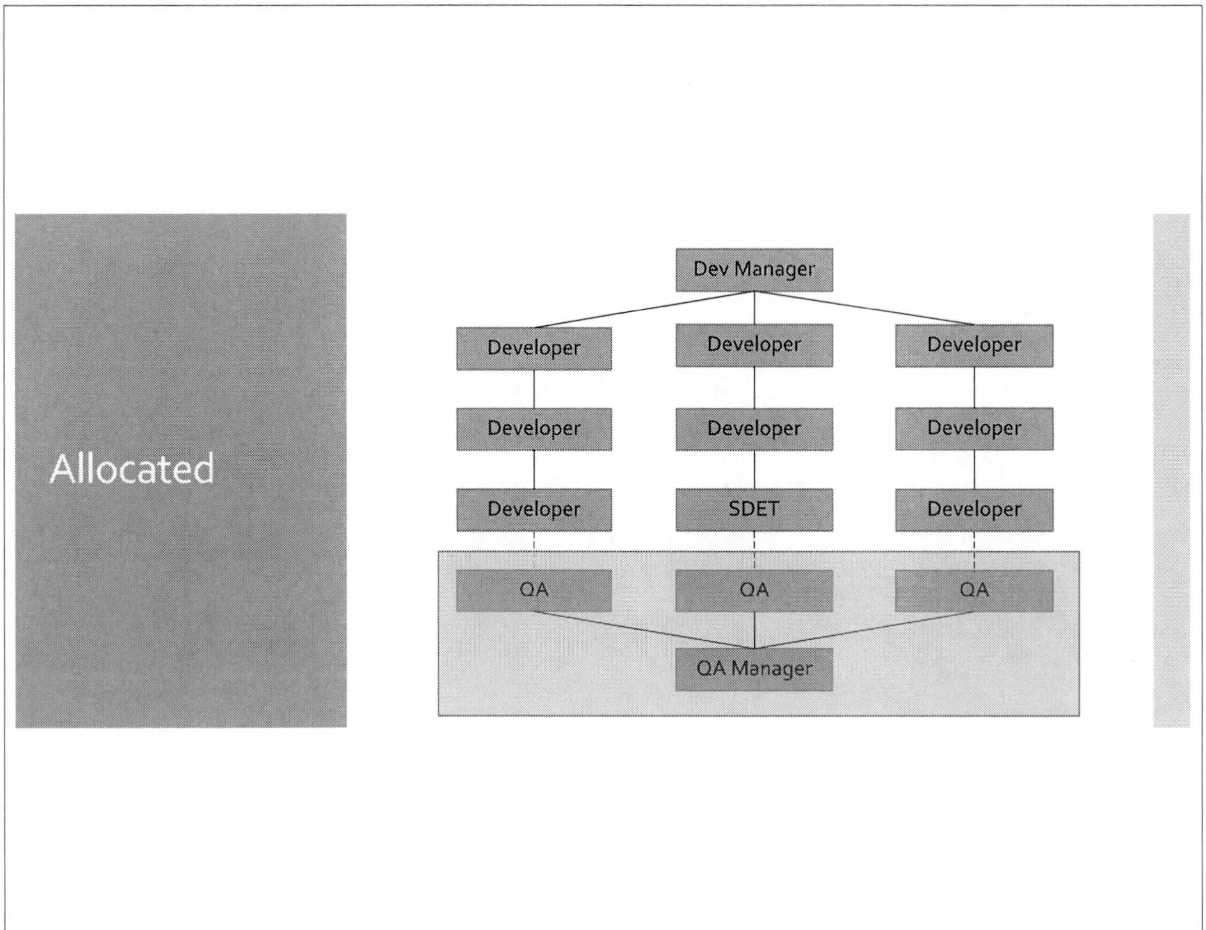
Allocated
Dev Manager
Developer
Developer
Developer
Developer
Developer
Developer
Developer
SDET
Developer
QA
QA
QA
QA Manager

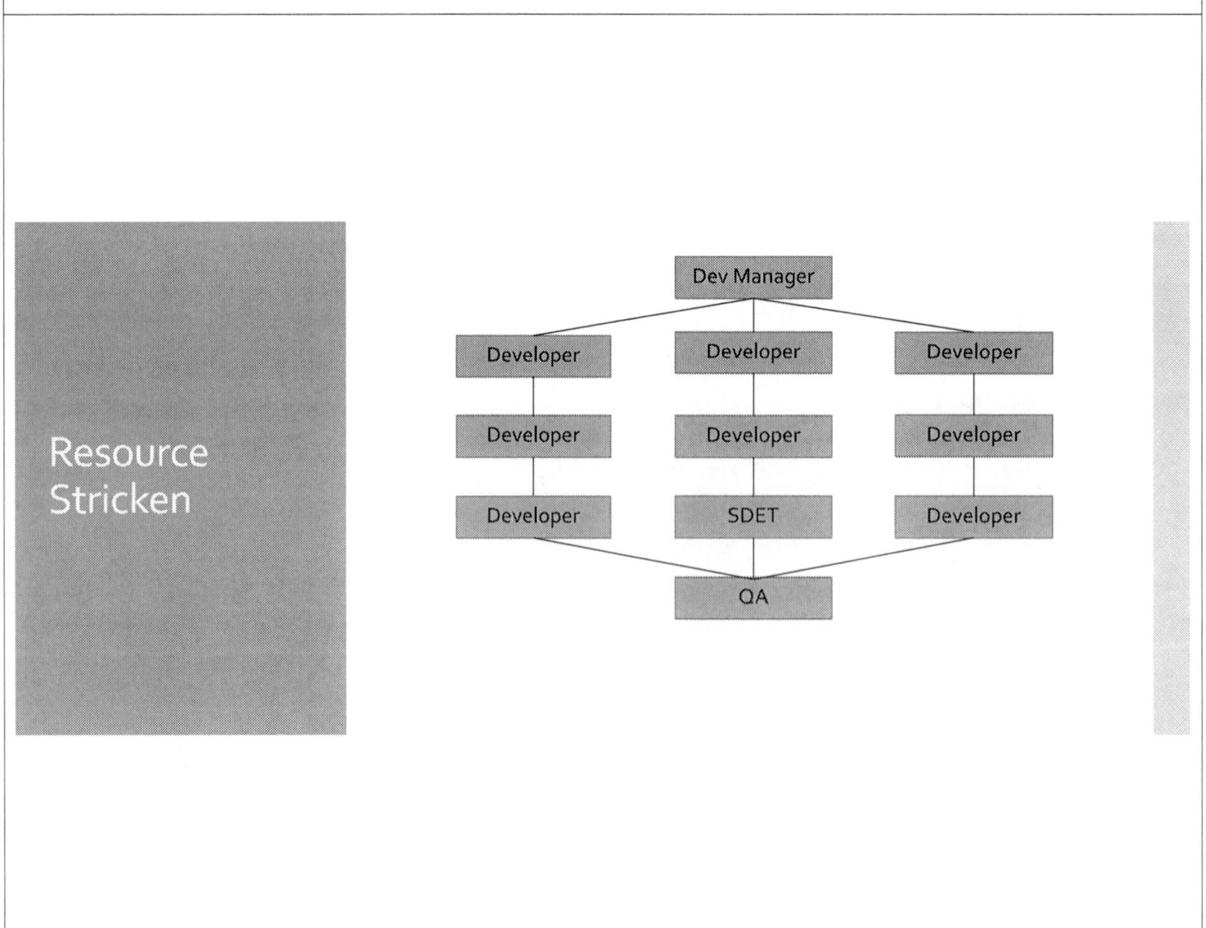
Resource Stricken
Dev Manager
Developer
Developer
Developer
Developer
Developer
Developer
Developer
SDET
Developer
QA

How does Your Org Test?

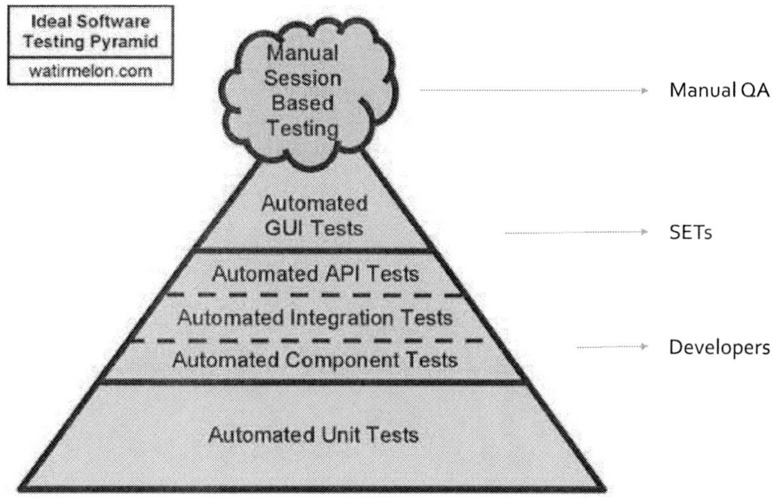

Hybrid Engineering

What is the Appeal?

What is the Benefit?

- Provides better career mobility
- Simplifies accountability by making the first-line manager/scrum master responsible for all the resources in the scrum team
- Drives consistency & efficiency across all engineering
- Addresses inconsistencies in testing execution
- Easier to hire

Testing Quadrants

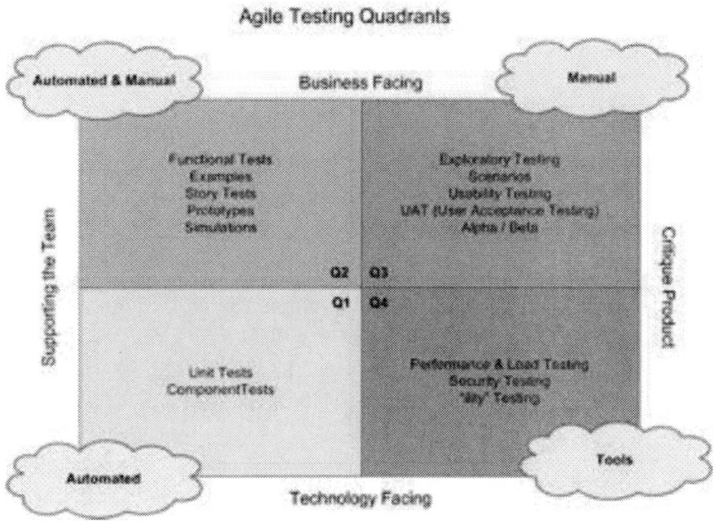

Transition Roles

- Development
- Design, develop, and deliver software
- High technical skills
- Troubleshoot and resolve problems, production issues
- Create functionality
- Single Team
- Help train QA on test automation
- Write test cases and assist with manual and exploratory testing
- Fully own quality

Transition Roles

- Quality Assurance
- Work with multiple teams
- Become quality consultants
- Review test cases and guide teams around manual and exploratory testing
- Train developers on writing test cases, test plans, and doing exploratory testing
- Get trained on test automation (and eventually feature development)

What's the Worst that could Happen?

Sources

- https://www.nytimes.com/2015/10/05/business/engine-shortfall-pushed-volkswagen-to-evade-emissions-testing.html?_r=0
- https://www.justice.gov/opa/pr/volkswagen-engineer-pleads-guilty-his-role-conspiracy-cheat-us-emissions-tests
- "The Passat" (PDF). UK: Volkswagen Group. 1 August 2008. Retrieved 23 May 2016
- http://lisacrispin.com/2011/11/08/using-the-agile-testing-quadrants/
- https://docs.google.com/presentation/d/15gNk21rjer3xo-b1ZqyQVGebOp_aPvHU3YH7YnOMxtE/edit#slide=id.g437663ce1_53_98

PNSQC/Pacific Agenda
PO Box 10733
Portland, OR 97296-0733
USA

ISBN 978-1-5108-5220-4

9 781510 852204

CURRAN ASSOCIATES INC.
proceedings.com

6th International High Performance Buildings Conference at Purdue 2021

West Lafayette, Indiana, USA
24-28 May 2021

Herrick Laboratories
PURDUE UNIVERSITY